With Compliments

Triton

Supertrends

Supertrends

Winning Investment Strategies for the Coming Decades

Lars Tvede

www.supertrends.com

A John Wiley and Sons, Ltd, Publication

A catalogue record for this book is available from the British Library.

ISBN 978-0-470-71014-2

Project Management by OPS Ltd, Gt Yarmouth, Norfolk, UK
Typeset in 10.5/13pt Bembo
Printed in Great Britain by TJ International Ltd, Padstow, Cornwall, UK

Contents

Note from the Author

Dear reader,

In writing this book I have relied on a range of data sources, and as an active investor, my search for new information and inspiration is ongoing. The references I have used, plus the many that will inspire me in the future, can be found on the website *www.supertrends.com*, where you will find not only links to relevant text sources, but also videos with global thought leaders, as well as interactive roadmaps of the future as I see it, overview of profit models, and much, much more.

Lars Tvede

Preface

What will the world be like in 2020? Or in 2030, 2040, and 2050? Where will it be most interesting to work, build businesses, or invest? Where will the greatest growth and biggest profits be?

During much of May 2009 I found myself pondering that question. A few years earlier I had co-founded a mobile communication company, which in January 2009 won the *Red Herring Global 100* award as one of the world's most promising technology companies. Following the award celebration, which took place in San Diego, I was invited to give a keynote speech to leading entrepreneurs and venture capital companies at the *Red Herring Europe 100* event in Berlin. It took place on April 1, 2009, and the title was "The Future of Technology".

After the speech I got the idea to write a book, not only about the future of technology, but about the future of politics, conflict, economics, demographics, environment, lifestyles, business, finance, and, yes, technology.

The reason was this: from time to time I have noticed how almost all business people—including myself—overwhelmingly seek information about the short to medium term. "What will 12-month forward consensus earnings be?" "Which mobile phone manufacturers are currently taking market share?" "Who will win the election in Japan?"

This kind of information is important, but I have discovered that the times in my life when I personally have made the best investments and had the greatest fun in business was when I got the really *big* picture right and took long-term positions against the prevailing mood or ahead of the game. I have also noticed that to have fun and to succeed, it's not enough to play your game well—it is far more important to *choose the right game to play*. When things worked for me, I really was in the right place at the right time, as they say.

What you are reading now is the resulting book. I have mostly looked toward 2050. For some parts, the indications of what will happen until then seem clear and strong, while, for others, I am venturing fairly far out on a limb. For instance, demographics in 2050 is far more predictable than information technology so far out.

During the months when I wrote this book, there were many who said that the world economy was in for a very, very long stagnation phase—"10 years", "20 years", something like that. After all, this is what happened to Japan after its crash in 1990, and as the Western world has accumulated excessive credit since 1980, even since World War II, won't this excess take just as long to reverse?

Personally, I don't think so. I think we are in for a big, global expansion, and while a few economies will struggle with debts, most countries either won't have debt problems or will be able to handle them. However, the economic crisis from 2007 to 2009 has some lessons for the future that we need to understand. So, even though this book is about the coming decades, I will start by addressing this enormous meltdown.

Part I

Superscares

- The path of human civilization has never been smooth, and the future won't be either. Some of this is due to unpredictable events, but some recurring phenomena also play a big role.
- Taking its cue from the 2007–2009 meltdown, this part explains and quantifies some of these phenomena and the irrationality, instability, and drama they will create in the future. It highlights in particular the economic and psychological drivers behind business cycles, bubbles, panics, and scares.
- Furthermore, it contains an explanation of what money and banking really is, and it shows how shadow money and shadow banking have contributed to extraordinary booms and crashes in the past and may do so again in the future.
- Finally, it shows that the world after 1980 has entered a structural deflationary boom phase, which is far from over. This dynamic condition will stimulate an unusually high frequency of financial bubbles going forward.

More information on
www.superscares.com

1

Crises

It was a cold day in January 2008, and I was sitting in Zurich airport waiting to board my plane, when I heard the sound of a U-boat sonar. It came from my pocket.

Piiiiiing, Piiiiiing.

It was my mobile phone. I pulled it out and pressed the green button. "Lars ...", I said. The voice on the other end was one of my friends. What he told me sounded alarming:

"Lars, I just came out from the bank seminar. They were the most bearish I have ever heard. In fact, it's the first time I heard them really worried—just thought you should know."

The seminar he referred to was an annual forecast seminar in Zurich, which as usual was held at a famous hotel by the shores of Lake Zurich. My friend and I used to go to this presentation every year, since it tended to be very good. But this time I couldn't come.

The message in my friend's call didn't come as a total surprise; I had in fact already sold a lot of my shares and hedged the rest by selling equity index futures at the end of 2007. But what he said still worried me. We kept talking for a while, and then we hung up. The plane was still not ready, so I sat and reflected for a while. "If this thing *really* tanks—and it could—then I don't want to get in trouble because of it," I thought. The issue was that I had invested in a lot of private equity, which you cannot sell easily, and I had committed myself to invest even more. And I also had hedge funds and small caps that you could not get out of quickly. I called a broker and sold more equity futures, before finally boarding the plane.

In retrospect I should have sold even more, of course. The meltdown that followed was even bigger than I feared, and probably also bigger than almost any investment banker would have guessed. It was the bust of a lifetime, and in spite of my foresight, my net equity ended up declining during its late phases, as I covered my hedge positions in futures too early.

So, what on Earth was it that happened in that crash? Some said it was *bubbles* that were bursting in 2007. However, even though some markets were too high at the top, I personally wouldn't call them by that name. U.S. real estate, for instance, wasn't in my opinion insanely expensive at the beginning of 2008, and nor were equities.

There were others who mainly saw the crises as a *systemic failure* in the financial system, which I think is definitely correct. Still others said it was a traditional *business cycle* event, which is clearly a part of the story. So, let's take that aspect first.

It would be risky to look into the future and not consider business cycles. There are two reasons for that. First, they have an enormous impact on our lives, so how they play out in the future will impact everything else. Second, the ways business cycles behave depend a lot on the longer term trends in innovation and inflation. And, third, I think that people often confuse cycles with trends, which is avoidable if you understand both. So, I will spend the next few pages going through the few facts that I think any investor or businessman needs to know.

The main reasons for business cycles are some phenomena that you may call "ketchup effects". A ketchup effect is when you keep hitting a ketchup bottle and nothing comes out—and then, suddenly, you get much too much. Similar effects will typically occur in three unstable areas of the economy

- inventories
- capital spending
- property.

Inventories is the most predictable and least troublesome of these. If you make a snapshot of any modern economy during normal economic times, you are likely to find that inventories constitute approx. 6% of annual GDP. Here is a step-by-step overview of how it creates cycles:

1. As we enter the last phases of a recession, inventories are lower than normal, because companies for a while haven't ordered anything.
2. As demand picks up from that point, companies will be forced to increase inventories. This catching up process increases new orders and thereby gives extra stimulus to the economy.
3. With an accelerating economy, companies keep trying to increase their inventories to still higher levels, but since their sales orders also increase, they get behind with restocking for a while. Furthermore, as the economy expands, delivery times for inventory get longer, which may compel companies to order more than they really need.
4. However, eventually they seem to have enough. Once that happens, the factory orders level off and suddenly many managers get worried that they actually overdid it now they have too much inventory. So, they stop ordering for a while, and the inventory-driven cycle turns down.

Inventory fluctuations tend to create a mild business cycle that turns down every 4–5 years, which makes it the shortest of business cycles. One reason that it is short is that inventories are easy to order and arrive fairly quickly (albeit slower in booms). You don't have a nuclear reactor or a skyscraper in your inventory; you have smaller or simpler stuff, like screws and bolts, raw materials, or simple products like shavers, vacuum cleaners, or cases of wine. If an economy is contracting 5% in a deep recession, then there is actually still 95% that is moving, so companies can fairly easily reduce their inventories. The reality is that once businesses panic at the beginning of a recession and start the de-stocking process, it will very rarely take more than 9–12 months before inventories are down to almost nothing, which is why the inventory cycle is short.

The next business cycle driver is *capital spending*, which is investments in machines and equipment like assembly lines, trucks, packing machines, and computers. Capital spending comprises approx. 9–10% of most modern economies, and more in high-growth emerging markets.

Why do capital investments cause economic fluctuations? Well, when the economy grows, companies will after a while decide that they need to increase their production capacity, so they order more equipment. This creates a boom among vendors of capital equipment, who then need to increase *their* capacity, so they will also order more equipment. The boom is, in other words, now self-feeding. Finally, when everyone feels that they have reached a sufficient capacity, the order flow is reduced, and many vendors will now suddenly sense that they have ordered too much equipment. Sales begin to fall, and then even more, and so on. This ketchup effect is very similar to the inventory phenomenon, but it is slower, since capital equipment is far more complicated and thus time-consuming to produce than inventory. The reason the capital-spending cycle is larger is that capital spending is a bigger part of the economy and because longer timelags make the excesses in both directions worse. Capital-spending cycles will on average create a downturn every 9–10 years.

Capital-spending cycles are serious, and the crash in information technology from 2000 to 2003 was a good example. However, the most violent business cycle is caused by inherent volatility in *property markets*. The typical developed economy spends on average around 9% of GDP on construction of residential property and 3% on commercial property. Around half of that is improvements and maintenance while the rest is new construction. Perhaps 20% is financed by government and thus fairly stable, but the rest is private, and it is here that this nasty cycle emerges.

So, how does it look? First, the average duration is 18–20 years. Just after a property market crash there is hardly any new construction activity—people are too scared, and existing property trades well below replacement cost anyway, so why build? Furthermore, a large proportion of developers are at this stage bankrupt, and financing for new development is difficult to get—developers or buyers will have to come up with large downpayments.

However, time passes and natural demand eventually catches up with the supply of unsold property. Property prices begin to rise and after a while reach levels where replacement becomes profitable. Developers now start looking for new plots, projects are drafted, building permits obtained, and construction begins. All of this takes years, of course. Meanwhile the market continues to improve and speculators join the fray. Furthermore, many private individuals may decide to purchase a second home now—partly for fun, perhaps, but also in the expectation that it will be a good and safe investment.

The final climax of the property cycle happens as a huge supply of new property is offered at price levels that only few can afford. Selling becomes difficult now, prices stall and trading volumes decline. Approximately a year after sales volumes have fallen, the prices start to drop too and continue down for 3–4 years.

It is in this phase that many banks realize to their horror that some of the speculators they have financed won't be able to repay their loans. As each speculator typically has several banks, the lenders conclude that the last to cancel loans will be left with the loss, so they make a competitive "run" on the client.

As property prices now are falling, the damage spreads from highly leveraged speculators to builders, brokers, and owners of real estate of all sorts. Bankruptcies follow, and lenders—who are typically themselves leveraged some 10 times—are forced to book mounting losses. Soon some of the weaker banks reach the brink, and whereas banks made runs on clients in the early phases of the crises, it's now clients that make runs on the banks. The weakest financial institutions are soon brought to their knees. Forced by risks of bankruptcies and declining asset bases, the banks will now cut off lending to all sectors, and the resulting contraction in overall liquidity leads to a severe recession, if not depression.

The property cycle has been known for more than 150 years and has been shown to behave in much the same way across different countries and regions as well as over the ages. Whereas each cycle can deviate substantially from the historical average, the typical scenario is this:

1. Beginning of a bust: One year where property prices stall and trading volume declines.
2. Then 3–4 years of price declines.
3. This is followed by a couple of years where trading resumes and prices slowly creep up.
4. Finally 10–15 years of rising prices, which accelerate just before the next bust.

As I said: This is the historical *average* and should only be understood as such. But, as mentioned, it has been robust over centuries and has been much the same in many different countries.

Here is a question: Why is it that property cycles are more dramatic than capital-spending cycles in developed countries? After all, we just saw that capital spending is approx. 9% of GDP and property approx. 12%. That's not such a huge difference, is it?

The answer relates partly to the so-called "wealth effect". When property prices go down, and as they pull equities with them, people suddenly feel a lot less wealthy, and that makes them stop spending. However, the bigger part of the reason why property downturns are so mean is that, whereas most other variable price assets are owned by non-leveraged investors such as pension funds, the property market rests on two layers of leverage. First, *the owners of property have normally borrowed a substantial part of the money for it*, and, second, *the institutions that lent them the money are typically themselves leveraged around 10 times* (excluding off-balance-sheet activities, which we review later).

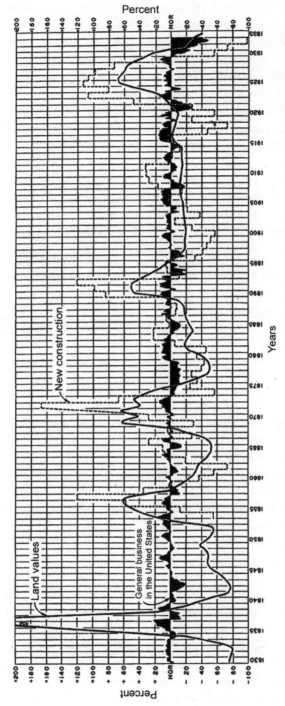

The Chicago property cycle over a 103-year period (1830–1933). It is fairly easy to see a pronounced, long-term cycle in land values and new construction in this long-term graph. *Source:* Hoyt, Homer: *One Hundred Years of Land Values in Chicago*, Chicago: Chicago University Press, 1933.

The three business cycles

There are three business cycles:

- *Inventory cycle.* Limited cycle with approx. 4.5-year average duration.
- *Capital-spending cycle.* Potentially strong cycle with approx. 9–10 year average duration.
- *Property cycle.* Strong cycle leading to banking crises. Average duration: 18–20 years.

There is a tendency that if one business cycle—say, the property cycle—turns down, the others turn down as well. This is called "mode-locking". Think about when people start clapping randomly after a concert and then quickly settle into a collective rhythm—it's something like that. Mode locking in business cycles happens because everything is connected, and it is especially pronounced during property crises, since these hurt the banking sector, which everyone depends on whether for financing inventory, capital spending, and, well, property.

I think that anybody who ever wants to invest or do business needs to be familiar with the cycles I just described. However, it is also extremely useful to know about normal "market rotation". This is a cyclical rotation between money markets, bond markets, and equities, and even within each of them. The typical overall sequence around (property-based) business cycles is given as a table on the next page.

The rotation around a capital spending–based business cycle is largely the same, except that with pure capital-spending or inventory-driven business cycles, the property market may not decline in the economic down phase, as benefits from falling interest rates more than offset the deteriorating economy.

Within each of the asset classes involved in market rotation there are also leaders and laggards. For the equity market, for instance, the sequence of outperformance before and during an economic upswing is typically that (1) financials and consumer discretionary rise first, then (2) information technology and industrials, and finally (3) resources. As the economy peaks, it is first consumer staples and then utilities that outperform.

Here is another thing that everyone should know (but many apparently don't): *Equities have on average peaked some 9 months before a peak in the economy* and then normally either gone into a trading range or

Financial market rotation over business cycles	
Boom	1. Increasing money rates (interest rates on bank loans)
	2. Declining bond prices (which means that interest rates for bonds go up)
	3. Declining stock prices
Decline	4. Declining economy
	5. Declining commodity prices
Crises	6. Declining real estate prices
	7. Low money rates
	8. Increasing bond prices
	9. Increasing stock prices
Recovery	10. Recovering economy
	11. Increasing commodity prices
	12. Increasing real estate prices

turned down. Goldman Sachs has measured that cyclical bear markets in the U.S. economy from 1847 to 1982 lasted an average of *23 months* and brought equity prices down an average of 30%. The behavior is somewhat different at troughs, where *equity markets on average turn back up some 5 months before the economic trough.*

So, equities are leading indicators at peaks as well as at troughs; in fact some of the best leading indicators we have. It can nevertheless be mentally challenging for those who bought near the bottom to hold on to their shares for 5 months while they see economic conditions continue to deteriorate. However (and this is often forgotten), when you buy a share it's not only the corporate profits or losses for the next 5 or 12 months you buy into, but discounted cashflows for the next 15 years or more. Seen in that light, financial markets overreact madly to cyclical fluctuations in the economy.

Why are lead times longer at peaks than at troughs? One reason can be that economic peaks are drawn out due to the momentum of capital spending and property construction activity, which is difficult to terminate quickly. For that reason equity markets will often commence a multi-month period with high volatility, but no clear trend, before they turn down before a peak in the economy. Financial price patterns at lower turning points are often more abrupt since the lower economic turning point can come quickly, mainly kick-started by inventory restocking. In any case, Baron Rothschild once said that the time to buy equities is "when there is blood in the streets—even if it's your own," which is very right. Equities should be bought even before the economy reaches its lowest point, and one of the early signals to do so is often a recovery in bond prices, including corporate bonds, followed, perhaps, by a period where equities stop falling in spite of deteriorating news.

Commodities also play a big role in market rotation. First, they are clearly laggers in the business cycle. Gordon & Rouwenhorst studied how different commodities fluctuated over U.S. business cycles from 1959 to 2004 (*Facts and Fantasies about Commodity Futures*). Below are their average price performance compared with bonds and equities, where I have highlighted strong performance phases in gray:

	Early expansion	Late expansion	Early recession	Late recession
Copper	2.3%	18.8%	11.3%	−21.6%
Zinc	3.3%	11.9%	−8.6%	−1.7%
Nickel	3.4%	14.1%	6.9%	−11.2%
Aluminum	−0.6%	4.6%	5.6%	−3.8%
Lead	2.6%	11.6%	−16%	−9.7%
Corporate bonds	11.5%	3.6%	−2.9%	25.7%
S&P Total return	18.1%	10.4%	−15.5%	17.3%
Source: Gordon & Rouwenhorst: *Facts and Fantasies about Commodity Futures*.				

The difference is clear. Corporate bonds explode upwards even during late recession and continue into the recovery, as inflation melts away, as liquidity expands, and as a better future is discounted. These are closely followed by equities, for the same reason and because the discount rate of futures earnings (which is bond yields) is dropping. Commodities kick in late in the expansion, where in particular copper and zinc perform well. Copper even stays high into early recession since construction projects that had been started during the expansion typically will be continued until they are finished.

Investing well over business cycles is not a question of whether one has invested at given times or not, but of *what* one has invested in during each phase. There is always a bull market. And a bear market.

————

Enough about business cycle theory. Let's instead give the great bust of 2007–2009 a closer look. It started with a peak in trading activity in U.S. residential real estate in 2006 followed by falling real estate prices from 2007. The timing is interesting here, because the previous time the U.S. experienced this was in 1986–1991, which was exactly 20 years earlier. This previous event was called the "savings and loan crises", and it was ugly: during that period so-called "housing starts" (new homes constructed) fell by 45% to its lowest level since World War II, and the savings and loan crises led to the default of no fewer than 745 savings and loan associations.

My point here is that what happened in 2007–2009 was textbook business cycle stuff, and since the banking sector as usual got paralyzed by its losses, it cut off funding for capital spending so that this also fell dramatically. The fact that there was a banking crisis was also in accordance with standard business cycle models—all property crises lead to banking crises, so that banks have to reduce lending. Needless to say, companies reacted by reducing inventory, which led to a synchronized collapse in all three business cycles. As I said: textbook stuff. However, there were other aspects of the 2007–2009 meltdown that wasn't by the book. To explain this I would like to tell a few fictive tales.

We start in good old Germany, where property wasn't expensive at all by 2006 (I invested with some friends a lot in German prime-location property in the previous years, at around 40% of replacement value and with annual cash yields of around 6–8%. That's very cheap!). Anyway, we imagine we are at a bank affiliate in the imaginary German village of Hochdorf, where Mr. Schmidt is responsible for the local mortgage department.

Just after lunch Mr. Schmidt receives a phone call from an old client, Mr. Müller, who says that he would like to buy a new house. "I have been saving up for a downpayment for a number of years", he says. "Aber gut", answers Mr. Schmidt, and adds that Mr. Müller can expect to get 70% financing, since the bank has known him for many years, and since they know that he is in a safe job and that he also has a stable marriage, life insurance, a healthy life style, and that he earns enough to handle this.

Mr. Schmidt and Mr. Müller are here both behaving responsibly and exhibiting what the Germans call "geschäftssinn", which means business acumen. The world is full of *geschäftssinn*.

However, let's now go across the pond and imagine that it is still 2006, but we are now in the U.S. A salesman called Daniel Williams works in *Golden Opportunity Finance, Inc.* in an imaginary city called Maimi. One sunny Monday morning Daniel makes a phone call to an unemployed man called Joe Johnson. Daniel now asks Joe if he would like to buy a condominium. It has already been arranged that he can get cheap financing from *Local Finance Inc.*, he explains; a financial package, where Joe doesn't even have to pay any interest the first few years. Not a single dollar! And furthermore, Joe can then sell his condo if he wants to, as soon as its price has gone up, which means that he can get rich without working. If the worst should happen and Joe can't pay (for which reason should that be, by the way?), then he can just send back the keys and all will be forgotten. The condo will be the only collateral for the loan; no personal guarantee.

Joe just had five beers and doesn't quite understand everything Daniel says (what does "collateral" mean, for instance?), so Daniel explains again that he doesn't really take any risk here. ". . . so if property prices go up, you get rich, and if they go down, you can just walk away."

Joe still doesn't fully get it, but the core of the story—that he can get rich without working—does resonate. So, they meet the next day, Joe signs the agreement soon after, and Daniel is pleased, because he works on commission only; the more loans, the more commissions. And Daniel isn't particularly worried about risk, because everyone knows that real estate always goes up, so what he just did was basically to do Joe a huge favor, wasn't it?

Daniel's boss in *Golden Opportunity Finance* may be a bit more cynical. He knows that you are not allowed to issue property loans that exceed the value of the real estate. So, he calls in a local appraiser to put a value on each property they deal with. Now, there are many of these appraisers around, and some have a more optimistic view on things than others, to put it that way. Fortunately Daniel's boss has found one who is distinctly forthcoming (which, by the way, is why this appraiser seems to get more business than his competitors).

All of this may sound very risky for *Golden Opportunity Finance*, but it really isn't, because they sell all of these loans to *Big Bank Ltd.* with a profit. So, whether Joe can repay the loan doesn't actually matter to *Golden Opportunity Finance*. Amazingly, it doesn't matter to *Big Bank* either, because they have a whole team of academics, who slice these loans into different financial products, like you would slice salami. Different slices of this salami are then sold on to "special-purpose vehicles" or "SPVs". *Big Bank* writes contracts that stipulate how payments from the lenders (Joe and others like him) first will go to the most privileged bundles and then be distributed to the others.

This sounds complex, perhaps, but brace yourself, because there is more. The SPVs are sold on to *Global Megabank Inc.*, which has some Ivy League people-class experts, who use them as a basis for creating "collateralized debt obligations", or "CDOs". The basis for the CDOs is the money flowing from the SPVs, but the CDOs are not directly tied to the underlying loans. There is no direct connection between Joe in Maimi and the CDOs, only an indirect one.

Now it gets really hairy, because *Global Megabank* calls *Global Rating Agency, Inc.* and asks if they could issue official credit ratings for each of the salami slices. *Global Rating Agency* agrees and asks for documentation, which *Global Megabank* sends over in the form of some enormous electronic spreadsheets containing information about

- how many of the transactions have reduced interest payments for the first years
- where the properties were located
- whether they were primary residences or second homes
- how much of the estimated property value was financed, or had no downpayments
- how many were made without any valid documentation for the buyer's economic status, etc.

Global Megabank has a good dialog with *Global Rating Agency*, which puts all of this into their computers to calculate the ratings. Because of the good relationship (*Global Megabank* is a great client), the bank knows exactly how the ratings models work. They also know how to create each salami slice so that it just—*just!*—qualifies for a given credit rating. The best bundles will now be rated "AAA" (barely), which to an investor means that they should be really, really safe. But there are typically around 12 risk layers, and some of those will evidently get low ratings and thus have a higher interest rate to compensate for the risk.

I promise to end this soon, but we aren't finished yet. *Global Megabank* has found a way to turn the junk slices of salami into financial gourmet food: Buy loss insurance from *Global Credit Insurance, Inc.* That has a price, of course, but it's worth it, since it turns financial toxic waste into AAA.

It doesn't stop here. The people at *Global Megabank* establish some empty CDO companies and give these some clear, written investment mandates and calls *Global Rating Agency* to get these CDO companies rated as well. That whole process is then repeated with other CDO companies intended to own car loans, credit card loans, student loans, and what not. All of this is called "asset-backed securities" or "ABS", and the CDOs that hold them don't need to appear on the bank's balance sheets.

And what does *Global Megabank* do with the loans it actually keeps? It establishes so-called special-purpose vehicles (SPVs), or "off-balance-sheet conduits", which buy (CDOs/ABSs) based on different loans from third parties and finances them with so-called "commercial paper"; a sort of very short-term bonds. In order to achieve high ratings on these, it issues credit default swaps (CDSs). These SPVs are incorporated in offshore locations, and *Global Megabank* doesn't need to put them on its balance sheet, as it neither owns the assets nor handles the financing. The idea is that these vehicles should simply run forever and generate an interest differential that can be brought back to the bank from time to time, which will be good for the stock price as well as for the bonuses and stock options of management.

I think you get the picture, and stuff like this *did* happen on a very large scale—the *financial sector was building the biggest house of cards in the history of business on a foundation of people like our Joe in Maimi.*

Did they know this? There is every indication that most of the players didn't fully comprehend it. After all, the salami slices were bundled, re-bundled and sold and resold globally, and spread to international pension funds, hedge funds, small banks, and even local counties. Some of these buyers would even use them as collateral for highly leveraged investments, which at times were funded though other departments in the same banks that sold the salami slices in the first place. When the crash came, apart from a few people from J.P. Morgan, Goldman Sachs, and Credit Suisse plus some hedge funds, I think very few market participants understood how dangerous the whole thing had become. If they had, would the banks have bought the stuff themselves?

We are done here, as far as the mechanics of the salami machine goes, even though my description was highly simplified. However, one may ask what the purpose of all this activity essentially was? The answer, I think, is predominantly two things: (1) to create fees and (2) to increase leverage. The former wasn't a systemic threat to society, but the latter was. Both will be repeated numerous times in the future, although I think it will take a long time before we see it on a scale similar to the runup of the 2007–2009 collapse.

Now, whereas this convoluted story was about excesses at *financial* institutions prior to the 2007–2009 collapse, the *commercial* business sector seemed much sounder. Commercial companies are car manufacturers, for instance, or courier services, food processors, and pharmaceutical companies—real stuff. Profits were here on average extremely high up to 2007. Furthermore, capital spending wasn't excessive, and balance sheets actually looked sounder than at almost any time since World War II.

However, there was also a problem within commercial companies—it was about how they funded themselves. The traditional sources of funding for a commercial corporation are either (1) to issue equity, or (2) to issue bonds, or (3) to arrange for bank loans, and collateral for the last two could be anything. It might be government bonds, high-grade corporate bonds, etc., which would be almost entirely financed after deduction of a so-called "haircut" of perhaps 10, 15, or 20%. The collateral could also be tangible assets of many kinds. Lots and lots of assets could be converted to cool cash in this way; a process that was called "securitization".

If you issue equity you have no legal obligation to pay anything back; and bonds are paid over a long time schedule according to predefined terms. So these two arrangements are fairly safe for the issuing company. The third option, funding via bank loans/credit lines may in principle be dicier, since the bank could terminate the agreement, or choose not to prolong ("roll") it after expiry. In reality the bank will often be interested in working with the company to solve any issues, unless the case is hopeless, since brutally turning off the tap may severely damage the value of any collateral and even hurt the bank's reputation.

Now, from 2004 to 2006 a change happened. The market witnessed a marked increase in the use of a fourth funding method: so-called "commercial paper", which was a sort of ultra-short-term bonds (or more correctly "promissory notes") that were not backed by any collateral. There was a good reason for this: Banks are expensive to run, you know, with their management bonuses, marble palaces and stuff, and with commercial paper you could essentially bypass them and thus avoid contributing indirectly to the overheads of banking.

However, whereas banks do have overheads, there are good reasons for that (apart from their palaces). They have management teams, for instance, who can negotiate with an issuer in trouble, and they have access to funds from central banks during liquidity squeezes.

The commercial paper market didn't have these safety valves. When you issued commercial paper you just hoped that someone picked them up. Every time some of these expired, you just issued some new ones, which would be snapped up in the market.

But what if one day nobody wanted to buy your commercial paper? When the crises broke out, the buyers vanished, and thousands of companies suddenly were left out of cash. Imagine your private economy was perfectly fine and that you had a short-term variable-rate mortgage on your house that was renewed every 6 months. And then imagine, that you suddenly couldn't renew it and had to come up with all you owed here and now. Just imagine! It was often like that.

So, there we have it: The property market had become too expensive and was beginning a natural, cyclical correction; the financial system had inadvertently built a huge house of cards, and due to securitization credit had expanded beyond anything meaningful. Furthermore, the commercial sector was increasingly funding itself through a system with no safety valves. The name for all of what happened in this financial house of cards was "shadow banking", and we can call the wealth that had piled up in variable price assets "shadow money". Some of this was very shady indeed, but all of it was fragile. It could go very wrong, and it did. Here are the 10 easy steps to disaster:

1. People like Joe from Maimi defaulted on mortgages they should never have had. They returned their keys ("jingle-mail") and abandoned their property.
2. Property prices began to decline, thus beginning the downturn phase of the property cycle. Leveraged players defaulted. Paper values for trillions disappeared.
3. Banks began fearing each other's exposure to collateralized debt obligations and special-purpose vehicles, etc. Consequently, they stopped lending to each other.

4. The stock market crashed, wiping out further trillions in paper wealth. Leveraged players were forced to sell.
5. Building construction declined and home builders and developers went bankrupt.
6. Rising fear and declining liquidity meant that the commercial paper market shut down, thus cutting off financing to the banks' off-balance-sheet structures as well as to the commercial sector.
7. Issuers of credit default swaps were overwhelmed by claims and became insolvent, thus rendering default-insured bonds far more risky than buyers had expected.
8. Credit ratings agencies got sued and downgraded instruments from AAA to junk status in a single step, thus forcing pension funds and others who were only allowed to own AAA-rated paper to dispose of them, which created new waves of forced selling.
9. Commercial companies terminated their capital spending due to lack of funding and because of fear of the future. At the same time they began reducing their inventories, which added to the overall contraction. The decline phase of the capital-spending and inventory cycles was in other words starting, and cyclical mode-locking was playing out.
10. Companies were forced to lay off people, which created unemployment. This meant falling demand and increasing defaults on credit cards, consumer loans, etc.

These events were not simply a case of one following the other as falling dominoes, but rather a global, vicious circle, where each and every part was simultaneously fueling the others, with the result that property prices, equity prices, corporate bond prices, capital spending, inventory, and credit in general all were brought down to levels that were far below the long-term trend.

While every property down cycle leads to banking crises, this one was unusual, because it was a real "bank run" like the ones that were common in the 19th century. The only difference was that this one started not as a retail bank run—like many of those had been—but in the wholesale sector. This particular run was instigated by institutional investors and by the banks themselves, as they stopped lending to each other.

As the collapse unfolded, the assets that could be securitized before and which therefore had appeared very "money-like" suddenly lost all collateral value. Meanwhile, money stopped changing hands—a phenomenon economists call "a decline in the velocity of money". It was probably the steepest such decline in money flows in 80 years, and one of the steepest declines in average global asset values for just as long. All of this made it an important lesson for the future, and so was the role of money and assets in it. The next chapter is about what money and assets are, and what they do.

2

Money and assets

During August 2009 I was on holiday with my family in Greece. Although there were clearly green seeds in the global economy at that time, it wasn't exactly difficult to get table reservations that summer. One day, when I was sitting in a the "1800" restaurant in the stunningly beautiful island of Santorini, my sister, who is a kindergarten teacher, asked me a good question:

> *"Lars, what I don't get is . . . why doesn't anyone seem to have any money now? Money can't just disappear, can it? It must be somewhere . . .?"*

In that moment it was too hot and beautiful to think very clearly about economics, so I answered fairly briefly that most of the money in a modern economy is credit, which actually can be canceled and thus can disappear. However, her question wasn't half-bad, so let's just take a closer look at what happens to money during crises, because it will actually lead us to some important points.

We can start with the definition of money. Virtually all economists agree that the functions of money are (1) mediums of exchange, (2) units of account, and (3) stores of value. Central banks typically refer to three basic categories of money, which they called M0, M1, and M2. These are jointly described as "narrow money", and they include cash and simple bank accounts—stuff that is simple and gives easy-to-use access for normal people. Furthermore, they use the terms M3, M4, and M5 for "broad money", which include institutional deposits, building society shares, etc.

I think the central bank definition of money is good when it comes to its function as mediums of exchange and units of account. However, it seems less complete when it comes to money's role as a store of value. Just think about how people store their wealth. Is it "money"? Some of it, yes. Some will indeed be stashed in savings—and money market accounts (M2), for instance, or in treasury bills (M5), or simply in cash (M0). But most people with meaningful savings will have a big part of their wealth in real estate, equities, bonds, jewellery, or perhaps in more exotic stuff such as collector cars, gold bars, or quality art. So, they will be placing their wealth in assets that aren't defined as "money" by central banks, but which does some of what money by definition should do: store value. These assets are called "variable-price assets".

One may think there is a clear difference between these assets and official money here, because a dollar is a dollar—it's not variable price. But the price of dollars measured in euros or yen does vary a lot over time—just like all those variable-price assets. Internationally, all stores of value are variable price.

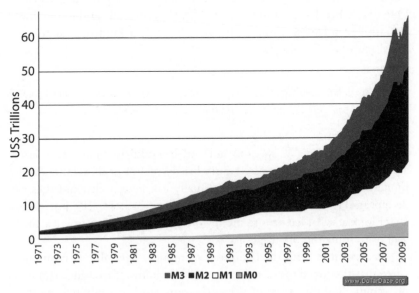

Estimated global monetary aggregates (Jan 1971–Dec 2009). *Source: www.dollardaze.org*

Let's just try to get our heads around some proportions here, starting with variable-price assets. I made the calculation which you will see below, using all reasonable variable-price assets. I excluded here all normal cars as well as aircraft and yachts, which tend to decline in value.

Estimate of global variable-price assets in 2004, in trillion dollars				
Variable-price asset class	*Total asset value* (U.S.$ trillion)		*Mid-range estimate* (% of global GDP)	
Residential property, OECD	*60–80*		*170%*	
Residential property, emerging markets	*15–25*		*49%*	
Global commercial property	15–25		49%	
Total property		*90–130*		*268%*
Bonds		45–55		122%
Equities		35–40		100%
Gold		1.6–2.0		4%
Collectibles		0.3–0.6		1%
Total, all variable-price assets		*172–228*		*488%*
− Estimated double-counting of assets owned by listed companies		(2–8)		(12%)
= *Total gross variable-price assets, excluding double-counting*		*170–220*		*476%*

The year for my calculation is 2004, where global GDP was $41 trillion. This may seem an oddly remote year to choose, but the reason is that 2004 was a very "normal" mid-cycle year, where global economies and asset markets were fairly calm—neither in a boom, nor a recession. Before we look at the details of these variable-price assets, I should add that the global money supply was just under $40 trillion in that year, so almost the same as global GDP.

Now, in this table you will see in the bottom row that my estimate of global variable-price assets in 2004 is around $170 trillion to $220 trillion. This means that *the value of variable-price assets is something like four to five times as big as GDP*. Furthermore, since money supply is approx. the same as one year's GDP, we can see that *the value of variable-price assets is also approx. four to five times as big as global money supply*.

Another key conclusion is that *property typically represents more than half of all variable-price wealth*—at least it did in my "normal" year 2004. The reason I think this is important, is that when the property cycle turns down, the decline in wealth is massive. If property prices fall 30% in my example, it may remove wealth equal to around 80% of all money (M5) in society.

Economists have tried many methods to calculate how big the effect of any wealth destruction is when asset prices fall, and the broad consensus is that the economy all-else-equal will contract by 6% of a wealth loss, unless it's very brief. And we should remember here that just before a crash, variable-asset values may be higher—perhaps five to six times global GDP, which makes the subsequent wealth loss even steeper. Let's imagine that variable-price wealth at the peak of a cyclical boom is five times GDP and that it subsequently does as follows:

- equities decline 50%
- property declines 35%
- bonds rise 20% (because of flight to safety).

The net effect of that would be a decline of total variable-price wealth of approx. 25% equaling roughly 125% of GDP (and 135% of money supply). Multiply that by the wealth effect and it gives an economic drag of ca. 7% of GDP.

The wealth effect is not immediate—it plays out over several years, and if asset prices recover fully within a short time, the wealth effect may not be that bad. However, it is not the only contraction of value that happens in a decline. People from a major Swiss bank told me that they estimated how much the abrupt stop to securitization during the crises in America reduced that country's money supply. They estimated this by taking all the common collaterals, apply standard haircuts, and assume that for a while none of these could be used anymore. The monetary loss was equal to approx. 25% of America's GDP!

I'd like to play a bit with the numbers, but this time looking at the real economy rather than the monetary sector. Let's assume that we have a really bad recession and that building construction and capital spending contract by 40% each, as declining asset prices destroy collateral, spread fear, and reduce commercial demand. That removes 5% and 4% of GDP, respectively. We can also assume that inventories are brought

Global variable-price wealth distribution

The pie chart below illustrates a typical distribution of different variable-price assets, and thus gives a feel for where meaningful wealth destruction can come from. A decline in the price of gold, for instance, does very little economic damage, but when commercial and residential property prices decline, it hurts.

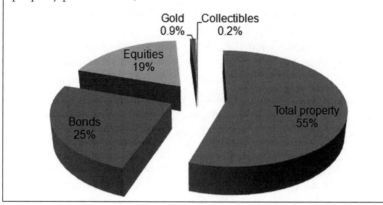

down by something equal to 2% of GDP and that private consumption declines 6% due to fear, wealth loss, and rising unemployment. If consumption starts at 70% of GDP, then this decline of 6% will remove approx. 4% from GDP. Let's just add these numbers up:

Decline in building construction:	5% of GDP
Decline in capital spending	4% of GDP
Decline in inventories	2% of GDP
Decline in private consumption	4% of GDP
Total decline	*15% of GDP*

There are all sorts of technical issues with what I just wrote above, and some economy professors might pull their hair out while reading it, but I think it does give a fairly decent back-of-the-envelope estimate of what can happen, when (1) the property cycle turns down and (2) the credit market consequently gets paralyzed, which leads to (3) a brutal decline in capital spending and (4) a rapid reduction of inventory as well as in (5) private consumption.

This total loss of 15% of GDP in my calculation example sounds truly horrifying, but fortunately it doesn't really happen like that. Let's say

that what I described is stretched out over 3 years, during which accumulated trend growth would otherwise be 6% (approx. 2% annually). The
15% loss above is "all-else-equal", but if real trend growth is 6%, then
that would pull the other way. Let's also assume that the government
starts running a large budget deficit to stimulate the economy and that
the central bank reduces interest rates to almost nothing and pumps liquidity into the system through purchase of bonds and by other means. The
effect of all this may be to turn a massive cyclical disaster into a briefer
and more shallow recession.

And this is exactly what happened in the subprime salami crisis (as I
will now call it) in 2007–2009, where interest rates were brought close to
zero in a number of countries, where central banks used all standard tools
(plus some that were made up on the fly) to support the banking system
and increase money supply, and where several governments began
running budget deficits of close to 10% of GDP or even more.

What if this entire stimulus hadn't happened, by the way? What if
authorities simply had let the crises run their course and "get all the rot
out of the system", as many suggested? I think we in this case would
have relearned the lessons from the Great Depression of the 1930s which
is that, whereas recessions tend to fade automatically, *depression* is a trap
you can't get easily out of. It's like when a golf ball goes into a lake
instead of the sand bunker.

Depression can in fact be a nasty equilibrium that persists until
authorities intervene. In a depression scenario, the baby would have been
thrown out with the bath water, as they say: entrepreneurs with great
ideas would get no funding; fragile companies would be wiped out;
well-educated and motivated people would see their time and talents
wasted; and great companies caught in the middle of major capital investments would suffocate for lack of funding. Furthermore, crime would
soar and intellectual and real assets, which had been developed over generations, would be sold off for a pittance to entities such as the sovereign
wealth funds of oil-producing nations that hadn't contributed to their
creation. Finally, the only lasting wealth loss from a recession comes
because of unemployment. This would have soared towards perhaps 20%
of the workforce, leading to permanent loss. Just letting the crises run
their course would have been a terrible and unnecessary waste.

Another objection to public intervention was raised: If central banks
pump that much money into the system, it will lead to inflation. This
objection sounds relevant in the sense that inflation always is, as the economist Milton Friedman rightly has claimed, "a monetary problem".
However, the authorities didn't try to *increase* liquidity; they merely tried

to prevent it from falling. How is that? Well, money is what money does. There exists a simple equation to explain this:

> **the amount of money**
> multiplied by
> **the velocity of its circulation**

equals

> **the amount of goods and services**
> multiplied by
> **the average price of goods and services**

This equation, which is called the "quantity theory of money", is actually not really a theory, but rather a statement of a dry fact. It applies in a household, a country, the whole world, or when you play Monopoly with your children.

What happens in a recession is not only that money supply (M) declines because credit is canceled, but also, as I mentioned in the previous chapter, that *the velocity (V) of money declines*—the speed with which it changes hands collapses. There is no direct way that authorities can force the private sector to move their money around faster, but they can compensate by (1) making it less attractive to sit on it by reducing interest rates, (2) allowing banks to increase their leverage, and (3) purchasing bonds, which drive down interest rates while increasing money supply and wealth.

So, as long as demand for products and services is far below production capacity, and as long as velocity of money is reduced, pumping out money will not create inflation. It is only when demand catches up with production capacity that central banks need to pull back their money.

Perhaps this is a good time to conclude with a short answer to my sister's question *"Lars, what I don't get is . . . why doesn't anyone seem to have any money now? Money can't just disappear, can it?"* I think a correct, short answer is this:

"Yes, money can actually disappear from an economy, for three main reasons:

1. First, most of the money in our economy is credit, which is based on promises to pay. Credit agreements can be reduced or canceled.

The expression that "a bank is an institution that lends you an umbrella when the sun is shining", is no misnomer. When a crisis is brewing, bankers and other creditors start doubting promises to pay, so they stop lending.

2. Second, if we accept that variable-price assets overlap with money as stores of wealth, then those do in fact decline. People's perception of their wealth changes, when prices of their real estate and financial holdings, etc. fall. They will then say that they "lost money" even if these holdings technically aren't called money. When asset prices fall, people will adjust their behaviors by spending less.

3. Third, the speed with which money changes hands can decline very rapidly, and money hidden under a mattress has no economic effect at all; it's as if it had disappeared."

I didn't say that, when my sister asked, but again: it was awfully hot in Santorini that day.

Time to wrap up. Whenever there is a cyclical crisis, there will be people expecting it to run for years on end, as it actually did in the Great Depression in the 1930s and in Japan after 1990. However, the conditions for that are fairly rare. When it does happen, it is either because the economy slips into real depression—which is entirely avoidable given that central banks ultimately have unlimited ability to create money—or because necessary restructuring in ailing companies is postponed forever through state subsidies, as we have actually seen in Japan. Revival, when it comes, has to be built on sound, internationally competitive businesses.

What I am getting at here is that business cycles essentially are what the word says: cyclical. This means that all the forces that can create a bust can also work in the opposite direction. The forces that in my hypothetical case gave a cyclical downdrift in an economy equal to "15% of GDP", may work in the opposite direction.

In fact, at some point they probably will. The statistics show that, normally, the bigger the preceding busts, the more powerful the following recoveries tend to be. Furthermore, revival after banking crises is typically very swift, because a banking crisis in itself isn't a symptom of overspending or overinvesting that has to be worked off over time. When such a snapback plays out, the only reason that our economies may not explode into inflationary overdrive can be that central banks and finance ministers manage to lean effectively into the wind. Central banks, in particular, can change from the accelerator to the brake pedal very quickly. So, that is the first conclusion: Cycles should not be confused with trends.

I think the other major conclusion is that the next thing to look for after a crisis such as the subprime salami calamity is not a long period of dull sluggishness, but a major revival. While it happens, I believe that this revival, which may be long and structural, will be fraught with numerous bubbles, scares, and crashes. So, that is what the next chapter will be about.

3

Bubbles, scares, and crashes

I think a bubble can be loosely defined as a group of assets whose price within a fairly short span of months or years rises to insane levels and then crashes. Below is a very good example: The IT bubble 1998–2000, in which NASDAQ, after a long and entirely justified bull market, accelerated and rose 360% in just two frantic years before collapsing completely. The graph below shows how NASDAQ behaved during this episode.

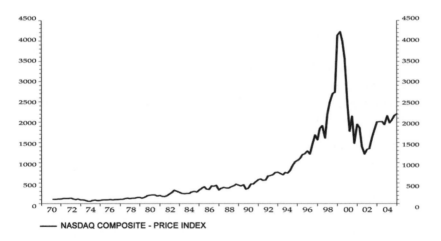

NASDAQ COMPOSITE - PRICE INDEX

If you look closely at the graph, you can see that up until early 1998 NASDAQ was in a nice, orderly bull market. When markets behave like NASDAQ did from 1981 to 1998, there are normally two factors in place: (1) cheap money and (2) a good "story". In the case of this particular bull market, the story was mainly the vast improvements in computer performance, the massive growth in the internet, and the global boom in mobile phones. Very exciting indeed, and a good reason for these stocks to rise.

However, what you also see from the graph is that the whole thing went mad from 1998 to 2000 and rose several hundred percent within two years. These were the days when, for instance, a company called Theglobe.com went public at $9 and rose to $97 during its first day of trading, reaching a market cap of $1 billion. I mention that particular company because it had only booked $2.7 million in revenues in its entire lifetime. Furthermore, it ran huge losses and had no proprietary technologies or patents. Another company with the name The Fantastic Corporation, of which I was a cofounder, reached a market cap of €4.6 billion just over 4 years after its foundation. Even though all we employees loved what we had created, there were times when we wondered how fast we might get a good return on such a market cap. (*That* company did in fact have numerous patents and meaningful revenues, I should add, plus financial and commercial backing from Intel, Deutsche Telekom, Reuters, Loral, BT, Telecom Italia, Lucent, KirchGroup, and Singapore Press Holdings).

––––––––––

The IT bubble was just a single example of financial exuberance among many. The way I count it, there have been 47 major bubbles and therefore 47 crashes in the world since 1557 (I have listed them all in *www.superscares.com*) Others may tabulate it differently, but I think my number is reasonably fair. I have tried to divide these calamities into categories. This gets a bit complicated by the fact that many bubbles and crashes involved more than one business area, so the total number below exceeds 47. Anyway, here they are:

- Finance and credit: 16
- Infrastructure: 13
- Property: 12
- Commodities: 11
- Trade-related activity: 9
- Agriculture: 9
- Collectibles: 3
- Mmanufacturing: 3.

It is hardly surprising that the four biggest categories among these bubble-drivers tie directly in with the main business cycles. After all, the most common category, *finance and credit* expansion, is part of major business cycles. It was, for instance, very central to the subprime salami fiasco, as I showed in the previous chapters. Furthermore, the second category in my list above, *infrastructure* investments, is related to 9-year to 10-year capital spending. *Property* is related to the 18-year to 20-year property cycle and *commodities* to the capital-spending and property cycles (as both activities require a lot of commodities). So, bubbles occur largely in those parts of the economy that by nature are most volatile. They tend to tie in with business cycles.

One day a few years ago, I attended a presentation by Jonathan Wilmot, the Chief Global Strategist at Credit Suisse, in which he mentioned that major asset price appreciation mainly happens during periods of globalization and innovation. He illustrated different economic phases with the longest continuing graph of any bond that exists: British Consols. These are bonds that never expire, and the graph gives a pretty good impression of interest rates and inflation expectations in the developed world since 1700. Here it is:

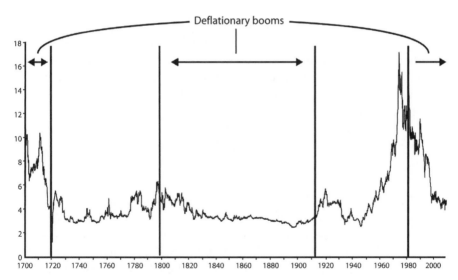

Yields on British Consols (1700–2009). *1700 to 1720*: This boom marked the first breakthroughs for the early industrial revolution in England, Scotland, and parts of Continental Europe. *1800 to 1913*: It was during these years that the Industrial Revolution really accelerated and started spreading across the globe. This went hand in hand with global trade expansion between the Old World and North and South America, India, Australia, New Zealand, and other areas. *1980–*: The fall of socialism coincided with innovative breakthroughs in IT to create the first truly global deflationary boom. *Source*: Consols graph by Credit Suisse; vertical lines inserted by Lars Tvede.

The graph shows three periods where the yields were generally falling: 1700–1720, 1800–1913, and 1970–2010. These three periods all exhibited "deflationary booms" driven by globalization and innovation.

I would like to get a bit technical here. Some of what happens during a deflationary boom can be explained with the quantity-of-money equation I mentioned earlier:

$$MV = PQ$$

where the left-hand side of the equation is M for money supply and V for velocity of money, and the right-hand side is P for prices of products and services sold, and Q for quantity of products and services sold. If globalization and innovation make it very unlikely that companies raise prices (P) due to high competition and productivity increases, then central banks can pump out a lot of money (MV) without getting inflation. Actually, they may even be forced to do this in order to avoid deflation (falling prices). One result of this is that the amount of money (MV) rises steeply, and this is reflected in fast growth in the amount of goods and services (Q). In other words: *the speed limit in the economy is high in deflationary environments.*

But there is another effect: A large part of the increase in money spills over to asset markets: you get "asset inflation". The quantity equation incorporates such asset inflation in the sense that P and Q not only concerns the prices and quantities of, say, cars and telephones produced, but also of assets such as equities and land. If the demand for assets exceeds their supply, their price goes up. So again: *The easy money of deflationary booms creates asset inflation.* Does past evidence support this thought? If you take the list of bubbles I referred to before, you will see an interesting pattern:

- There were two bubbles during the deflationary boom in 1700–1720. This is perhaps not a very large number, but both were absolutely massive. There was the South Sea Bubble, on the one hand, and the so-called "Mississippi Bubble" along with the crash of Banque Général and Banque Royale, on the other. So, two bubbles in 20 years is *one every 10 years.*
- Over the next 80 years there were just six bubbles—*one every 13 years.*
- Then, during the deflationary boom between 1800 and 1913 there were no fewer than 21 bubbles, which means *one every 5 years.*
- Between 1913 and 1980 there were only four—*one every 17 years.*
- Between 1980 and 2010 there were 12, and some of them have been huge. That amounts to . . . *one every 3 years!*

So, now the world is in the biggest, most coordinated deflationary boom ever, and therefore there are more bubbles than ever before, and since I will argue later that low inflation and high growth will be with us for several decades, the numerous financial bubbles and crashes will be as well. *I would guess that one bubble–crash pair every 3 years on average is a reasonable expectation.*

However, bubbles and crashes are not the only turbulence we can expect. There will also be numerous so-called "scares". When I was a teenager, I sat at home one day doing my homework with the radio on in the background. It was airing an interview with an environmentalist, but I was barely listening until he said something that caught my attention. He said that by year 2000 he expected the Mediterranean Sea would be so polluted, that you could not get closer than 25 km from its shores without smelling the rotten stench. Personally, I had been to the beaches of Cote D'Azur, and I knew that they let untreated sewage right out in the sea there, so to me what this environmentalist just said didn't sound implausible. I got scared.

It was also around that time that the international bestseller *Limits to Growth* came out. My parents got the 1974 edition, which, among other things, contained forecasts for when we would run out of different resources if the world economy continued its exponential growth rate. The book was based on findings from a huge computer model of the world from MIT (Massachusetts Institute of Technology), and it showed, that given known reserves, gold would run out in 1983, silver and mercury in 1987, tin in 1989, zinc in 1992, lead and copper in 1995, and aluminum in 2005. Somewhat reassuringly, the book also contained a second and far more optimistic forecast, assuming that reserves actually were five times as large as known at the time of publication. Under those assumptions we would run out of gold in 2003, mercury in 2005, silver in 2016, and petroleum in 2024, etc. This also scared me, because how would my generation get by if the world ran out of one commodity after another as I grew up?

However, the biggest scare in that same year (1974) was about an imminent ice age. The scare had begun a bit earlier. *Science Digest* had in 1973 published an article about the subject which stated:

> "At this point, the world's climatologists are agreed on only two things: That we do not have tens of thousands of years to prepare for the next ice age, and that how carefully we monitor our atmospheric

pollution will have direct bearing on the arrival and nature of this weather crisis. The sooner man confronts these facts, these scientists say, the safer he'll be."

We had learned in school that my country, Denmark, had been totally covered with ice during parts of the previous ice age, and now people said it was likely to happen again and could come very quickly. Anne and Paul Ehrlich published a book called *The End of Affluence* where they predicted how global cooling would diminish agricultural output. On April 28, 1975 *Newsweek* wrote a big piece about it proclaiming:

"There are ominous signs that the Earth's weather patterns have begun to change dramatically and that these changes may portend a drastic decline in food production with serious political implications for just about every nation on Earth. The drop in food output could begin quite soon, perhaps only 10 years from now."

And furthermore:

"Last April, in the most devastating outbreak of tornadoes ever recorded, 148 twisters killed more than 300 people and caused half a billion dollars' worth of damage in 13 U.S. states . . . Meteorologists disagree about the cause and extent of the cooling trend, as well as over its specific impact on local weather conditions. But they are almost unanimous in the view that the trend will reduce agricultural productivity for the rest of the century. If the climatic change is as profound as some of the pessimists fear, the resulting famines could be catastrophic . . . Climatologists are pessimistic that political leaders will take any positive action to compensate for the climatic change, or even to allay its effects."

Actually, if I had studied my history I would have known that we had been there before. At the top of the next page is the beginning of an article from the *New York Times* from February 24, 1895.

———

As we approached 2000 I had gotten over my first scare (about the stinking Mediterranean), for not only was the Mediterranean Sea (as well as the coastlines around Denmark and all the lakes I knew) far cleaner than when I was a child, but so was the air, due to better car engines and catalyzers and better cleaning of factory smoke. I was also by now less

---

PROSPECTS OF ANOTHER GLACIAL PERIOD

Geologists Think the World May Be
Frozen Up Again.

The question is again being discussed
whether recent and long-continued observations do not point to the advent of a second glacial period, when the countries now
basking in the fostering warmth of a tropical sun will ultimately give way to the
perennial frost and snow of the polar regions. The researches of geologists have
proved the existence in Greenland and other arctic lands of fossil palms and other
tropical plants, which show that these regions were once covered with a rich vege-
tation, which only equatorial climes can
now produce.

---

scared of mankind running out of resources, since commodity prices had generally been falling due to surplus production, or at least not keeping up with inflation. After *Limits to Growth* was published, fears about the imminence of an ice age had changed since temperatures had begun to rise again. But I had a new worry: The millennium bug, or "Y2K", as it was called. It was widely predicted in the press that large parts of the world economy would grind to a halt after 12:01 AM on the first day of 2000, since computers would think the year was "00".

So, there my family was, celebrating New Year's Eve in the French Alps on the last day of the millennium, wondering if the world's computers would all stop when the clock ticked past midnight.

Nothing happened. The next day our credit cards still worked. The mobile phones too, and the ski lifts. Globally there were virtually no Y2K incidents. It was another "scare".

Scares, the way I see them, are episodes where an initial concern over an existing or potential problem evolves into a media frenzy that is out of any proportion to the actual problem. Furthermore, many if not most scares lead to a public response that is also out of proportion with the problem, and which for that reason does more harm than good. Christopher Booker, a columnist for the *Sunday Telegraph*, and Dr. Richard North, a former research director in the European Parliament wrote the book *Scared to Death* in which they mapped the following clear

Quotes from the great ice age scare

Science News in 1975 (headline):

"The Ice Age Cometh."

The *New York Times*, May 21, 1975:

"Scientists Ponder Why the World's Climate is Changing: A Major Cooling Widely Considered to Be Inevitable."

International Wildlife, July 1975:

"The facts have emerged, in recent years and months, from research into past ice ages. They imply that the threat of a new ice age must now stand alongside nuclear war as a likely source of wholesale death and misery for mankind."

Lowe Ponte, *The Cooling*, 1976:

"The cooling has already killed thousands of people in poor nations ... If it continues, and no strong measures are taken to deal with it, the cooling will cause world famine, world chaos, and probably world war, and this could all come about by the year 2000."

Newsweek, April 1975:

"They concede that some of the more spectacular solutions proposed, such as melting the Arctic ice cap by covering it with black soot or diverting arctic rivers, might create problems far greater than those they solve. But the scientists see few signs that government leaders anywhere are even prepared to take the simple measures of stockpiling food or of introducing the variables of climatic uncertainty into economic projections of future food supplies. The longer the planners delay, the more difficult will they find it to cope with climatic change once the results become grim reality."

Time Magazine, January 1994:

" The last (ice age) ended 10,000 years ago; the next one—for there will be a next one—could start tens of thousands of years from now. Or tens of years. Or it may have already started."

scares since 1980:

- Killer eggs
- Listeria hysteria
- Mad cow disease
- Meat, cheese, and *E. coli*
- The Belgian dioxins debacle
- Ritualized child abuse
- Leaded gasoline
- Passive smoking
- Asbestos
- Global warming
- The millennium bug
- Bird flu.

Each of these seemed horrifying at some point. For instance, the World Health Organization called bird flu the greatest single health threat to mankind, and their senior official in charge of the issue predicted that the death toll might be anywhere up to 150 million people. That was an astronomical number; far more than the combined killings during World Wars I and II. In fact, in order to be the biggest contemporary health threat to mankind it would have to beat malaria, which caused about 250 million cases of fever annually. Fewer than 200 people died from bird flu in the 4 years following the WHO statement.

As for mad cow disease, the chairman of the British Spongiform Encephalopathy Advisory Committee agreed in a TV interview that the death toll might be as high as 500,000 and *The Observer* ran a major story describing how this disease might kill half a million Brits a year, leading to the country being sealed off from other nations and disintegrating. When it was thought that some people in the U.K. had been infected by salmonella in eggs, a government advisor proposed killing 50 million birds, even though the actual number of people dying from food poisoning had already begun to decrease naturally and despite the fact that there was no evidence at all that the infections came from eggs. The birds were still killed, though.

As for the impending threat of global food shortages due to a coming cooling or ice age, this didn't happen, of course, and agricultural food production has since increased more than 50% and the global fish catch by approx. 75%. Since the cooling stopped naturally, it is great in retrospect that we didn't listen to scientists suggesting that we should divert rivers and cover Arctic ice in soot to heat up the planet.

I believe that there are many commonalities between financial bubbles/crashes and public scares. Each has five groups of participants: (1) those who first seed the idea; (2) those who promote and amplify it; (3) star agitators who crave the attention by putting forward the most radical interpretations; (4) the millions of people who get impressed about it; and finally (5) the powerful elite, who must be seen to react:

Social role	Financial bubble	Public scare
Seed the idea	Financial analysts	Scientists
Promote the idea	Public media, banks	Public media, pressure groups
Star agitators	Key analysts and visionaries/evangelizers	Key scientists/ politicians
Create mass hysteria	Investors	Voters
Forced or convinced to respond irrationally	Fund managers, business leaders, regulators, politicians	Regulators, politicians

These systems are potentially extremely powerful. To understand why, we must look at the psychology involved. Let's take bubbles as an example and look at two so-called psychological "framing" factors that come into play when prices have been rising steadily for some time:

- *Representativeness effect.* We tend to think that trends we observe are likely to continue.
- *Anchoring.* Our decisions are influenced by input that seems to suggest the correct answer.

We will also get involved in so-called *groupthink*, where we end up blindly following the crowd:

- *False consensus effect.* We generally overestimate the number of other people that share our attitudes.
- *Adaptive attitudes.* We develop the same attitudes as people we associate with.

- *Social comparison.* We use the behavior of others as a source of information about a subject that we find difficult to understand.

The third and perhaps most painful group of psychological phenomena explain how we get caught in *self-deception*:

- *Confirmatory bias.* Our conclusions are unduly biased by what we want to believe.
- *Cognitive dissonance.* When evidence shows that our assumptions have been wrong, we try to avoid such information, or distort it, and we try to avoid action that highlights the dissonance.
- *Ego-defensive attitudes.* We adapt our attitudes, so that they seem to confirm the decision we have made.
- *Assimilation error.* We misinterpret information that we receive, so that it seems to confirm what we have done.
- *Selective exposure.* We try only to expose ourselves to information that seems to confirm our behavior and attitudes.
- *Selective perception.* We misinterpret information in a way that seems to confirm our behavior and attitudes.

As if all of this wasn't enough, there is a fourth category of phenomena concerning our tendency to overestimate our own talents and thereby gamble too hard:

- *Overconfident behavior.* We overestimate our ability to make correct decisions.
- *Hindsight bias.* We overestimate the likeliness that we would have been able to predict the outcome of a past series of events.

When all of this combines, it gets powerful enough to create a mania such as that we saw in NASDAQ 1998–2000 or a scare such as *Listeria* hysteria. As such a mass mania develops, we get bombarded with the same views and data again and again from all kinds of media as well as perhaps from colleagues, family, and friends. Resistance becomes more and more difficult.

However, there comes a point where there is no more evidence to support the scare, or no more money to support the financial trend. When the latter happens—when financial bubbles run out of fresh money—they often start falling fairly rapidly. A market that falls quickly is as mentally engaging as a roaring bull market. There exist psychological theories about that as well, and some of the most important are about "attitudes". Attitudes are a sort of simplification and data compression the brain uses for drawing simple conclusions from many impressions. Experiments show that it not only takes lots of new information to change an attitude, but also a lot of time—typically at least months. However, a *panicky* person—a person so struck by what happens that he has a high heartbeat, sweaty palms, and acute concentration problems—can change attitudes within minutes or even seconds. When millions of investors get caught in panic, they react much faster than normal, and this creates the freefall in prices. Resistance, when *this* happens, is more than difficult. It's futile.

A scare may seem very unlike a bubble in the sense that it initially involves fear rather than greed, but the psychological drivers are largely the same. They include (1) framing, (2) groupthink, (3) self-deception, (4) personal overestimation, and at times even (5) panic. The result of this is that people blindly ignore any calls for calm consideration of the costs versus benefits of proposed actions. Furthermore, if somebody comes up with evidence indicating that the fear may be exaggerated or even without any merit, it is quickly brushed off. As a part of this process they may even use so-called "contrast errors", where people view their opponents as much inferior to what they really are. They may, for instance, consider them less clever, honest, or well-intentioned, or they may go through their work with magnifying glasses to find errors that can be used as a pretext to discount their lines of thought. Or, perhaps most common of all, they may assume that they are part of a conspiracy and paid off by big companies or political parties.

Apart from the psychological effects, the buildup of bubbles or scares is vastly amplified by information filtering and social/financial pressure. No one in society has anywhere near the time needed to personally study all the new ideas and scares we are bombarded with. Who can sit down and carefully examine thousands of pages of research documents to form a qualified, personal opinion? Indeed, who has the skill to do so? Almost all research, whether financial or scientific, is full of odd terms and mathematical equations. So, what we get is what the press feeds us, and the press gets what banks or pressure groups feed them.

But a popular and successful journalist doesn't just serve facts. They have to be dramatized and perhaps amplified, so that they become good stories. Therefore, much of what some media do can be better described as story telling than fact finding. A good story needs saints and sinners, and the media will often choose these and amplify their roles. Furthermore, if they can show (or claim), that there is a conspiracy or cover-up that they—the journalists—have uncovered, then the heroes of their story become themselves, which isn't half-bad.

All of this creates social pressure, which can quickly mutate into financial pressure. This has been the case, for instance, when financial analysts, who warned against investment mania, were excluded from access to media and clients or were even fired, since they ruined the bank's business. Or when scientists interested in issues that may go against the grain were excluded from getting grants and thus effectively threatened by unemployment and ruined careers. The people who questioned conventional wisdom were often financial experts working in smaller organizations such as hedge funds or investing for themselves, or in the case of scares, often retired scientists who didn't have a career risk.

The irony comes when such scientists in the end can only get funding from the industry which may be under threat by the hysteria, in which case they inadvertently give perfect ammunition for conspiracy theories.

Since the book *Scared to Death* was published in 2007 it couldn't include the 2009 swine flu. But if we add this plus nuclear energy (which has turned out to be far safer than coal, since coal has killed hundreds of thousands in addition to polluting the air massively), then we reach 14 scares from 1980 to 2010, which is approx. one scare every 3 years. It seems a coincidence that this is so close to the number of bubbles/crashes in the same period (also one every 3 years), but there is an interesting aspect about the timing of both: According to the two authors of *Scared to Death*, the high frequency of scares started at the beginning of the 1980s, which happens to be the same time that the high frequency of bubbles began.

I have already argued that the bubbles were related to the latest deflationary boom, which was triggered mainly by the end of socialism. But why did the scares start at the same time? Whereas bubbles are errors of financial optimism, scares are errors of pessimism. To be optimistic is fun (until the market crash), but one may wonder why so many people get excessively scared and pessimistic, which shouldn't be pleasant?

Perhaps it has deep roots. People are typically fairly optimistic about their own life and community and their personal capabilities. When asked if they are better drivers than the average person, most will say they are, for instance. However, they are pessimistic about what is not within their personal vicinity or control. When you ask people about whether they think the environment in their own community, their country as a whole, or the world is good or bad, they will almost consistently rate their local environment as better than that of their country, which they again will rate as better than that of the world as a whole. This applies in almost all parts of the world. So, the more remote or general an issue is, the bigger the pessimistic bias.

A contributing reason for this negative worldview may be the speed of change in society. Until recent generations, society was in most ways static, which meant that people saw no structural change at all during their entire lifetime. You sowed your fields and then you harvested; some were born, some died, but it was all cyclical; there was *no trend forward*, into something unknown. It is only within the last hundred years or so that people really would notice clear change in society during their lifetime, and this is now going faster and faster, such that society is constantly changing before our eyes. It is like moving quickly forward through a dark, misty forest—we see shadows and shapes and hear sounds that we cannot completely make out. So, in our fantasy, we complete the picture and imagine them to be beasts and monsters that threaten us. Of course, if in fact we were chased by *real* monsters, such as a pack of wolves biting our heels, we wouldn't care at all about odd shapes and sounds in the distance. In olden days, some of your children would most likely die young, and if you got pneumonia or any other serious infection, you were very likely doomed.

There may be another explanation to the many scares: We need them. It does seem odd that movies about horror, death, and destruction sell so well, or that newspapers generally print more bad news than good. However, I think it's all because we are genetically built to fight, and if society doesn't pose major threats anymore, then we end up inventing some ourselves.

The third group of explanations is about guilt, cleansing, and religion. Man may well have an underlying sense of being guilty and dirty. This is probably because we are torn between our animal life and urges on one side, and our human knowledge on the other. We live, but are the only animals that know they must die. We kill, but can feel compassion. We are ego-centric, but have a moral sense as well. Religions provide a way of cleansing ourselves by confessions, prayers, fasting, and deliberate ascetic living. Viewing our civilization and lifestyle as a sin that must be cleansed can tie in with those emotions.

And this brings me back to the question of why the intense series of scares began at the same time as the intense series of bubbles: They both relate to the fall of socialism/communism. This transition did not only set in motion the intense deflationary boom that has dominated since, and which enabled the many bubbles, it also removed the massive threat of global nuclear war that had dominated before. After 1980 there wasn't much left to be afraid of in the developed world, so we started to exaggerate our fears of all sorts of things.

Society is an extremely complex system. Economists once thought that the economy as well as financial markets could best be modeled under the assumption of rational people interacting to create predictable equilibriums (something called classical, and later neoclassical, economics). When you put assumed rationality into mathematical equations you would expect so-called "linear" relationships. If the price of something went up, for instance, you would expect people to buy less of it. If price rose even further, they would buy even less.

Today the view is much more nuanced, and it is understood that whereas people *mostly* are rational, the individual as well as society as a whole can for long stretches of time end up doing things that are highly irrational. We may, perversely, sell equities because their prices go down and buy them because they are advancing rapidly, or we may get caught in irrational scares, panics, and whatnot.

In dynamic terms, all this gets described as cascades, positive (self-reinforcing) feedback loops, and dis-inhibitors (natural modifying forces are prevented from working). These so-called "non-linearities" have an impact on how you model economic phenomena statistically. Academics and financial engineers had long assumed that probabilities in these markets had so-called "normal" or Gaussian distributions—the ones that are illustrated with bell-curve graphs. However, because of non-linearities, there is a bigger risk of extreme events than these models predict. When referring to bell-curved distribution patterns, people talk about "fat tails" to illustrate this, and the slang for extreme events in financial circles is today simply "tail events". Systems that have many positive feedback loops and tail events tend to become somewhat chaotic, or, as they say, "exhibit high-dimensional deterministic chaos". But not everything is messy, and the appropriate way to view our economies, social trends, financial markets, etc. is as a combination of cycles, trends, and high-dimensional chaos.

To gauge the future in these conditions is evidently hard, but a large part of it is to try to separate out what are either (1) cycles, (2) bubbles, (3) scares, or (4) trends. Often, for instance, when a mania starts to build or a bubble bursts, people think that a trend has stopped. When the IT bubble evolved in 1998–2000, many thought that the "old" economy would almost disappear.

When the bubble burst, some saw the new economy as a joke. But this was a Wall Street crash, not a main street crash: IT continued to evolve during and after the bust, and innovation didn't stop. The financial *cycle* had turned, but the innovation *trend* continued. After the 2007–2009 subprime salami crash, lots of people believed the trend towards free market economies was over. I would argue that the property *cycle* turned, but that the globalization/innovation *trend* continues.

So, yes, distinguishing between these phenomena is essential, if not always easy. However, the clearer the picture of each phenomenon, the clearer is our sense of the whole. In the next chapters we shall turn to long-term trends.

Part II

Supertrends

This part addresses the greatest fundamental trends in demographics, macro-economics, environmental matters, resources, and basic science that will shape the future:

- Global population growth is decelerating, but approx. 2 billion—or 30%—will be added before global population stabilizes around 2050.
- Urban population will grow by approx. 3 billion.
- Rural population will decline, and many villages will become deserted.
- From 2010 to 2050 the global population will age, and the number of retirees will grow by 1.6 billion. Some 90% of this growth will be in emerging markets.
- Global life expectancy will grow approx. 2.5 years per decade, so 10 years from 2010 to 2050. However, towards the end of that period, it will start growing much faster, as age prevention becomes an information technology through use of advanced biotech and genomics.
- Global GDP will grow approx. 400% in real terms from 2010 to 2050.
- Average real income in developed countries will rise between 200% and 300% during that period.
- Average real income in most emerging markets will rise between 400% and 600%. This economic expansion in emerging markets

exceeds the current size of the six largest economies (annum 2010) by 2030.

- Global wealth will grow approx. 400% from 2010 to 2050, adding approx. $800 trillion in variable-price assets.
- The global middle class will increase by 70 to 90 million people a year and will rise from 1 billion in 2010 to 2.5 billion in 2050.
- The economic expansion in emerging markets will exceed the current size of the six largest economies (annum 2010) by 2030.
- China will become the world's biggest economy.
- Average incomes in the bottom billion nations will hardly rise at all, and some will decline.
- The number of people with tertiary education will double every 15 years.
- Emancipation of women will evolve extremely fast and they will often outnumber men in tertiary education.
- Many developed countries will lack savings to pay for retirement booms. Several Western economies plus possibly Japan will undergo acute debt crises.
- Labor forces will decline rapidly in Russia, Japan, and some parts of Eastern and Southern Europe.
- Human knowledge will double every 8–9 years and grow approx. 4,500% from 2010 to 2050. The fastest growth will be in genomics/biotech, IT, and alternative energy.
- Pollution will generally decline, but carbon emissions will take several decades to get under control, and the planet may heat 1–2°C, while sea levels will rise modestly.
- We will not run out of any resources, but due to explosive economic growth, some will experience temporary shortages and thus price spikes.
- Crop yields per land unit will begin to grow faster than demand for farm products, leading to an eventual contraction in the amount of farmland needed.

More information in
www.supertrends.com

4

Population growth, female emancipation, and aging

When I was born in 1957 the global population was 2.8 billion people. By 2010 we have reached almost 7 billion, which means more than a doubling in my lifetime—so far. Around 2050, the global population is expected to peak at around 9 billion people—almost a quadrupling since my birth and an increase from 2010 to 2050 of approx. 30%. *Global population growth is now around 80 million people per year, which is roughly equal to the number of inhabitants in Germany.*

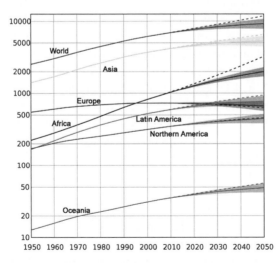

World Population (1950–2050), historical and U.N. forecast. The vertical axis is exponential for better illustration of changes to growth trends. The forecasts are indicated as probable range with central estimates drawn as solid lines. *Source:* Wikipedia Commons.

Let's just look at where all the 7 billion people inhabiting the Earth live today. We can start with the European Union plus other developed countries such as the U.S.A., Japan, Canada, Australia, etc. The combined population in these mature economies totals approx. 1 billion people, or around 14% of the world's population. Now compare that with China, which has 1.3 billion inhabitants, equal to 20% of the global population—*there are more people in China than in the combined developed world.*

How about India? India is home to 17% of the world's population, so *India also has more inhabitants than the combined developed world.* It even has more honor roll kids than there are kids in America. Let's take some other examples. There are 230 million people in Indonesia, 190 million in Brazil, 141 in Russia, and 87 in Vietnam. That is a lot.

Jim O'Neill, the head of global economic research at Goldman Sachs coined the term "BRIC" in 2001 as an abbreviation for four emerging market countries, namely Brazil, Russia, India, and China. The reason for his interest in these countries was that he thought that they not only could do well in the short run, but that they would become a dominant theme for global investors during the next many decades. Between them these four countries represent a quarter of all the land mass on Earth and no fewer than 40% of the global population—they have a total of 2.5 billion inhabitants.

So, they are huge. But another reason that they are interesting is that they have growth potential. Unlike, for instance, most of Africa, all four have demonstrated that they can manufacture products that can compete globally. We should not forget that Russia was the first nation on Earth to send a satellite into orbit—unmanned and manned—and they have a number of talented IT experts and engineers today. India is well known for its software industry in Bangalore and elsewhere. The Indian economy annum 2010 is actually still not as big as Italy's, but it is expected to overtake Germany by 2025 and after that its beneficial demographics will give it a huge comparative advantage. We shall come back to that later in this chapter.

Brazil has its own "Silicon Valley" in Campinas outside São Paulo, and it manufactures airplanes that compete globally—even in the luxury private jet segment. It has one of the largest groups of Germans and Japanese outside Germany and Japan, and we all know what that means in terms of engineering talent. While the Japanese constitute 1% of Brazil's population, they make up approx. 15% of student enrolments. Brazil's largest company Petróleo Brasiliero is a world leader in deep sea drilling. São Paulo's and Río de Janeiro's urban art is funky and cool and everyone knows the Brazilian samba and bossa nova. Brazil rocks.

And China? I can still recall a time in my career where people brushed off the potential of China by saying that its economy was smaller than that of Belgium. It is hard to believe today but, until the early 1970s, the average income in China was about the same as in Somalia. However, since then it has evidently blasted past Belgium's economy, and then that of the Netherlands. After that it passed Italy, and then England and Germany in short order. It is now poised to overtake the Japanese economy around 2016, which will make it the world's second largest economy.

The list of China's abilities seems very long, but perhaps the best indication of China's potential comes from all the Chinese that are currently living outside the country. This is 60 million people, and if they were a nation, then it would have the third largest economy in the world. Wherever the Chinese have been living in free market economies, they have on average done very well indeed, whether it is in Taiwan, Hong Kong, Singapore, Malaysia, or the United States. They constitute approx. 25% of the population of Malaysia, for instance, but in spite of affirmative action policies by the Malaysian government to protect the rights of ethnic Malays, it's the Chinese that dominate in the middle- and high-income segments. As for Singapore, 78% of the population is Chinese. Singapore, as we know, made the most stunning transformation from a primitive jungle community to one of the four richest nations on the planet within a few generations. All of this seems even more extraordinary if you consider that almost all of the Chinese abroad are refugees who left their country empty-handed and perhaps even starving.

Speaking of food: In 1995 I had a business dinner at a good restaurant in Hong Kong. At one point we ran out of wine, so I looked across the room, spotted a waiter, and gave a very discreet signal that I would like him to come over. Then he ran across the room to our table. While I appreciated the dedication, I thought running was a bit exaggerated, but that is not my point here. My point is that he . . . ran!

The conclusion is that the four BRIC countries constitute 2.5 billion people with the drive and knowledge to get far. Furthermore, they control considerable natural resources as well—especially Russia and Brazil. However, there is also a "next billion" which includes Bangladesh, Egypt, Indonesia, Iran, Korea, Mexico, Nigeria, Pakistan, Philippines, Turkey, and Vietnam (Goldman Sachs refers to these as the "N-11"). Add these to the 2.5 billion inhabitants of the BRIC countries, and we have approx. 3.5 billion people who are storming ahead, which means 3.5 economic sprint runners for each financial marathon runner in the Old World.

Expected GDP development in selected economies (2010—2030), billion dollars

	Brazil	China	India	Russia	Total, BRIC	France	Germany	Italy	Japan	U.K.	U.S.A.	Total, G6
2010	668	2,998	929	847	7,452	1,622	2,212	1,337	4,601	1,876	13,271	24,919
2015	952	4,754	1,411	1,232	9,364	1,767	2,386	1,447	4,858	2,089	14,786	27,333
2020	1,333	7,070	2,104	1,741	14,268	1,930	2,524	1,553	5,221	2,285	16,415	29,928
2025	1,695	10,213	3,174	2,264	19,371	2,095	2,604	1,625	2,267	2,456	18,340	29,387
2030	2,189	14,312	4,935	2,980	26,446	2,267	2,697	1,671	5,810	2,649	20,833	35,927
Change, 2010–2030	1,521	11,314	4,006	2,133	18,994	645	485	334	1,209	773	7,562	11,008

Source: *Dreaming with the BRICs: The Path to 2050*, Goldman Sachs Global Economic Paper No. 99, Goldman Sachs, 2003.

What is important is not only how big these economies are, but how much they contribute to global economic growth. The table opposite, which has been created by Goldman Sachs, gives a comparison between expected growth in the BRIC countries and the six largest mature economies, respectively, from 2010 to 2030.

I think it is worthwhile to study that table quite carefully, because it shows something remarkable. Just look at the two numbers in the bottom line that I have written in italic: "18,994" and "11,008". Here is what these two numbers show: According to this Goldman Sachs model, the four BRIC countries will produce a combined economic growth of approx. $19 trillion ("18,994") over this 20-year period, whereas the six leading mature countries will only grow by $11 trillion ("11,008") over the same period.

If we look further ahead (as Goldman has done), the indication is that *China will overtake the United States around 2040.* Not per capita, I should add, but in total GDP. Ten years later, by the way—in 2050—its economy will be approx. 25% larger than America's. Between 2010 and 2050 the G6 countries should grow by $29 trillion and the BRIC countries by $78 trillion. *Again adding the N-11 may take emerging market economic growth to around $100 trillion,* which means that the world economy will quadruple within 40 years. Read it again: *The world economy will quadruple in the next 40 years.*

Conclusion? *The next booms will be large, and they will be largely driven first by China and to a lesser degree Russia, and then by India and Brazil as well as countries such as Mexico, Indonesia, and Vietnam.* I think that to invest in China now is a bit like investing in Japan in the 1960s or in South Korea in the mid-1970s. It's like a new Japan story, but with 10 times as many inhabitants. It is really, truly . . . huge.

Are GDP numbers real?

GDP numbers summarize what people buy and pay for. They don't reflect whether it has any value or how good it is. You could argue that if Americans spend an insane amount on suing each other, or Europeans on collecting taxes or avoiding tax payments, it adds to GDP, but not to overall wellbeing.

On the other hand, GDP doesn't reflect the improved performance and quality of many products. The coffee I drink, or the bread and fruit I buy today, is vastly better than when I was a younger, but in real terms it costs less. Some IT products have consistently fallen approx. 50% in price every year, which all-else-equal reduces GDP, while giving us better products. The smartphone you carry in your pocket

may be more powerful and infinitely more user-friendly than a
multimillion dollar mainframe 30 years ago, and yet it cost a tiny fraction.

What will be the impact of all this emerging market growth? When
economies grow as these do, a lot of people are lifted up from poverty,
to a level where some income is available for discretionary spending. The
Brookings Institute predicts that the global middle class will grow by 1.8
billion from 2008 to 2020. Goldman Sachs estimates that *the global middle
class will grow by 70–90 million people a year annually between 2010 and 2030.*
This—Goldman's number—is equal to 220,000 people daily, and the
effect after 20 years will be to *increase the global middle class from a level of
approx. 1 billion in 2010 to around 2.5 billion by 2030.* That, of course, will
have significant effects on our environment and our natural resources,
and also on demand for products and services. I will cover this later.

It will also have many other important investment implications,
which we shall address continuously as we proceed. To understand these,
it can be useful to think of what is called Maslow's Pyramid. This
diagram, which is shown below, describes how people prioritize different
needs, starting from the most basic physical ones such as food and water.

Maslow's hierarchy of needs. *Source*: Creative Commons.

In a way we can simplify what the pyramid says and divide it into four levels, which you should read from the bottom up:

- Self-fulfilling: "We wish to live our dream . . ."
- Esthetic: "We wish to sense beauty and artistry . . ."
- Emotional: "We need love and caring . . ."
- Physical: "We need food and shelter . . .".

A common critique of Maslow's Pyramid is that all people in fact have a great desire for all groups of needs, which sounds roughly right to me. After all, people in Turkey started building enormous T-shaped monolithic pillars of limestone in Göbekli Tepe just after the last ice age—around 11,500 years ago. Most weighed 10 to 50 tons, and the work to cut them out of the rocks, decorate them with beautiful carvings, and drag them from local quarries must have been crushing for these Stone Age men. It was the same, of course, with the construction of the pyramids, the first of which was built more than 4,600 years ago, or the cathedrals in Europe, which often took generations to construct. Some of the most ornate elements in many cathedrals are hidden toward the top, where they are barely visible, if not entirely shielded from the human eye. They, it is said, were built by the masons "for the eyes of God". This is esthetic and self-fulfilling work done by sometimes very poor people.

However, the point for our purpose is that people's *ability* to satisfy needs that are higher up in Maslow's Pyramid can be severely hampered, if lower down needs are not met first. How much do you think about self-esteem if your children are starving? Might you steal to feed them?

Anyway, here is what I think will happen: As people move to the middle class they can spend money on real property instead of slums, better health, scooters, motorcycles, or cars, etc. This is all physical, and as perhaps 70 million to 90 million people a year move up from satisfying basic physiological needs to obtaining safety and security, they will buy hundreds of millions of cars, houses, and apartments. China has between 300 and 500 million people in the countryside who are expected to move to the cities within a few decades. The higher of these numbers is not far from the entire population of the EU plus countries currently applying to join the EU.

Furthermore, as many move from poverty to middle class, there are also quite a few who move from lower to higher middle class, and from there to affluent, rich, and very rich levels, which means that products and services that are aesthetic, emotional, and self-fulfilling become more common. I think this will give an explosion in 12 areas of private leisure activity:

The 12 cornerstones of leisure			
Objects you buy	*Things you do*	*Media you use*	*Places you meet*
Fashion	Travel	Movies and music	Restaurants
Art	Sport	Web/print	Bars
Luxury	Wellness	Electronic games	Night clubs

Whereas these phenomena are virtually non-existent or very basic among the world's poorest, they play a huge role in richer societies. Just to be clear: By *fashion* I mean primarily clothes/apparel, but it can be anything that involves deliberate and carefully planned change of styling over time. By *art* I mean here art for the sake of it, such as abstract paintings, sculptures, artistic music, etc. *Luxury* is objects of a unique quality and international reputation, which each seems to be in a class of its own. *Travel, wellness, sport, music, movies, restaurants, bars,* and *night clubs* speak for themselves, and by *web* I mean the internet plus mobile media and networking.

I should add, of course, that all these areas often overlap each other. I will later argue that luxury is the one among these 12 sectors where the big money is. I will show, for instance, how the big luxury brands generate profits that are completely out of proportion with their revenues and how the luxury business grows much faster than almost any other sector in the global economy.

We cannot speak of emerging markets without mentioning their enormous future demand for commodities and alternative energy. Nobody who really knows much about these markets believes that we are close to running out of resources—that is not the issue (I will address this later as well). The issue is that demand for some natural resources probably for a number of years will grow substantially faster than we can meet it in *conventional* ways. Furthermore, for the energy market there will be pressure to reduce global emissions and the huge transfers of wealth to oil-producing nations. So, we shall have to innovate, and we shall have to do it rather quickly, and this may become a constraint.

There are two other great constraints. One is about financial imbalances and the other one about aging. Let's look at aging first.

———

To understand aging, we need to start with a few important numbers. From a purely biological standpoint, a woman may be able to have *16–20* children during her reproductive lifetime (a few have even had more).

Another important number is *2.1*, which is the so-called "replacement fertility" in modern societies. If a woman on average has 2.1 children, then the population is stable (the 0.1 extra comes because some will be infertile, or die before reaching fertility and because nature creates a slight overweight of boys). However, as mentioned, the number "2.1" is only valid in modern societies. This so-called "replacement fertility" number is higher than 2.1 in developing countries, because of higher mortality rates and because the girl/boy ratio may be different in some places. In those countries replacement fertility ranges from *2.5* to *3.3*. There is a third important number: Globally, the average replacement fertility is a bit over *2.3* children per woman as of 2010.

That number—the 2.3 fertility rate—has changed. Actual fertility rates in Europe 200 years ago seem to have been 6.5–8 children per woman. Most people were farmers at that time and in medieval farming you had a strong economic incentive to have children, since they would work for you on your farm from an early age, and in particular handle the farm when you got old, and thus also take care of you. Actually, your children pretty much had to take care of you, even if you were a grumpy old son of a bitch, because you probably owned the land they were farming! Of course, there was an initial net burden related to raising the children, but that was fairly brief, since they could start helping out at the farm from their early teens or even before. Child labor was quite OK back then. I have read my great grandad's memoirs, and he often tended the cattle all day as a child. Lots of children died young in those days, and if we go back a few centuries, the population was actually relatively stable at this fertility rate of 5.6–8. It was brutal, but at least it was stable, and in that sense ecologically viable.

———

I think it would be useful at this point to introduce a sort of classification system for population growth. Let me start with what happened in the Western World a very few hundred years ago and still happens in a few countries today. I would call this "Stage 1: Pre-industrial stable stage population"

Stage 1 society: Pre-industrial stable stage population

- No contraception; high child mortality
- Very limited healthcare technology
- No institutionalized pensions
- Child-raising is brief and children start working at early age
- Children tied to parents through use of land. They are only income source for retirees
- Fertility rate: 5–8
- Population: Stable
- Productivity and wealth: Stable or slowly rising
- Unemployment and underemployment: Stable and low
- Examples:
  - Most medieval societies
  - Isolated parts of the Amazon and Borneo jungle.

I guess a good name for the next stage is "Stage 2a: Knowhow-driven population explosion" (I shall come to a Stage "2b" later). This stage was largely driven by industrialization. Furthermore, the curiosity, technical and commercial ingenuity, and entrepreneurship that brought industrialization also brought international trade and banking. All of this increased incomes, which improved hygiene and healthcare, which again reduced mortality, and especially child mortality. The result? Populations began to grow rapidly, and so did average incomes.

Stage 2a society: Knowhow-driven population explosion

- Limited or no contraception; low child mortality
- Reasonable healthcare technology
- Limited institutionalized pensions
- Children require more and longer education
- Children more often living away from parents, but were expected to take care of retirees
- Fertility rate: 3–8
- Population: Exponential growth
- Productivity and wealth: Growing exponentially
- Unemployment and underemployment: Structurally stable
- Examples:
  - Most of emerging Asia
  - Parts of Latin America.

Technology evolved further, though, and so did the social structure in society. Machines began competing with people for the simpler jobs, and in order for children to prepare for meaningful jobs, they needed some education, and then more, and then a lot more. The initial cost of having many children thus rose. At the same time, farming lost importance and children would in any case most likely create their own lives away from their parents, who increasingly depended on public and private pension plans to pay for their retirement. Furthermore, contraception became widely available. All of this meant that children became something you had only for love—a high-maintenance expense, really. They moved up Maslow's Pyramid, if you like. Instead of having eight and burying three of them before they reached their teens and using the rest for hard child labor, you would perhaps have two or three, whom you would shower with love and endow with education. Let us call this stage "Stage 3: Education and social infrastructure–driven population stabilization".

Stage 3 society: Education and social infrastructure–driven population stabilization

- Contraception fully available; low child mortality
- Good healthcare technology
- Institutionalized pensions
- Children require more and longer education
- Children more often living away from parents and only partly, if at all, expected to take care of parents' retirements
- Fertility rate: ~2.1
- Population: Stable, but aging
- Productivity and wealth: Growing rapidly
- Unemployment and underemployment: Structurally low and stable
- Examples:
  - Canada
  - Scandinavia.

The fourth stage came when society developed infrastructures that made women less economically dependent on either their husband or their children. For instance, communities began now to offer new mass infrastructure to assist women with childcare. At the same time the state would offer pensions for all, and the banking system facilitated supplementary savings for even more pension, which meant economic independency from children.

Another aspect was that as life expectancy grew, a woman with two children would often only be restricted by late pregnancy and baby nursing (and perhaps only partially because of daycare centers, etc.) for a total of around only 8 years, which now meant just 10% of her life. This meant that suddenly it became viable to get an education and pursue an interesting career, and since it became viable, there also evolved a movement pushing for it. And so, gradually, women achieved equal rights, which meant that more and more women chose to have an intellectually interesting life over having numerous children. Also, since childbearing women no longer were entirely dependent on men, divorces became more common and were often a reason not to have more children.

Furthermore, when people did have children, they wanted them not only to have a long, solid education, but also to play the piano, tennis, and football, get their teeth fixed properly, have sleepovers with friends, celebrate their birthdays in good company, see the world, speak many languages, etc. Ambitions rose, in other words, and many of those who wanted children opted for only one or two, so they could dedicate them enough time. Let's call this "Stage 4: Education and aspiration–driven population decline".

Stage 4 society: Education and aspiration–driven population decline

- Contraception fully available; low child mortality
- Good healthcare technology
- Institutionalized pensions
- Children require more and longer education. Extra-curriculum activities also expected
- Children more often living away from parents and only partly, if at all, expected to take care of parents' retirements
- Fertility rate: <2.1
- Population: Declining and aging rapidly
- Productivity and wealth: Growing per capita, but stagnating overall
- Unemployment and underemployment: Structurally low and stable
- Examples:
  - Eastern Europe
  - Japan
  - Southern Europe, Germany.

I have to rewind here and introduce one more category: "Stage 2b:

Healthcare-driven medieval population explosion". The key word here is "medieval". This happened when modern healthcare was introduced from outside into societies that were not otherwise undergoing any sort of economic and social progress. The result was a population explosion that was not in any way matched by increasing production or social infrastructure development. While healthcare was desirable from a humanitarian perspective, the long-term social and environmental consequences were highly problematic.

Stage 2b society: Healthcare-driven medieval population explosion

- Limited or low contraception; low child mortality
- Reasonable healthcare technology
- Limited institutionalized pensions
- Child-raising is brief and children start working at early age
- Children often tied to parents through use of land and are only income source for retirees
- Fertility rate: 3-8
- Population: Exponential growth
- Production and wealth: Stable or slowly rising
- Unemployment and underemployment: Rapidly rising
- Examples:
  - Subsaharan Africa
  - Parts of the Middle East.

To conclude on my 4 + 1 stages of population development, in a sense it is about enabling each and every child to have a fulfilling life, and in another about the increasing cost of education and organized social security replacing children as the main means of support for the elderly. But more than anything, it's perhaps about the role of women.

I already mentioned the role of women in declining birthrates, but I think this needs some elaboration. Goldman Sachs, Boston Consulting Group, the World Bank, and the National Bureau of Economic Research are some of the numerous institutions that have investigated the changes in women's role in society across the globe. What they have found is a clear trend almost everywhere towards more equal rights and opportunities for women.

A part of it seems to involve television. A team from the National Bureau of Economic Research studied in 2007 how the introduction of cable television affected different rural communities in India. The results were remarkable: within just 1–2 years of gaining access to cable television, local families became more likely to send their children, and in particular their daughters, to school. Furthermore, it also made it less likely that these girls dropped out of school. Finally, the women who had access to cable television started having fewer children.

So, how fast is female emancipation happening? The World Bank has made an international study of the ratio of female to male enrolment in different categories of education and found some dramatic changes in this balance. Let's look at the first table here, which shows the number for "rich" nations.

Proportion of girls to boys in enrolment for different levels of education in developed regions, 1998–1999 and 2006–2007

	1999	2007
Primary education	100	100
Secondary education	100	100
Tertiary education	119	129

Source: The Millennium Development Goals Report, 2009, U.N.

There is no surprise for primary education here, because each and every boy and girl has to go to school in developed countries, and their numbers are approximately equal. Nor are the numbers for secondary education interesting.

But now take a look at *tertiary* education. This is what comes after graduation from, say, high school, and it involves colleges, universities, plus institutes of technology and polytechnics. In 1999 there was a 20% *overweight* of women in tertiary education in developed countries. This means that women had not only reached equality with men here—they had blasted right past them, and *within just 8 years, they had increased their lead from almost 1.2 to 1.3 women per man in tertiary education.* I find the level of female achievement remarkable and the speed of change truly stunning.

The next table gives us similar figures for developing nations. This shows that girls have been catching up with boys in primary education

(+4 percentage points), and more in secondary (+5). And even more in tertiary; much, much more, in fact: +18% in just 8 years!

Proportion of girls to boys in enrolment for different levels of education in developing regions, 1998–1999 and 2006–2007		
	1999	*2007*
Primary education	91	95
Secondary education	89	94
Tertiary education	78	96
Source: *The Millennium Development Goals Report*, 2009, U.N.		

It is very rare that you ever see anything change 18% in 8 years in demographics, but this did, and *the trend towards female emancipation is dramatic, important, and widespread.*

Let me give you an example. I think many, or perhaps most, people living outside the Middle East hold the view that women in many Muslim countries are very repressed, and it is certainly true that members of the Taliban at times have thrown acid in the faces of young girls because they went to school, or even bombed such schools, and that women are not allowed to drive cars in Saudi Arabia. However, according to the *Arab Human Development Report 2005*, which is published by the United Nations, women had by 2005 come close to or achieved gender parity in tertiary education in Egypt, Lebanon, Jordan, Palestine, and Oman, and university enrolment in the Gulf States now exceeded that of men. No fewer than 3.4 times more women were, for instance, enrolled in universities in Qatar than were men. Now, the same report mentioned that many men often studied in universities abroad and that many universities in the area were single-sex, and that those for women didn't have the same choices as those for men. But the trend is nevertheless clear, it is universal and it is evolving much faster than population growth and aging.

There is a saying that if you educate a boy, then you have just educated that boy. But if you educate a girl you will educate the whole family, because that girl will insist that her children also get educated. Female emancipation and all that comes with it is an important supertrend. As women get more education, they also get more jobs, higher income, and a greater say in their families. Furthermore, children of educated women also get more education and are generally healthier. When women decide how to spend a family's money, they are less likely to buy tobacco and alcohol than men, and more oriented towards food, health-care, education, clothing, and personal-care products. It seems likely that emancipation of women is contributing strongly to defusing the global population bomb, ensuring a better future for our children, and increasing per capita incomes. And finally, *a world with more powerful women and more retired people might turn out to be more peaceful.*

I mentioned before that the world's population is poised to increase approx. 30%, or by approx. 2 billion people between 2010 and 2050. During those years it will rise in all emerging markets except Russia and Eastern Europe (see the table below).

Expected population changes around the globe from 2010 to 2050 are, in order of growth rate

Africa	+93%
West Asia (Turkey plus Middle East nations)	+60%
Oceania (Australia, New Zealand, and Pacific islands)	+43%
India	+33%
North America	+28%
Latin America and the Caribbean	+24%
China	+5%
Western Europe	−2%
Eastern Europe, including Russia	−18%
Japan	−20%

Source: *World Population Prospects*, 2008 revision, U.N.

If we look at the name at the top of the list above, we see that the demographic profile of *Africa* is environmentally scary, but in a sense economically promising. However, before we get too thrilled about that economic promise here, we should recall that the total GDP of the approx. 1 billion people living in Subsaharan Africa is less than that of Spain, in spite of Africa's huge natural resources. Africa is still, to a large degree, performing an unsustainable "Stage 2b; Healthcare-driven medieval population explosion". I will address the reasons for this in the next chapter.

What does look promising for Africa, though, is that its exports to Asia have been growing rapidly and that Asians increasingly are engaging in farming in Africa, which should transfer technical and commercial knowledge and management. Furthermore, rising commodity prices have helped many countries to bring down their foreign debt, and new technologies such as mobile phones have enabled them to bypass legacy technologies all together and use new and cheaper systems. Indeed, one famous 2007 study by Harvard University showed what happened, when fishermen in Southern India got mobile phones. They would now start calling prospective buyers even before reaching shore, and as a consequence, their profits on average rose 8%, whereas retail fish prices declined by 4%. The London Business School has estimated that each time mobile phone penetration rises by 10% in the population, it increases GDP by 0.5%.

Next on the population growth list is the *Middle East*, where the number of inhabitants is set to explode. It was only 100 million in 1950 but is approx. 430 million as of 2010. Like most of Africa, much of the population growth in the Middle East is also Stage 2b.

Amazingly, only 47% of the potential working population in the Middle East is actually working, and 25% are outright unemployed. There are many reasons for this, but one is discrimination against women and insufficient education, which prevents transition to Stage 2a and eventually Stages 3 and 4. Strangely, it isn't particularly the uneducated that are unemployed—there are a fairly large percentage of those with some skills and education who are also out of work. Those Middle Eastern countries that don't have oil have fallen further and further behind other emerging markets. For instance, 40 years ago Egypt exported approximately as much as Taiwan or South Korea. As of 2010 their exports are fewer than 1% of those the Asian Tigers handle.

Apart from working women, it seems to be largely skilled entrepreneurship and scientific curiosity that is missing in some parts of the Middle East. The *2002 Arab Human Development Report* concluded:

> "The figures for translated books are also discouraging. The Arab world translates about 330 books annually, one-fifth of the number that Greece translates."

Another statistic that reveals a lot is the number of patents granted in Arab countries each year. In 2006, Morocco issued 133 patents, Saudi Arabia 73, Algeria 79, the Emirates 16, Kuwait 7, Egypt 6, Tunisia 3, Syria 3, Qatar 2, Lebanon 2, Jordan 1, Libya 0, Oman 0, Sudan 0,

Somalia 0, Djibouti 0, and Iraq 0 patents. If we add Iran's 45 for good measure (Iran is Persian, not Arab), we get a total of 370 patents granted to a combined population of almost 400 million people in 2006. During the same year, Holland, with a population of fewer than 16 million, was granted more than 30 times as many patents, or 9,949 to be precise. *A Dutchman was almost 1,000 times as likely to file a patent as an Arab/Persian.*

However, all hope is not lost, as especially Saudi Arabia and (even more) the Gulf States, and some northern African nations have taken initiatives to improve education, create new businesses, and in some cases motivate women. Modernization in the Emirates is in fact exceptionally fast.

In North America, the U.S. stands out as having fairly strong population growth prospects in spite of its mature economy. Apart from immigration, one reason is that the American economy in a way has a degree of the emerging market mentality embedded in it. The country has fairly uneven income distribution and a very large number of first- and second-generation immigrants from emerging markets such as Mexico, who may still have more children per family than the average for the rest of America's population.

India's fertility rate is twice as high as China's (about three children per woman). Now, since the Indians have so many children, they actually have a fairly high dependency ratio (number of people depending on other people's income), but children cost only one-third to one-quarter to take care of than old people. Furthermore—and this is important—as fertility levels will begin to drop around 2025, *India will enjoy a huge demographic benefit*: fewer children but still not many elderly. However, one concern for India is that it is largely divided into a rich, sophisticated south with an older population and a more populous but less educated north, where fertility also is higher. In order to benefit from their overall demographic upside, the Indians need to spread education, or move people.

China has low fertility rates and will actually have an aging problem fairly soon and a workforce that will begin to decline from 2020. Furthermore, its dependency ratio is bottoming out around 2010, where it is just below 50% (meaning that fewer than 50% are aged 0–14 or 65+). By 2050, that ratio will have grown to 80%. *China is already beginning to experience demographic headwinds now.*

If we move down the growth list to slow-growing or contracting regions, then we see that in *Europe* the population is expected to rise by approx. 10 million until 2025. However, afterwards it will actually start to decline, resulting in an overall net growth of just 2% between 2010 and 2050.

Populations in *Japan* and *Eastern Europe* are declining considerably. The *Russian* population, for instance, is already dwindling. It is around 140 million at present (2010) and could decline to 80–90 million by 2050. Fertility reached a low of just 1.17 in 1999 before starting to climb modestly, and there is very little chance that it will recover to a level that can stabilize the population within this century. *Russia's working population is currently approx. 100 million and should decline to 65 million by 2050.* By 2025 the decline will be around 15 million.

The overall population growth numbers I described earlier (+ approx. 2 billion from 2010 to 2050) sounds like a lot, but these numbers are actually masking another trend that looks rather different: *The rate of population growth is declining.*

The natural development for developing societies is to move from the "Pre-industrial stable stage population" to the "Knowhow-driven population explosion", which is economically sustainable, but environmentally potentially unsustainable. From there they will grow economically to a point—typically when GDP/capita passes U.S.$15,000—when they enter "Education and social infrastructure–driven population stabilization". Finally, as aspiration and sophistication evolve further, they are likely to enter "Education and ambition–driven population decline".

The alternative path is for medieval societies that are in the "Pre-industrial stable stage population" to be lifted into the "Healthcare-driven population explosion", which in their case is economically as well as environmentally unsustainable, since they cannot develop their economy and society to deal with a growing population. However, even such countries will eventually see pockets of society that start to work, and may then take the same path as other industrializing countries.

In any case: the global growth rate is declining. Global fertility rates were 4.5 in 1970 and fell to 2.7 in 2000. They should reach 2.05 by 2050, which is slightly below the replacement rate. Correspondingly, global population growth rate is approx. 1.2% as of 2010 but should slow steadily towards 2050. It actually peaked out once in the 1950s and then made a new and apparently final peak at 2.2% in 1963. It has since been declining continuously, and it is now expected to reach 0.7% by 2020. So, in other words, *world population growth has already been decelerating steadily for around 50 years.* Furthermore, *this trend can be seen virtually over the globe,* and it is fortunately, for the first time in history, overwhelmingly voluntary. That is indeed a good thing, or else we would drown in people.

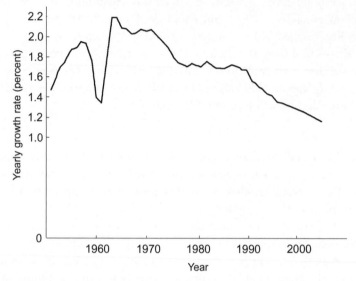

World population increase history (1959—2009). *Source*: Wikimedia Commons.

However, with the deceleration in population growth comes the problem of aging. There are really two factors behind this: declining fertility and rising life expectancy. Children born in the United States in 1900 could expect to live to around 47 years, and in 1950 this number had grown to 68 years. The U.S. Census Bureau estimate life expectancy for those born in 2050 to be 84 years. In Japan it is expected to be 91 years by that time. For America the increase from 47 to 84 years within 15 decades equals an almost 2.5-year increase in average longevity per decade. However, *globally, the increase from 1850 to 2010 has been almost linear with 2.5 years added every decade.* In Europe, life expectancy will probably rise by around 6–7 years from 2010 to 2050 and in Asia by around 10 years. Improved healthcare, hygiene, and nutrition are among the main explanations, but this improvement in most developed countries is decelerating as obesity, smoking, and lack of exercise take their toll. However, *it will probably be possible to massively increase human longevity through genomics and biotech, taking the average lifespan toward perhaps 150 years or longer.* I would guess that some of these procedures will be seen before 2050, meaning that we may see the beginning of a transition period, where life expectancy grows more than one year per year.

The number of elderly (over 60) is expected to increase from around 680 million people in 2010 to reach one billion by 2020. One billion old people! That is equal to the entire population in mature economies today. And the increase of over 300 million in 10 years is approximately equal to the population in the U.S. as of 2010. By 2030 there will be three times as many old people in the developing world as there are inhabitants in the OECD countries today.

It won't stop there. By 2050 there will be almost 2 billion people aged 60 or more, and that will be equal to some 22% of the world population. In Japan, which admittedly is a radical case, the proportion of old will have grown to 38% of the population by then. Indeed, *approx. 80% of the increase in the world population until 2050 will be people over 60.* Even the number of people over 80 will be massive: It will grow from around 90 million today to over 400 million.

What about emerging markets? Although most of these will experience continued population growth for a long time, they will not escape aging at all. Less developed countries are home to 50% of the over-80s today, but that will grow to over 70% by 2050. In 2005 the over-65s in Asia and Latin America accounted for just about 6% of the population, and in Africa it was only 3%. However, by 2030, those proportions will have almost doubled, and by 2050 they will have tripled. In fact, *when we reach 2050, most emerging markets will have age structures that resemble what we have in developed countries today.* China today (2010) has just fewer than 150 million elderly, but this number will grow to 438 million or so by 2050.

The two tables below provide the fuller perspective. The first one shows total numbers of elderly, and the second shows the change—both measured in million people. The first one shows that the number of elderly will grow from 728 million in 2006 to 1.4 billion in 2030 and 2.4 billion in 2050.

Total number of people who are 60 years or older, millions			
	2006	*2030*	*2050*
Developed economies	248	363	400
Developing economies	480	1,014	1,968
Total	*728*	*1,377*	*2,368*
Source: United Nations Population Division, *Population Aging*, 2006.			

However, the next table shows the growth in these numbers and indicates how this growth is divided between developed and developing countries in the rightmost column. No fewer than 90% of it will be in emerging markets:

Total growth in number of people who are 60 years or older, millions				
	2006–2030	2030–2050	Total	Growth (%)
Developed economies	125	37	162	10
Developing economies	531	954	1,485	90
Total growth	656	991	1,647	100
Source: United Nations Population Division, Population Aging, 2006.				

If there should be a single number that sticks in your mind here, then perhaps it should be that *over 40 years, the global number of people of retirement age will grow by much more than the entire population in all developed nations today.* This is a big, fat market, if you are in the healthcare business. Let's just look at how much people over 65 on average spend on some items and services compared with the rest of the population:

- Nursing care: 30 times
- Home healthcare: 10 times
- Hospital services: 4 times
- Prescription drugs: 3 times
- Doctors services: 2.5 times

However, it is also a large financial burden to society as a whole. Both the OECD and IMF have estimated that age-related spending in developed countries will rise by the equivalent of 7% of GDP from 2010 until 2050, taking it from around 20% of GDP in 2010 to around 27% of GDP in 2050. The table below shows the change in expected old age spending in different countries over a medium-term and long-term horizon, respectively. I have listed them in order of how problematic it is.

Country/Area	Total change in age-related spending as % of GDP, 2005–2025	Total change in age-related spending as % of GDP, 2005–2050
Spain	4.5	13.5
New Zealand	5.7	12
Australia	3.3	7.9
Canada	3.3	7.9
Germany	2.2	7.5
France	3.1	7.3
U.K.	2.8	7.2
Japan	3.4	7.1
U.S.	2.9	7
Italy	3.1	7
Sweden	1.8	5.1

Source: Cournede, Boris: *The Political Economy of Delaying Fiscal Consolidation*, Economics Working Paper No. 548, OECD, Paris, March 9, 2007.

As I mentioned, the list is ordered by how problematic the numbers are, and Spain tops it. According to these forecasts, the Spanish will need to find 13.5% of GDP to pay for aging. However, none of the numbers in the list are set in stone. The EU has, for instance, made some more favorable assumptions that show that age-related spending in the EU area will only grow by 4.3%. Who will be right, OECD or the EU? This will depend, of course, on which age people retire at, on how big their pensions are, and how expensive medical aid will be.

In the U.S. the Congressional Budget Office made a study which projected that social security and healthcare spending would rise from 8.4% of GDP in 2005 to 19% in 2050—an increase of 11%. Total federal revenues were 18.5% of GDP in 2008, so an increase of 11% means a *40% increase in necessary taxation*. I found a rather good illustration of this on The Heritage Foundation webpage:

It is important that you read this graph correctly. What it shows is

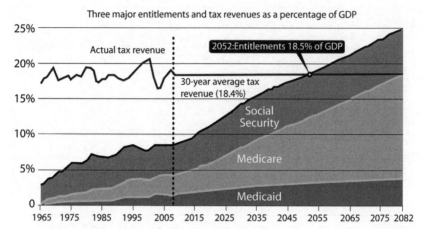

Three major entitlements and tax revenues as a percentage of GDP

U.S. social spending entitlements versus historical and projected total tax revenues 1965–2082 (est.). The illustration shows that such entitlements alone will eclipse tax receipts by 2052, unless radical change is made. The graph does not include spending on interest payments, infrastructure, education, armed forces, etc. *Source*: The Heritage Foundation's *2009 Federal Revenue and Spending Book of Charts*.

social/healthcare spending compared with federal revenues, but it doesn't show other federal expenses such as the military, transportation infrastructure, environment, etc. Actually, the total federal costs already exceeded revenues by 10% of GDP in 2009, so it wasn't as if they were diligently saving up for the coming aging as they should. No, while facing this future problem, they had instead increased national debt. But we will come back to that later (I should add, by the way, that the "11%" cited by the U.S. Congressional Budget Office was a central estimate and they actually gave a range from an increase of just 7% to a whopping 22%, depending on which actions were taken). What may seem odd here is that their central estimate is so high considering that their dependency ratio will not evolve as badly as in Europe and Japan—we shall recall that their workforce will increase steadily by 0.5% annually through 2050. A big part of the explanation is that Americans have massive healthcare costs per capita compared with other nations.

One thing we know for sure: Global dependency ratios will explode. The question is how difficult it will be to cope with this aging of the population. The answer is that it all depends on the economic capability of those who have to pay. The first thing economists might look at here is the number of children that have to be taken care of. The cost of nursing/educating children is much smaller than that of taking care of the elderly. Having said that, there are a number of countries, including Eastern and Southern Europe, which right now enjoy reduced child-nursing costs, since they don't have that many children.

Economists will also look at how many of the people of working age actually do work ("labor participation"), how much their productivity grows ("unit labor cost"), and, as an indicator of unit labor growth, how much capital is deployed per working person, since man plus machine obviously gives higher productivity than man without machine.

Let's look at the potential workforce first. The outlook for the workforce is bad in most countries. For the U.S., the rapid growth in the workforce during the last two generations has to some degree been driven by increasing participation in labor markets by women as well as increasing work hours. Those two forces are now largely spent, but the picture is nevertheless not too alarming; the U.S. working population should grow fairly steadily by approx. 0.5% a year until 2050, as mentioned earlier. Furthermore, there are strong indications that many Americans intend to work beyond their normal retirement age. At the beginning of 2008 about 30% of those between 65 and 69 were in fact either working or looking for work, according to the Bureau of Labor Statistics. This was up from 24% in 2000. The number of people aged 60–64 who were working had also grown from 47% to 54%. The first so-called "baby-boomers"—people born between 1945 and approx. 1965—are approaching official retirement age, but many choose to carry on working.

However, about two thirds of Americans are not sufficiently prepared financially for retirement, and around a quarter tend to say in opinion polls that they will "never" retire. Whether that is because they like working or need to is another matter. On the other hand, it should be said that because of increased female labor market participation since World War II, there are also more two-pension households, which may actually do rather well.

The workforce situation is very different in Japan, where the number of working people actually began declining in 1999 and will continue to do so at a rate of 1–1.5% annually until 2050 and possibly beyond. Europe's should begin to decline after 2011 and the decline will afterwards accelerate gradually towards 0.7% annually.

In emerging markets Russia stands out. Its workforce is set to decline rapidly from around 2014 at a typical pace of 1–1.5% annually. China comes next. The country has long pursued a one-child policy, which until now has prevented a population increase of 400 million, and thus probably prevented economic and ecological disaster. However, with this policy comes an economically painful demographic transition phase. As previously mentioned, China's workforce will keep growing until around 2020, and then it will start declining, albeit only modestly until 2030.

But then faster. *While there are 6.5 workers per retiree in China today, the number will fall to fewer than two in 2050.* China, by the way, provides an example of a phenomenon which can hamper economic development: the disproportion between the number of male and female children. The global average is 105 boys per 100 women, but China has an extreme ratio of 120 boys for every 100 women. One reason is that local tradition says that it's the son who has to care for the elderly.

The data I mentioned above were about the number of people in workforces. But how about labor productivity? Globally it grew 25% between 1996 and 2006, according to the International Labor Organization—a rather impressive number for just 10 years.

Past and forecast real economic growth, Eurozone and U.S.A.		
	Annual productivity growth, Eurozone	*Annual productivity growth, U.S.A.*
1960–1980	4.8	2.1
1981–2000	2.1	1.5
2001–2005	0.8	2.5
2006–2010	1.1	1.5
2011–2030	*1.8*	*2.2*
2031–2050	*1.7*	*2.2*
Source: Macroeconomic Implications of Demographic Developments in the Euro Area, Occasional Paper No. 51, European Central Bank, August 2006, and Magnus, George: *The Age of Ageing,* John Wiley & Sons, 2009.		

The expectation is an average productivity growth of around 2% annually, with the U.S. somewhat ahead of Europe. At that rate, the per capita income corrected for inflation could continue to grow more than 20% every 10 years. In fact, for a girl who lives 80 years in a society where annual productivity growth is 2% the productivity per capita when she dies will be 4.8 times as high as on the day she was born. It really does add up, and people will be far, far richer when she dies than they were when she was born. *The world of future generations will be extremely wealthy by our standards.*

Most emerging markets will evidently have much higher productivity growth than 2% annually, as they catch up and adapt new technologies that already exist at competitive prices. Furthermore, there is a huge labor reserve in emerging markets—today, for instance, there are 600 million people, who often produce very little, living in Asian slum districts. There are also hundreds of millions practicing very old-fashioned farming who will move to the cities. We are already seeing the effects of this urbanization in China and other places.

There is evidently another solution to consider for developed countries with a declining workforce: Encourage immigration. However, the reality is that immigrants on average only have a slightly higher propensity to work than the local population, and that they often bring in their (perhaps very extended) families after a while, who may then add to social burdens. In particular, immigrants coming from disintegrating societies may lack the basic understanding and acceptance of how modern societies work and may, for instance, be opposed to democracy, tolerance, and pluralism. Furthermore, immigrants add to congestion, and they will often produce more children than the locals. There are even many cases where those children do not assimilate as well in society as their parents did and become unemployed or criminals. Germany and other countries have also experienced another problem: That the children of immigrants perform considerably worse in the education system than natives. While immigration may help in the short term, the longer term effect of immigration may for the reasons I just mentioned very well be to worsen the dependency ratio and increase public expenditure disproportionally.

There is an exception to this problem: High earners. These are typically people with high-education or entrepreneurial skills. Such people will not only come to fill vacant jobs, but will often create new products and services, and perhaps new companies which lead to growth, income, and taxes. They will aim for destination countries with low taxes and high business opportunities. In the U.S., for instance, no fewer than 40% of PhDs are immigrants. Furthermore, studies from the U.S.A.

have indicated that immigrants are more likely than locals to start their own companies. According to Vivek Wadhwa of Harvard Law School, a quarter of the engineering and technology firms founded in America between 1995 and 2005 had an immigrant founder. I can see three reasons for that. One is that it takes some initiative to immigrate in the first place, which means that immigrants may not be typical of the average population. Second, immigrants will be somewhat isolated from the society they arrive at, and they will thus have a stronger need to create their own future. The third possible explanation is that they immigrated because they believed that they had high potential, which would be better rewarded in their destination country.

––––––––––

I have already mentioned the issue of the financial burden aging will bring. Now I would like to review it a bit closer, starting with a question: Is the following statement right or wrong?

"Mature, market leading companies typically generate a lot of free cash. They run big surpluses, in other words. Some of this is invested in new startups".

This statement is correct. Now let's try another one:

"OECD countries typically save a lot of money, which they invest in exciting emerging markets. Furthermore, they set aside large amounts to pay for future pensions and healthcare for an aging population."

That statement ought to be correct, but it isn't. Perversely, it is actually the poor, emerging market countries which pump money into the rich, and as we approach an explosion in retirement costs, most affected developed nations save little or nothing to handle it.

This appears really strange, but I can think of some reasons why this is so. The first is that mature markets had a great expansion from 1980 to 2007, and in such an environment people have a natural tendency to get carried away and assume that it will continue without major disruptions, so why save? Another part is perhaps that most people in developed economies have never seen war or depression and expect the state to be there for them if things go wrong, which means that they think they don't need to save. However, the most important reason is perhaps that asset prices, and in particular real estate, rose quickly, which meant that *many people got richer without actually saving*—for as long as it lasted. They thought they were saving. Inhabitants in emerging markets, on the other hand, have felt a lot less secure due to the absence of social security systems and memories of recent crises, so they saved a lot.

The lack of saving in developed nations is a very large threat. How large? Sometimes I read a magazine called *Financial Analysts Journal*. In its March/April issue (Vol. 63, No. 2, 2007) it contained an alarming story. Here is the official abstract in its full wording:

"If the U.S. federal government properly accounted for its explicit and promised liabilities, it would record a national debt of $64 trillion and a national deficit of $2.4 trillion in 2006. Although capital markets seem to care about the officially reported budget deficit—a metric that is backward looking and quite misleading—the markets have done little more than yawn at the federal government's mammoth, and growing, forward-looking budget imbalance. Are investors uninformed? They should remember that the common belief that capital markets cannot fail is precisely the reason why they can."

Let me rephrase this: If you take the view that the US should actually raise the money now to cover for the liabilities it is adding up every year, then the annual budget deficit was approx. 20% of GDP in 2006 (and, by the way, a whopping 30% in 2009). The total liabilities by 2006 were $63.7 trillion, and that was equal to the entire value of all land, all buildings, all roads, all cars, all factories, all financial assets, and for that matter all the jewelry of all the women in America. The country was, by that measurement, completely insolvent. And that was *before* the crises of 2007–2009. So, one day America will really blow up. T-bonds will go to zero. The world will almost go under—financially at least. Or, so one should think.

This is serious stuff, but perhaps not as serious as it was put above, because after all, who isn't insolvent if they take their current assets and compare them with all the liabilities for the next 40 years? What keeps most people, most companies, and most states going is that they have future income as well. America isn't saving as it should, but it isn't insolvent either.

However, there really is a savings problem in most of the developed world. According to Credit Action (*www.creditaction.org.uk*), Britain's consumer debt was increasing by ~£1 million every 5 minutes in April 2008. Here is some of how their website described the U.K.'s national statistics over one day in that year:

- "Consumers will borrow an additional £304m today
- Consumers will pay £259m in interest today
- The average household debt will increase by over £12.22 today
- 74 properties will be repossessed today
- 292 people will be declared insolvent or bankrupt today
- 388 mortgage repossession claims will be issued and 272 mortgage repossession orders will be made today
- 404 landlord repossession claims will be issued and 306 landlord repossession orders will be made today."

An amusing symptom of the whole problem was that when 18 to 24-year-olds were asked what an "ISA" (individual tax-free savings account) was, approx. 15% suggested it was an "iPod accessory" and 10% that it was an "energy drink".

There was once a time when most people died fairly soon after they stopped working. Now there are many who live a substantial part of their life in the "golden years"—happy and long-lasting retirement. This is great, but people and governments need to save enough for that, and they don't. While the savings rate in the U.S. for many years had been around 8%, which was too low, it started to decline until actually going *negative* from the spring of 2005.

How about Japan? I think that most people regard the Japanese as savers, and they really were for many years. After World War II their savings averaged around 15% of GDP, followed by an increase to around 20% in the 1970s. But then it peaked and nosedived to just 3% of GDP in 2005–2006. As of 2010, the people in Japan aged 30-40 saved 6–7% of their income. To put that into perspective, when their parents were at that age, they saved 25–28%. There is another problem with Japan's savings: Most of it is kept in cash and deposits, which gave close to zero return—only approx. 15% are in shares. This means that savings in Japan do not accumulate to the same extent that is seen elsewhere.

In Europe it has been the U.K. and Spain that have had some of the lowest savings rates, which, as I already mentioned, probably is partly related to their property market booms. On the other hand, it has been more reasonable in continental European countries such as Germany, France, and Italy, where it has been stable around a more responsible 8–11%. However, generally, the farther south you go in Europe, the less likely savers are to invest in something that gives a good, long-term return. While most northern Europeans would opt for mainly equities and investment funds, southern Europeans are more likely to hold their savings in bonds, second properties, or cash, which on average gives lower returns.

Do aging and declining workforces offer any silver linings? I can think of a few. When a society ages, there will be fewer descendants to share inheritances. In many cases the fruits of two people's labor will be given to one child. Also, there will be less competition for skilled jobs and for university places. Furthermore, eventually housing can become more affordable.

And are there solutions to the problems? Indeed, there are. The problems can be solved by a combination of higher retirement age, lower pensions, higher taxes, and compulsory individual pension savings programs. However, it's not easy. High income taxes lead to a brain drain, tax evasion, and declining work effort and will thus defeat itself over the long run, and higher VAT encourages moonlighting. Lower pensions are difficult to enforce, since the old represent many votes and thus political power. The most realistic way forward is probably a combination of consumption-related taxes (real estate, automobiles, energy, etc.), mandatory savings accounts, and a higher and more flexible retirement age (after all, people have become healthier).

The question is whether such solutions will be implemented to a degree and at a time that will prevent meltdowns. My guess is that they will in most countries, but that there may be some smaller nations that eventually go over the cliff. It starts to feel uncomfortable when national debt exceeds around 60% of GDP, and the panic zone may not be far off when interest payments exceed the nominal growth rate in GDP. As of 2010 the most indebted developed countries are Italy and Greece with levels around 120%. Japan seems even higher with 180%, but more than half of it is held by government agencies. Countries with medium-level debt include the U.S.A., Canada, Germany, France, Sweden, Holland, and Portugal, and the less indebted countries include Norway, Australia, New Zealand, Ireland, Denmark, Spain, the U.K., and Finland.

One more thing about aging: There is a widespread theory that when people get older they will save less and therefore sell their bonds and shares, which will drive markets down. This, however, is not necessarily so. The table overleaf shows the results from a study of how people save during different phases of their lives.

The Americans do in fact save a lot less when they age, and the Germans save a bit less. But then again, the Japanese and English actually save *more* as they get older, and the Italians just stay the course. There is, in other words, no strong indication that aging will lead to financial selloffs.

Savings as a percentage of income in different age groups						
Age	*U.K.*	*Canada*	*Japan*	*Germany*	*Italy*	*U.S.*
25–34	6	2	11	11	13	9
35–44	9	4	20	14	17	14
45–54	12	7	18	16	18	15
55–64	8	10	20	10	18	11
65–74	11	6	20	8	17	−5
Over 75	20	8	26	10	16	−7

Source: Stephen A. Nyce and Sylveter J. Schreiber: *The Economic Implications of Aging Societies: The Cost of Living Happily Forever After*, New York: Cambridge University Press, 2006.

Nor, by the way, is there empirical evidence that this has happened before. There was a relative increase of people of working age in America during the 1920s and 1930s, and while share prices rose strongly up to 1929, they fell 85% during the subsequent crash and stayed depressed for years after. Conversely, during the years from the end of World War II and into the 1970s the working age group fell in proportion to the total population—but share prices rose steadily.

5

Globalization, urbanization, and wealth explosion

By the late 1970s the large majority of the world's population lived in communist and socialist systems, led by China, Russia, and the Warsaw Pact countries. However, it was slowly getting clearer that these systems were fundamentally dysfunctional. The Soviet Union, for instance, found it ever harder to meet basic requirements of its people—let alone to compete militarily with the U.S.A. Meanwhile, communist China had fallen so far behind its peers that its GDP per capita was only 13% of that of Taiwan and 6% of Hong Kong's. As previously mnentioned, it was as a matter of fact about the same as in Somalia.

When the change finally came, it started in China. After an internal power struggle, Deng Xiaoping initiated a radical change of direction in the late 1970s, which soon brought its growth rates up to levels similar to those of Taiwan and Hong Kong. Even though China's change of economic policy was radical, it was implemented through a long series of incremental steps.

The Warsaw Pact countries were next. On August 23, 1989, Hungary surprisingly removed its border defenses with Austria, and the following month more than 13,000 East German tourists took the chance and escaped to Austria. When the Hungarian authorities tried to stop the flood by sending the remaining East German tourists to Budapest, they entered the compounds of the West German Embassy and refused to be sent back to their own country. East Germany now forbade travel to Hungary. People got furious: mass demonstrations followed within East Germany, where people chanted *"Wir wollen raus!"* ("We want to leave!") and *"Wir sind das Volk!"* ("We are the people!"). On November 9, the East German government gave up and allowed its citizens to pass directly through the border posts to West Germany. No longer able or willing to prevent its citizens from escaping, the system collapsed.

The consequence was a global trend towards economic freedom and in most cases fairly radical versions of market economies, characterized by low or flat taxation and free trade. This trend became international after the fall of the Berlin Wall in 1989, and then became solidly institutionalized with support from organizations such as the IMF, World Bank, WTO (World Trade Organization), EU, G8, U.N., ILO (International Labor Organization), North American Free Trade Organization, etc., which acted as arbiters in conflicts of interest and supporters of the weak.

The economic impact was enormous. Between 1945 and 1975 international statistics indicated that global capital flows between nations were approx. 1% of GDP. However, as soon as movement of capital became free, it was as if a dam had broken. Between 1975 and 2000, global capital flows grew to just over 5% of global GDP, which had meanwhile exploded upwards.

It didn't stop there: By 2005, global capital flows reached no fewer than 16% of global GDP, and the trend toward economic freedom had clearly become something more: *a supertrend toward globalization.* The rapid development of the new economies involved a hitherto unseen collaboration between peoples, cultures, companies, and nations. Everything became international. You could drive up alongside a burger restaurant in America and order your meal through the car window to a loudspeaker. What you might not know could be that the person answering you and typing the order into the restaurant's computer wasn't present in the building. She was sitting in a service company in India.

————

I don't know if you saw the movie *Independence Day*, but if you did then you will surely recall the scenes showing a gigantic alien mother ship, about a quarter the size of the moon, which goes into orbit around the Earth while deploying several dozen smaller spacecraft, each being 15 miles, or 24 km wide. Very impressive.

Now, imagine that something like this really happened and that there were "people" inside these spacecraft—a civilization that produced as much as the combined GDP of the U.S.A., Germany, Japan, the U.K., France, and Italy. That would be something. Their demand for all sorts of products would be massive. Their production, too. It would be an immense shock for the world economy—for better and for worse.

And, yet, this is in fact not far from what we will face. The combined GDP of the G6 as of 2010 will be a bit under $25 trillion, and the GDP of the four leading emerging markets a bit over $5 trillion. So, the global economy in 2010 is still very much dominated by the Old World. But let's fast-forward. By 2030 the BRIC countries will produce a GDP of around $25 trillion, when adjusted for inflation. So, by that time they will be as big as the six old economies of today.

That change will happen within just 20 years. However, after that the BRICs will still steam ahead, and just 2–3 years after reaching the current G6 volume, it's not their size, but their *growth* since 2010 that will equal the entire size of the economies of the U.S.A., Germany, Japan, the U.K., France, and Italy in 2010. The giant spaceship will have landed. Actually, if we include the "N-11", the *emerging market growth will exceed the current output of G6 within fewer than 20 years.* What they *add* will be what the G6 now *produce.*

So, that's what we are facing: If you take a plane and criss-cross over every part of America, then another one cruising over the U.K., Germany, France, and Italy, and then a third one criss-crossing Japan, the size of everything you see below and everything else in these countries will equal the size of the new civilization that the emerging markets will build in fewer than 20 years. The houses, roads, automobiles, every-thing—they will make that within 20 years. And when the 20 years are up, they will do it again, just faster.

Some numbers in business and investing aren't that important, but others are mind-boggling, and it's those that you really have to comprehend. The expected emerging market growth is mind-boggling.

One may ask, of course, if all of this is really realistic. What if Goldman Sachs and all the other forecasters are plain wrong? Many of them (but not Goldman Sachs) were totally blindsided by the subprime salami crises, for instance, so how smart are these guys?

My answer to that would be that it doesn't take a Houdini-style miracle for emerging markets to do what I described. Japan, Singapore, Hong Kong, South Korea, and others have already shown how it's done, and the recipe is no secret: free markets, education, savings, and low taxes. The Western world did it too, but the emerging markets that are catching up now have a huge advantage over the currently rich nations: They can leapfrog. They can skip whole generations of technology and go straight to the newest and most productive. Their first trains are not steam locomotives like ours were. Their first mobile phones will not weigh 25 kg. They will follow in the slipstream of what the rich countries did, and that is much easier than going in front. So, take that and add the fact that 85% of the world's population live in these nations, and we get our GDP explosion.

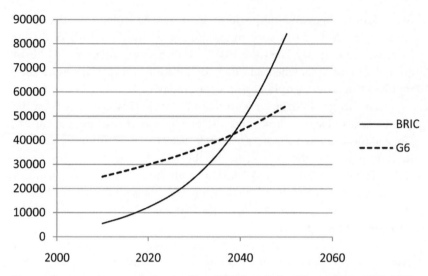

Expected economic growth in the four BRIC and six G6 countries, 2010–2050 (thousands). The illustration shows the addition of wealth in BRIC markets as compared with those of the G6. BRIC is illustrated by the lower graphs which show that BRIC growth will contribute more to the world economy by 2040 than G6 growth. The wall of money from these new markets can already be felt, but it will intensify over time. *Source: Dreaming with the BRICs*, Goldman Sachs, 2003.

However, the Goldman Sachs numbers I referred to above were a case presented in 2003. In late 2009, Goldman Sachs sent out a new report, where they indicated that they might have miscalculated quite a lot. The emerging markets had grown much, much faster since 2003 than they had originally imagined, whereas developed markets had grown less. This story is very solid indeed.

––––––––––

The expected growth in emerging market income will go hand in hand with a radical change of lifestyle: Urbanization. In 1800 only 3% of the world's population lived in cities. By 1950 that had grown to about one-third. If you look at the chart on p. 86, you will clearly see why this is an important change. The graph shows the development of global rural and urban populations starting in 1950, when one-third of the world's population already lived in towns and cities and continuing with forecasts until 2050 when two-thirds will do so.

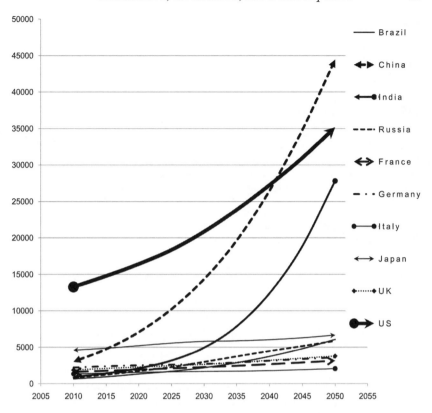

As the graph (p. 86) shows, *the number of people living in cities will grow by about 3 billion over 40 years, equal to almost 75 million per year.* Urbanization is a supertrend, and it means that a lot of people will suddenly get exposed to everything associated with urban lifestyle—automobiles, apartments, shops, media, and brands. A lot of bad things can be said about urbanization, including of course that cities are noisy, and in some cases polluted, and may be bad environments for children to grow up in. However, it also has its advantages. People living in urban environments tend to use a lot less energy per capita than those living in suburban or rural places. Furthermore, in emerging markets they are more likely to get access to clean water, healthcare, and education for children, and they will be exposed to new ideas and new knowhow. They are also less likely to produce many children, since children can't help out in the farm because there isn't any farm, and the children have to go to

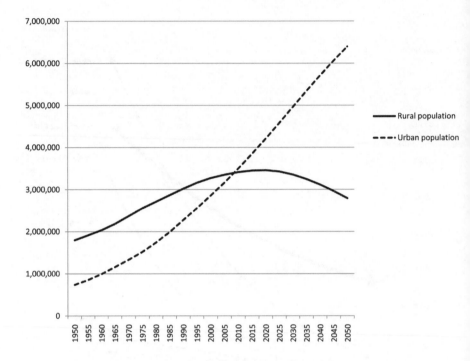

school anyway. Finally, as urbanization outpaces global growth, we will actually see some rural areas get less populated.

———

One way that emerging market economic growth will be felt is as what I would call a global "wall of money". The combination of rapid economic growth and currency appreciation in emerging markets will lead to a massive increase in international purchasing power among emerging market consumers as a whole. In some places it will be felt like it must have been to live in parts of Spain when all the Northern Europeans turned up, bought a lot of the land (a process which the locals often managed very badly, by the way), and filled it with houses and apartments. Some Europeans have also experienced rich Russians suddenly turning up from seemingly nowhere and outbidding everyone for property, yachts, aircraft, and collectibles.

Speaking of rich people: Merrill Lynch and Cap Gemini produced for many years a study of the number of so-called "high net worth individuals" ("HNWIs"); people with more than $1 million in net assets, excluding their primary residence and consumables. This was, in other words, a study of wealth available for investments (Cap Gemini now produces the report alone).

The reports show that the number of wealthy people grew substantially in 2006 to reach 9.5 million people who were managing $37 trillion in financial wealth, or an average of $3.8 million per person. Note here that this does not include their property or other fixed assets, nor the assets of less wealthy people. By 2008 the assets of HNWIs had risen to $40.7 trillion with the average HNWI's wealth surpassing $4 million for the first time. Furthermore, the number of people with more than $30 million in freely disposable private wealth (so-called "ultra-HNWIs", or "U-HNWIs") rose to 10.1 million individuals, with the fastest growth recorded in India, China, and Brazil.

Then came the crises. At the start of 2009, the world's population of HNWIs was down 14.9% from the year before, while their wealth had dropped 19.5%. Furthermore, there were now "only" 8.6 million U-HNWIs. However, by 2013 it was forecast that global high net wealth would have grown to $48.5 trillion, after advancing at a sustained annual rate of 8.1%. The following HNWI distribution was expected by 2013:

Forecast freely available assets held by HNWIs plus U-HNWIs by region (USD, 2013)		
Region	*Amount* ($ trillion)	*Percent of total*
Asia/Pacific	13.5	28.07
U.S.A.	12.7	26.40
Europe	11.4	23.70
Latin America	7.6	15.80
Middle East	1.9	3.95
Africa	1.0	2.08
Source: World Wealth Report 2009, Cap Gemini.		

What is striking here is that total wealth in these groups should be approx. 20% higher than the peak before the 2008–2009 crash, and also that Asia/Pacific should take the lead as the world's largest region for free wealth, increasing its share from 23% of the total in 2006 to 28% in 2013.

How big will the global wall of money of the coming decades be? Let's start with the assumption that the BRIC economy plus the "third billion" or "next 11" grow a combined $25 trillion from 2010 to 2030 (even though this may now seem conservative). Now, if we add the OECD countries we should get to around $40 trillion.

Now, we have seen that variable-price assets normally constitute some four to five times GDP. It takes time to generate savings and assets, which speaks for slow asset growth, but on the other hand, most emerging markets save a lot, which speaks for rapid asset growth. To make it simple let's assume that emerging market assets will grow in normal proportion to their GDP growth. This will mean that the order of magnitude in asset growth in emerging markets over the 20 years from 2010 to 2030 would be $160 trillion to $200 trillion in real terms. A trillion has 12 zeros, so $160,000,000,000,000–$200,000,000,000,000. What I am going to say now is not very serious, but I found a website (*http:// 87billion.com/*), which illustrated how big different piles of $100 bills were. The biggest one it showed was $315 billion. That pile, it claimed, would be "125 feet wide, 200 feet deep, and 450 feet tall". That is the size of a large skyscraper in Manhattan, so $160 trillion to $200 trillion in $100 bills would be the size of around 450–500 such skyscrapers. A Manhattan of money, really.

If we instead look farther ahead—to 2050—and concern ourselves with real GDP and wealth in the entire world, then the numbers get even more interesting. PricewaterhouseCoopers in 2006 published a study entitled *How Big Will the Major Emerging Market Economies Get and How Can the OECD Compete?* I have shown some of their numbers in the table opposite.

I think the most informative columns here are the two at the right, which compare per capita GDP corrected for inflation in 2005 and 2050. If you look at the U.S. at the top, you will see that *the Americans will more than double their real income per capita. Most other developed countries will be somewhere between doubling and tripling their average incomes.* As for the seven last countries in the table, which are developing nations, they will do far better. *The typical pattern is that these developing countries with a combined population currently close to 4 billion will increase average personal purchasing power by 400–600%.*

There are a few other details in the table that I find interesting. The first is that GDP per capita will rise far more in nominal terms than in purchasing power parity (PPP) terms in the emerging markets. This is a way of saying that their currencies will go up at the same time as their income will rise. If you live in an OECD country and invest in these countries

Expected GDP development 2005–2050, major economies				
	GDP per capita at market exchange rates		*GDP per capita in PPP[a] terms*	
	2005	*2050*	*2005*	*2050*
U.S.	40,339	88,443	40,339	88,443
Canada	31,466	75,425	31,874	75,425
U.K.	36,675	75,855	31,489	75,855
Australia	32,364	74,000	31,109	74,000
Japan	36,686	70,646	30,081	70,646
France	33,978	74,685	29,674	74,685
Germany	33,457	68,261	28,770	68,261
Italy	29,455	66,165	28,576	66,165
Spain	23,982	66,552	25,283	66,552
Korea	15,154	66,489	21,434	66,489
Russia	4,383	41,876	10,358	43,586
Mexico	6,673	42,879	9,939	42,879
Brazil	3,415	26,924	8,311	34,448
Turkey	4,369	35,861	7,920	35,861
China	1,664	23,534	6,949	35,851
Indonesia	1,249	23,097	3,702	23,686
India	674	12,773	3,224	21,872

Source: *How Big Will the Major Emerging Market Economies Get and How Can the OECD Compete?* PricewaterhouseCoopers, 2006.
[a] PPP stands for Purchasing Power Parity.

for the very long term (let's say in equities and real estate), then you will benefit from both.

I would also like to highlight what emerging market living standards will be in 2050. If you look at GDP per capita in real terms in 2005, you see that in Germany, for instance, it is 28,770, and in France it is 29,674. Now jump down to emerging markets in 2050 and you see that in Russia and Mexico it will be over 40,000 and that in Brazil, Turkey, and China it will be around 35,000. *Living standards in many emerging markets, including the five largest, will be higher in 2050 than they were in Germany, France, or Italy in 2005. The future world will be overwhelmingly rich when seen with the eyes of today. Also, by 2050, global income distribution between nations will be far more equal than it is today.*

The report doesn't focus on wealth development until 2050, but I would like to use its numbers to make a guess. The implication of the report is that *global GDP will grow by roughly 400% in terms of purchasing power from 2010 to 2050*, which means from approx. $60 trillion to $240 trillion per year, or an increase of around $180 trillion. Now, 2010 is a year where assets have just been hammered by crises, but if we work with "normalized" variable-price assets of four to five times GDP, then *total variable-price asset growth will be something like $800 trillion in real terms.* Some of the asset markets will easily expand to absorb that. There will surely be more equities, corporate bonds, and buildings to buy, for instance. But there are other assets where supply cannot go up, such as good coastal land, or most auction-class or museum-class collector items. Some of these could go silly, as in bubble-silly.

————————

I have addressed the problems of aging and peaking/declining workforces earlier in this chapter and proceeded afterwards to describe a scenario of solid, economic growth. Does that make sense? Can the world really get four times richer in 40 years given such a backdrop? Or, in Europe can wealth more than double in the absence of population growth?

Let's look at the table for the Eurozone opposite, which addresses changes in (1) working age population, (2) annual productivity growth, (3) change in hours worked per worker, and (4) real GDP change per annum.

The column at the right shows inflation-adjusted GDP change, which grew rapidly from 1960 to 1980, but slowed afterwards. The forecast for 2010–2030 is 1.7% growth and for 2031–2050 just 1.2% annually, which is really low. Now, I will argue later in this book that productivity could do rather well due to innovations in IT and genomics, but the second column in the table ("annual productivity growth") actually assumes the same. So, to put it simply, *aging will cut growth in the Eurozone by 0.3%*

Past and forecast real economic growth, Eurozone				
	Annual working age population change	*Annual productivity growth*	*Annual change in total hours worked per worker*	*Annual inflation-adjusted GDP change*
1960–1980	0.7	4.8	−1.2	4.3
1981–2000	0.5	2.1	−0.3	2.3
2001–2005	0.4	0.8	0.1	1.3
2006–2010	0.2	1.1	0.8	2.1
2011–2030	*−0.3*	*1.8*	*0.2*	*1.7*
2031–2050	*−0.6*	*1.7*	*0.1*	*1.2*

Source: *Macroeconomic Implications of Demographic Developments in the Euro Area*, Occasional Paper No. 51, European Central Bank, August 2006, and Magnus, George: *The Age of Aging*, John Wiley & Sons, 2009.

initially and then by 0.6% annually. Compared with the recent past—from 1980 to 2000—growth will almost be cut in half.

The next table shows the same calculation for America, and the results are more encouraging here. America should cruise along with a real growth rate of approx. 2.5%, which is one reason that I don't believe in the meltdown scenarios for the American economy you often hear about. If I put an average growth rate of 2.55% into my spreadsheet and run it for 40 years, it shows that adjusted for inflation the *American economy will be 2.6 times as big in 2050 as in 2010.* America has balance issues that need to be tackled, but it will remain mighty.

I don't have the same calculations for Japan, but given that (1) its working population is in tailspin, (2) its national debt is at critical levels, and (3) its productivity growth is low, the prognosis can't be good. It could end up like the American car manufacturers whose social obligations became ever more unmanageable as they downsized their business. If you can grow out of debt problems, then you can also shrink into them. Japan is the first major economy in modern times to have entered a long period with declining nominal GDP. So, this is one major conclusion: *America will be OK, Europe will be slower, and Japan will be in rapid, relative decline.*

Past and forecast real economic growth, USA				
	Annual working age population change	Annual productivity growth	Annual change in total hours worked per worker	Annual inflation-adjusted GDP change
1960–1980	1.6	2.1	−0.1	3.6
1981–2000	1.1	1.5	0.6	3.2
2001–2005	1.1	2.5	−1.1	2.5
2006–2010	0.7	1.5	−0.5	1.7
2011–2030	0.3	2.2	0	2.5
2031–2050	0.2	2.2	0.2	2.6

Source: Macroeconomic Implications of Demographic Developments in the Euro Area, Occasional Paper No. 51, European Central Bank, August 2006, and Magnus, George: The Age of Aging, John Wiley & Sons, 2009.

Now, for emerging markets the economic story is very different. Here is a list of characteristics that are common in most emerging markets:

1. In the process of liberalization
2. High economic growth
3. High savings rate
4. Sound government finances
5. Surplus on current account
6. Undervalued currency
7. Early stages of credit culture
8. High level of aspiration
9. Low average age
10. Low taxes.

Not all emerging markets score 10 out of 10 here, but some do and many come close. They will grow rapidly and on a global basis; the effect of this will more than offset the effect of global aging.

One interesting aspect that I have already briefly mentioned is that as they expand, their currencies should appreciate. Personally I believe this will happen until they reach a point where their cost of living is close to—or perhaps higher—than that of most OECD countries. Think Spain. When I was 19 years of age (in 1976), a friend of mine and I worked for 4 months in two dairies in Iceland. After we finished, we went to Spain, where we used the money earned over these 4 months as a downpayment for a house on the Costa del Sol with 30,000 m^2 of land on a mountain top. The total cost of the property was around U.S.$12,000. It didn't have running water, a kitchen, or bathroom, but we had that retrofitted for approx. $6,000. We were just university students who had worked for a bit on the side, but down there we were almost rich. Spain was an emerging market and *really* cheap.

In 2007—21 years later—I came to the Spanish island of Majorca with my (Spanish) wife to buy a summer house, and this time I expected extreme luxury for what we could now afford. We were surprised. The house prices were now on a par with the most expensive prices in Switzerland and far higher than, say, Germany. Someone offered us a 600 m^2 house with 10,000 m^2 land going down to the sea. Very nice indeed, but the asking price was €22 million (we bought a cheaper one).

The issue is that capital will flow to where the economic growth is, and to where people want to live. As most of the growth in the future will come from emerging markets, their currencies will appreciate a lot. How fast and how much is hard to say, but as I write I am part-owner of a software company with offices in Zug (Switzerland), New York, Hong Kong, and Shenzhen. I know the company's cost structure inside out and can see that salaries for skilled software developers as well as office rent cost us in China one-seventh of what it might have cost in Switzerland or New York. So, Chinese price levels would have to go up some 700% in order to reach parity—either through inflation or currency appreciation.

———

Maybe when you read this chapter, you had a nagging thought that it's all forecasts made by economists, and none of it mentions what will actually drive the expected growth in wealth and income. "How can we be so sure that the global economy will expand so much?" you may rightly ask. "Which technologies should make that even remotely possible?" You may also have other concerns: "Hasn't growth reached the limits of what mother Earth will allow? Will environmental pressure and resource shortages not force us to stop economic growth or even scale back to a more sustainable level?"

I will address the first question in the next chapter and the second in the one after.

6

Intelligence, knowledge, and innovation

The human race (*Homo sapiens*) is somewhere around 200,000 years old, and for almost all that time we lived as hunters and gatherers. It took thousands of years before people had the idea to sharpen rocks on one side and use them as tools, and additional thousands of years before it occurred to someone to start sharpening them on both sides. And then again, it took thousands of years until they began attaching them to a branch to create axes.

However, after the last ice age, approx. 11,500 years ago, we invented farming. Then came the industrial society a couple of hundred years ago. Then trains, automobiles, and aircraft. The chemical industry. Electricity. It goes faster and faster, and while it took 120 years from the time the first railroad was invented until it was within practical reach of 80% of the population in the U.S., it only took 100 years for the telephone and 70 years for the radio. Then came television which reached 80% of the population after 60 years.

The IBM PC entered the scene in 1981, and was followed by the internet, which had an 80% penetration in the U.S. within 20 years. The next key innovation, mobile phones, took just 15 years to achieve an 80% coverage. After the launch of the iPhone, the so-called "app-store" opened. This was a market place, where independent software companies could sell software and services based on Apple's mobile technology. During the first 12 months, around 35,000 different software packages were launched, which gave rise to more than a billion software downloads from users. During this year, approximately 100 new software programs for the iPhone were launched per day, and almost 3 million were downloaded daily. This meant 125,000 software downloads every hour, 2,000 per minute, and approximately 33 per second. And this was just what happened the first year, and only to one of many mobile platforms. This explosion in creativity ought to be mentioned in the *Guinness Book of Records*. Not only is the rate of new inventions accelerating, so is the speed at which we roll out new stuff to the market.

Our accumulation of knowledge is also accelerating. According to a study by the University of California at Berkeley in 2005, the global amount of digital information in the world had grown 60% during the previous year, which happened to mean that it grew by 57,000 times as much as the existing information available in the Library of Congress within just one year (why does this make me think that libraries have a limited future?). Every year about a million new book titles are printed. There are approx. 80,000 mass-market periodicals, 40,000 scholarly journals, 40,000 newsletters, and 25,000 newspaper titles. It's massive. Our innovation and knowledge seem to be in exponential growth.

How is that possible? One reason is our proliferation of so-called "meta-ideas"—new ways to inspire, develop, test, capture, distribute, and utilize ideas. The first printing press, for instance, was a meta-idea that enabled fast and efficient distribution of other ideas of any kind. Gutenberg's printing press came into operation in 1450, a time which marked the start of Europe's global ascent. Ocean-going ships like the Spanish caravel served that function as well. When the Spanish arrived in America, they passed their ideas to the indians. They also brought back ideas garnered from the indians—the cultivation of potatoes, tomatoes, corn, chocolate, vanilla, tobacco, and many other crops.

There have been numerous other meta-ideas such as the whole complex of thought that leads to the pursuit of truth: logic, the scientific method, mathematics, statistics, peer-reviewed scientific publications, freedom of speech, and free press, etc. Some newer meta-ideas include universities, patent and copyright laws, satellite television, international banking, the venture capital industry, and the internet. Meta-ideas create a huge network effect which puts a booster behind everything.

Before these ideas evolved, people would live insular lives and would be subject to superstition and severe groupthink. They would think of events around them, such as thunderstorms, as simply controlled by divine beings and not connected to any logical and natural sequence of events. They would assume the presence of mysterious ethers, fluids, or spirits, rather than of tangible forces abiding to mathematical/physical/chemical laws. If they had discovered something new, they would keep it to themselves and try to sell it in private sessions. If they came across new data, they would torture these data (or those who discovered them) until they confessed to preconceived opinions.

The 15 greatest meta-ideas

Without great meta-ideas, new ideas are likely to be lost quickly, or to find no useful application. The best meta-ideas ever are listed below.

1. *Logic.* Develop systematic tools to distinguish between the true and the false through coherent thinking.
2. *Writing and printing.* Capture ideas in text, code, musical notes, or illustrations, thus enabling them to transcend time and place.
3. *Observation of nature.* The ideas to systematically record what happens in nature.
4. *The basic scientific method.* The acquisition of knowledge as a cumulative, disinterested enterprise. Formulate logical hypothesis to explain observable phenomena, describe possible ways to prove that they are either wrong or right, and test systematically for both these possibilities.
5. *Controlled data replication.* Isolate phenomena from their complex surroundings and test them in controlled environments.
6. *Occam's Razor.* Reduce scientific explanations to the simplest, true form.
7. *Formal reviews.* Have formal science papers critically reviewed by competent peers, and operate a large structure of informal peer reviews in the media. Maintain a free press.
8. *Mathematical structure of nature.* Describe, if at all possible, any scientific observation in terms of statistical probabilities and correlations and/or mathematical equations (this does not exclude other forms of description). Use this to provide mathematical/statistical proof or rejection of hypotheses.
9. *Assigning credit through publication.* Recognize that the first person to describe a new observation or theory in scientific terms in a recognized, peer-reviewed publication can lay claim to be its discoverer.
10. *Reserving rights.* The ability to take out patents and to reserve copyright and trademarks.
11. *Traveling and migration.* The movement of people, which enables them to exchange ideas and make new observations.
12. *Banking and venture capital.* The infrastructure to allocate money to where the best ideas are.

13. *Telecommunication.* Enabling the rapid one-to-many or interactive dissemination of ideas.
14. *Science-based education.* Schools and universities, etc., which provide scientifically based skills, and test and record them so that others can rely upon them.
15. *Private enterprise and property rights.* The personal financial incentive to turn ideas into products and services for others.

Science-based education is the greatest meta-idea of all. *The number of people taking tertiary education worldwide seems to double every 15 years or so,* which means that there are simply more and more people around to think, spread knowledge, and implement innovation. And what's more: These people are getting smarter and smarter. It was the New Zealand–based James R. Flynn, who discovered what is now called the "Flynn Effect", which is a continuous, year-on-year rise of intelligence quotient (IQ) scores in virtually all parts of the world. Before this phenomenon was discovered, scientists trying to evaluate how our IQ declines as we age simply compared intelligence from different age groups and concluded that it declined fairly much with age. It does indeed decline as a person ages, but what Flynn discovered was that some of the measured age differences were actually baseline errors, since average IQ was increasing with each new generation.

Why do IQs rise? A natural assumption might be that this is entirely driven by better education. However, the parts of IQ tests that are most influenced by education, such as vocabulary, arithmetic, and general knowledge, have actually not really improved. Where we do find improvements are instead in what we could call "raw" intelligence or simply mental firepower. This is shown through so-called "general intelligence factor loaded" (g-loaded) tests such as the so-called "Raven's Progressive Matrices". The concept of general intelligence, or "g", is based on the extremely common observation that if you are smart in one area, you are also likely to be smart in many others.

So, yes, we are getting smarter in a very broad way, and it cannot be explained very well with education. One likely factor is increasing heterosis, which in this case means the mixing of genes through interbreeding of people from different places and races. This can create something called "hybrid vigor" or "outbreeding enhancement", which means that mixing strengthens the genes (the opposite is inbreeding, which leads to deterioration). Whereas inbreeding can lead to rapid genetic decay, heterosis—the result of increased traveling and migration—can strengthen the genetic makeup over generations. However, genetics definitely cannot explain all the increase in human intelligence, because natural genetics doesn't evolve nearly that fast. Environmental factors such as better nutrition, smaller families, and better upbringing are probably important. These are factors that would also explain why people get taller and live longer, and it would seem intuitively surprising if healthier, taller, better nourished people didn't also exhibit improved intelligence. What's good for the body should be good for the brain.

The global rate of IQ increase is approx. 3 % per decade, but with large differences. In some places it's really radical. Flynn used the mean scores of Raven's test from 1952 in some Dutch tests and calibrated them so that the average score in 1952 was 100. He then looked at subsequent identical tests and found that the average in 1982 had risen to 121.10. That is a gain of 21 points in just 30 years, which means about 7 points per decade. He found data from around a dozen other countries that showed similar trends. Whereas a 20-point gain is clearly impressive, one may think that 3% per decade, which is the global norm, isn't that much, but I actually think the scale is deceptive. One might intuitively imagine, for instance, that a person with an IQ of 140 can do an arithmetic calculation twice as fast as one with an IQ of 70, but there is a lot more to it. Here is a common translation of the numbers into plain words:

Human intelligence ratings	
IQ range	*Classification*
140 and over	Genius or near genius
120–140	Very superior intelligence
110–120	Superior intelligence
90–110	Normal or average intelligence
80–90	Dullness
70–80	Borderline deficiency
Below 70	Definite feeble-mindedness

Source: Wechsler, D.: *The Measurement of Adult Intelligence*, Williams & Wilkins, Baltimore, 1944.

As the descriptions of each IQ bracket shows, the differences have vast implications. A person with an IQ of 140 may be a top scientist or a business-man with an annual income in the millions of dollars, whereas one with 70 most likely is struggling at the fringes of a society he hardly understands.

The highest intelligence recorded, according to the *Guinness Book of Records*, belongs to a young Korean named Kim Ung-Yong, who scored 210. Kim was able to read (read!) Japanese, Korean, German, and English by his third birthday, which meant 24 months after his birth. He studied physics at Hanyang University from the age of 3 until he was 6 and could solve an advanced stochastic differential equation at the age of 4. Somehow I can imagine how it must have felt for the other students to sit next to a toddler during lectures. I wonder if he was sucking a pacifier. At the age of 7, Kim was invited to America by NASA and he earned his Ph.D. in physics at Colorado State University at the age of 15. So, again, someone with an IQ of half Kim's (i.e., 105) is really far less capable. It's not that with an IQ of 105 (instead of 210) you can only read 2 languages on your third birthday instead of 4, or that you begin your university physics studies at the age of 6 instead of 3. No, the differences in human intelligence are much bigger than that.

In 1995 the American Psychological Association assembled a taskforce headed by Ulric Neisser to create an overall assessment of all research made on the state of intelligence research—a so-called "meta-study". One of the conclusions in the report was truly remarkable: If the American children of 1932 could take an IQ test normed in 1997, their average IQ would have been only about 80 (against 100 in 1997). The reason I find that so important is that if the average was 80 in 1932, then most people were actually "dull" or suffered from "borderline deficiency", when measured by modern standards. I believe that the increase in mental cap-abilities must play an important role in the acceleration of human knowledge creation and innovation.

Let me summarize: Human knowledge and innovation is growing exponentially for the following reasons:

- The number of people in tertiary education doubles every third year
- The continued development and spread of meta-ideas
- The average IQ grows approx. 0.3% per annum.

I think all of this adds up to a global network effect of smartness. It feeds on itself. So, how fast does our knowledge actually grow? If you check that question on the internet, you find numerous suggestions, almost all without any source quoted, but they range from a doubling every year to every 15 years, with many quoting 5 years. I found an interesting source, though. In 2007 Thomas Fuller published a league table for 25 points of measurements of the growth of human knowledge, which is shown overleaf.

Based on this he suggested that doubling took longer than the 5 years some people claim. I would like to offer my own wild guess, taking my own experiences as an example. In 1983, when I taught economics at a university, I wrote a large compendium about operational planning in the food industry for my students. It wrote it by hand (!) and it was then typed on a typewriter by a secretary—it took ages, and the secretary gave me evil stares whenever I entered the office with a new pile of scribbles. Afterwards we added the illustrations with glue, before we photocopied and bound it for my students. Big, big work.

A few years later I wrote a book about international market research for a publisher, and for that purpose I needed to visit libraries, where I ordered books and photocopies that I could then pick up the day after. I would then read them, get new ideas, and come back for more the day after. I typed the whole thing on my new Olivetti computer, which unfortunately crashed a few times every week. Big work again, but it was now a lot easier than the previous handwriting and gluing.

Today, with modern computers, the internet, Google, and all that, I work much faster than I did in those days. If I have a question, I normally find the answer within a few minutes. To read and think takes exactly the same time as before, of course, but if I see a reference to an interesting book, I download it from Amazon to my Kindle and start reading it straightaway. My PC doesn't crash and the spellchecker saves my skin. If I can't recall where in the book I covered something, I do a quick word search. If I can't recall where I stored a document about something, I do a quick word search of my computers and servers. If I don't know if a large document I find on the internet deals with what I am looking for, I do a couple of word searches within it. When the manuscript is done, I email it to the publisher while sitting in a chalet in the mountains. When they have questions, I read them on my Blackberry and answer straightaway, no matter what day or time of the day it is.

So, let's say that my productivity as a knowledge worker has increased tenfold from 1985 to 2010. That is a compound annual growth rate of around 10%. I would guess that the parts of human knowledge gathering that involve real-world experiments, such as interviewing people or mixing chemicals have a slower average productivity growth—let's say

Growth rates and doubling rates of indicators of human knowledge

Field	Annual growth rate	Knowledge doubling time, years
Nanotechnology patents	44.91	1.87
Nanotechnology journals	42.03	1.98
Global-warming patents	38.62	2.12
Prion patents	33.76	2.38
Programming patents	33.53	2.40
Stem cell patents	26.47	2.95
Prion journals	25.57	3.04
Global-warming journals	24.71	3.14
Epidemiology patents	17.37	4.33
Stem cell journals	16.63	4.51
Programming journals	12.55	5.86
Alzheimer's disease patents	11.26	6.50
Oncology patents	10.02	7.26
Alzheimer's disease journals	9.65	7.52
Oncology journals	9.23	7.85
DeSolla Price estimate of world literature growth	7.00	10.24
Epidemiology journals	6.22	11.49
Mars journals	5.78	12.34
Shale oil journals	5.53	12.88
U.S. patent grants	5.21	13.65
University enrollment worldwide	4.85	14.64
U.S. patent applications	3.88	18.21
U.S. book publishing	3.65	19.33
Shale oil patents	2.58	27.21
All publications in astrophysics since 1970	4.01	17.67

Source: Thomas Fuller, *http://newsfan.typepad.co.uk/does.human.knowledge.doub/2007/05/league.tables.a.html*

5% annually. Perhaps what we should estimate is that personal productivity in knowledge creation grows 6–7% annually.

Moore's law: one of many

Ray Kurzweil is one of America's leading technologists. He holds no fewer than 16 honorary doctorates and has been awarded by three American presidents. Kurzweil has been a serial entrepreneur and developed, among other things, the CCD flatbed scanner, the text-to-speech synthesizer, and music synthesizers capable of accurately duplicating the sounds of real instruments.

Early in his career he realized that among startups with good ideas and teams, the few that eventually succeeded wildly did so mainly because their *timing* was right. He thought that in order to achieve this in high tech you have to start development before the necessary core technologies for commercial rollout exist, so that you are ready to launch exactly when it gets technically feasible.

Inspired by this conclusion, he began tracking developments in all sorts of technologies, such as clock speeds, cost, density performance, and unit sales of microprocessors, supercomputer power, DNA-sequencing cost, mapped gene bank, price reduction per bit of random access memory, wireless price/performance, hosts, traffic, and backbone bandwidth of the internet, patents, resolution of 3D brain scans, and much more. He found that *most of what involves development of intelligence in any form evolves exponentially*, which means constantly accelerating, like in Moore's Law for computers.

Exponential growth is difficult to comprehend for humans. We tend to think in static or linear dimensions, and we will thus very often massively underestimate what an intelligent product will be capable of doing 20–30 years later.

If the number of people working with knowledge has more than tripled from 1985 to 2010 (doubling every 15 years), and if the average productivity of such people has almost quadrupled during the same time (improving 6–7% annually), then we have knowledge output that is around 12 times faster in 2010 than it was in 1985, taking *overall compound annual growth in human knowledge to around 10% and the doubling time for knowledge to 8–9 years*. If we believe that human knowledge will continue to expand at that speed (I shall come back to that), then we shall know six to seven times as much in 2030 than we do in 2010, and in 2050 we shall know approx. 45 times as much. So, while I talked about a "wall of money" in a previous chapter, I think it is fair to refer to a "wave of knowledge" that we will surf in the future, and as for predictions that global GDP will grow 400% within 40 years, these appear a lot more plausible if we factor in that human knowledge will grow 4,500% during the same period.

But human knowledge about what? Which knowledge is growing fastest and which will have the greatest impact in the future? To answer this, I would like to take a few steps back and look at the status of basic natural sciences. These are, in my opinion, (1) mathematics, (2) statistics, (3) classical physics, (4) chemistry, (5) quantum mechanics, and (6) genetics. Others might disagree and argue, for instance, that astronomy or geology qualify as well, but astronomy draws widely on math and physics and geology on chemistry and classical physics. I do think the six I mentioned are the really basic ones.

Now, if you think about them, it seems that the first four are fairly mature. The initial important breakthroughs in *mathematics* were made by the Greeks no fewer than 2,300–2,500 years ago, and parts of the *statistical* models we use today were developed as far back as the 18th and 19th centuries. I am not saying that these disciplines are no longer evolving, because they definitely are, but they are probably not accelerating any longer—most of the best discoveries in these disciplines are behind us now, I think. *Classical physics* has also been mature for a long time, and *chemistry* is largely based on our understanding of the periodic system, which was first described in 1869—around 150 years ago, although I have to stress that the discipline still has intense challenges in areas such as supporting new generations of computer chips.

The progress we have achieved in these four disciplines has totally changed our lives. Most of the products we buy today, from toothpaste to automobiles, soap, magazines, airplanes, food, and our houses, would not be possible without application of some or all of these four sciences— not with the current quality and price anyway. So, from that perspective at least, one would be forgiven for not expecting massive innovation over the coming decades.

However, it gets more interesting when we get to quantum mechanics, which is the discipline that deals with atomic and subatomic systems. The common trait of quantum mechanics and Einstein's relativity theory (and certain types of modern art, for that matter) is that it is almost impossible to explain and even harder to understand. However, it is easily proved that quantum mechanics theories are true. Quantum mechanics forms the deeper basis of many parts of chemistry and classical physics and includes such subdisciplines as quantum chemistry, particle physics, nuclear physics, condensed matter physics, solid-state physics, atomic physics, molecular physics, and computational chemistry. It has come far, but it is not mature by any means. Scientists working with quantum mechanics are actually struggling with answering some big and basic questions. "How many dimensions exist in the universe?", for instance (definitely more than 3!), or

- "Which are the smallest particles that exist?"
- "What on Earth is dark matter, which calculations show must exist but which we can't find?"
- "Does dark energy also exist?"
- "What was there before the Big Bang?"

These are very important questions, and the answers are not yet known, although I do believe that we shall have positive identification of dark matter and the smallest particles in the universe by 2030 or so. In fact, I suspect that physicists will have formed a consensus about a "grand unifying theory" by then. But they haven't at the moment.

Particle accelerators

Nuclear scientists have long known that there were smaller particles than protons, electrons, and neutrons, and they are today routinely discussing particles they give such names as "positive kaon", "Y(3940)", "sigma-minus", "lambda-C-plus", "charm-quark (c)", "strange-quark (s)", etc. They are now referring to a "standard model", which in a way corresponds to the periodic system used in chemistry. Just as the development of the periodic system enabled scientists to correctly predict the existence of atoms they hadn't yet seen in nature, the standard model of nuclear science has enabled scientists to predict the existence of particles they give further weird names to such as "charmed-pentaquark", "xi-minus-minus", "X(3872)", "mystery meson", and not least the much anticipated "Higgs' boson".

Nuclear scientists use the Hadron Collider, a 27 km long particle accelerator close to Geneva, to search for some of these missing particles, and the budget for the first planned experiments runs into billions of euros.

What new innovations will come out of the work in quantum physics over the coming decades? The one that is most anticipated is a commercially viable fusion reactor, which heats up particles to 120,000,000°K. If we can get it to work, we would have access to unlimited, clean energy for several million years. That is radical, but scientists have been working on it for decades. The most optimistic case is probably commercial rollout around 2030, but the uncertainties are huge and it may well take 50 or 100 years. The website of the Culham Center for Fusion Energy contained this formulation in December 2009:

> "Experimental fusion machines have now produced fusion powers of more than ten megawatts. A new machine under construction, called ITER, will be capable of producing 500 megawatts of fusion power. ITER is expected to start operating in 2018. Although it will be on the scale needed for a power station, there will still be technological issues to address to produce steady, reliable electricity, so it is anticipated that a prototype power station will be needed after ITER. Electricity generation is expected in 30 to 40 years, depending on how focused the research and funding decisions remain."

So, *perhaps the most probable outcome is that it will work by 2050 and will be rolled out over the following decades.* It should be mentioned that there have been efforts to create fusion energy without high temperatures—perhaps in collapsing bubbles. However, so far the results have not been encouraging.

Another example: The quantum computer is one that uses the so-called "spin state" of electrons to represent bits of information (each electron can have four intermittent stages). If scientists can get this to work, then a single computer might have more processing power than all computers that exist on Earth today. Scientists are working on quantum computers too.

There are also attempts to create superconductors that work at normal temperatures. I do not know if that is possible, but if it is, then it will radically change the economics and geography of energy transportation and enable us to make 3D computer chips that are much, much faster and more compact than the human brain. It may sound like science fiction stuff, but again scientists are working on it.

However, the two more predictable and probably most promising innovation areas over the next few decades will probably be biotechnology and information technology. Why biotechnology? Because we have just made a series of ground-breaking discoveries that will radically change the scope of what we can do with life. In order to get biotechnology to the same level as traditional chemistry, we have needed to do what the chemists did: get to fully understand what happens at the smallest level. In biotechnology this started by mapping the exact code of life—the genomes. We needed to do this for all life, and then we needed to find out what each of the genes in an organism actually does, and then proceed to map how proteins are created and how they interact. All of this was until very recently practically impossible because of the sheer complexity. (Human DNA contains 1.3 billion base-pairs, for instance, and it can take a mainframe computer a year to calculate how a single protein folds in 3D space.)

But the door to this world has just swung wide open. It is not long ago that biotech was more an experimental technology that evolved much like other "old economy" businesses—increasing its productivity linearly. However, it has now become an information technology, since we are beginning to know the software of life. The *Human Genome Project* started in 1990 with a budget of $3 billion and a timeframe of 13 years to map human DNA (using four samples). This can now be done for $60,000 in 2 weeks and probably soon for $1,000 or less in a few days or even hours. That is equal to *performance doubling every 16 months*, which makes it easily comparable with what we have seen with computer chips—if anything even a bit faster.

Wet and dry nanotechnology

So-called "nanotechnology" is a manufacturing process, where atoms or molecules are manipulated one at a time. It can be used to produce superconductor components in microchips, materials with extraordinary qualities, or, for instance, artificial red blood cells that are 100 times more efficient than the ones nature gave us (so that you can dive for 30 minutes without using scubadiving compressed air bottles). Industrial production of nanotech devices and materials is sometimes called "dry nanotech". The alternative is "wet nanotech", or bioengineering. This has a massive advantage over dry nanotech inasmuch as nature has already given us a huge library of useful code plus the ability to quickly and exponentially self-replicate a design.

Wet nanotech has already taken off, whereas dry nanotech probably won't become a particularly large business until after 2030.

The implications are massive. We can use this to create far cheaper and more environmentally friendly food. Whereas global population growth is decelerating, due to genomics, farming yield will accelerate, so that we will eventually be able to feed a growing population using less farmland. In Africa, average yields are just a third of what they are globally, and since global yields can increase massively due to gene technology, African yields could technically quadruple or more. Healthcare will also be improved beyond recognition, which will be much needed given the coming increase in the number of elderly. It even seems that we will be able to recreate extinct species such as the mammoth (I am not joking here). I have dedicated a whole chapter later to genomics and biotech.

Another spectacular innovation area is information technology. After the IT crash in 2000–2003, there were many who believed that the party for IT was just about over. Then came the massive successes of cloud computing, mobile broadband, Google, Skype, Amazon, and Apple, etc., and it became clear that innovation in IT hadn't stopped at all. The crash was just temporary indigestion in the investment community. So, it continues, but will the coming decades for IT be . . . *great?*

They will. In 1965 Gordon E. Moore, one of the founders of Intel, wrote a paper describing that the number of transistors that could be placed inexpensively on a chip (or integrated circuit) had doubled approximately every two years. Furthermore, he predicted that this doubling speed could continue for some time. Other people soon started to refer this phenomenon as "Moore's Law". There is now strong reason to expect that Moore's Law can continue to work for a while based on current technological concepts (probably until just after 2020). Eventually we need to make some radical changes based on 3D chip designs, optical computing, superconductors, or quantum computing to keep or accelerate the pace of performance improvement, or else the doubling time will rise to perhaps 5 years. But with what is already in the development pipeline we will see computers that approach the human brain in sheer data-processing capacity fairly soon. There are, in fact, several major projects underway to imitate how the brain works with computers. DARPA and IBM are, for instance, working on it. These are very credible players. DARPA, just to put this in perspective, played a large part in developing the early versions of the internet, and IBM developed the computer that beat world champion Gary Kasparov at chess; so, these are smart people working on serious stuff. The list of what we can expect from information technology over the next 20–40 years is very long, and I have also devoted another chapter just to that.

Core sciences, discovery, and innovation

The next few decades will provide extremely rapid development in scientific and technical discovery and innovation.

Discovery	*Innovation*
	● Computer hardware
● Mathematics	● Software
● Statistics	● Telecommunication
● Classical physics	● Electronic media
● Chemistry $\longrightarrow$	● Chemical products
● Quantum physics	● Nuclear fusion power
● Genomics	● Bioengineering
	● Human brain simulation
	● Nanotechnologies
	● Alternative energy

One way to track how and where our collective ingenuity has evolved is to look at patents filed or granted. The World Intellectual Property Organization tracks all patent filings and has found that these grew rapidly from 1991 to 2006, as shown in the graph at the top of the next page—in fact they roughly doubled during these 15 years.

Just after World War II, the creative dominance of the West was complete. However, with the rise of Japan and South Korea, they showed up strongly in international patent statistics. The statistics show that by 2006 the overwhelming proportion of all patents was held by Japan, the U.S.A., Europe, Korea, and China—equally split between Western and Eastern nations. Chinese residents/businesses increased their share of total worldwide patent filings from 1.8% to 7.3% between 2000 and 2006. Due to this rapid increase in patent applications from China, it appears likely that Asia will lead in patents granted over the coming decades.

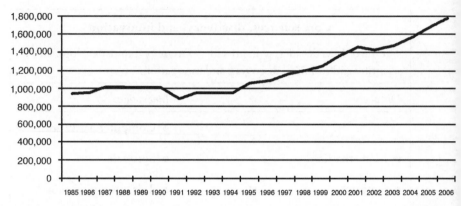

Global patent filings, 1985–2006. Patent filings are not direct indicators of human knowledge growth, since their numbers don't quantify innovation, performance, quality, or productivity growth. A new patent in computer technology may represent a tenfold performance jump whereas other patents are less significant or even commercially irrelevant. *Source: World Patent Report: A Statistical Review (2008)*, World Intellectual Property Organization.

The subject matter of this chapter was intelligence, knowledge, and innovation, and I think the most important conclusions are these:

- Average human intelligence will continue to rise approx. *0.3%* every year.
- The number of knowledge workers will continue to grow *5%* a year.
- The performance of computer chips and genomic sequencing will grow *50–75%* a year for a number of years.
- The total amount of scientific and technical knowledge will grow approx. *10%* a year, driven by the two factors above plus the continued development of meta-ideas.

What all of this amounts to is an amazing development in our collective ingenuity. I asked earlier how our economies can grow as fast as expected in the future, and these numbers provide the answer.

Let's now reverse the question: If the creation of ideas proceeds so quickly, then why don't our economies grow even faster than they do? First, many ideas do not lead to growth in output, but simply to *savings in costs, or to improvements in quality that do not show up in GDP statistics.* Second, much of what we do is hardly affected by innovation at all. The best example I can think of is Stradivarius' violins, the best of which were made between 1698 and 1720, and which sell for millions of dollars each today. In blind tests, they aren't any better than the best violins

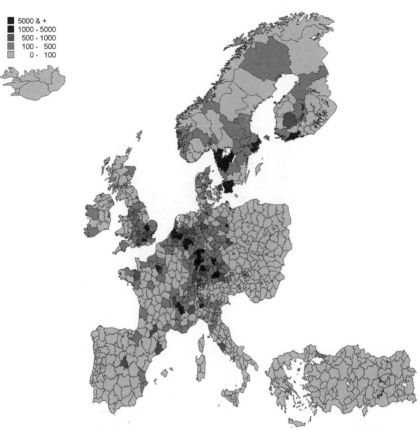

Number of patent applications filed under the Patent Cooperation Treaty (PCT), 2003–2005. Patent counts are based on the priority date, the inventor's region of residence, and use fractional counts on PCT filings at the international phase—European Patent Organization (EPO) designations. Data are graphically presented according to Territorial Level 3 (U.S.). Data for Iceland are not available at the regional level. Interestingly, the geographical concentrations of patent applications in this recent period coincide largely with where the Industrial Revolution, the Enlightenment, etc. first took hold several hundred years ago, as I shall address later. *Source: OECD 2008 Compendium of Patent Statistics.*

made today, but they aren't worse either. Finally, we work fewer hours than before.

These reasons are why, for instance, measured unit labor productivity in Europe and the U.S.A. "only" grows around 25% per decade, even though the knowledge at our disposal may more than double within the same time. The combination of massive growth in future wealth and knowledge will create products and services in the future that would seem magical to us if we could see them today.

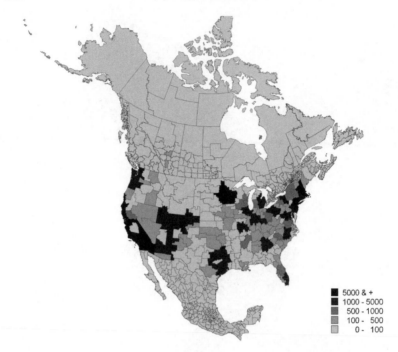

Number of patent applications filed under the PCT, North America, 2003–2005. Patent counts are based on the priority date, the inventor's region of residence, and use fractional counts on PCT filings at the international phase (EPO designations). Data for Mexico are not yet available at the regional level. Data are graphically presented according to level 3 of the Nomenclature of Territorial Units for Statistics (NUTS 3) for Canada, and use Territorial Level 3 for the United States. *Source*: *OECD 2008 Compendium of Patent Statistics.*

The list of what they may be is very long indeed. How about roads that collect solar power or are made by material that automatically glues back together when cracks have appeared? Holographic television and internet. Or noise cancellation systems in your garden? Or could you imagine

- Mobile phones that enable you to look at the real world through a transparent screen and get the world in front of you explained/conceptualized
- Entire walls or large parts of walls that can turn into displays, or "media walls", displaying video, images, or perhaps just an ambience
- The ability to easily project content from any intelligent device to any screen near you (e.g., from a smartphone to a media wall)
- Vaccines against asthma, multiple sclerosis, leukemia, arthritis, malaria,

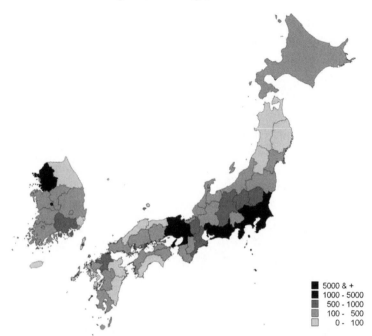

Number of patents filed under the PCT, Japan and Korea (2003–2005). Patent counts are based on the priority date, the inventor's region of residence, and use fractional counts on PCT filings at the international phase (EPO designations). Data are graphically presented according to Territorial Level 3 (U.S.). *Source: OECD 2008 Compendium of Patent Statistics.*

high blood pressure, rheumatoid arthritis, salmonella infection, and substance addiction, etc.

- Computers that scan the internet for information about a subject and write a summary of scientific consensus
- Back seat and passenger seat online entertainment with movies, television, internet, etc.
- Artificial blood cells that enable you to dive for 30 minutes without breathing
- Computers with human-level intelligence working as private tutors for children
- A soft, bendable e-reader that can download and display any media
- Bacteria that absorb CO_2 from the atmosphere and turn it into jetfuel
- Smart perimeter control, intrusion detection, and access control
- Entire roofs and walls made of photovoltaic cells
- Diets tailored to your personal genetic makeup
- Remote controlled/robotic cargo airplanes
- Anti-noise technology in gardens

- Plants that grow 10 times faster
- Face recognition doors
- Self-driving cars
- ... magic?

7

Environmental and
resource strain

It is hardly surprising that all the new people and new money I have
mentioned so far will constitute a severe challenge to the world's resources
and environment. Simply put, the issues we have to deal with are that
over the next 40 years

- The world's population will increase by approx. 2 billion people
- The world's urban population will increase by approx. 3 billion people
- The world's real purchasing power and wealth will grow 400%.

I guess the third of these observations is what matters most.
Civilization, and all that goes with it, will quadruple within 40 years. Now
think about the pollution that will come from that, and of the increasing
shortage of water that will be felt in many places. And of fish stock depletion. Loss of biodiversity. Global warming. And here is a big one: How
do we double our agricultural production within 40 years to meet the
demand for more and better food, more meat, and biofuels? How on
Earth do we handle that? How . . .?

There is more. Instead of predominantly living together in often large
families, people will increasingly live as young, unmarried singles, or as
retirees. Living alone means freedom without responsibility and it probably makes many people more egocentric and isolated, and some may
even lock themselves completely off from the outside world and just play
computer games, watch TV, or surf the net all day. However, for others,
it means a greater social nightlife than if they were married, and many of
those will seek to live in inner cities rather than in suburbs. Indeed, there
has been a reversal of the previous trend of people who could afford it

moving out from city centers to the opposite. So, this means that not only is our current infrastructure much too small for the future population, but it is also largely useless. Big family houses in the countryside are of zero use to yuppies living the urban life. So, we will need to build, build, build. Add to that an explosion in tourism, second houses, and automobile use. All the stuff that these people will want. Can we handle it?

When you industrialize a country you use an enormous quantity of industrial commodities such as metals, and once people get richer they use more and more energy. It is, in fact, really difficult to think of a way to spend money that doesn't directly or indirectly involve the use of energy, and there are people who measure the sophistication of a society by that simple metric—how much energy they expend. A rich civilization = big energy consumption.

Global oil production in 2010 is approx. 85 million barrels daily. A barrel contains circa 165 liters of oil, and if you want to move a single day's consumption in ships, you would need 50 supertankers, each the length of three football pitches. And this is just our oil consumption— our global energy infrastructure is simply enormous, and in addition to oil it includes coal, gas, and whatnot.

Let me give a few numbers about energy to indicate some of what we will confront. China has only about 56 million automobiles as of 2010, and their oil consumption per capita is just a tenth of what it is in the U.S. Most analysts estimate that the Chinese car park will grow to almost 400 million automobiles around 2030 and 500 million by 2050. India starts from much lower numbers but should reach approx. 800 million automobiles in 2050. Russia and Brazil should have a bit over 200 million automobiles combined in 2050, and the total growth in automobile penetration in those four countries should be 1.4 billion over the coming 40 years. Add the other emerging markets, plus the increased wealth in developed markets, and the global automobile park could easily grow by 2 billion to 2.5 billion. Let's say now that each of these automobiles use 6 barrels of oil per year (the typical figure at the moment is 9 barrels, so fuel efficiency would need to improve a lot to get to 6). If we take the low number—2 billion new automobiles—we need 12 billion barrels of oil per year for these additional vehicles, or approx. 33 million barrels per day, or we need to power them with something completely different.

A lot of people will have to be really clever to solve this. Not just inventors, but business people, project managers, workers, technicians, financiers.

Fortunately it seems that a lot of people really are quite clever. I mentioned at the beginning of this chapter that global population is set to increase by approx. 2 billion people within the 40 years from 2010 to 2050, which sounds enormous. However, we should consider that *mankind just managed to go through a similar population expansion within approx. 25 years.* The reality is that we passed the peak growth rate in terms of percentage increase in the 1960s and the peak growth in absolute numbers in the 1980s. We have already taken our hardest exam.

And how did that go? In spite of an endless stream of warnings that we were close to the "limits to growth", it was "5 minutes to 12", "high noon", or that we were reaching the "end of prosperity", the actual numbers are surprising:

- Calorie intake per capita has grown rapidly in emerging markets— from approx. 2,430 calories in 1970 to an estimated 2,730 in 2010 (it peaked in the developed world in the late 1980s, which is good because of obesity problems).
- The percentage of global population that is starving fell from 35% in 1970 to below 15% in 2010—a decrease not only in percentage but also in absolute numbers.
- Whereas only 30% of the world's population had access to clean water in 1970, the number has increased to approx. 80% in 2010.
- Life expectancy grew in almost every part of the world, and particularly rapidly in fast-growing Asia. The only exceptions were a few African nations plagued by rampant AIDS.
- Illiteracy fell dramatically.

Economically, what we can look back at is an amazing triumph. In the past 50 years poverty has fallen more than in the previous 500, and this has been going on in the vast majority of poor countries. Furthermore, since the fall of communism, the economic gap between rich and poor countries has narrowed significantly as most developing nations have had far higher growth rates than developed countries. This doesn't mean that all is good, or that no countries are in decline, but it shows that we could increase the global population by 2 billion within 25 years while vastly improving average conditions at the same time.

Work weeks have fallen and holiday time has grown, on average. Fewer than a hundred years ago Europeans spent on average 6 hours a week carrying coal into their houses and on cleaning coal dust from carpets, removing ashes from stoves, etc. They spent about an equal amount of time carrying water to wash clothes, which was done manually on washboards. They maintained the latrine, provisioned fresh food every day (since they didn't have refrigerators), had poor teeth with often constantly painful decay, and were living in constant fear of infections for lack of antibiotics. Today we have shorter working weeks, longer holidays, and many more years of expected retirement. In fact, in the old days, simply surviving until retirement age was a pretty mean feat.

Living longer

So far, mankind has always succeeded in finding new ways to generate more wealth and to replace one type of raw material with another. After the last ice age, there were only between one and 10 million people on the Earth. People often lived in small bands of hunter–gatherers, and a group of 20–30 of these would need several thousand square kilometers of hunting ground to themselves in order to sustain a living. Today, we are between 700 and 7,000 times as many.

We know from examining skeletons that life expectancy in the Stone Age in North Africa was just 21 years. In imperial Rome it was about the same—22 years. In England it was around 30 to 40 years from the mid–16th century to the mid–19th century. Then it started to rise dramatically. In China in 1930 it was 24 years.

We have also become better and better at fighting diseases. Malaria, still the world's second deadliest disease after AIDS, was endemic in Europe until the late 17th century and remained present until fairly recently. The last Dutch malaria epidemic occurred, for instance, during World War II. In the 1920s almost 2% of America's population was infected by malaria every year. In the mid-1930s the country still experienced more than 400,000 cases each year and in 1933 almost a third of the inhabitants in Tennessee River valley were infected by this decease. Now it's virtually gone.

The reason? Money. Studies show that when countries get an average income above 3,000 dollars per capita per year, they start to eradicate malaria.

What about degradation of the environment? Some of what people often bring up in normal conversation is that we are cutting down the forests—which is certainly true. At its highest point, forest is estimated to have covered around 37% of the Earth's landmass, and today it only covers 30%. In other words, over the last 10,000 years man has chopped down a fifth of our forests, mainly to make room for farming, and this must have accelerated into the first part of the last century, even though no one measured it accurately at the time.

However, we do measure it now. The FAO, an organization set up by the United Nations, does the laborious work of examining the amount of forest in the world at regular intervals. Its statistics show that global forest cover declined a total of 3% between 1985 and 2000, equal to 0.2% per year. However, in their *Global Forest Assessment* report from 2005, the researchers found that forest stocks had actually expanded over the past 15 years in 22 of the world's 50 most forested nations and that overall decline from 2000 to 2005 had slowed to 0.18%, or 0.036% per year. Subsequent studies by the Smithsonian Institute have indicated that as people move to cities and abandon marginal farmland, the addition of rainforest in some places may now exceed its destruction in others. These things are difficult to measure, but I think the overall impression isn't one of accelerating destruction—rather of a beginning stabilization. Furthermore, if we look at where that happens, we can see that forest cover is growing in most rich nations, which is promising since more countries will get rich.

China is an example. Although it is not particularly rich yet, it now has the world's largest tree-planting program, involving mandatory planting of at least three trees each year for most people aged between 11 and 60. In 2008 a total of 540 million people participated in this activity, planting 2.31 billion trees in mountain areas, city parks, campuses, and along highways and railways. China's tree cover began to grow in 2000.

The long-term trends in air pollution have also been encouraging. One of the places that have been best studied is English cities, where air pollution has been declining massively. Old reports talk about air that was so full of smoke and soot from residential coal fires and coal-fired factories that one could hardly breathe. We know that the Queen of England visited Nottingham in 1257 and found the stench of smoke from coal burning so awful, that she feared for her life and left. In those years, human waste was often dumped in the streets and left to rot to the delight of rats. However, in spite of the massive increase in the number of people and automobiles over the years, and in spite of a huge increase in consumption and housing, urban air pollution in London has decreased by more than 90% since 1930. How much it has decreased since the earlier Industrial Revolution we do not know. But probably a lot more.

The picture is the same for water quality. Previously, sewage was discharged directly into the Thames, which stank so much that the curtains in the Houses of Parliament had to be soaked in lime to stop the odor from preventing government from getting on with its business. In 1855 a letter from Michael Faraday in *The Times* newspaper, London, described the River Thames, from his observations on a boat trip, in this way

> "The whole of the river was an opaque pale brown fluid ... surely the river which flows for so many miles through London ought not to be allowed to become a fermenting sewer. Despite the foul smell, people continued to wash and bathe and drink from the river."

He should at least have been glad that his boat didn't capsize during that trip. In 1878 the steamship *Princess Alice* actually did, and most of the approx. 600 passengers who died from that incident were not killed by drowning, but because of the pollution in the river. In fact, from 1830 to 1860, tens of thousands of people had died of cholera as a result of pollution in the Thames. Today, it's a world apart. On July 14th, 2009, *The London Evening Standard* brought this news story:

> "The Thames is packed full of fish and cleaner than it has been for 200 years, fishing experts say. More than 125 species, including wild salmon, trout, Dover sole, plaice, haddock and bass, now live in the 215-mile waterway which was declared biologically dead in 1957. The stocks are attracting predators including porpoise, seals and dolphins which have been spotted as far upstream as London Bridge."

In 1999 two of the world's leading universities, Yale and Cornell, plus the World Economic Forum and the European Commission decided jointly to create a uniform measure of how environmentally responsible different nations were. The teams of scientists developed jointly a statistical measurement method, which they called the *Environmental Sustainability Index*. This was further refined over the years so that it is now called the *Environmental Performance Index*, or "EPI" and is based on 25 different indicators for each country in the world. These indicators fall within six main categories: environmental health, air pollution, water resources, biodiversity and habitat, productive natural resources, plus climate change, and they include everything from water quality and water stress to outdoor and indoor air pollution, pesticide regulation, and much more. What they have found is that we start polluting less after our incomes reach a given threshold. According to the EPI website, the threshold for improvement is annual incomes around U.S.$10,000 per capita:

> "Not surprisingly, per capita GDP is correlated with higher performance on the EPI. In particular, overall EPI scores are higher in countries that have a per capita GDP of $10,000 or higher."

They reached this conclusion from comparing their environmental index scores with national GDP/capita numbers. I would guess that the appropriate number today is probably around U.S.$15,000 due to inflation and decline in the dollar exchange rate. In any case, this rich-means-clean tendency is also reflected in their 2010 rankings of the 15 cleanest countries in the world.

The 15 cleanest countries in the world

1. Iceland	6. Mauritius	11. Malta
2. Switzerland	7. France	12. Finland
3. Costa Rica	8. Austria	13. Slovakia
4. Sweden	9. Cuba	14. United Kingdom
5. Norway	10. Colombia	15. New Zealand

Source: *The Environmental Performance Index 2010*, Yale Center for Environmental Law & Policy, and Center for International Earth Science Information Network at Columbia University.

Of these 15 countries 14 were among the world's richest. So, which were the 15 worst performing countries—the ones ranked between 135 and 149?

The 15 least clean countries in the world

149. Botswana	154. Benin	159. Togo
150. Iraq	155. Haiti	160. Angola
151. Chad	156. Mali	161. Mauritania
152. United Arab Emirates	157. Turkmenistan	162. Central African Republic
153. Nigeria	158. Niger	163. Sierra Leone

Source: *The Environmental Performance Index 2008*, Yale Center for Environmental Law & Policy, and Center for International Earth Science Information Network at Columbia University.

The most polluting countries in the world were, with the exception of the Emirates, all dirt-poor, if you will excuse the expression. It should be mentioned here that the ratings do not take into account that rich countries often outsource production that results in pollution to developing countries, who then take disproportionate blame. However, this is probably more than offset by the fact that population growth isn't factored in either, even though this evidently is an extremely important driver of lack of sustainability. As we have seen before, rapid population growth is closely related to being poor, whereas many of the richest countries have or will soon have declining populations.

So, all in all, I think the overwhelming impression one gets from studying environmental problems is this:

- When countries reach a high level of average income, their population stops growing or goes into decline. This evidently does more than almost anything else to take the pressure off the environment and resource problems.

- Furthermore, as they get richer, they become far more efficient at providing resources for their people, and their pollution declines. They use cleaner technology, start to recycle, protect their landscapes, undertake tree-planting programs, etc. Furthermore, they start cleaning up what they had previously destroyed and they start exporting clean technology to poor countries that can't develop it themselves.

This is actually illustrated by an international study called *Development and the Environment* which was published by the World Bank in 1992. This showed a very clear *negative* correlation between income and such pollution as sulfur dioxide and particulate matter in the air, or access to clean water. The higher the average income, the cleaner the environment.

However, that same study showed that there was a flipside—positive correlation—between income and carbon dioxide emission, which brings me to the subject of global warming; a complex story that has evolved considerably over the latest years, and which raises emotions like virtually no other subject apart from perhaps terrorism.

———————

Before we dig into the global-warming discussion, let me just bring a few facts that most scientists clearly agree on. First, the air in the atmosphere has roughly the following composition:

- 78.08% nitrogen
- 20.95% oxygen
- 0.93% argon
- 0.038% carbon dioxide
- 0.002% other.

Suspended in this air is a minuscule number of particles plus water vapor, which on average is equal to approx. 1% of the mass of the atmosphere.

Among the components of the atmosphere, nitrogen and oxygen have virtually no greenhouse effect, but other components, including carbon dioxide (CO_2) do. This doesn't make CO_2 a pollutant. Whereas people, animals, and many bacteria depend on oxygen for energy, plants depend on CO_2 for nutrition (building their body with the carbon, while typically getting their energy from sunlight).

The Earth receives its external energy through Sun rays, and approx. 30% of this is reflected back into space by clouds, etc. before reaching the ground. The part of the light from the Sun that does reach Earth arrives in a broad spectrum of wavelengths, from ultraviolet to infrared. Ultraviolet, which is pretty rough and can cause skin cancer, spans from 100–280 nm wavelength. Depending on time and place, 93–99% of the ultraviolet light that comes from the Sun is blocked by our ozone layer. You didn't see ozone listed above because the amount of ozone that does this trick is absolutely tiny—if it was concentrated at the bottom of the atmosphere, it would only be a few millimeters thick.

Next in the wavelength spectrum comes ultraviolet B (280–315 nm), ultraviolet A (315–400 nm), and then visible light (400–700 nm). Below visible comes infrared, which goes from 700 nm to 1 mm. We cannot see that either, but we use it for infrared heating. It feels warm.

Outgoing energy from the Earth is less eschewed towards visible light and more towards infrared than what comes in, and this means that the filtering effect of the atmosphere works differently on the way out from that on the way in. Specifically, it traps some of the infrared light trying to escape, thereby creating the greenhouse effect. However, when water vapor forms clouds, this reflects daylight sunshine back into space before it reaches the ground, whereas its net effect at night is warming. Greenhouse effects are in themselves not a negative, because without them the Earth would be a ball of frozen ice. However, what is discussed is manmade *change* to CO_2 concentrations and what that may do to our climate.

The components in the atmosphere that create the greenhouse effect are listed below, and I have indicated after each component how much they probably contribute to potential warming. The numbers I have given are broad intervals, because this if where the first scientific disagreements (which are not small) start:

- Water vapor, droplets, and ice crystals account for approx. 36–70% of the greenhouse effect, but—as the percentages indicate—there is obviously much variability.
- Carbon dioxide contributes 9–26%. A large part of this—somewhere between 7.5 and 10%—circulates through plants and oceans, etc. each year, and if we stopped emitting it approx. half would be reabsorbed by oceans and plants within 30 years.
- Methane contributes 4–9% (some say a lot more). More than half of the methane comes from agriculture, and the rest from fossil energy production processes, as well as landfills, waste treatment, and fuel combustion. I am not kidding when I say that eeehhh . . . gases from cows are significant contributors, because they really are. The concentration of methane in the atmosphere is tiny, but it is a very potent greenhouse gas. Fortunately methane interacts with other chemicals in the atmosphere that break it down over an average of 10–12 years. The result is reduced CO_2 plus water vapor, which soon after falls back to Earth as raindrops.
- Black carbon may be responsible for 5–10% of the greenhouse effect. It is the visible dirt of smoke from an unclean burning process from old or bad engines or forest fires (deliberate or natural). It is an exceptionally powerful greenhouse gas, but fortunately it is washed out of the atmosphere within days or weeks.
- Nitrous oxide, ozone, and CFCs (the stuff we used to put in aerosols until they got outlawed): a total of 3–7%.

If you consider this list of greenhouse contributors, you can see that black carbon emissions and their effect could be reduced fairly quickly if some time in the future we reduced deliberate forest clearing using fire to a minimum and if we switched to better engines—both of which sound plausible. Methane stays a long time in the atmosphere until it is broken down into water and fairly limited quantities of carbon dioxide, but if we reduce its emissions, this would return to previous levels fairly quickly. The bigger problem is carbon dioxide, which is only partially reabsorbed. In the following pages I will focus on CO_2.

We know with high certainty (from measuring bubbles in ice cores and other sources) that the CO_2 concentration shortly before humans developed farming was around 0.028%. It has since increased because of land clearing (destroying 20% of our forests, fossil fuel burning, cement production, clearing of peatlands, and soil cultivation, which often reduces the carbon content in the soil). Current CO_2 levels are being recorded at 0.038% (380 parts per million, or "ppm"), and by 2050 carbon dioxide is expected to register between 0.045% and 0.055% unless a radical process to stop it is put in place. I believe this is the single part of the discussion that almost everyone agrees on.

The theory that CO_2 is a greenhouse gas and that mankind is heating up the atmosphere is fairly old, but it started to create interest in the 1980s after the global cooling from 1940 to 1970 (which caused the ice age scare I mentioned earlier) reversed. It is possible to estimate old climate fluctuations in many ways, including studies of

- The composition of air trapped in ice cores
- Thickness of seasonal layers of ice in glaciers
- Thickness and composition of seasonal layers of lake and ocean sediments
- Concentrations of pollen and seeds in seasonal ice and earth/rock layers
- Size of tree rings in old or even fossilized trees
- Old human descriptions of weather and lifestyles in books and paintings.

It is clear that there have been very large climate fluctuations in the past. Studies of individual glaciers show that many of them had been ice-free in the past and that areas that are ice-free now have been ice-covered before. Mean temperatures in Alaska seem to have been 3–5°C higher than today. There had been significant warming periods during the Roman Empire, where archeological evidence suggests that people were growing wine in Great Britain. Furthermore, as Alpine glacier ice retreats, archeologists have found many Roman artifacts that show that Romans frequently walked across passes that are now ice-covered. There were also indications of northern warming around the times when the Vikings populated Greenland and briefly settled in Newfoundland, near L'Anse aux Meadows.

There also seems to have been a so-called "Medieval Warm Period" in the North Atlantic region from about 800 to 1300, and even a warming as recently as the 1930s. However, there have also been cooling periods since the last ice age. In the so-called "Little Ice Age" from the 16th century to the mid–19th century, temperatures apparently cooled very significantly, and amazingly we have six recordings of Eskimos landing their kayaks in Scotland, which suggests that ice reached from Greenland to very close to Scotland. During this cold period, the Thames regularly froze over, and people held fairs on it, and it was here that Dutch painters developed their tradition for paintings of ice-covered landscapes. Going even further back, there had been an abrupt global cooling of approx.

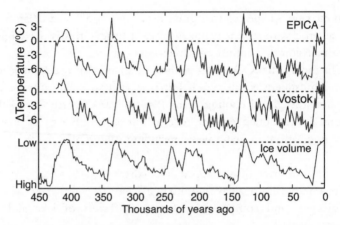

Ice age temperature changes. This figure shows estimates of Antarctic temperature changes during the last several glacial/interglacial cycles and a comparison with changes in global ice volume. The present day is at the right end of the graph, and the horizontal lines show present levels. The last steep rise in temperature is the exit from the last ice age approx. 12,000 years ago and the small ups and downs at the extreme right include the Little Ice Age, the many periods of modest warming, etc. *Source*: Wikipedia Commons.

2.3°C as an absolutely enormous amount of meltwater trapped by ice in North America had broken through and for a time disrupted the Gulf Stream.

While longer term statistics were made by combining all sorts of proxies (such as ice core data) newer ones were based on direct measurements. The most reliable long-term statistics were generally assumed to be those from America, which showed a clear warming in the 1930s, followed by a modest cooling between approx. 1950 and 1970 (the time of the ice age scare), and then warming again. All in all the indications are that there have been 50–60 warming and cooling periods since the end of the last ice age.

————

I am going to take a little diversion here, because most of what I've written above was conventional wisdom until the so-called "hockey stick" entered the picture and created the seeds of a panic. This became so central to the debate that I must devote a bit of space to explain this event, also because this hockey stick is still in frequent use as I write this.

Here we go: the stick, or "MBH98" as it was soon known, was published in 1998 in *Nature*, one of the two most prestigious science journals in the world, by Michael E. Mann and two co-workers. It was a graph which, contrary to conventional wisdom, showed that the global climate had in fact been very stable—if anything declining a bit—from 1000 AD until around the middle of the 20th century. After around 1970 it had risen very strongly, and towards the end of the century it was shooting almost straight up. The graph was made by combining all sorts of proxy data such as ice core measurements, tree rings, etc, which were analyzed through a so-called "multiproxy technique" using "principal component analysis", which is a good and normal—but very complicated—way to combine numerous proxy data into a single estimate.

This graph soon created a huge stir and appeared on thousands of websites. In the 2001 *Third Assessment Report* (TAR) from the Intergovernmental Panel on Climate Change (IPCC) it appeared in very large format on page 29 (as shown overleaf). Actually, on the preceding page there were two alternative temperature graphs based on satellite measurements and balloons that suggested that temperatures either had declined in the last part of the 20th century or had been oscillating around the same level but with a spike in 1998, which was an El Niño year. However, these graphs were not given the same prominence. The hockey stick graph was the only long-term climate reconstruction shown in the report, and it was the only graph that was shown several times, and it was in color.

After this display, the hockey stick became by far the most widely used illustration of the global-warming problem. It was featured, for instance, in the British Government's 2003 energy white paper.

However, in that same year two Canadians, Stephen McIntyre and Ross McKitrick, asked Mann if they could get access to the model and the data behind it. The two Canadians were not climate experts, but they had substantial experience in the evaluation of statistical models. After some difficulty, they managed to get hold of the material and first did something that I also like to do with statistically modeled data: Look at the raw data. When doing that they noticed that this actually didn't seem to suggest that there was a hockey stick. Stephen McIntyre decided then to spend more time on the matter and got Ross McKitrick, a Canadian economist specializing in environmental economics and policy analysis, to join him in his efforts. The two tried now to replicate the graph using Mann's model—but couldn't. In 2003 they published these disturbing findings in the magazine *Environment and Energy*. Mann responded that the

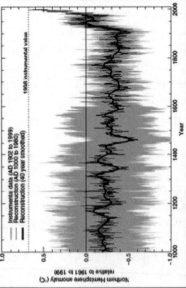

Figure 5: Millennial Northern Hemisphere (NH) temperature reconstruction (blue – tree-rings, corals, ice cores, and historical records) and instrumental data (red) from AD 1000 to 1999. Smoother version of NH series (black), and two standard error limits (grey shaded) are shown. (Based on Figure 2.20)

data he had sent them were in fact not the right ones and gave them access to another database. However, when testing these data, the two Canadians came up with virtually the same results. They supplied a list of the errors they had found to *Nature*, which chose not the print them, but instead to ask Mann for a corrigendum.

This is where it gets interesting, because now the two Canadians did something scientists often do: carry out a "null test" by running random data, or so-called "red noise", through Mann's model and also through a standard principal component analysis. As they made 10,000 different repetitions of this test, they found that, as expected, the standard model almost never showed a hockey stick. However, Mann's model showed hockey stocks in the random data over 99% of the time. His model was in a very literal sense—well, a hockey stick model. You could feed it random telephone numbers from your local directory, and it would in all likelihood show a hockey stick.

How did this happen? The Canadians discovered the secret: Mann had inserted an unusual rule which vastly amplified the weighting of time series that were particularly volatile in the 20th century. This meant that such data could be assigned several hundred times as much weight as other data that had been more flat in the last 100 years. So, McIntyre and McKitrick zoomed in on which data it was that this rule amplified enough to create the hockey stick.

It was Gaspé cedar tree rings in California. Mann had taken these data from a study called *Detecting the Aerial Fertilization Effect of Atmospheric CO_2 Enrichment in Tree-Ring Chronologies*, which went back to 1404, where it covered but a single tree. He had then added fictive observations for year 1403, 1402, 1401 and 1400 so that his time series could begin in that round year. From 1421 until 1447 the original study had two trees. The two scientists who had made the original study had ignored these early observations in their conclusion reports, as you would normally not publish statistics based on just one or two trees (let alone a fictional one). In fact, they had only included numbers starting in 1600.

McIntyre and McKitrick decided now to check what happened to the hockey stick if they simply ignored the dubious tree ring observations from before 1450, basically removing the data for (1) first a fictional tree, (2) then the single tree, and (3) then the two trees. This had a dramatic effect: The hockey stick disappeared. However, even leaving these tree rings in at all was dubious, since the authors of the original study of the tree rings had stated that they could not be correlated with local temperature fluctuations. What tree rings can be correlated to is the so-called "areal fertilization effect" of CO_2 in the air, as the name of the original tree ring study actually suggested. It is well known that increased CO_2 concentration in the atmosphere increases plant growth, and this is some-times used in greenhouses. So, the fact that trees in Californian mountains grew faster in the 20th century might simply be because of increased CO_2 concentrations, and thus driven by the areal fertilization effect. Hard to say, really, if you ask me.

Following the critique from McIntyre and McKitrick, international climate scientists started a heated debate. We have an interesting insight into this, as some hackers stole and anonymously distributed approx. 3,000 emails and other documents made over the course of 13 years by the Climatic Research Unit (CRU) of the University of East Anglia (UEA) in Norwich, England. It appeared that some of the scientists saw some merit in the critique, and others discussed how to ensure that relevant data did not get out. The email below might appear to be a case of the latter:

> "And don't leave stuff lying around on ftp sites—you never know who is trawling them. The two MMs have been after the CRU station data for years."

———————

The reasons that I just went into so much detail with the case of the hockey stick model and the tree rings are twofold. First, it shows how difficult it is to get to the bottom of this matter, especially if some of the scientists involved (on both sides of the debate) have motives that go beyond the disinterested pursuit of truth. Second, it is important simply because it changed history. It was the hockey stick that changed the rising concern to an outright panic and anger against the "skeptics". A writer for *Grist Magazine* wrote this on his blog:

> "When we've finally gotten serious about global warming, when the impacts are really hitting us and we're in a full worldwide scramble to minimize the damage, we should have war crimes trials for these bastards—some sort of climate Nuremberg."

After the hockey stick, one politician after the other rushed out and made statements about how global warming was no longer something we should fear for the future, but a disaster playing out in the present.

Scientists with differing views were ignored, ridiculed, and frequently starved of funds. People who disagreed were called "deniers", as in "holocaust deniers". It got very rough, in other words. However, in spite of all this, the debate did continue, and as I write this book, it seems that there are four main camps (the names are my own):

- "The Al Gore view": Global warming is the largest threat facing mankind, and indeed the planet, and we should pull out all the stops to prevent it. If we don't, the consequences may be disastrous.
- "The Henrik Svensmark view": Virtually all the temperature fluctuations we have seen recently and in the distant past can be explained by fluctuations in cosmic rays and other natural phenomena. Global warming (and cooling) occurs frequently, but it is natural.
- "The Bjorn Lomborg view": Manmade global warming is real, but there have always been considerable temperature fluctuations on Earth, and we have coped. Trying to prevent global warming through rapid action is a monumental waste of money. This could be far better spent on trying to generate economic growth in emerging markets, alleviating the negative effects of global warming, and doing research in alternative energies.
- "The Ray Kurzweil view": Solar power capacity deployment is doubling every 2 years and has essentially become an information technology. With this doubling speed, it will supply virtually all our energy by 2030.

The first-named camp is by far the strongest and is backed by numerous environmental organizations and almost all governments (in words, if perhaps not in deeds). Al Gore has money, movies, books, and a Nobel Prize to back him, and his view is mainstream and based on IPCC reports (while exaggerating some of these rather massively, though).

The 2007 IPCC report offers alternative scenarios showing average global temperatures between 2090 and 2099 relative to the period 1980–1999 to be *between 1.1°C and 6.4°C higher*. As for global sea levels, these have been rising for as long as scientific records exist, averaging approx. 2 mm annually in the first half of the 20th century and 1.5 mm in the second—perhaps because we are still exiting the Little Ice Age, or perhaps due to manmade warming. The IPCC estimates that they will rise *18–59 cm* within the time interval mentioned above. It should be added here that if all glaciers and icecaps in the world melted, it would only raise the sea level by approx. 30 cm. The big potential rise in sea level comes from the melting of land-based ice in Greenland and Antarctica plus some from the slight expansion of water when it heats. If all of Antarctica's land-based ice melted, sea levels would rise a whopping 57 meters (186 feet). However, it is likely that rising temperatures will increase the amount of precipitation but will not increase enough to melt the ice. Such a scenario would lead to melting along the edges but increasing thickness in the middle, which has in fact already been seen.

There is also a cost factor for the world economy. The IPCC has come up with six scenarios. If you take the most gloomy of these, which assumes 3.4°C warming and world population growth to 15 billion (more than 50% higher than most estimates), you can calculate the cost of global warming as 3% of GDP in the developed world and 10% in the poor part.

Al Gore's view is that we need to reduce emissions by more than 70% to stop global warming, and that, even as we do that, the reaction will be delayed, which means that we need to move quickly. This can be done through (1) more efficient energy use, (2) new energy sources, (3) raising energy/carbon taxes, and (4) carbon sequestering (= burying).

He points out that many initiatives *to save energy through more efficient technology will have very short payback times and thus be good business as well as good for the environment.* As for alternative forms of energy, he goes through a long list which I will cover in the later chapter on alternative energy. He mentions, for instance, that solar influx is approx. 7,000 times as large as our energy consumption and that, as an example calculation, covering just 2.6% of the Sahara Desert with solar panels would satisfy global energy consumption. Approx. 1% could deliver the same amount of power as all the world's power plants combined, and less than 0.15% could meet all of Europe's power demands.

He believes that if we combine solar, geothermal, wind, second and third-generation biofuels and other alternative sources, and link them up to "intelligent" grids, where everyone can buy or sell power, we can make the energy transition away from fossil fuels within a reasonable span of time. Over time, he says, alternative forms of energy will get cheaper as the technologies evolve and they begin to enjoy economies of scale. Carbon-based energy, on the other hand, will get more and more expensive, as more marginal sources have to be brought into use.

As for carbon sequestering, he points out that farmers have reduced the carbon content in their soil because of ploughing or turning it. This has not only contributed to global warming, but has also reduced the fertility of soil for farming and has even contributed to soil erosion. The U.S. "dust bowl" in the 1930s is perhaps the clearest example of this. He suggests a complete conversion to no-till farming, which is possible if combined with genetically engineered herbicides (I will cover these later). Only a small fraction of world farming is based on no-till—virtually all in North and South America.

Another solution is to create biocharcoal. This is made by burning biomass in near anaerobic conditions, so that only the gases and oils burn, whereas the solid material doesn't. The char can then be mixed into the soil, where it apparently improves quality considerably. The most obvious way to do this is to plant fast-growing plants or trees on degraded land, and then burn them to make biochar. Another method for fixing CO_2 in the soil is to mix *Rhizobium* bacteria and *Mycorrhiza* fungi, which both do this naturally, albeit more slowly. These organisms are the real reason why crop rotation is an efficient way to regenerate soil, and they could perhaps be enhanced through genetic engineering.

The most direct opposition to Al Gore's line of thought comes from scientists who believe that global warming is a natural phenomenon that has very little correlation with human activity. One scientist, whose thoughts on the matter have gained ground, is Henrik Svensmark, who is director of the Center for Sun–Climate Research at the Danish Space Research Institute (a part of the Danish National Space Center). Svensmark discovered in the early 1990s that there was an uncanny correlation between historical solar activity (sunspots) and average temperatures on Earth, but couldn't initially see why. However, he soon realized that high solar activity created a magnetic field which partially shielded the Earth against so-called cosmic rays.

Cosmic rays are, in spite of their name, actually not rays, but charged particles—approx. 90% are protons, fewer than 10% are helium nuclei, and just under 1% heavy elements and electrons. There are two types of cosmic rays: primary and secondary. Primary cosmic rays are a combination of remnants from the Big Bang, particles that have been ejected from exploding stars, and particles from the Sun and other living stars. When these particles emerge from somewhere within the Milky Way, they will be trapped by the combined gravity of all the billions of stars and will on average hurl around for 10 million to 20 million years before they hit a solid object such as the Earth. They are very energetic; some as high as $\sim 10^{20}$ eV. When they enter the atmosphere, often at close to the speed of light, they create a shower of secondary particles which consist of muons, positrons, electrons, neutrinos, etc.

So, let's imagine such a particle approaching Earth at, say, 200,000 km per second. What happens? To find out, Svensmark uses the so-called Frauenhofer Model (which was developed by other scientists at the Frauenhofer Institute in Germany). This model says that such a particle typically creates a chain reaction of approx. *one billion* subatomic chemical reactions—most of them at around 3 km altitude. The result of this is the creation of a very large number of charged particles in the atmosphere. This is interesting, because water molecules have very strong dipolar properties—they form an angle, with hydrogen atoms at the tips and oxygen at the vertex. Since oxygen has a higher electronegativity than hydrogen, you have a high dipolar charge, like a tiny magnet. Because of that, water will be attracted to charged particles, like one magnet to another. A lot of charged particles in the air due to incoming cosmic rays will cause water to form droplets, which then become clouds.

So, in other words, *the more cosmic waves entering the atmosphere, the more clouds and the colder the climate.* We all know the effect clouds have—when the weather changes from sunny to overcast. Also, the effect of charged particles on cloud cover can be easily tested by exposing clean, humid air to X-rays. Water droplets form immediately and it gets misty.

So far, so good. But how would that explain long-term climate variation? Svensmark's explanation is that we are subject to three types of external forcing relevant to cosmic rays:

- The position of our solar system within the four major "arms" of the Milky Way. When we pass through one of the arms, there will be more stars close to us, which means more cosmic waves and thus more cloud cover.
- The oscillation of the solar system up and down relative to the galactic plane. This happens approximately 2.7 times per orbit. When we pass the center there are more stars close by, so again more cloud cover.
- The magnetic field from the Sun, which fluctuates with sunspot activity. This shields the Earth from cosmic waves, so more sunspots means less cloud cover.

This could explain the natural climate fluctuations we have always had, including ice ages. Of particular interest is that there was unusual sunspot activity throughout much of the 20th century, which could have explained the two phases of warming. And, finally, sunspot activity decreased markedly towards the end of the century, and this was followed by a leveling off in average temperatures after 1998.

Whereas many think that global warming is manmade and a threat, and others that it is natural and thus less of a concern, there is a third

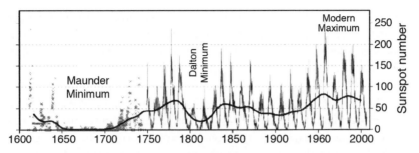

Sunspot activity from 1600 to the present day, actual observations plus continuous monthly averages of sunspot activity. These figures are based on an average of measurements from many different observatories around the world. Prior to 1749, the observations are sporadic and not very reliable. *Source*: Wikipedia Commons.

school of thought lead by Bjørn Lomborg, who is best known for his book *The Skeptical Environmentalist*. Lomborg was a Greenpeace member, an active environmentalist, and a professor of statistics, when he realized through his work that the environment seemed to evolve much better than many environmentalists as well as the media suggest. He has since been director of the Environmental Assessment Institute in Copenhagen and has founded the Copenhagen Consensus Center, a thinktank advising governments and philanthropists about the best ways to spend aid and development money.

Lomborg accepts the IPCC estimates of possible climate changes but adds that the consequences are not fairly portrayed by the IPCC and many others. The IPCC mentions, for instance, that there will be more heat-related deaths, but ignores the fact that far more people die from cold than heat every year, so why doesn't the IPCC write it in that way? In Europe, about 200,000 people die from excessive heat each year and 1.5 million die from excessive cold. This means that a warming would lead to fewer temperature-related deaths. Actually it seems that a warmer world would save millions of lives worldwide every year, at least until 2200. Another example: Al Gore points out that with global warming there will be 28 million additional people in central Africa who get water-stressed, and another 15 million in southern and northern Africa. But he doesn't mention the 23 million in West Africa and 44 million in Africa overall who will get less water-stressed. The total outcome is that the number of people under water stress will go down, not up, as a consequence of global warming.

Furthermore, many of the negative effects are blown out of proportion. The total expected drop in agricultural output by 2100 due to potential global warming is in the most pessimistic IPCC case 1.4%, which is less than the 1.7% *annual* increase it has produced per year over the last 30 years. So, the loss will mean that instead of reaching a given production level in 2100, we will reach it in 2101. Some of his other views include:

- Humans are used to enormous temperature variations. We cope easily with differences between day and night temperature, summer and winter, and we have set up thriving societies north of the Arctic Circle and close to the Equator. Furthermore, we have survived and even thrived through substantial natural climate changes in the past.
- In warming scenarios, it is the coldest places that will heat up most and, furthermore, temperatures will rise more at night time than during the days.
- When weighing the costs and benefits to society of combating global warming aggressively, it should be considered that the slower economic growth is, the more poverty, higher population growth, and more conflict there will be. Furthermore, the economics of it is terrible. If we try to stabilize emissions, the economic payback will only be met in 2250, so a payback time of 250 years.
- When it comes to the alternative cost of ignoring global warming (or significantly limiting the effort to prevent it) it should be borne in mind that all it will mean is that within 90 years people in the rich world will only be 2.6 times as rich as today, instead of 2.7 times, and people in poor countries will only be 8.5 instead of 9.5 times as rich. To ask people, and especially people in poor nations, to make large economic sacrifices now to avoid a slight reduction in wealth within 90 years would be similar to have gotten poor people 90 years ago to sacrifice themselves so that we could live in even higher luxury than we actually do today.

Apart from pointing out that the environmental debate is often based on far too negative assumptions, Lomborg makes the obvious point that before deciding to spend money on one issue, one should consider if alternative projects would have more beneficial outcomes—*one should make a series of comparative cost–benefit studies*, in other words. He argues in this connection that the number of malnourished and starving people will depend much more on population growth and economic growth than on global warming. The harsh consequences in Lomborg's view are that if we spend a lot of money on global-warming prevention instead of economic growth and emerging market assistance, the number of people starving will rise as a consequence. Each time our investment in climate

stabilization saves one person from starvation, he argues, you could alternatively save 5,000 people by investing in direct hunger prevention
policies, and this is far better than indirectly letting a poor man pay for a
rich man's scare, as they have done before with DDT. In poor countries,
3 million die from HIV/AIDS, 2.5 million from indoor and outdoor
air pollution, more than 2 million from lack of nutrition, and almost
2 million from lack of clean drinking water. Malaria kills more than
1 million a year.

**Imagine you had $50 billion to donate to worthwhile causes.
What would you do, and where would you start?**

The following is the priorities list made by economists:

1. Micronutrient supplements for children (vitamin A and zinc)
2. The Doha development agenda
3. Micronutrient fortification (iron and salt iodization)
4. Expanded immunization coverage for children
5. Biofortification
6. Deworming and other nutrition programs at school
7. Lowering the price of schooling
8. Increase and improve schooling for girls
9. Community-based nutrition promotion
10. Provide support for women's reproductive role
11. Heart attack acute management
12. Malaria prevention and treatment
13. Tuberculosis case finding and treatment
14. R&D in low-carbon energy technologies
15. Biosand filters for household water treatment
16. Rural water supply
17. Conditional cash transfer
18. Peace-keeping in post-conflict situations
19. HIV combination prevention
20. Total sanitation campaign

To follow up on his view about priorities, Lomborg created the Copenhagen Consensus Center project, which sought answers to the following question: "Imagine you had $50 billion to donate to worthwhile causes. What would you do, and where would you start?"

The exercise was first set up in 2004 and then repeated in 2008. In preparation for the 2008 session, more than 50 economists with different expertise spent 2 years finding the best solution to each of a number of global challenges. During the last week, an expert panel of eight top economists, including five Nobel laureates, sat down to assess the research. Interestingly, they found that investing heavily to mitigate global warming did not belong among the top-20 priorities and made little sense. However, they did suggest that investments in alternative energy *research* could have very high returns.

In order to test whether their views were vastly different from those of other people given the same information, the Copenhagen Consensus Center team asked 80 students, 70% of whom came from emerging markets, the same questions. Before making their priority lists, the students had access to world-class experts on each of the issues. Similarly, in 2006 they asked a number of U.N. ambassadors from the U.S.A., China, India, Angola, Australia, Azerbaidjan, Canada, Chile, Egypt, Iraq, Mexico, Nigeria, Poland, Somalia, South Korea, Tanzania, Vietnam, Zimbabwe, and many other countries the same questions. Interestingly, the students and the U.N. ambassadors ended up making priority lists that were very similar to what the economists had done. In neither case was investing in global-warming mitigation seen as a worthwhile priority.

The last main school of thought concerning global warming essentially states that we are already well on our way to solving it through innovation which will soon make fossil fuel uncompetitive. A leading proponent for that view is Ray Kurzweil, whom I mentioned in the previous chapter. Kurzweil points out that there is far more sunlight than we need to meet all our energy needs, and he thinks that the technology needed for collecting and storing it is evolving so fast that such a technology could deliver all the world's energy by around 2030. He believes that solar voltaic technologies are information technologies comparable with IT and genomics. Their installed capacity is doubling every 2 years, which means that it will grow 1,000 times larger within just 20 years. In addition to power-generating solar panels ("photovoltaic" or "PV" solar), he believes that sales of solar concentrators made of parabolic mirrors that focus very large areas of sunlight onto a small collector or a small efficient steam turbine will grow dramatically. The energy from these and PV solar can be stored using nano-engineered fuel cells.

———

It seems to me that there is merit in all four lines of thought—Al Gore's, Bjørn Lomborg's, Henrik Svensmark's, and Ray Kurzweil's. If Svensmark is entirely right, then the global-warming campaign will turn out to be the biggest scare of all time. Svensmark's view has the merit that it actually can explain the wild climate fluctuations in the distant and more recent past.

As for Lomborg's view, few want to support it publicly, but the most likely actual outcome may be that we will do roughly what he recommends (which is not much). Just think about what we have seen so far. At the Earth summit in Rio in 1992, leaders promised to cut back their emissions to 1990 levels by 2000. On average, OECD countries overshot their target by a whopping 12%. The Kyoto Agreement, had all countries ratified it, would have postponed global warming by only 5 years as of 2100. However, the only Kyoto ratifier that has met its targets is Russia. The reason is that its extremely inefficient heavy industries, and in particular its defence industry, has been scaled back because it couldn't compete. Russia has earned billions of dollars by selling emission rights (known in the emission right trading industry as "hot air"). Since no one else lived up to their Kyoto promises, the agreement probably only gained for the world little more than a warming postponement of a single week by 2001, and at huge cost. Absurdly, the U.S., which didn't ratify the agreement, actually restricted its emission growth better than the EU over the Kyoto Agreement period.

Here are some possible conclusions to the whole discussion, at least as I see it:

- A distinct possibility is that the warming in the latter part of the 20th century came from a combination of manmade activity and high sunspot activity, in which case there is a manmade global-warming problem, but perhaps not entirely as dramatic as previously thought. Since the climate is so complex, it will probably take several generations before we can separate out the effects of difficult variables.
- There are in any case several reasons to develop and deploy alternative energy, including the explosive increase in energy demand, excessive dependency on oil producers, and the risk that CO_2 really can get us in big trouble.

- It is true that some alternative energy forms will get much cheaper, but they are only partly information technologies. There is a lot of physical "old-economy" stuff involved—such as mounting PV solar panels, making transmission grids, putting up windmills, constructing biofuel farms, etc.—because of that, making a significant change to new-energy forms will probably takes 30–50 years.
- If rich countries impose hefty carbon taxes and put emission trading schemes in place, they simply export their heavy industries to emerging markets, which care less about the environment. China is building a new coal-fired power plant every 5 days, and it is increasing its power capacity each year with something equal to Britain's total capacity. However, moving the tax burden from work to energy consumption can stimulate creativity and increase savings.

Environmentalism has become very powerful, and it has done the Earth a lot of good, and occasionally some damage. It seems today to exist in three basic forms, which the American futurist Alex Steffen famously entitled "light", "dark", and "bright" greens, respectively.

"Light greens" are concerned with the environment and see protecting it first and foremost as a personal responsibility. They try to contribute to a better world by, for instance, buying carbon offsets when they fly or by driving hybrid cars, and insulating their houses better, all of which they see as a lifestyle choice. A critique of this is that many companies will use "greenwashing" to claim that their products are green whereas they in fact are only slightly less polluting than before (e.g., unleaded gasoline is often sold with strong environmental branding, as if suggesting that burning it is good for the environment).

"Dark greens" believe that environmental problems are primarily caused by capitalism and economic growth, and that the solution is radical regime change and relinquishment of technology such as genomics. The main critique is that rich, capitalist countries actually are the cleanest and that socialist countries were extremely polluting.

"Bright greens" are environmentalists who believe that the problems must and can be solved through the application of new technologies such as clean energy systems, genetically modified plants, etc. and that neither personal shopping restraints nor protests or totalitarian control will help the environment much, if at all.

If "light" is understood as "not very", "dark" as in "dark ages", and "bright" as in "bright minds", then I don't think this whole distinction is far off the mark.

———

Let's now move on from the issue of environmental damage to the problem of resources. Can we really provide all the food, energy, metals, etc. that the markets will demand?

The fear of running out is not new. In 1939 the Department of the Interior in the U.S. predicted that America's oil would run out within 13 years. It didn't, but nevertheless the selfsame prediction was made in 1951: 13 years left!

No one wants to repeat that prediction now, because it is now known that, in addition to its considerable conventional oil reserves, America has untapped shale oil reserves that exceed all conventional oil reserves in the world and could alone supply it for well over a century, should it decide to pursue this avenue. Furthermore, it turns out that where there is shale oil there is also shale gas—huge amounts of it. U.S. planners realized around 2007–2009 that the country had such large supplies of this gas that, instead of importing gas from the Middle East and other places, it might in fact end up as a net gas exporter. So far, they believe that there is enough for 90 years' domestic supply. As for resources outside the U.S., a study by IHS Cambridge Energy Research Associates calculated that recoverable shale gas outside North America could turn out to be equivalent to between 211 and 690 times the present annual gas consumption in the U.S. This would be equal to somewhere between a 50% and a 160% increase in the world's known gas reserves.

These are just examples, but they are typical of our accelerating ability to find new resources. So far, mankind has always succeeded in finding new ways to generate more wealth and to replace one type of raw material with another, or to find more of the same. Recently we have also begun to use IT-based virtualization to eliminate the need for more and more physical products. We can download music instead of going to a shop and purchase it on a physical device, for instance.

As for water, there are shortages in many places in the world, and even though these have been reduced massively over the last few generations, the number of people living in so-called water-stressed areas will increase due to population expansion, so there will be lots to do in terms of moving over to drip irrigation, reducing pipe leaks, building dams, pipes, and water collection systems, etc. But again it's not is if we are running out of this resource either. After all, 71% of the Earth's surface is covered with water, totaling $13,600,000 \, km^3$. Only 1% of that is freshwater, but that is still far more than $1,000,000 \, km^3$. With solar-powered desalination plants we could in principle convert any amount of the total amount to freshwater and pump it to where it's needed. And water, unlike oil, is not chemically altered by its use, so it doesn't disappear.

We may also think that we are chopping down forests to make wood and paper. However, the global consumption of wood for timber and paper within any timeframe is equal to just 5% of actual tree *growth* within that period. The problem with forest cover is mainly that we clear it for agriculture, not that forests can't continuously produce the wood we need.

How about copper? This metal constitutes 0.0058% of the Earth's crust, which actually means that there is enough for 83 *million* years of consumption, if we could find ways to mine it all (which of course, we can't). But it's not running out. One exotic way is to start mining the bottom of the ocean floor with robots. This is scattered with metal nodules 5–10 cm in diameter made of copper, manganese, iron, nickel, cobalt, and zinc.

Agricultural crop yields? I will address this in detail later, but one indication is interesting. Companies like Monsanto have for many decades managed to increase corn yields approx. 1% annually due to genetic modification and active seed selection. That equals a bit over *10% per decade*. Now, world population grew 20% from 1970 to 1980, so twice as fast as these crop yields. The world population grew 19% the following decade, then 15% from 1990 to 2000, and finally 14% until 2010. The next decades should bring growth rates of 11%, 8%, 6%, and 4%, respectively, which means less than historic corn productivity growth. However, that's not the whole story. Monsanto now expects that, due to the genomics revolution, corn productivity growth will *increase* dramatically to over 3.5% annually, which means over 40% per decade—four times faster than population growth from 2010–2020, and 10 times faster by mid-century, if this growth rate can be maintained.

In a sense, the issue with resources is that while our demand for some of them may double every 20–25 years, our knowledge doubles much faster (every 8-9 years, if my estimates in the previous chapter are correct). In other words: *There is a race between the demand driven by economic growth, and supply driven by knowledge growth, and knowledge is winning this race hands down.*

————

However, while we may not be anywhere near running out of resources, and while our available resources will continue to grow as we get ever smarter, we might face a *temporary* blip over the next few decades. The reason is that the industrialization of emerging markets is on a speed and scale that hasn't been seen before. The best would be if governments put a floor under a number of commodity prices—as they do in Europe for oil and gas—and guaranteed that any drop in wholesale prices would be offset by increasing taxes. That would not only be a far more effective way to tax people than income tax, but it would possibly deflect a chaotic situation a few years down the line by stimulating a fairly steep ramp-up in new investments. In addition, Europe should allow bio-engineered foods and open its markets further to emerging market food imports.

However, none of this will probably happen anytime soon, and what seems most likely to me is that commodity prices will go sky high, partly driven by an investment mania, thus triggering a secondary mania in alternative energy businesses such as biofuels and solar power.

Would a crash replacement of fossil fuel be possible?

During World War II, which lasted about 5 years, the warring nations produced 5.7 million machine guns, 3.7 million trucks, 900,000 aircraft, and 1,700 submarines. Furthermore, they used almost 40 million tons of steel and other materials to construct new boats, including 169 new aircraft carriers, and they used approx. 10 million tons of cement on the construction of landing strips alone.

This was done by a population that was slightly less than a third of what it is today and under working conditions that were as bad as they can possibly get: constant bombing, sabotage, and sinking of transport ships. If we adjust this to today's world population, it would be equal to producing 2.7 million aircraft and more than 500 aircraft carriers in 5 years. If we also adjust for real GDP growth, what happened during World War II simply becomes surreal. So, yes, we could probably change the world's energy infrastructure fairly quickly, *if it made sense.*

Part III

Superempires

A tribe is a community of people, bound by common nationality, religion, lifestyles, or other bonds. Throughout history, there have always been some tribes that did exceedingly well and gained influence far beyond their own numbers, whereas others failed. This part is about these supertribes, and their superempires. It is also about the problems that arise when other tribes are failing.

- The world has approx. 1 billion people living in rich and successful nations, and 5 billion that have fast or explosive economic growth and will get rich.
- Approx. 55 nations with a current population of around 1 billion missed the boat of globalization, and some of these will not get onboard for many decades.
- There will be approx. 100 new wars; almost all originating or happening in these lost countries.
- The same nations will originate approx. 5,000 acts of terror, kidnappings, and piracy until 2050.
- Robotic warfare will become common.
- War between any two uniformed armies will virtually disappear.
- The U.S.A. will remain the world's dominant military power by a considerable margin.
- Large powers will sponsor dictators in return for access to resources.
- International legal tribunals will be set up for terrorists, as exist for human rights abuses, crime, and war.

- The great empires of 2050 will not be defined by clear national borderlines, because they will be virtual, and they will grow organically—not through military confrontation, but by the voluntary merger of tribes.
- By 2050 there will be two such virtual empires: One will be predominantly Chinese, and the other Latin/Germanic/Anglo-Saxon. Many people will feel attachment to both.

For more information:
www.superempires.com

8

Tribes and empires

There are countless ways to describe world history, but one that always fascinated me is the story of how small tribes occasionally manage to spread their influence and build empires. This is not because I think they necessarily are a good (sometimes they are; sometimes not), but because they have been showpieces of civilization. It's incredibly challenging to create and maintain an empire, so any civilization that managed this over long periods of time has at least in some senses been superior to its peers. So, this is the question: How did they do it? If we understand that, perhaps we can guess which will be the empires of the future.

Let's start with some facts and definitions. A supertribe to me is a people that has enormous influence over others. An empire exists, when different people, tribes, or nations are united under a single rule within an extensive geographical area. I find empires most fascinating since they bring different people together, which isn't easy. For instance, the EU will probably be defined as a great empire by future historians, since it replaces a group of nationalistic nation states, the tribes of which were previously constantly at war with each other.

Depending on how you define them, there have been somewhere between 200 and 250 empires through history.

In the table (overleaf) I have highlighted some of the most important empires and their milestones in gray. We can start with *duration*, where the ancient Egyptian Empire was the first in history to last over 300 years—in fact, it lasted for 500. Even long before the start of their empire, Egypt had become by far the most sophisticated civilization in the world in terms of technologies and artistic skills. In its so-called Third Dynasty from 2737 BC to 2717 BC, for instance, the ruler Zoser developed

List of some of the greatest empires in the world, in chronological order from time of start

Name	Period	Duration (years)	Max. landmass (km^2)	Max. population (% of world population)
Egyptian Empire	1570 BC–1070 BC	500	1.0	4
Achaemenid Empire or Persian Empire	550-330 BC	220	8.0	44[1]
Chinese/Quing Empire	221 BC–1912	2,133	14.7	37[2]
Roman Empire	27 BC–1453	1,480	6.5	36[3]
Byzantine Empire	330–1453	1,123	1.35	5[4]
Umayyad Caliphate	622–750	138	13.0	30[5]
Mongolian Empire	1206–1260	54	33.0	26[6]
Ottoman Empire	1299–1922	623	5.2	7[7]
Portuguese Empire	1415–1999	584	10.4	1[8]
Spanish Empire	1492–1975	483	20.0	12[9]
British Empire	1583–1997	414	33.7	23[10]
Mughal Empire	1526–1857	341	4.6	29[11]
Russian Empire	1721–1917	196	23.7	10[12]
Second French Empire	1830–1960	130	13.3	5[13]

Source: Wikipedia.

[1] 49.4 million out of 112.4 million in the 5th century BC.
[2] 381.0 million out of 1.041 billion in 1820.
[3] 80.0 million out of 223 million in the 2nd century AD.
[4] 12 million out of 180 million in 1025.
[5] 62 million out of 210 million in the 7th century.
[6] 1,10.0 million out of 429 million in the 13th century.
[7] 39.0 million out of 556 million in the 17th century.
[8] 7 million out of 985 million.
[9] 68.2 million out of 556 million.
[10] 531.3 million out of 2.295 billion in 1938.
[11] 175.0 million out of 600 million in 1700.
[12] 176.4 million out of 1.791 billion in 1913.
[13] 112.9 million out of 2.295 billion in 1938.

an efficient bureaucracy and introduced stone blocks rather than traditional mud bricks for building construction. When he died, he was buried within the Step Pyramid, a 62-meter tall construction which still stands today.

His successors promoted international commerce and mining and began construction of the huge pyramids that are today world-famous. Consider this: The Great Pyramid of Giza was built of approx. 2.3 million cut stone blocks with an average weight of approx. 2.6 tons. Each of these had been created far away and shipped to the construction site. On top of this base construction there were originally 115,000 polished casing stones, each weighing approx. 10 tons. This means that, incredibly, the Egyptians (and their slaves) cut, shipped, and in many cases polished more than 7 million tons of stone—7 billion kilos. And they did it all with great precision. Each of the sides of the Great Pyramid is approx. 2.5 football fields long, and yet the difference in the length of the longest and the shortest is less than 2 centimeters. Equally, and perhaps more impressive, *the entire base is level to within less than 2 centimeters*, and the four corners of the construction are aligned with the cardinal points of the compass (north, east, south, west) to within *0.02%*.

It evidently required an incredible skill to bring this about, and thus a very sophisticated civilization. And yet, the pyramids were far from the Egyptians' only accomplishments. In fact, they were leaders in astronomy, navigation, sculpture, painting, physiology, industrial arts, and sciences.

While Egypt arguably remained the greatest nation on Earth for more than two millennia and ruled an empire for 500 years, it is China that takes the prize as the world's longest lasting empire (2,133 years) and probably also for running an empire consisting of the largest percentage of the world's population (37%). During the Song Dynasty, which lasted from 960 to 1279, Hangzhou served as the national capital and became the most advanced city anywhere. Here you could find hundreds of restaurants, hotels, and theaters. There were tea houses with landscaped gardens, large colored lamps, fine porcelain, and calligraphy and paintings by famous artists. The night life was rich and varied, and there were professional puppeteers, sword swallowers, theater actors, acrobats, musicians, snake charmers, storytellers, and whatnot. People with special interests could join exotic food clubs, antiquarian and art collector clubs, music clubs, horse-loving clubs, and poetry clubs. All of that about 1,000 years ago.

They pioneered numerous phenomena that we take for granted today. The Chinese developed the world's first paper, paper money and bank notes, the first printing mechanisms, gunpowder and the compass. They studied biology, botany, zoology, geology, mineralogy, astronomy, pharmaceutical medicine, archeology, mathematics, cartography, and optics, and they maintained social welfare programs, including retirement homes, public clinics, and graveyards. They had an efficient postal service and public cleaning, construction and maintenance cadres. They also developed an intricate system of national roads and had thousands of ships criss-crossing the rivers and coast lines, including some that acted as floating restaurants.

And they were great explorers. Let me give an example: We know the story of Christopher Columbus, who sailed to America in 1492 with three ships of approximately 20 meters in length and a total crew of 90 men. I have seen replicas of them in Spain and they were really, really small, which speaks for the courage of the sailors, but perhaps less for the craftsmanship or resources of the boat builders. But how many people know that many years earlier, between 1405 and 1433, the Chinese emperor asked a man by the name of 鄭和 (OK, his name was "Zheng He") to head seven international expeditions, and that Zheng He for this purpose gathered a crew of approximately 30,000 men and equipped around 300 ships?

According to records at the time, some of these ships were 150 meters long and had nine masts (some scientists believe that the ships might only have been 60 meters long, which is still three times as much as Columbus' ships. When a boat is three times as long, it normally means it is nine times as big). Zheng He returned from his journey—and this was 600 years ago—with a load of luxury goods including gold, silver, copper, and silk. The reality is that from many hundred years prior to the birth of Christ and around 1,900 years after, China had an upper class that cultivated and appreciated products of extraordinary beauty and quality—products such as enameled porcelain, gold, opulent jewelry, refined writing paper and pens, calligraphy, paintings, pearls, silver, ivory, and of course the world-famous Ming vases. There were large art collections, who were advised by art experts, and they had art critics and art catalogs. What an empire!

While it has been estimated that China at its peak controlled 37% of the world's population, the Roman Empire comes very close (36%). In fact, we shall never know for sure which of the two was largest. But Rome was as amazing as China. During its heyday period under Antoninus Pius (who reigned from 138 to 161), Rome had over 25 public libraries, where people could check out books for reading at home—in fact, most people of means even had their own, private libraries. Many houses had running water, art and book collections, and floors decorated with fine mosaics and walls with frescos. Rome developed, like China, a complex system of highways, and these would often include stretches of many kilometers that were completely straight, and at points along their length they cut tunnels through hills or built viaducts and bridges to cross valleys or passes. The Romans collected wine and raved about the 121 BC vintage, which people kept in their collections for centuries after. Roman military, bureaucracy, trading, architecture, etc. were all far more advanced than those of its neighbors, and we still admire their art. A visit to the excavated Roman town of Pompeii is nothing less than breathtaking.

When you look at the empires in my list above you will see that among the first six, founded between 221 BC and 1299, there was a mix of Middle Eastern, Asian, and European. However, from around 1400, it was overwhelmingly Europeans who built great empires.

Spain played a special role. The first seeds of the creation of the Spanish Empire started in 1492, when the repossession of Granada from the Arabs coincided with Columbus' first expedition to the West. During the next 300 years, Spain built possessions in North and South America, Africa, Europe, and Asia.

However, the greatest European empire was the British, which at its peak in 1922 included more than one-quarter of the world's population and had possessions in every continent, climate, and time zone. Britain had, like Egypt, China, and Rome before it, a thriving and diverse culture. In 1785 there were 650 businesses in London making their money from producing or selling books, and the London art fairs, theater plays, and concerts drew huge crowds. England was home to Darwin, Newton, Rutherford, Watt, Shakespeare, Purcell, and countless other leaders in science, visual arts, literature, music, and not least in technical innovation.

The Russian Empire also had a great influence on recent history even though it has now largely dissolved. It was the successor to the tsardom and prevailed from 1721 to the revolution in 1917, when it was transformed into the Soviet Union. In terms of landmass, it was the third largest empire ever, after the British and Mongolian.

What makes an empire? It would be obvious to think that empires evolve, when an overwhelming force of angry young men attack a

Geographical giants

The largest empire in terms of landmass was the British, followed by the Mongolian, Russian, and Spanish—all other empires have been substantially smaller in terms of controlled landmass.

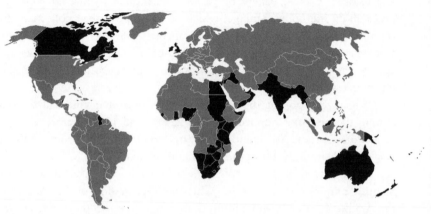

The British Empire. As the anachronistic map shows, this empire (indicated in black) comprised at different times India, parts of the United States, Canada, Australia, New Zealand, large parts of Africa, plus a number of other areas. By 1922, it held sway over approx. one-quarter of the world population, and it was said that "the sun never sets on the British Empire", because it actually didn't.

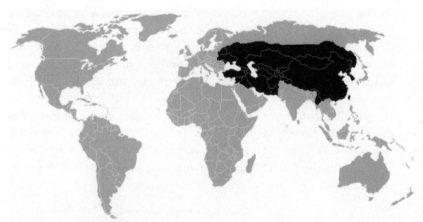

The Mongolian Empire at its greatest extent (indicated in black). This is the second largest empire that ever existed in terms of landmass. However, after just 54 years it split into several smaller units.

The Spanish Empire. Begun in 1492, it reached its peak approx. 300 years later. The map includes some Portuguese possessions owing to the Iberian Union (1580–1640).

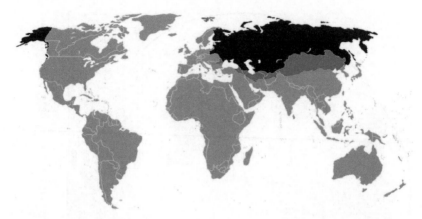

The Russian Empire (indicated in black). This was built largely through the 17th and 18th centuries, and it prevails in different forms even today, despite lost parts during the collapse of the Soviet Union.

weaker population and then subvert them. However, that would be quite misleading. It is true that the empires listed earlier mostly evolved through war and conquest. However, the overwhelming majority of all wars are followed by a return to the previous *status quo* or some sort of dis-integration. The Vikings, for instance, waged countless wars and made numerous conquests, but they rarely held the areas they took for long, and perhaps they didn't have much interest in it either, because in terms of organizing a society, they didn't have much new to offer. Empires, on the other hand, develop when the conquering people possess a set of technologies, cultural achievement, and/or organizing principles that are vastly superior to what exists in the areas they amass. It is, in other words, the power of ideas and sophisticated knowhow that make empires possible. Examples:

- Leadership in international trade and naval power
- Superior administrative systems
- Admirable cultural/artistic achievements
- New technologies (ships, arms, communication technologies)

Let us examine this in the context of the European empires. The American scientist Charles Murray published in 2003 a book called *Human Accomplishment: The Pursuit of Excellence in the Arts and Sciences, 800 BC to 1950*. This contained an elaborate attempt to quantify human achievements within disciplines such as astronomy, biology, chemistry, physics, mathematics, medicine, technology, philosophy, art, and literature, starting when individual names could first be assigned to human achievements.

Charles Murray's methodology

The task of quantifying human achievement objectively (or even at all) may seem impossible, but Murray used so-called historiometric methods, which in this case involved checking more than 150 leading international reference works such as Asimov's *Chronology of Science and Discovery*, *The Heritage of Japanese Art*, or *Histoire de la Musique*. By going through these, he could identify 19,794 important contributors to human advancement through history. In order to eliminate more superficial sources or sources with home bias, he now selected statistically those references that had broad coverage of the important people identified overall.

And then he indexed the accomplishments. Let's say, for instance, that in "Western music" Chopin was on average allocated 1.06% of the total reference descriptions, in terms of number of words used, of that subject in all the reference books. That would then be his "raw score". He would then for each category change these raw scores to "index scores", so that the person given the lowest score was allocated "1" and the one with the highest "100". In this way, everything became easily comparable within and across categories. Furthermore, while Murray had no predefined start point, he deliberately made 1950 the endpoint to avoid bias for people who may be popular when they live, but will not stand the test of time. Finally, he decided to only classify people as significant if they had been mentioned in at least 50% of all the reference sources he checked. The result was a list of 4,002 significant figures, from Confucius to Aristotle, Darwin, Newton, Beethoven, etc.

The entire study was very interesting, but I think three observations stood out. The first was that *until around year 1450, there were as many periods of actual decline in new human achievement as of progress.* For example, the Egyptians took giant steps forward, but began a steady process of decline from around 2300 BC, and when the Romans finally conquered them in 30 BC, they were a shadow of their former glory. In fact, during this period, it was almost only China that progressed—the rest of the world bar Greece was largely static or in fact declining. Nevertheless, it is stunning how China evolved from being the world's most sophisticated nation by far into a period of stagnation followed by a decline culminating with the cultural revolution in the 1960s, where people were murdered, worked to death, starved, imprisoned, raped, tortured, and plundered in the name of the revolution, and where antiques, historical sites, and other traces of previous culture were deliberately destroyed. Decline, it seems, can be as overwhelming as advancement.

The second and perhaps most striking observation was that *no fewer than 97% of all accomplishments of all times were made in Europe and the rest of the West* (mainly North America). Bear in mind here that this was not Murray's subjective judgment, but the statistically objective, implied consensus from a wide range of leading, international reference works. The third clear observation in Murray's study was, as one might guess, that *the rate of human achievement took off from around 1450.*

I guess these observations raise two good questions: (1) Why does decline happen?, and (2) Why did Europe and the West become the completely dominant empire builders and achievers in science art, etc. after 1450?

Let me start with decline. There is something very odd about a society falling apart, because in order to do so, their inhabitants need to accomplish less and less. The reason this seems so strange is that excelling is highly pleasurable. So, why, once you have learned to excel, would a society stop doing it? Just think about it: Whether people are craftsmen, artists, scientists, nurses, or anything else, one of the greatest pleasures in their life is when they produce the very best they can. People often speak of a sense of "flow", when describing how they successfully do things that are difficult. So, again: How can an empire have a lot of that, and 50 or 500 years later, it's virtually gone?

I think that for the individual to excel there has to be a receptive environment—an audience, a market, an encouragement to go further. And there has to be a reason. After all, while achievement is fun, it is also often incredibly hard and can be fraught with risks. These conditions can disappear in four different ways:

- The *need* to achieve disappears. When Spain conquered much of Latin America and brought back 200 tons of gold, the Spanish became immensely rich, with the effect that few people had any interest in normal business anymore. In fact this problem is widespread among nations enjoying work-free windfalls. Oil-producing nations are here at risk.
- The *will* to achieve disappears. Overconfidence is often a reason here. It can also come from, simply, long stretches of time without major sense of danger, which leads to increasing overspending, indifference,

and lack of will to defend anything—a cultural and military pacifism. Europe springs to mind.

- The *opportunity* to achieve disappears. Lack of opportunity can come simply from a very strong sense of commitment to parents, extended family, and the community at large, which means that risk taking and migration is strongly discouraged. Furthermore, it is also an inevitable consequence of totalitarian regimes. These will often experience an initial enthusiasm with leads to amazing achievements within a short timespan. Whether we speak of the Soviet Union, Nazi Germany, or strongly religious empires, this pattern is very clear. However, it is equally clear that whenever such an empire manages to stay in place for a longer time, decay sets in, since totalitarian systems suppress individual initiative and diversity. Iran, perhaps?

- The *incentive* to achieve disappears. If risk-taking and hard work is not rewarded, people will rarely do it. Socialism is the obvious way to strangle initiative, and when socialist countries have indeed excelled after the initial burst of energy, it has only been because socialism produced "freedom islands" within the system, where select people did not have all the constraints of society as a whole. Apart from socialism as such, another impediment to incentive is overwhelming consensus orientation, where people who are original and different are viewed with suspicion and discriminated against. Cuba and North Korea?

To sum up these reasons for failure, they can be described as lack of "need", "will", "opportunity", and "incentive" but the deeper reasons can simply be described by just four words: (1) windfalls, (2) decadence, (3) suppression, and (4) envy.

As for decadence and suppression, religion can play a role. The case of taoism is here illustrative. Taoism is beautiful and attractive, but there is a snag. It describes how the universe works harmoniously and why it is therefore wrong for anyone to change what already is. This doesn't mean that people should be completely passive, but letting things be as they are is seen as important. This is spelled out in the Tao Te Ching: "To seek the Tao one loses day by day, losing and yet losing some more, till one has reached the state of wu wei (doing nothing or inaction)." This concept of defeatism and inaction as a route to divinity is also found in Buddhism, where some men still today will choose to leave their family to fend for themselves while they personally seek truth through an ascetic life as beggars. That's hardly how empires are made. Also, in many religions, the thought that everything that happens is directed from above and that life on Earth is nothing but a short prelude to eternal afterlife may lead to inaction and indifference. Why bother, if you are not in charge anyway, and if life doesn't matter much?

The 10 golden rules of tyranny

1. Establish taboo views that can never be questioned.
2. Discredit everybody who offers deviant views.
3. Cut off access to any alternative source of affection and information.
4. Intermix police, justice, military, central banking, church. and law-making powers under a single, central command.
5. Create a superior class of ultra-loyalists who are not subject to the law. Use that force to suppress alternative thinking.
6. Invent an enemy that you can blame for everything.
7. Use staged events to create support and develop hatred of imagined enemies.
8. Increase dependency on the state through handouts, food, and fuel subsidies, etc.
9. Make political correctness the main determinant of advancement in society.
10. Mix up crime and calls for freedom, and fight both as if they were the same.

So, these are the reasons why empires can decline, and they may help us understand why Europe was falling behind between the end of the Roman Empire and 1400–1450. In 285, Rome had been split into an Eastern part which later became Byzantine, and a Western part. After Rome's defeat to the Goths at the Battle of Adrianople in 378, the Western Roman Empire went into a gradual decline and finally disintegrated.

This was followed by what we today call the Middle Ages. Western Europe was now largely ruled through feudalism, where fairly weak monarchs ruled through agreement with strong, local leaders (similar to Afghanistan today). This was combined with a very strong influence by an often aggressive, repressive, and militarized church, as witnessed by the crusades and local persecution against heretics such as in the Spanish Inquisition. While progress was made on some fronts, Europe was behind Islam in terms of science throughout the first parts of the Middle Ages, and from a global perspective, this period was for Europe one of relative decline. When compared with the achievements of the Roman Empire, it was even in some respects a period of absolute decline.

So, how did Europe rise from the ashes after that and come into the position of being the world's leading light in science, arts, engineering, trade, and many other disciplines, and to become the only major empire-builders? I think this can mainly be explained by four new developments:

- The Renaissance
- The Reformation
- The Enlightenment
- Female emancipation.

The *Renaissance*, which spanned from the end of the 13th century to around 1600, was a separation process from the previously totally dominant church. As the name "renaissance" indicates, it was a rediscovery of earlier artistic and humanistic values created by the Romans and, before them, the Greeks. The most important inspiration for this movement was perhaps the monk Thomas Aquinas, who lived from approx. 1225 to 1274. Aquinas claimed that humans had natural talents for discovering things without divine guidance and that they should use that talent. He was impressed with the Greek philosopher Aristotle who was a proponent of empiricism—the concept of gaining knowledge from practical experience.

Aquinas was Italian and the Renaissance started there, where it led to new publications and translations of books by writers such as Plato and Aristotle. Their profound thoughts on ethics, logic, scientific observation, politics, and the nature of living a satisfying human life gained ground. All of this eventually evolved into the mass publication of compact books that people could carry in a pocket. It even led to a veritable book collection craze. Also, artists began to emulate older art styles, which in many ways had been more sophisticated than medieval ones. The movement fostered thriving communities of humanists and artists, who inspired a sense of individualism and creativity that had not existed before, and with that also the sense that man can shape his own destiny. After its start in north Italian cities like Florence, Siena, and Lucca, the Renaissance movement spread through the rest of Italy and then Europe.

It is possible that the Black Death, which killed a third of Europe's population, contributed to this process for three reasons: (1) The church was seen as helpless in tackling the plague problem, which undermined its authority; (2) it created labor shortages, which gave individuals enhanced power over institutions; and (3) decimation of the population

made the survivors richer, and gave them more resources to invest in art
and literature.

The *Reformation* was a revolt against the institutions of the Catholic
Church, which were seen as increasingly corrupt and as placing too much
emphasis on ritual and money. It was possible to buy offices at the
church, for instance, and one could even buy salvation. All of this led to
an accumulation of capital and wealth in the church, which was extreme.
Of course, it didn't help when people discovered that some clerics held
several offices at the same time and lived very well from the combined
income. As more people moved to cities, they could first of all see this
wealth and corruption with their own eyes and, furthermore, they had
the ability to network with many others, which made collective resent-
ment grow. A contributing factor here was evidently the tendency
towards individual thought that the Renaissance had created. People
began to question whether clerics actually were better judges of what was
right and moral than they were themselves.

The Reformation process started as an attempt to change the Catholic
Church, but it soon spawned the creation of the Protestant Church,
which again splintered into the Lutheran, the Calvinist, the Reformed,
and the Presbyterian churches. People were now forced to choose a side,
and their decisions could have great impact on their future and perhaps
even cost them their lives. All of this again fostered the increasing propensity towards individual thought. Furthermore, while Catholics confessed
to priests, and did their penance under the guidance of priests, protestants
practiced their faith directly—they read the Bible themselves, prayed in
private, and received their absolution directly from God. Because of this,
they could all develop their own interpretation of religion. This was yet
another stimulus for individual thought.

The Catholic Church eventually reacted to the Reformation by
instituting a counter-reformation, including better training of the clerics,
nicer decoration of churches, more appealing and comprehensible
sermons, and much more. They also decided to update their calendar,
which seemed to be around 10 days out of step with the seasons. One of
the astronomers they asked to work on the project was Nicolaus
Copernicus. He published his *De Revolutionibus* in 1543, which became
the first of a series of scientific breakthroughs that culminated in
Newton's Laws at the end of the 17th century. All of this became part
of the process of *Enlightenment*, which put freedom, democracy, science,
religious tolerance, the rule of law, and reason as primary values of society.

The final step in Europe's transition was the *emancipation of women*. The
first steps in that direction had come when women were given conditional

suffrage during Sweden's so-called age of liberty, which lasted from 1718 to 1771. However, emancipation began in earnest in the 1840s when state legislatures in the United States and the British Parliament began passing so-called "Married Women's Property Acts", which protected women's property from their husbands and their husbands' creditors. In 1893 New Zealand became the first country to give women voting rights at national elections, and this was followed by Australia in 1902, while the U.S.A., Britain, and Canada gave women the vote after the First World War. This gave women a much greater influence and resulted in the workforce being much better educated and provided a higher incentive for children to excel in education.

I have already argued that it is not hordes of angry young men that create empires, but great ideas. Winston Churchill, whom I count as one of the greatest political minds of all times, actually saw this at the end of World War II, as he stated that: "The empires of the future are the empires of the mind." The Egyptian, Chinese, Roman, or British empires all brought administrative systems, art, science, and discovery to their subjects, and it was for that reason that they could run their empires. When you study the history of empires, it should therefore not be entirely surprising how often it is tiny groups of people with superior knowledge that controlled far larger groups. Take Portugal as an example. Portugal was a small nation—almost tiny—with just a few hundred thousand inhabitants, when it started building the world's first global empire. Portugal's seafarers were among the best at the time, and they knew how to build caravels and how to navigate using cartography and other maritime technologies.

The empire they built lasted for almost six centuries, from the capture of Ceuta in 1415 to the handover of Macau to China in 1999. At the top of p. 163 is an illustration of all the possessions this empire had at its peak.

You will notice on the map that they had numerous small colonies along coastlines in South America, Africa, India, the Middle East, India, and the Far East. So, how many men did this tiny nation deploy to build such a global empire? The British historian Charles Boxer has estimated that at the end of the 16th century the number of able-bodied Portuguese working overseas did not exceed 10,000. I don't know if you can think of a place with 10,000 inhabitants, but this would be little more than a single village or a small suburb. And yet, such a contingent held a global empire together. So, again, it was not hordes of angry young men who brought it about; it was ideas and the contingent superiority accompanying them, whether in terms of arms, ships, commercial skills, arts, or other strengths.

Creating Europe's advantage

The dominance of Europe after 1400–1450 can largely be explained by four processes:

- The Renaissance (1200–1600) fostered artistic activity, humanistic thought, individualism, and creativity.
- The Reformation (1517–1648) broke the dominance of the Church as an economic and political powerhouse. Furthermore, the splintering of the church into competing branches forced people to think about what each of them actually stood for and created the idea that individuals might be as good judges of spirituality as clerics.
- The Enlightenment (mainly from 1543 to 1800) placed the ideals of freedom, democracy, science, religious tolerance, rule of law, and reason as the primary values of society.
- Female emancipation (mainly from 1840 to 1920) brought education and political clout to women.

Each of these processes inspired the next, but they were probably all stimulated by urbanization, which contributed to enlightenment, periods of labor shortage, which gave workers a stronger sense of power versus landowners, state, and church, and a tradition for seafaring, which reduced the bonds between parents and sons. The overall result was a rapid development of science, technology, social systems, and cultural achievements, which gave Europe military, economic, cultural, and social advantages, all of which could be used in the development of global empires.

The European countries that created empires after 1400 included the U.K., Spain, Russia, Portugal, France, Holland, Germany, Sweden, Denmark, Austria–Hungary, and Italy. Together, these nations ended up controlling the majority of the global landmass, population, and economy.

There are many other examples. Venice, for instance, was not on my list of great empires earlier, because it wasn't that big, but it did control most of the Greek islands plus Croatia and parts of northern Italy, even though Venice is a place you can easily walk across in 30 minutes or less. Rome, which became perhaps the greatest empire of all time (considering its durability and level of sophistication) was initially a tiny village. The Spanish conquistador Pizarro beat around 7,000 Inca warriors at Cajamarca with a force of just 168 men, and Hernando Cortes conquered

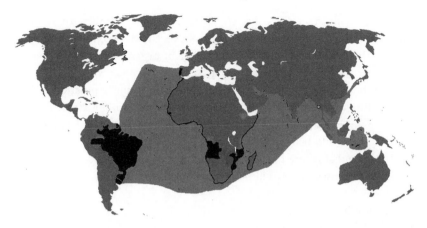

The Portuguese Empire (indicated in black, with gray indicating its sea domain). Held together by a tiny contingent of men, it spanned five continents and held dominance over much of the sea. *Source*: Wikipedia Commons.

more than 5 million Aztecs with a force of only 1,000 soldiers, which means that his troops won while being outnumbered 5,000 to 1.

I started this chapter by drawing maps of some of history's largest empires. You can buy books and read articles today where people make forecasts of the borders of future empires, but personally I think this is largely beside the point. The age of empire building by land conquest in North America came to an end when the Confederates surrendered at the end of the Civil War (1861–1865). As for Western Europe and Japan, the end of World War II and the fall of the Berlin Wall marked the end of violent land conquest, and in Eastern Europe the Yugoslavian wars hopefully have been the last major land battles we shall ever see there. In the Middle East and Africa there are still many ongoing land-grab attempts, but it seems highly unlikely that anyone will succeed in building new empires through conquest—the existing superpowers would not let it happen.

The age of rivalry between capitalism and socialism is also essentially over. Socialism is so utterly discredited that even most political parties that have the word "social" in their name do not believe in the idea of a command economy. What has already happened in most countries is a convergence around a central position based on free markets but with a social network. While this is essentially a good thing, it is also very boring, and fewer people vote at national elections. What might come, instead, is a drift towards the Swiss model of a mind-numbingly boring national coalition that virtually never changes, but with the highly exciting addition of direct democracy voting on single issues which can be called by political parties or by a fairly small number of voters. Furthermore, given that the big issues have largely been resolved, we may see the establishment of non-government organizations that propose global best practices of how to run a country. In other words: Who has the best health system in the world? The best traffic regulations? Tax system? Environmental system? Privacy laws? Emigration system? I think it will come. Perhaps a big bank or consulting company could sponsor it, or perhaps it could become a Wikipedia kind of thing.

I believe that future *empires will be virtual in a geographical sense*, but very real in other senses. They will be created through

- economic power
- social fascination.

It may be a trivial observation, but in most of the world land can actually now be bought legally and peacefully in free markets. So can companies, mines, farming rights, precious metals, brands, equities, bonds, and much more. A country that consistently produces more than it consumes will be able to invest the surplus in acquisition of such assets abroad; and thus expand its empire quietly. The most obvious example of this has been China's massive purchase of U.S. treasury bonds, which means that the American people owe the Chinese people ever larger amounts.

This transfer of wealth, and thus economic empire building, shows up in foreign exchange reserves, private holdings, and sovereign wealth funds. The latter are state-owned investment funds which often use sophisticated investment vehicles, including private equity and hedge fund portfolios. During the subprime salami crises, numerous emerging market companies and sovereign wealth funds took over entire Western companies, or acquired significant stakes in major banks, for instance—at rock bottom prices. While investment bankers worthy of their names will never reveal their clients, if I ask those I know how sovereign wealth funds are doing, they tend to describe them as "smart", or "clever". These funds have a long-term perspective and, unlike private investors who often sell when equity prices are low and economic news is bad, sovereign wealth funds will often be strong buyers in such situations.

As of 2010, China plus Hong Kong has almost $1 trillion stashed away in four sovereign wealth funds and around $2 trillion in foreign exhange reserves. Other very large net accumulators of foreign assets include Saudi Arabia, the Gulf States, Norway, Russia, and Singapore, as well as Switzerland and Germany in central Europe. The single biggest loser is the United States, although some of the headline numbers hide the fact that America's holdings abroad seem to perform better than foreign holdings in America.

One way to enhance a country's balance of payments is to force down your own currency, as China has done. However, while this has positive impact on the annual flow of capital, it simultaneuosly cheapens your own assets and makes foreign assets more expensive. The single most efficient way to become an economic empire builder is perhaps to combine growth-oriented policies with very high domestic consumption taxes such as VAT and energy taxes. One reason that central Europe has done better than America in terms of net asset accumulation may be exactly that.

As for social fascination as a driver of virtual empires, things get a bit fluffier, of course. But let me give an example of what I mean by it: After World War II the U.S. State Department organized a series of international jazz concerts by some of its country's finest musicians, including Dave Brubeck, Louis Armstrong, Benny Goodman, and Duke Ellington. They was soon unofficially dubbed "the real ambassadors" because it worked wonders. When Greek students threw rocks at the American embassy in Greece, for instance, the incredibly charming and talented Dizzy Gillespie showed up and gave a hilarious concert. After this, the attacks on America died down. Simultaneously Norman Granz organized the so-called "Jazz at the Philharmonic" (JATP), which also included America's very best jazz musicians. There is a wonderful concert recording, *J.A.T.P—in Tokyo 1953*, where the Japanese audience is clearly extremely enthusiastic. What makes this so exceptional is that the event took place just 7 years after the end of an exceptionally brutal war between the U.S.A. and Japan.

Fascination is the amazement you feel when you listen to music that touches your heart, see architecture that strikes you with its beauty or charm, taste food that only an artist could have made, or use products that ooze luxury. It may come from dining in a superb French restaurant, admiring an Italian supercar, seeing a Chinese sports team perform amazingly, or enjoying the refinement of a hotel in Vietnam or Thailand. The combination of wealth and mutual fascination can create a very strong concept, the so-called "fabric of society". This fabric works when

- People essentially feel that society is fair
- People with different lifestyles and views have a right to be there, as long as they don't harm others
- It's felt that the vast majority contribute as best they can

- People feel that tax money is reasonably well spent
- People think that public employees are honest, well-meaning, and not corrupt
- Society creates products, services, and events that make people proud of belonging
- Humor and gestures are universally understood and accepted
- Politeness and respect is frequently exchanged
- People are often seen to excel in arts, science, sports, and philosophy
- Society is clearly progressing
- The environment is respected
- Government decisions are made by the people and for the people.

When the fabric of society works, the large majority of society's inhabitants feel that the community they belong to is great, worthwhile, and just, and they will therefore each contribute to its progress, and each defend it against abuse. I do not believe future empires will be built by the barrel of a gun, but by a barrage of fun, and not by moving border posts, but by removing them. Once the social fabric between two communities has become close enough to blend, you can take down the border posts, and an empire begins to form. Once people like and accept each other, there will be no point in guns.

The foundation of the European Union (starting with the European Coal and Steel Community, followed by the European Economic Community) was largely created to prevent nationalism, and it has as such been hugely successful. Germanic, Anglo-Saxon, Hispanic, Celtic, Gallic, and other tribes are today mixing and bonding like never before, and there is a general feeling of shared values and belonging—not to the EU as an institution, but between the people. A good joke told by an Irishman will seem funny to an Italian, and a gesture by a German will be understood by a Swede. A product produced by a Belgian can be purchased duty-free by a Dane, and a good English TV program will have viewers across the continent. Anyone can work in any other country, and people of different nationalities will increasingly marry and get international children. We are witnessing the creation of a new empire.

However, while virtual empires that are built on tolerance and acceptance rather than force can be extremely powerful, they cannot be rushed. The fabric can be stretched to certain limits, and it will still work. People may think "I don't like the way these guys dress," but they may still essentially accept them; a general tolerant mindset bridges the gap. Or they may think "why pay taxes, if the money goes to leeches," but if the vast majority of the population clearly work and obey the laws, most people will accept the system as a whole. Again, tolerance bridges the gaps.

However, any social fabric does have limits and when many people, who are themselves intolerant or who don't seem to contribute like others, join or evolve in a society, the general acceptance of state, community, and taxes breaks down. What follows is like a social allergic reaction, where society either goes into a defense position by scaling back its tolerance until the issue has been reversed or resolved, or it dissolves.

I guess the overall pattern for the coming decades may be that commodity producers and northeast Asian nations will expand their virtual *economic* empires—often massively. However, when it comes to virtual social empires, the predominantly Western ideas of individuality, creativity, and tolerance will continue to succeed. In the very long term, the largest renewable resource and growth industry will be knowledge, and countries that are most capable of inspiring knowledge will continue to thrive. This speaks for Europe and the rest of the "West", such as America, Australia, and Canada, etc.

The great empires by 2050 will not be defined by clear national borders, because they will be virtual, and they will grow organically. There will be two: One will be predominantly Chinese, and the other Latin/Germanic/Anglo-Saxon. Many people will feel attachment to both.

9

War, terror, and the bottom billion

Humans have always been aggressive towards each other. A part of the reason can be, quite simply, fear—each of two groups is afraid of the other, and each thus wants to strike before the other one does. Many think that World War I essentially started in that way.

The anthropologist Lawrence Keeley, who authored the important book *War before Civilization*, estimates that approx. 25% of all people were killed in war or war-like events before the emergence of civilization. Early hunter–gatherers and tribal societies, such as the Yanomamo in Amazonia and the Enga in New Guinea, would often make raids against neighbors with very high fatalities. War and state-sponsored genocide was also clearly widespread during the first part of the 20th century, where it killed approx. 190 million people, with its culmination in World War II.

Common defects in human psychology have surely contributed. Psychopathologists estimate that 3–5% of the general population has anti-social personality disorder ("psychopaths" among laymen), and that approx. 15% have sadistic tendencies. The former lack human empathy and regard people as playthings or toys, and the latter get sexually stimulated by hurting others. The problems caused by these personality disorders (which may overlap) have surely been aggravated by the fact that many psychopaths often are clever and charming and will frequently manage to become leaders. And, finally, there is a tendency for psychopaths and sadists to often seek the kinds of work that can give them most power over other people, so that they can more easily abuse and manipulate them, such as becoming judges, teachers, politicians, and priests, or gaining high rank in the military. The Aztecs routinely made thousands of sacrifices where they sliced the living victim's abdomen open with a flint knife, then pulled out the still-beating heart with their hands. It is hard to imagine that those who thought up these acts or engaged in them did not take sexual pleasure from it. Or, to put it differently, it is impossible to imagine normal people doing such things.

However, whereas we regard people with antisocial and sadistic personalities as deviant and, in severe cases, suffering from clinical disorders, there are also general aspects of the normal human mind that contribute to violence. Humans are fighters and predators by nature, like cats or wolves, and if we don't have to fight for survival and catch our prey, our instincts—or at least many young men's instincts—are to seek something to replace these fights. We may, for instance, indulge ourselves in violent movies and computer games and perhaps also in aggressive sports, to feed our aggressive instincts. The violent urges are clearly in our genes.

I come from Scandinavia, which I think is one of the most peace-loving areas on Earth, but if you look back in history, it wasn't always so. My own ancestors, the Danes, attacked England and other neighboring countries virtually every year, over long periods of time. They plundered, raped, extorted, and stole. This was reinforced by a religion that said that you would go to the Viking heaven of Valhalla if you died in battle.

Between 1276 and 1658, long after the Viking age had ended, a small enclave of Danish-minded people living in "Scania", which is now a part of southern Sweden, were attacked by Swedish armies no fewer than 34 times, until the Treaty of Roskilde, when they finally ceded to Sweden. To put this into perspective: *The 34 attacks equalled one every 11 years over a period of almost 400 years.* Furthermore, during the same years Sweden and Denmark-proper engaged in a long series of wars.

The reality is that most of the history of Europe is one of an endless series of wars, culminating in World War II in which over 60 million people were killed. The last war between Denmark and Sweden ended in 1721; after the end of World War II, Northern and Western Europe have enjoyed the longest period of peace measured historically.

Finally, I think average intelligence (or lack of it) matters too. Within any country, and between nations, there seems to be a fairly strong tendency that the less intelligent are more prone to violence. There is actually hope in this observation, because of the Flynn Effect that I described earlier. IQ scales are reset in different countries with regular intervals to compensate for gradually rising intelligence scores. Average IQ in the U.S. today is around 100, for instance, because the scales have been calibrated there to make it 100. However, if we study similar IQ tests made in the U.S. in the 1930s and calibrate them per modern standards, it seems that average IQ at that time was around 80. That is a huge difference in 80 years. This makes me think that average IQ may have been closer to 70 when the American Civil War took place in 1861–1865. That, I think, might actually be a part of the reason that such a meaningless event could occur. After all, 70–75 is normally considered borderline retarded today; and 70 is the minimum level of IQ necessary to complete basic school education without major difficulties.

World War II brought an end to most of the British Empire and left a world with two power centers: America and the Soviet Union, both of which were associated with a large number of allies. The Soviet Empire was the stronger of the two in the sense of landmass and people it controlled or dominated—America actually withdrew fairly quickly from the areas it had conquered after ensuring creation of democracies there. However, when the Soviet Union and the Warsaw Pact later fell apart, America was the only superpower left.

America was (and is) frequently described as a superpower, but one might also call it an empire, because of its global influence. At the end of the war it was in fact the most dominant such empire in terms of military and economic power before it. In 1945 it controlled 35% of global GDP—more than any other empire in world history. The second most economically dominant empire ever, China's Qing Empire in 1820, came closest (33%), but that was more than 120 years earlier. The British controlled 24% in 1870.

The five most economically dominating empires of all times

1. American Empire in 1945:   35% ($1,644.8 billion out of $4,699 billion)
2. Qing Empire in 1820:   33% ($228.6 billion out of $694.4 billion)
3. Mughal Empire in 1700:   25% ($90.8 billion out of $371 billion)
4. British Empire in 1870:   24% ($265 billion out of $1,111 billion)
5. Russian Empire in 1913:   9% ($257.7 billion out of $2,733 billion)

American military superiority since the end of World War II has been unrivaled in history. Its military policy has, since the fall of the Berlin Wall, predominantly been driven by two considerations:

- Humanitarian: protect weak people or states, when they were attacked by stronger ones. The two Balkan interventions in Bosnia and Kosovo to protect Muslims against attacks from Christians, intervention in Somalia to deliver food aid to starving people, invasion in Haiti to maintain democracy, participation in various U.N. peacekeeping operations, etc. are examples. Somalia was a fiasco, but most of the others succeeded.

- Defensive: prevent the rise of new, strong tyrants who were hostile to America, or prevent existing ones from gaining more power. The prime examples were the wars in Vietnam, Korea, Kuwait, Afghanistan, and Iraq, where only the Korean War and the liberation of Kuwait can be deemed undisputed successes (Afghanistan and Iraq remain open).

It seems that the main intellectual inspiration for the latter part of America's military activities comes from Niccolò di Bernardo dei Machiavelli, the Italian who authored a short political treatise called *The Prince*, which was published in 1513 (5 years after his death). We shall never know if it was meant as a satire or a handbook for cynical politicians, but it has since been widely used as the latter. It describes how a leader (his imaginary prince), in order to be effective, must be seen to be good and moral in public, while some of what he must do is actually amoral. For this amoral action to work, Machiavelli concludes, it has to be (1) decisive, (2) swift, (3) effective, and (4) short-lived.

The Machiavellian part of America's foreign policy has gained it a huge number of friends (mainly in Eastern Europe) and enemies (mainly in Latin America and the Middle East). It has also created endless chain reactions of unintended consequences.

———

Let's take the case of Afghanistan, Iran, and Iraq. I promise to make this short, but the story of the geopolitics and U.S. intervention there makes a Swiss complication watch look simple.

Let us start at the time that U.S. supported the removal of Iran's democratically elected Prime Minister Mohammed Mosaddeq in 1953 due to (you guessed it) disputes about sharing of oil revenues. This operation was decisive, swift, and effective, as Machiavelli would have it. However, the problem was that, whereas most Americans probably can't recall that incident, most Iranians remain very well aware of it. Anyway, after the coup the country was run by the Iranian monarch Mohammed Reza Pahlavi. Pahlavi modernized the country and extended suffrage to women, among other things, and seemed generally friendly to other nations, but he was also brutal against his internal enemies. However,

Pahlavi was unseated in the 1979 Islamic revolution, where students also attacked the American embassy and took its employees hostage for 444 days. During the same year the Soviet Union attacked Afghanistan, which inspired America to support the Islamist mujahedin (if the embedded "jahed" in this word sounds like "jihad", it's no coincidence).

Here is an important fact: Iran is a Shiite nation. Neighboring Iraq is mainly Shiite too, but at the time of the Iranian revolution Iraq was ruled almost entirely by its Sunni minority, under the leadership of Saddam Hussein. Hussein got seriously worried that the Shiite revolutionary fever in Iran might spread to his own country and, besides, he seemed to like the idea of expanding his own empire. So, he attacked. The war that followed lasted for 8 years and brought about half a million fatalities. America supported Saddam Hussein here, since your enemy's enemy is your friend. However, this caused Iran to send two missiles into an American warship, and America to accidentally shoot down a civilian Iranian aircraft. By the way, Iran and Iraq also started sinking each other's oil tankers, and Iraq apparently used nerve gas against Iranians. It was exceptionally brutal.

A new important fact: Saudi Arabia is a Sunni country, and the Saudis probably liked the idea of a Sunni ruler in Iraq. However, Saudi Arabia, Kuwait, and the Emirates constitute the most inviting military targets on this planet, because of all that oil and gas plus a geography that is difficult to defend: flat desert. So, they made defense alliances with America. Hussein and his sons, who apparently shared great appetite for violence (such as shooting a cabinet minister during a meeting), had noticed the apparent military vulnerability of the Gulf States. So, Iraq attacked Kuwait and sent a few missiles into Israel in the hope that Israel would counterattack and thereby create justification for the whole thing. America and its allies quickly drove Saddam Hussein back out, but not before he set the Kuwaiti oil wells ablaze and started pumping 450 million liters of oil directly into the sea to show his displeasure.

A number of Islamists wanted to create a regime change in Saudi Arabia and were upset because America was present and cooperating with the Saudi family (the Saudis contributed 118,000 troops to the Gulf War). So, they set up training camps in Afghanistan from where they organized numerous terror attacks across the globe, culminating with 9/11 in New York, which was perpetrated by Saudis, Yemenis, and Egyptians. America and its allies attacked Afghanistan to stop the terror camps and capture Osama Bin Laden, which alienated members of the Pashtun tribe, who live in parts of Afghanistan plus parts of Pakistan. The Pashtun started to organize terror campaigns in both countries.

Shortly after, the Americans also attacked their own previous ally, Iraq. Before the offensive, they asked Turkey for permission to invade from their side, which was declined because the Turkish were concerned that the Kurds would take the opportunity to revolt. Did I mention the Kurds before? They live in Iran, Iraq, Syria, and Turkey and want their own state.

This will go on and on, and no matter what anyone does about it, there will be ever-escalating cascades of unintended consequences. And, if nothing is done, it may get even worse. If Saddam had gotten away with taking Kuwait, for instance, would he not have grabbed Saudi and the other Gulf States afterwards? No one can know, but the Saudis clearly feared it. How it will all end is impossible to say. It could eventually fade, it could go on like it has in eternity, or it could culminate in an apocalyptic war.

———————

In spite of this mess, America will remain extremely strong. After the fall of the Berlin Wall, America reigned supreme, and its military budget exceeded the combined budgets of the next 20 nations. *No other empire has ever before come anywhere near America's military dominance after 1980.*

The latest numbers, which are estimates from 2009, show that *America has approx. 45% of world military spending*, whereas China is a very distant second with 6%. India is responsible for just 2% of world military spending. Furthermore, the U.S. is a partner in NATO which in total controls around 60% of global military spending.

As if this wasn't enough, America has extensive experience in all sorts of military operations, which is essential, because the projection of large-scale military power involves very considerable training plus the most complex logistic operation of any human endeavor. Military planners operate with an unpleasant term called "kill ratio" (i.e., the proportion of casualties on each side in a battle). During World War II, The Soviet Union lost between 9 million and 11 million soldiers, Germany approx. 5.5 million, and Japan 2.1 million. Incredibly, the U.S. invaded Africa, Europe, and Japan simultaneously, and yet it suffered far fewer casualties than the other major combatants—America lost just over 400,000. During subsequent wars America has seen very high kill ratios. American casualties for the first Gulf War were 148 killed in action, and its 36 allies lost 77. However, estimates of Iraqi casualties range from 30,000 to 100,000.

Another way to understand the dominance of America is by looking at a very small part of its combined war machine: the so-called carrier strike groups (CSGs). Such a group normally consist of 1 aircraft carrier, which is like a heavily defended floating airport, plus 2 guided missile cruisers, 2 anti-aircraft warships, and 1 or 2 anti-submarine destroyers or frigates. The only times in world history that such groups have engaged in direct battle with each other were during World War II, notably at the Battle of Coral Sea, and a month later at the famous Battle of Midway, where the U.S. destroyed 3 of Japan's 4 aircraft carriers within 7 minutes and the last one shortly after.

A modern American battle group carries stealth warplanes, cruise missiles, bunker busters, and much more, and any of these may be equipped with tactical or strategic nuclear bombs. In essence, a carrier group can deliver bombs with unrivaled precision, literally through windows, or it can wipe out megacities within minutes. America has close to 10,000 nuclear bombs and has 11 of these battle groups.

Another aspect of America's power is that since America is surrounded by large oceans to the east and west, which are patrolled by its vastly superior navy, and since it has two friendly neighbors to the south and north, there is no possibility of anyone invading it militarily. Nor can it be starved into surrender; America is the world's third largest conventional oil producer and sits on some of the world's largest oil reserves in the form of shale oil. It is scarcely populated (its population density is 34 inhabitants per square kilometer against 230 for Germany and 338 for Japan) and is a net exporter of agricultural products.

Finally, America has made great strides in developing robots for military purposes, which may further reduce its potential battle losses. These intelligent machines include

- Unmanned aerial vehicles, which can take surveillance photographs and launch precision-guided missiles.
- Unmanned combat air vehicles, which are remote-controlled fighter planes. By eliminating the functions necessary for pilots, these may have higher speed, maneuverability and range than normal aircraft, while at the same time eliminating the risks of pilot loss.
- Autonomous rotorcraft sniper systems. These are small, remotely operated sniper rifles that can be quickly launched into the air to attack opposing ground forces shielded behind buildings or in the landscape.
- Armed robotic vehicle assault light machines. Essentially robots with machine guns, bazookas, and rifles, which can control an area and return sniper fire almost instantly and with greater precision than any soldier.

American robot warfare technology is evolving extremely rapidly. Whereas the U.S. brought a handful of drones to the second Gulf War, it had thousands just a few years after. There are similar projects to enable enhanced situational awareness of the theater of war, including "smart dust": very small, camouflaged sensors (perhaps looking like pebbles or grains of sand) which listen to conversations, track motion, self-organize into virtual communication and tracking networks, and beam data to central interceptors. Ultimately, very large supercomputers could track all such data to flag what might require human attention.

Furthermore, America has pioneered a very efficient "privatization" of war by using so-called "PMFs" (private military firms) for facility protection, training, interrogation, etc.

So, in summary, America is big and mighty, and as war increasingly becomes information technology, America will retain or even further strengthen its leadership. It will in all likelihood remain the strongest military power in the world until 2050 and possibly far beyond.

However, within the foreseeable future, it will cease to be the world's *only* strong military power. China will eventually gain significant military strength too, and with two major military powers, we will probably see a replay of some of what we experienced during the Cold War: proxy wars about natural resources. It seems highly unlikely that nations will engage in direct military battle for access to water, energy, metals, etc., although such issues will cause frustration. Different Chinese authorities have from time to time seeded clouds to create local rainfall which has caused anger among those downwind.

Instead of outright resource wars, I think we will see unscrupulous Machiavellian politics, where the superpowers will support dictators militarily and economically, in return for long-term commodity purchase deals or land utilization rights—sorts of protection racket schemes, if you will. Furthermore, commodity price fluctuations may in themselves lead to economic upheaval in some countries. Very high oil prices could, for instance, lead to state failure in weak oil-importing nations such as Nepal, Laos, the Central African Republic, and the Congo.

———

However, there will be lots of wars, civil wars, and terror too, and most of it will come from poor nations that are stagnant, in decline, or which have disintegrated and "failed". In earlier chapters I described the economic future of wealthy and emerging nations, without giving any attention to this troubled minority. There are approx. 55 smaller nations with a combined population of approx. 1 billion, which means that, simply put, there are 1 billion rich people, 5 billion in rapid ascent, and 1 billion who are lost.

Most of the people in the bottom billion live in conditions that are reminiscent of Europe prior to 1450. Their leaders are tyrants, their knowledge is very limited, their health is poor, their environments filthy, their income minimal, and they are typically unhappy. They are also, as we shall see later, often aggressive and dangerous. Most of them live in Africa and the Middle East.

Much of the violence generated within and from these societies seems to revolve around religion. The largest religion in the world is Christianity, which has approx. 2.1 billion adherents, followed by Islam (approx. 1.5 billion), secularism/irreligious/agnostic/atheism (approx. 1.1 billion), Hinduism (0.9 billion), Chinese folk religion (0.4 billion), and Buddhism (0.4 billion).

While it is evident that many warriors cite religious dispute as their motive, I believe that the typical, real driver is other factors: desperation and decline in the poorest nations.

Paul Collier, who is professor of economics at Oxford University and former director of development research at the World Bank (which actually is not a bank, but an aid organization), has spent his entire career studying with different co-workers what causes the lack of progress in these nations. *The Bottom Billion,* as he calls them in a book of the same name, grew their economies by just 0.5% annually in the 1970s, declined 0.4% each year in the 1980s, and declined 0.5% in the 1990s. This is in stark contrast to the developing nations (the 5 billion in rapid ascent), whose economies on average grew 2.5% in the 1970s, then 4% in the 1980s and 1990s. Evidently, poverty is in itself not a trap, since all nations have been poor, and most are now either rich or in the process of becoming so.

Collier points out that those countries that have not taken part in globalization may simply have missed the boat and will be forced to wait for several decades before a new opportunity emerges for them. The reason, which Paul Krugman and Anthony Vanbales also pointed out in their 2000 study *Globalization and the Inequality of Nations* is simple. Imagine that you are a software company annum 1980 and you want to move some of your development to a country where salaries are 90% lower—say, to India. This sounds like a good business decision, but if you are the very first one to do so, you will be extremely concerned about access to talent mass, local legal environment, cultural gaps, etc. Doing so may be great, but it is very high risk. Twenty years later, the salary gap has halved but, on the other hand, thousands of companies

Map of the distribution of Christians of the world. *Sources*: Wikipedia; TheGreenEditor; CIA, *The World Factbook*; Census Bureau's statistical agencies.

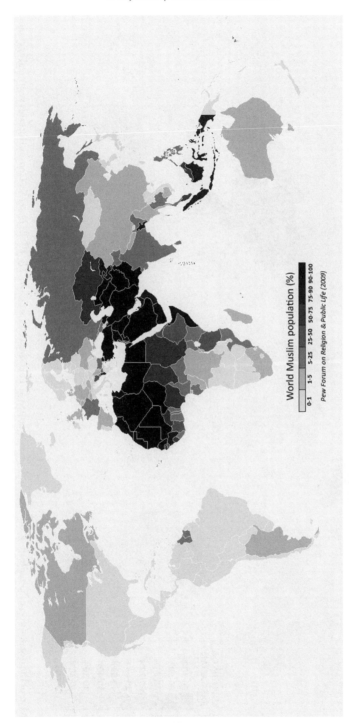

Map of the distribution of Muslims of the world. *Sources*: Wikipedia; TheGreenEditor; CIA, *The World Factbook*; Census Bureau's statistical agencies.

Map of the distribution of Buddhists of the world. *Sources*: Wikipedia; TheGreenEditor; CIA, *The World Factbook*; Census Bureau's statistical agencies.

Map of the distribution of Hindus of the world. *Sources:* Wikipedia; TheGreenEditor; CIA, *The World Factbook*; Census Bureau's statistical agencies.

have outsourced their development to India, the infrastructure and pitfalls are well-known, the talent base has grown, etc. India is now enjoying a great network effect, which feeds on itself. Outsourcing of biotech, auto-mobile manufacturing, IT services, etc. is now all going to developing nations that enjoy such network effects, and other poor nations are there-fore no longer considered as alternatives. And this will only change when the income gap between nations such as China or India, on the one hand, and bottom billion nations, on the other, has become very large—perhaps 1:10. *However, and this is the ultimate horror scenario: When we reach that point, robots will be far more efficient and reliable than the workers in these poor countries. They may simply be locked out for good.*

So, why did these poor nations miss the boat of globalization in the first place? Collier has narrowed the explanations to the misery of the lost billion down to five main problems: (1) being landlocked (2), having bad neighbors (3) having economies dominated by natural resource extraction, (4) having bad governance, and (5) having frequent conflicts, such as civil war.

If a country is landlocked, it needs to transport its exports via trucks or trains through a neighbor's territory, or perhaps focus on selling to its neighbors only. Both situations can be a hindrance to growth, especially if the neighboring countries are poor and have lousy infrastructure. If you look at a world map you will discover that there are surprisingly few landlocked countries. Latin America has just 2 landlocked countries out of 20 (Bolivia and Paraguay), Eastern Europe has some, and Asia very few. In fact, outside Africa, only 1% of the population lives in land-locked countries. But Africa is another matter—approx. 30% of Africa's population live in landlocked nations.

The problem of bad neighbors speaks for itself, and economies dominated by natural resource extraction are indicative of the traditional windfall problem, which discourages work and creativity. As for bad governance, this can include everything from kleptocracies (government corruption) to general corruption, psychopathic or incompetent leader-ship, socialism, or religious tyranny. Many such regimes are entirely unmanageable. The World Bank investigated in 2004 what happened to money released by the Ministry of Health in Chad to regional adminis-trations and 281 primary health care centers. Although regional administrations were officially allocated 60% of the Ministry's non-wage recurrent expenditures, the share that actually reached them was only 18%. Health centers, which are the frontline providers and the entry point for the population, received less than 1% of the Ministry's non-wage recurrent expenditures.

All of these problems can destroy the fabric of society and lead to a brain drain and money migration. Collier and his co-workers calculated, for instance, that approx. 38% of Africa's wealth was held abroad, even though Africa itself is capital-scarce and needs investments. The flight of money and minds from such countries will often accelerate over time. It is far easier to migrate once you have already gotten your money out (which is typically illegal), and it is much easier to settle in when you arrive, if some of your friends or family are already there to help you.

Collier's fifth bottom billion problem was conflict. *The typical low-income country is at peace 61% of the time, at war 24%, and in post-war conflict condition 15% of the time.* The latter is characterized by a tense social atmosphere, very high military spending, and massively elevated murder rates. Whereas the average cross-border conflict lasts approx. 6 months, the typical civil war will rage on for 5–6 years. It will lead to death, a capital and brain drain, disease, fear, elevated military spending, and will scare foreign investors away, etc. The typical civil war costs $64 billion and cuts 15% off GDP, much of it due to after-effects. Since there are on average approx. 2 new civil wars starting in poor countries each year, their combined cost is approx. $100 billion annually. There are also very long-term effects. Countries or areas undergoing civil war are very attractive for criminals and terrorists, because there is no functional law or police. This is why Osama Bin Laden was located in Afghanistan and why 95% of all drug production comes from civil war areas.

Collier has found no statistical correlation between civil war and political repression, colonial history, income inequality, or any of the numerous other ideological reasons given when one group attacks another. Nor is ethnic diversity a normal reason. Somalia is one of the most ethnically homogeneous populations in the world, and yet one of the most frequently engaged in civil conflict. Instead, what mattered was poverty and low-income growth. The math is simple: *If income in a poor country is half that in a rich country, then the poor country has twice the risk of civil war if they have an equal growth rate. Slow growth or negative growth adds considerably to war risk.* An average bottom billion country has a 14% risk of civil war in any 5-year period. If its annual economic growth rate is 3%, it reduces that risk to 12%. If it is −3%, the risk grows to 17%. Or if its economic growth rate is 10%, the risk of civil war within any 5-year period falls to 3%.

The leaders and instigators of a civil war will always claim some specific grievances or ideology to justify the violence, and they may in some cases believe in those. However, a rebellious movement will always attract sadists, drug dealers, common criminals, bounty hunters, etc. and, after some time, the ideology means very little. It becomes a financial protection racket, organized theft, a drug cartel, a death cult, a lifestyle, or a combination of them. Access to primary, exportable commodities such as gold or diamonds can increase the incentive for civil war and can prolong it by providing finance.

The number of civil wars in Latin America has declined very substantially since 1990, but it has risen in Subsaharan Africa and has for long been elevated in the Middle East and some parts of Asia. Collier published in 2003 the now famous report *Breaking the Conflict Trap: Civil War and the Development Policy* under the auspices of the World Bank. This included a statistical model to forecast the prevalence of conflict worldwide from 2003 to 2050. It predicted that *the number of civil wars would fall from a peak of 17 in the late 1980s to 15 in 2020 and 13 in 2050.* Furthermore, most failed states would remain in despair for a very long time. *The average duration of such a failed state has been 59 years.*

So, to conclude, it seems that *we shall see an average of approx. 14 ongoing civil wars between 2010 and 2050,* and as the average duration of these will be 5–6 years the implication is that *we will witness 2–3 new civil wars per year, with a total of around 100 new such wars starting during these 40 years.*

––––––––––

There is another common driver of violence: youth bulges. History tells us that if a society has a "male youth bulge" (a surplus of young men in the typical fighting age range of 15–29), it is extremely likely to have a big problem, unless the economy is really booming or the cultural life very rich. When people live on the countryside, the oldest son may inherit the farm or small family business, but for the 3 or 4 sons that perhaps follow in type 2b societies, there may be nothing meaningful to do at home, and the younger sons may even become envious of their older brother. So, they choose between four alternative ways to earn prestige and get a mission:

- emigrate
- start killing each other in gang wars or tribal wars
- start a civil war
- attack neighboring countries and civilizations.

After the bubonic plague outbreaks in the 15th century, Europe entered into an era of rapid population growth, which continued for several hundred years. A large number of local wars followed, but fortunately there was plenty of newly discovered land where the surplus population could settle, so they populated South and North America, Australia, New Zealand, South Africa, Rhodesia (now Zimbabwe), and many other countries, as I have described before. The European youth bulk came at a fortunate time, and while their migrations did create wars with indigenous populations like the American Indians, it also enabled the largely successful resettling of huge population surpluses. All of this worked, because Europe had already developed the rule of law (albeit in rustic forms), education systems, monetary and banking infrastructures, cultural diversity and splendor, and, most importantly, a tradition for technical innovation. The settlers created new business and prospered over time. So much so, in fact, that many of their new colonies even overtook their mother countries in terms of prosperity and are now among the richest countries in the world. America, Canada, Australia, and New Zealand are prime examples.

A youth bulk tends to become critical if those between age 15 and 29 constitute more than 30% of the population. When that is the case, and when it cannot be resolved by migration, the risk of mass killings seems to be around 90%. The worst example in modern times was Rwanda, where in 1994 between 500,000 to 1 million of its approx. 8 million inhabitants were killed in internal battles within a few months.

A few other examples: Palestine has approx. 25% unemployment. When Ariel Sharon erected walls to cut off Palestinian terrorists from their Israeli targets, the Palestinians almost immediately started fighting each other with the same brutality that they had used against the Jews, even deliberately targeting each other's children. Or when the Soviet Union decided to pull out of Afghanistan, the Afghani soldiers just changed from fighting Russians to fighting each other in endless battles. These fights are carried out by angry young men with no meaningful jobs, income, or honor. So, they turn to military heroism, which may even turn out to be a business, when someone pays them for fighting or per kill, as is often the case. There will always be an official justification, of course, but as we have seen in Afghanistan and other places, a warlord would often be willing to switch sides for money. Fighting was mainly about battle as a business, for revenge, honor, or as a lifestyle.

According to the *Arab Human Development Report 2009*, youth unemployment for Arab nations as a whole was a mind-boggling 30% in 2005–2006, with Iraq, Somalia, Algeria, and Sudan among the worst hit countries. *Each of these countries had over 40% youth unemployment.* Somalia had 47% unemployment in 2002.

A study by Population Action International, a Washington-based private advocacy group, showed that between 1970 and 1999 *80% of all civil conflicts in the world* occurred in countries where at least 60% of the population were under the age of 30. Another study by the National Intelligence Council in the U.S. showed that by 2008 there were 67 countries in the world with youth bulges and that 60 of them were undergoing some kind of civil war or mass killing.

The problem seems most acute when a population makes the transition from very high population growth to lower fertility—the stage when huge groups of young men reach working or fighting age, or when there is very high unemployment. In September 1928, a year before the Great Crash of 1929, Germany had 650,000 unemployed. Two years later it was 3,000,000, and by then Germany's manufacturing had fallen 17% from its 1927 level. In 1932 unemployment reached 30% of the workforce, or 5,102,000 in September of that year, and when Hitler came to power in 1933, the number had increased to over 6 million which created a very fertile ground for hatred, scapegoating, and aggression. One of Hitler's election promises had been to eliminate unemployment and one of his methods for doing so was to increase arms production and expand the army from 100,000 in 1933 to 1.4 million in 1939. The number of Germans killed during the subsequent war was roughly equal to the number of unemployed when Hitler took over.

The diversion of unemployed men to violence does not only directly affect these men and their enemies, but also creates a pervasive aggressive culture throughout society. Exactly this phenomenon is happening in much of Africa and the Middle East.

The NATO nations fighting in Afghanistan have first-hand experience of the symptoms of youth bulge. Many of the soldiers coming from, say, America or Poland, are the only sons of their families, but many of those they fight may be one of many sons from very large families, who do not value life equally highly. While virtually all parents love their children, the willingness in society to potentially sacrifice a son probably increases when each family has many. And whereas the NATO forces have huge military superiority in direct conflict, the number of enemies just keeps growing. About 500,000 Afghan boys reach fighting age every year, and at least 200,000 of those have no jobs.

The maps on the next page show youth bulges in different countries around the world—the ones with the darkest tints have the highest proportion of young people. What this shows is that most of Northern Africa, Iran, Pakistan and many other nations will likely come off the boil by 2025 or sooner, whereas the current conflict zones of Afghanistan,

Iraq, Yemen, Somalia, and Sudan will remain among the countries that continue to produce huge surpluses of young men. Unlike the case of Europe which had its youth bulge several hundred years ago, these men will have very limited opportunity to migrate, so it seems very likely that many of them will turn to violence. This in turn will prevent their societies from developing and will thus keep them trapped in misery.

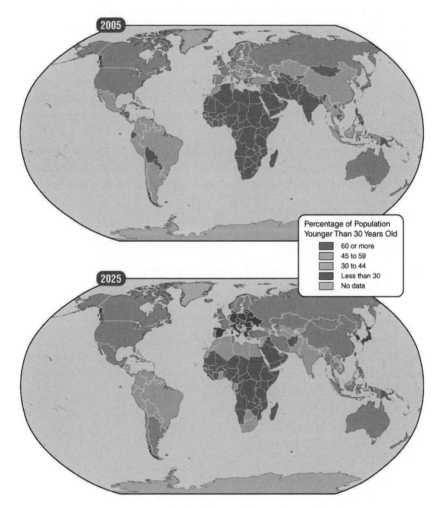

Youth bulges across the world, 2005 and 2025 (estimated) *Source*: *Global Trends 2025: A Transformed World*, National Intelligence Council, 2008.

In addition to the predictable effects of a youth bulge combined with extremely high unemployment, many Arab countries struggle with an internal conflict between so-called "secular" forces favoring some of the transitions that Europe went through over a number of centuries (Renaissance, Reformation, Enlightenment, and female emancipation), and others who fiercely oppose these forces (and perhaps more than anything the increasing emancipation of women). Furthermore, there may also be social dimensions to this, where poor people are upset by the wealth of the ruling classes, hatred of Israel for occupying Arab land, and of Western nations for protecting Israel, let alone invading Iraq and Afghanistan, etc. Furthermore, lots of young men in some of these places are not allowed to listen to music, dance, watch movies, have girlfriends, or congregate with girls outside their immediate family in public places. So, in addition to having no jobs, no source of income, and no pride, they may not have much to do. Combine that with a large youth bulge and we are almost certain to see even more violence over the coming decades.

The number of wars and terror in Africa and the Middle East is truly horrible. The list below is by no means complete, but it illustrates the relentless process of violence in these two regions in just 10 years (2000–2010):

- South Lebanon conflict (2000)
- Al-Aqsa Intifada (2000)
- Central African Republic Civil War (2001–2003)
- Afghanistan War (2001–)
- Ivory Coast Civil War (2002–2003)
- Islamic insurgency in the Maghreb (2002–)
- Operation Enduring Freedom—Horn of Africa (2002–)
- War in Darfur (2003–)
- Iraq War (2003–)
- France–Ivory Coast clashes (2004–)
- Conflict in the Niger Delta (2004–)
- Central African Republic Bush War (2004–)
- Kivu conflict (2004–)
- Civil War in Chad (2005–)
- Mount Elgon insurgency (2005–2008)
- Lebanon War (2006)
- Rise of the Islamic Courts Union (2006)
- Fatah al-Islam and the Lebanese Army (2007)
- Ethiopian War in Somalia (2006–2009)
- Operation Enduring Freedom—Trans Sahara (2007–)
- Second Tuareg Rebellion (2007–)

- Kenyan crisis (2007–2008)
- Invasion of Anjouan (2008)
- Israel–Gaza conflict (2008–2009)
- Djibouti–Eritrea border conflict (2008)
- Islamist civil war in Somalia (2009–)
- Taliban insurgency in Nigeria (2009–)
- Israeli bombing of Sudan (2009).

In addition to these 28 larger conflicts, several military coups as well as *more than a thousand individual acts of terror, kidnappings, and piracy*—committed by Middle Easterners and North Africans—took place during these 10 years. The problem is enormous—a new major conflict every 4 months, and an attack on innocent civilians several times per week.

It should be said here, of course, that terror as a concept is far from new, although the current extent of it is. In the 1880s America experienced a wave of anarchist terror, which continued until around 1920. It was about that time that international anti-colonial terrorism began, only to fade around 1960, whereas a new wave of terrorism—Marxist terror—broke out in Europe and other places. While there are still remnants of the latter in some emerging markets, it has largely disappeared and is completely absent in developed nations. The IRA laid down its arms after 40 years of terror. ETA in Spain is still active, but perhaps fading. So, yes, there have been many terror movements, and four commonalities about them are that

- They have typically suffered from significant internal strife (with members often killing each other).
- The have almost always become increasingly dominated by career criminals, psychopaths, and sadists.
- They have on average lasted approx. 40 years.

None of this should be taken as a forecast, of course, and given the magnitude of the youth bulk issue and the complexity of underlying issues, the current wave of terror might very well continue for longer. Islamic terrorism began in earnest in 1979, which sent some of the Islamic world into decline at exactly the same time as much of Asia and Latin America began their rapid ascent. However, the fact that Islamic terror took off in 1979 does not make it likely that it will only last 40 years, like average terror movements have; there exist a whole spectrum of independent terror movements which may each have their own destiny and timeline. It seems technically impossible for terrorists to achieve anything from their acts and in the short term it is equally technically impossible for governments to stop the process, as long as it is nourished by youth bulges. Neither side can win, and it seems that the only way it can end is by eventually fading with the passage of time.

———

In addition to looking at why violence may occur, it is interesting to consider the conditions for peace. Why, for instance, has most of Europe been peaceful since 1945, given the previous history of constant internal wars? I can see several reasons for this transition.

First, the most basic change is that the European youth bulge and hordes of unemployed young men has disappeared because of changing demographics combined with a healthy, creative business environment. Also, society offers an abundance of outlets for young men's energies, whether in fashion, art, luxury, travel, sport, wellness, movies, music, web/print media, bars, restaurants, or night clubs, as well as endless opportunities to engage in education, politics, altruistic projects, or professional careers.

In contrast, there is now the beginnings of an old people bulge, but the elderly are very rarely warmongers. They don't want war, nor do most women. Furthermore, people travel a lot, typically have friends or perhaps even holiday homes in neighboring countries, and, as a result of globalization, may also be financially, commercially, and personally engaged in foreign nations. The number of cross-country marriages and mixed nationality children is booming. For all these reasons, populations in neighboring countries are no longer stereotyped, which eliminates the desire to wage war against them. A third reason why people don't want war may be rising IQs—people are probably significantly more intelligent on average than they were during the two world wars. And, finally, as society has become more pluralistic and diverse, it is virtually impossible to mobilize large hordes in pursuit of a single, aggressive cause.

Another factor is that European countries have all become democratic, which means that if a psychopathic politician should call for offensive aggression, people can avoid it by not electing or re-electing him. This may be important, because many wars in the past have probably been started by megalomaniac, psychopathic, sadistic, imbecile, or incompetent leaders looking for a diversion from their own failures, or seeking personal glory.

Drivers of war and peace	
War	*Peace*
Lack of entrepreneurship, high unemployment	Healthy business environment, low unemployment
Youth bulge	Aging population; no youth bulge
Low status of females	Female emancipation
Male surplus	Natural male–female balance
Low average IQs	High average IQs
Insular mentality, limited international tourism	Increased overseas traveling and property ownership
Limited/restricted leisure life	Diverse leisure life opportunities
Protectionist/nationalist business policies	Commercial globalization
Totalitarian rule	Democracy
Low income and/or low growth	High income and/or high growth
Primarily commodity-dependent economy	Economy depending on creative sectors, service, or manufacturing

However, some Islamic nations may actually be heading for calmer waters within the foreseeable future. Most of the North African nations have demographic profiles similar to those the Asian Tiger countries had just before they took off economically. Iran has seen one of the steepest declines in fertility anywhere, which should lead it to a demographic profile that is typically associated with more peaceful behavior. It may in fact be that these countries develop much as Southern and Eastern Europe have done. It should not be forgotten that it wasn't very long ago that Greece, Italy, Spain, Yugoslavia, Rumania, Bulgaria, Albania, etc. were under totalitarian rule. Now it seems like that was light-years ago.

Other totalitarian nations may change relatively peacefully. The most likely candidate seems to be *North Korea*, which could collapse like the Soviet Bloc—abruptly and with very little prior warning. *Cuba* could liberalize, and leadership changes in *Sudan, Zimbabwe, Belarus, Myanmar,* and *Turkmenistan* could lead to less misery for their peoples.

In spite of all the violence we have experienced and can expect, the reality is that the decades following World War II have been exceptionally peaceful compared with almost any previous era of historical time. One of the main reasons may be that the number of democratic nations grew from 20 in 1945 to more than 80. Over the last 200 years there have barely been any cases of two democratic nations fighting each other. Other contributing factors to this relative peace may be increased wealth, women's education, and globalization.

It seems likely that the age where two uniformed, state-sponsored armies engage in war is virtually over. I think a likely scenario will be one of almost entirely asymmetric warfare. On one side will be terror, insurgencies, politically motivated kidnappings, piracy, and other individual acts of violence, where none of the international conventions of warfare is respected. Women, children, embassy staff, aid workers, journalists, and places of worship will be deliberately targeted.

On the other side will be robotic, remote-controlled forces, which will seek to respect human rights conventions, but which will fight without risks to its soldiers. In other words: *War and terror will become dual-asymmetric,* and for as long as youth bulge problems increase and many nations are excluded from participation in globalization, there will be violence.

I believe that nations suffering from terrorism at some point will agree on a set of rules to regulate how terrorists can legally be dealt with. To date, our legal system is prepared to deal with three concepts of malfeasance: (1) crimes against humanity, (2) normal crime, and (3) war. The main issue with terrorism is that it's the only sort of crime where the objective is to inflict maximum pain on the largest possible number of innocent civilians. This means that states with the threat of terrorism hanging over them have enormous incentive to arrest the terrorists *before* they commit their planned acts, which is antithetical to the conventions of common criminal law. Furthermore, since terrorists neither declare war, nor surrender like armies, you cannot release them and trust that they will not try again—in fact, they often will. So, the rules of warfare do not work here. As for international regulations relating to crimes against humanity, first, terrorism doesn't fit some of the definitions, such as being condoned or ordered by governments or de facto powers, and, second, the legal system is far too slow to prevent anything. Therefore, I believe that a number of nations will agree to develop a fourth system to regulate this issue.

———————

I can imagine a positive scenario in which *youth bulges fade, emerging market incomes increase, women become liberated, and the average age of the global population increases—all of which will lead to a much more peaceful planet.*

However, there is a more disturbing scenario, where some of the bottom billion nations remain stuck in cycles of violence, where they get excluded from globalization because robots will surpass them, before the income gap makes them attractive for international businesses, and where, as I shall explain later, people in rich nations start to modify their own genes to create super-intelligence, thus *leaving the losers not only culturally, economically, and politically handicapped, but even massively outclassed biologically.* In this scenario, these nations missed the boat, which will not come back.

I think we will see some of both scenarios.

Likely geopolitical events over the coming decades

- There will be between 100 and 150 acts of terror, kidnappings, and piracy per year, perhaps totaling around 5,000 between 2010 and 2050. The most likely sources will be youth bulge/conflict cycle countries like Pakistan, Afghanistan, Yemen, and Somalia.
- Global power politics will become more cynical, as several power centers finance ruthless dictators in exchange for commodity/land use deals.
- Some bottom billion regimes, including Nepal, Laos, the Central African Republic, and Congo could fail if oil prices go very high.
- Several totalitarian states, including Cuba, Sudan, Zimbabwe, Belarus, Myanmar, Turkmenistan. and North African states may become more democratic and start integrating more into the international community. The North Korean regime may collapse.
- Between 2 and 3 new civil wars may start per year, reaching a total of around 100 between 2010 to 2050, and ongoing civil wars may average out at approx. 14 over the same period.

Part IV

Supersectors

This part summarizes the effects of supertrends and concludes that seven sectors will do particularly well between 2010 and 2050:

- Finance, which is an information business, will benefit from economic growth and development of a credit and trading culture in emerging markets. Furthermore, it will participate in the funding of a massive construction boom plus the financing of countless high-tech startups in genomics, IT, and alternative energy.
- The real estate sector will construct new housing for 100 million people per year between 2010 and 2050, and will construct the commercial infrastructure necessary to quadruple global income. As global wealth also quadruples while land supply is static, some land prices will rise very dramatically.
- The resources industry—in particular, the mining of industrial metals—will struggle to keep up with demand, which will lead to occasional large price spikes. Fossil energy will shift towards shale gas and oil, as well as tar oil.
- Alternative energy will be an exciting and innovative growth industry driven by exploding energy demand, desires to achieve energy independence, and fear of global warming. Third-generation nuclear energy, and second, third, and fourth-generation biofuels and photovoltaic solar power will be among the most exciting technologies.
- Genomics and biotech will evolve exponentially and will create huge advantages in healthcare (which will be sorely needed due to

global aging), farming, and biofuel. There will also be controversial developments such as attempts to create superhumans and re-create extinct species.

- IT will continue to evolve exponentially, and the best computers will rival the human brain around 2020. We will simulate the human neocortex (analytical and intuitive intelligence, but not emotion). The products and services coming out of IT will be amazing and will include robots, creative computers, and software that can provide scientifically based answers to almost any questions within a very short time.

- The market for luxury will grow extremely rapidly and will generate outsize profits for its lead players. Demand will be driven by an overall increase in human wealth and in particular by a brand hunger from the rapidly growing middle and upper classes in emerging markets.

People will increasingly feel free to define their own identity, spirituality, and way of life. In terms of lifestyles, there will be a trend towards creativity, individuality, and authentic charm. The throw-away culture will give way to a preference for things that last and age well. Patina will be more valued.

Furthermore, the market for experiences and storytelling will grow rapidly, and leading companies will hire media professionals to create and tell their stories. This will be particularly popular in sport, finance, luxury, and food/health.

The fastest growing job markets will be creative jobs and storytelling, plus service jobs, where the human touch is valued as such.

For more information:
www.supersectors.com

10

The shape of things to come

I would like to summarize now what I have described regarding the cycles and trends that we can expect, and I think a good angle is to think of development curves and their shapes, starting with exponential curves.

There is something that tends to strike people when they look at exponential curves: The last part to the right will often seem to go straight up—almost as if it will fall backwards. Take a look at this population graph, for instance

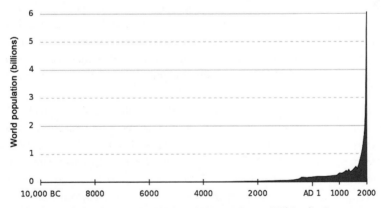

World population (estimate) 10000 BC–2000 AD. *Source*: Wikipedia Commons.

The last part of that curve is indeed extreme, and the whole thing looks overwhelming. Alternatively, take a look at curves of computer performance development, average incomes, or consumption of numerous products, and they look very similar; like everything has been very dull for ages, but then they took off and right now we are in a spike phase.

However, if you cut off the same curves at an earlier time and optimized the graph space as computers automatically do, they would look the same. The population growth 30 years ago would (in 1980) show that "now, right now we are in the spike phase!" Same in 2010.

There is another issue with exponential curves that captivates people: If the curves continue as they visually seem poised to do, the numbers become so unreal that you can't make sense of them. Scary!

However, the reality is that things that can't continue indefinitely, won't. Sometimes they just fade, and the curve becomes "S"-shaped, and at other times they crash, making the curve a spike, but real-life exponential processes cannot last. The population curve above, for instance, has (as previously described) already started to decelerate, although it is difficult to see in the graph. It should, as discussed earlier, peak at close to 9 billion around 2050. What comes after is hard to say, but if the recent fertility or population decline in an increasing number of rich countries is any indicator, then it should actually begin to decline when more and more countries get rich. The spike we see on the graphs will then smooth out to be an S-shaped growth phase which after 2050 gets replaced with stabilization, or most likely a gradual decline.

———

So, how will all the different phenomena I have discussed so far shape up? Let's start with the most obvious: The three categories of *business cycles*. These are inherently cyclical, of course, and I am convinced that they will remain with us for the foreseeable future. There will be a continued tendency towards mode-locking, which means that we may have a major crash every 18–20 years on average, and a significant one every 9–10 years.

I think *bubbles*, *crashes*, and *scares* could be called "semi-cyclical". The conditions for bubbles are largely created by economic booms, which make them partially forced by business cycles. It takes a bit of time after there has been a crash before people are silly enough to create a new bubble, but apparently not much. As for the scares, there is zero cyclicality concerning when the events that scare us are discovered, but there seems to be some basic lust for scares, which means that if there hasn't been one for a while, we will just invent one.

Other phenomena include S-shapes. We can start with the ones we can be most sure about. I have already mentioned the first of these: global *population growth*, which, simply stated, began to accelerate around 1000 BC. It then added momentum approx. 2,000 years later, or around 1000 AD, and accelerated further towards 1500, until it finally began to decelerate in 1963. Since we already number 7 billion people and the peak should be 9 billion, we are obviously around two-thirds of the way through the S here.

The next S-shape is global *aging*, which is evidently lagging the deceleration and subsequent stagnation of the global population. We are still in the early stages of this process.

What about *female emancipation*? I believe that we have moved into the late part of that process for mature societies but are still in the early part for many emerging markets, especially in many Islamic communities. Globally we may be around the midpoint of the S. Once women reach parity with men or perhaps surpass them in a few areas like tertiary education, it has to stabilize.

As for *human intelligence*, it gets more interesting. Perhaps we are slowly approaching a natural leveling phase in the most developed countries—there are indications that the rise has stopped in Denmark and the U.K. However, if we begin to manipulate our own genes for higher IQ as I would expect, we will start on a new and much faster IQ growth phase later—perhaps from approx. 2050. I will address human intelligence later, but there are records of people with IQs beyond 200, which may enable them to read and write numerous languages by the age of 3 or 4, for instance, and attend university at the age of 10. So, biologically, extreme intelligence is clearly possible—it's just still rare.

Human knowledge and *cultural diversity* should both continue to rise in what are probably S-curves—they are both very far from any leveling.

I think it is also pretty obvious that *urbanization* follows an S-curve, since not everyone on Earth will need to or want to live in cities. It may even be that it reverses once global population peaks. One factor that could facilitate such a reversal would be continuous improvements in IT, which makes it even easier to telecommute not only for intellectual work, but also for physical work done through the remote management of robots. The way military drones are operated via satellite from across the globe is an extreme example of this.

How about *wealth*? As long as the world population keeps growing, we keep innovating, and emerging markets keep catching up, I think it will be supercharged, However, population growth is decelerating and emerging markets will catch up one by one. I think the next 20–30 years might be the steepest point in the S-curve of wealth creation, after which it will decelerate somewhat. Having said that, even if the world population begins to decline after 2050, income per capita may continue to rise, at least for several more centuries if not almost forever, as people will still innovate.

Globalization? Globalization is roaring ahead but, as all societies open up and as opportunities of utilizing differences in exchange rates, knowledge, labor costs, etc. get arbitraged away through the free flow of people, money, and ideas, the globalization process will start to decelerate. Deceleration may simply be triggered by currency appreciation in emerging markets. I would guess we will see a peak in globalization between 2020 and 2040.

Will inflation come back?

The deflationary forces of the post-1980 structural boom are driven by innovation and globalization. However, as savings rates begin to decline in emerging markets such as China, and as their salaries and currencies advance, the deflationary globalization force will be spent. Assuming that this cannot be entirely compensated for by increased use of robots, we may see an increasing inflationary pressure emerge later in the boom.

It all becomes a bit more difficult when we look at innovation in *IT*. For how long will we be able to deliver ever-faster computer hardware? Will we succeed with quantum computers or not? What I think might happen here is what one often sees in any given industry: A period with S-shaped growth, followed by some leveling until a new paradigm is invented, which starts the next S-shaped advance. Ultimately it may turn out that we are still very much in the early stages of what we will achieve.

As for *biotech* I think it is obvious that we are in the early stages, and progress will probably be extremely intense until around 2050.

The question, which is perhaps most politically charged, is how we will fare in terms of *environmental strain* and *resource shortage*. As regards pollution, we know the following:

- Primitive populations can destroy their own environment and often do so by forest clearance for agricultural purposes. However, this normally doesn't start until their population grows out of control.
- We also know that populations that go through early industrialization always create huge pollution.
- We know that once countries reach GDP per capita levels somewhere around $10,000–$15,000, they will start to pollute less per person, and that their populations will at the same time typically stabilize.

- We know that when nations get even richer, their environment will improve further, and their population will often begin to decline.

I think that the conclusion to draw from this is that environmental strain as a whole in a country tends to be bell-shaped, and that the growth phase lags economic growth by a few decades. However, that doesn't mean that every aspect of the environment moves in parallel. Some environmental damage may simply not be understood initially and will thus be left unaddressed for longer than more obvious problems. One example of this was the depletion of the ozone layer, which went on until it was discovered and regulation against damaging CFC production was introduced, resulting in a sharp emission reduction in 1987 and total phaseout by 1996, which should lead to resolving the ozone problem with the passage of time. Potential issues with carbon dioxide were also unaddressed for a very long time and will continue to build for decades before the trend finally turns.

What about *resources*? The human use of resources has generally moved in an exponential slope upwards. Despite the world population peaking around 9 billion people, its wealth may continue to grow for a very long time beyond that. It therefore seems that our demand for resources will continue to grow. But can supply meet demand forever?

I think it is useful to divide supply into three main categories: (1) food and water, (2) energy, and (3) metals. As for food and water, we know that this is renewable, but also that it may not be available in sufficient quantities where parts of the population live, and that drinking water can get contaminated by pollution. I think it is reasonable to expect that we have the technology to solve both problems, but that poor people may not be able to pay for that.

Regarding energy, I think there will be increased demand for many centuries, but that we will go through a series of technology transitions which will move us away from fossil fuel and toward renewable sources and fusion energy. During this process prices may spike very high for periods. However, ultimately energy will be virtually limitless and very, very cheap.

Finally, let us look at metals; there is no way that we can keep ramping production up exponentially. Ultimately, the Earth is one huge ball of commodities, of course, and we are only scratching the surface to get them. So, yes, ultimately the resources are in a sense virtually unlimited. However, from a practical point of view there will come times when the cost of extracting gets ever more prohibitive (even though the cost of energy may become minimal and robots abundant), and the result will be that we increasingly replace metals with synthetic materials such as carbon, plastic, etc. Apart from that we will evidently get better at recycling what has already been extracted, and there may also come a time in the very distant future when we start mining comets and other planets. But meanwhile there may be some real supply squeezes which drive prices sky high.

What all of this amounts to is a world that will be characterized by the 20 dynamic drivers shown in the table on pp. 204–205.

It is important to note that for each of these drivers there is a countertrend. When financial markets tank, there are bearish hedge funds making money by going against the grain. When panic is at its most extreme, the vultures buy while almost everyone else seems to sell. Similarly, when telecommunication seems to penetrate every corner of society more people seek holidays and leave their mobiles at home. When cities are built of concrete, steel, and glass, the prices of rustic holiday homes made of wood and stone go up. When human wealth explodes, an increasing number choose the money-less life of hippies. When building control systems become more and more sophisticated and sometimes trigger cascading failures, some will go back to simple, standalone things with nothing but on/off buttons.

Another aspect that is always relevant is that the new often doesn't replace the old. What mostly happens is that it becomes an added choice, which means that it adds to the diversity.

However, through all of it, one thing seems clear. Mankind is heading towards an extremely intense phase in our development. There will be huge challenges and much of it will be dreadful and scary. However, the primary driver of the world is, and always has been, what completely normal people do every day. This may not end up in the history books or news broadcasts. However, it does show in the statistics, which may tell a completely different story than the news.

––––––––

Over the coming generation there will be lots and lots to do for these normal people. There will be huge opportunities for entrepreneurs, businessmen, and investors. There will also be a large growth in creative and interesting job opportunities.

The question is: In which sectors will it be? If you are a student considering a scientific or commercial/financial career, where should you look? If you are a skilled entrepreneur, where is it that you may start up with very little money and get to see your venture become a great company, maybe even within relatively few years—perhaps getting your initial investment back 1,000 times?

Or, if you are an investor, which assets and which sectors will be most profitable in the coming decades? Where is it that you may get your money back 10 times in 10 years, if your timing and selection is good?

I think that there are always two factors to look out for: rapid growth and a great profit model. As for rapid growth, the big drivers will be population growth, urbanization, aging, global middle-class and upper-class expansion, and innovation in IT, genomics/biotech, and alternative energy. Regarding great profit models, I can think of 40 which are frequently practiced, and which can be divided into 8 main categories:

- *Asset-based.* Invent, create, or acquire a desirable asset.
- *Network-based.* Let the commercial ecosystem around you drive your business forward.
- *Speed-based.* Do things generally faster than the competition, or be first with something new, or buy and sell when the timing is just right.
- *Customer relationship–based.* Instead of selling products, think about the client and sell them what they really need: solutions.
- *Cost-based.* Find a way to produce cheaper than the competition.
- *Financial timing–based.* Actively time investment around business cycles, sentiment fluctuations, etc.
- *Financial arbitrage–based.* Utilize differences in the value or yield of two investment objects or asset classes.
- *Active financial–based.* As you invest, involve yourself actively in the underlying asset and enhance it.

I have listed all 40 in the table at the top of p. 206, and there is further explanation to each of them at *www.supersectors.com*

One of the markets that springs to mind is real estate, which will benefit from the wall of money from emerging markets plus urbanization, population growth, changing age structure, etc. There will be opportunities in building all that new property, of course, but perhaps more in investing in land. As the amount of attractive land is virtually static, prices may go extremely high in some areas. Some common profit models in real estate will include active business cycle timing, prime asset collecting, and asset enhancing. For developers, they will also involve wholesale to retail.

When people build real estate on a massive scale, when 70–90 million people enter the middle class every year, and when we need to finance a new energy infrastructure, we need funding, which opens up a huge

#	Driver	Description	Shape
		The 20 main drivers of civilization for the coming decades	
1	Inventory cycles	Small economic cycles	Cyclical; peaks every 4–5 years on average
2	Capital spending cycles	Larger economic cycles driven by investments in machinery, equipment, etc.	Cyclical; peaking on average every 9–10 years
3	Property cycles	Very large economic cycles driven by construction of and investment in property and leading to banking crises	Cyclical; peaking on average every 18–20 years
4	Bubbles and crashes	Financial bubbles followed by crashes, happening on average every 3 years	Semi-cyclical; on average every 3 years
5	Scares	Excessive panic waves relating to the environment, technology, and health	Semi-cyclical; on average every 3 years
6	Population growth	World population grows by 2 billion from 2010 to 2050. This is approx. 30% growth	Either partly bell-shaped or S-shaped. In either case peaking around 2050
7	Aging	Number of elderly more than trebles between 2020 and 2050 as it grows by 1.6 billion	Bell-shaped with peak some decades after 2050
8	Female emancipation	Women will vastly outnumber men in tertiary education and will want to have more of a career and fewer children	S-shaped followed by leveling, perhaps between 2030 and 2040
9	Human intelligence	Average human intelligence increases 0.3% annually as societies develop	S-shaped followed by leveling as human health reaches natural peak. However, new and steeper cycle will take over when genetic engineering of humans becomes common
10	Human knowledge	Probably doubling every 8–9 years	Doubling speed may accelerate as computers become creative. Doubling time may subsequently increase, but probably not before 2050
11	Cultural diversity	Continued fusion of cultures and ideas across most of the globe	S-shaped, but may be disrupted by war and terror

\#	Driver	Description	Shape
		The 20 main drivers of civilization for the coming decades (*cont.*)	
12	Urbanization	The number of people living in urban environments will grow by 3 billion between 2010 and 2050	S-shaped followed by leveling perhaps around 2050
13	Emerging market wealth growth	Emerging market GDP will grow by more than $100 trillion from 2010 to 2050, and their wealth will increase by 4–5 times that much	S-shaped, perhaps followed by less pronounced growth after 2040
14	Globalization	Continued increase in the flow of money, people, ideas, and products between and within nations	S-curve followed by leveling or cyclical fluctuations. Perhaps reaching plateaus between 2020 and 2040
15	IT innovation	Exponential increase in chip performance; computers exceeding human brain around 2020	Probably a series of S-curves interrupted by leveling
16	Bio-technology innovation	Exponential increase in biotechnological knowledge and products; gene manipulation	S-curve and then leveling, perhaps around 2050
17	Environmental strain	Improving environments in most developed economies overshadowed by deteriorating environments in many emerging markets	Bell-shaped curves, with different overall peaks depending on issue
18	Resource shortage	Supply constraints on resources leading to price spikes. Food and water eventually resolved. Eventually access to virtually unlimited cheap and clean energy	Supply is a series of S-curves extending almost infinitely
19	Wars and terror	Between 100 and 150 acts of terror, kidnappings, and piracy per year, perhaps totaling around 5,000 from 2010 to 2050. Furthermore, between 2 and 3 new civil wars starting per year, with a total of around 100 new such wars starting from 2010 to 2050, and an average of ongoing civil wars of approx. 14	Very long bell-shaped curve
20	Governmental protection rackets for commodity producers	Governments support dictators who control natural resources with arms and money in return for guaranteed access to resources	Bell-shaped curve

The 40 leading profit models in the world			
Overall strategy category	*Specific strategy*	*Overall strategy category*	*Specific strategy*
Asset-based	• Mining and farming • Brand-building • Disruptive invention • Build-to-be-bought • Blockbuster • Asset enhancing • Profit multiplier • Converting to luxury	Customer relationship-based	• Wholesale to retail • Secondary sales • Mass customizing • Central aggregator • Solutions provider • Niche dominator • Price differentiator • Converting to service • Converting to sharing • Converting to digital
Cost control-based	• Critical scaling • Low-cost business • Location arbitrage	Speed-based	• First-mover advantage • Organized for speed
Financial timing-based	• Business cycle timing • Technical timing • Vulture investing	Network-based	• Community-building • Platform and standard creating • Digital exchange
Financial arbitrage-based	• Carry trading • Prime asset collecting • Relative value arbitrage • Event-driven trading • Liquidity arbitrage	Active financial-based	• Venture capital • Turnaround • Buyout • Activist investment • Risk averaging • Consolidation play

growth market for *global finance*—especially in emerging markets. Many of these growth markets haven't developed a credit culture yet, and as they do their banks might benefit. Furthermore, financing as a whole will be able to pursue the financial strategies described among the 40 above. Finance is in a way a sector that can play across a very wide spectrum of all the main developments in the future.

The growth in emerging markets will also drive the demand for *commodities*. This story is fairly simple: It could very well be that supply cannot be ramped up fast enough, in which case prices and producer profits may go very high, which will make business cycle timing and mining strategies very interesting. There will also be great opportunities for disruptive innovation such as using genomics and advanced recovery technologies.

The demand for alternative energy will be driven by emerging market demand, requirements to reduce emissions, and by the desire to reduce or stop transfers of wealth to aggressive nations. The most important commercial business models here will be disruptive innovation, first-mover advantage, build-to-be-bought, and venture capital. As the market matures there will also be huge opportunities for consolidation plays.

Information technology is interesting because of its incredible speed of innovation, which creates ever more new and compelling products. It provides rich opportunities to do disruptive inventions, and for startups to build-to-be-bought. One extremely important aspect here is the possibility to create network effects by creating, for instance, online communities or acting as a central aggregator.

Genomics and biotech are facing an innovation speed that is probably as fast as, or even faster than IT; it has many of the same characteristics as IT, even though network effects are far less common here. Three commercial business models that work particularly well here are disruptive innovation, blockbuster, and critical scaling. Financially there will be a lot of small companies pursuing build-to-be-bought and a lot of consolidation plays, since biotech tends to work best in very large companies due to enormous single-product risks and very large overheads.

I have earlier defined leisure as 12 different business areas (travel, fashion, wellness, luxury, sports, restaurants, etc.), but there is one among those 12 that I think will stand out: *Luxury*. Luxury will benefit from the coming wealth explosion; it will also be able to protect very high margins due to brand-building effects. The relevant value strategies in luxury include asset enhancing, converting to luxury, community-building, critical scaling, consolidation plays, and prime asset collecting.

The following seven chapters will be dedicated to the seven sectors I have just listed, and for each of them I will try to explain what is going on and why. I will start with what is the world's biggest sector by a huge margin if you measure by trading volume: finance.

The seven supersectors		
Sector	*Core drivers*	*Profit drivers*
1. Finance	Plays key roles in emerging market expansion, innovation, and energy infrastructure transition	• Business cycle timing • Technical timing • Vulture investing • Carry trading • Prime asset collecting • Relative value arbitrage • Event-driven trading • Liquidity arbitrage
2. Real estate	Accommodates global urbanization, age transition, population growth, and wealth growth	• Business cycle timing • Prime asset collecting • Asset enhancing • Wholesale to retail
3. Commodities	Meets massive demand from emerging market expansion	• Business cycle timing • Mining and farming strategies • Disruptive innovation • Consolidation plays
4. Alternative energy	Meets emerging market demand, reduces carbon emissions, reduces wealth transfers to aggressive nations	• Disruptive innovation • First-mover advantage • Build-to-be-bought • Venture capital • Consolidation plays

The seven supersectors (*cont.*)		
Sector	*Core drivers*	*Profit drivers*
5. Genomics and biotech	Incredible innovation enables second green revolution, break-throughs in healthcare, third- and fourth-generation biofuels and more	• Disruptive innovation • Blockbuster • Critical scaling • Build-to-be-bought • Consolidation plays
6. Information technology	Computers soon to match and surpass human intelligence; bandwidth, storage, mobile batteries, etc. continue to become better and cheaper. Enormous numbers of new applications will be possible	• Organized for speed • Disruptive inventions • Build-to-be-bought • Community-building • Platform and standard creating • Digital exchange
7. Luxury	Benefits from coming wealth explosion and extreme demand from emerging markets	• Asset enhancing • Converting to luxury • Community-building • Critical scaling • Consolidation • Prime asset collecting

11

Finance

When I was young I was excited when I got accepted at a university in Denmark to study for an M.Sc. in engineering. Soon after, I took out subscriptions to various business newspapers and magazines, so I could begin to familiarize myself with how the real world worked before I joined it. However, from reading these every day, I slowly developed the impression the world didn't seem to be run by engineers. An engineer, it seemed, was typically a nice guy with velvet jeans and a Volvo, who was passionate for his technology and for what it could achieve. However, the engineer would very often have a boss, who was a marketing guy with a suit, a tight-knotted silk tie, and perhaps a BMW. That guy decided what companies were supposed to do, which meant that he decided what the engineers should do, or indeed if they should do anything at all.

But the marketing guy would ultimately report to a finance guy, who shaved twice daily and made a lot of money. This guy decided which companies should be sold, merged, expanded, or even shut down. So, no money; no marketing guy. No marketing guy; no engineer. The finance people ran the world.

I know this is a simplification, but it impressed me enough to start studying for an MBA during evenings, and today, having worked as engineer, marketing guy, and finance guy for 30 years, I still see it mainly that way. The finance guys (or girls) are typically the kings.

———

Finance is huge. In 2004 the total trading in derivatives/forex (which I will explain later) constituted almost 30 times global GDP, and in 2007 it had grown to approx. 46 times global GDP. If we add in trading in bonds and equities, we reach approx. *50 times GDP*. That's what I mean by "huge". Derivatives trading actually turns around something equal to America's annual GDP every three days, which is why these markets are so liquid. If you want to move a billion dollars in the foreign exchange markets, it shouldn't take more than a couple of minutes, and you will probably not detect any change in the prices because of what you just did. In these markets a billion is a drop in the ocean. It is, to be more precise, less than what the global financial markets on average churn in 10 seconds.

In the years before the 2007–2009 crash, the banking sector alone generated around 20% of the profits of all listed companies in the world. According to *Institutional Investor's Alpha* magazine, the 25 highest paid hedge fund managers in the U.S. had an average income of $540 million in 2006, or nearly $1.5 million per person, per day, every day, for the entire year. No manager of any commercial enterprise came even remotely close. In fact, the top-25 hedge fund managers combined appeared to have earned more than all the S&P 500's CEOs combined. That, again, is rather huge.

So, evidently you can earn a lot if you run a hedge fund, but the financial sector as a whole can also make huge profits when conditions are right. They will soon be again. I estimated in a previous chapter that total variable price asset growth in the world over the coming 40 years will be something like $800 trillion in real terms. That is about 12 times as much as global GDP in 2010—coming in as new assets. The money going into these assets will pass through banks and other financial institutions. Much of it will in fact churn rapidly all the time. I shall come back to that, but again, it's huge, huge, huge.

I also wrote previously that we will need to build accommodation for 3 billion new urban dwellers, in addition to the expansion of commercial property, upgrading of existing property, etc. That's about real estate, of course, but also about finance, because real estate means mortgages. Many emerging countries do not even have a credit culture today—so, as they develop one, their financial sectors will grow much faster than their economies as a whole.

I also claimed that there will be intense innovation, primarily in IT, biotech, and alternative energy. This will need risk-financing from venture capital funds. I added that emerging market currencies would rise—a great arbitrage opportunity for hedge funds. I could go on, but I think the core of the matter is that whatever happens at any time and place, and in any sector, it creates opportunities in finance. Here are the main players in the sector:

- *Insurance and reinsurance companies*, which insure people, households, and companies, and which also operate large investment funds.
- *Commercial banks*. These do "normal" banking stuff like safekeeping; consumer, mortgage, and commercial loans; credit card business; and financial trading support.
- *Investment banks* are there to help companies raise money through the issuance of bonds or equity, or to get listed though initial public offerings. They may also help with mergers and acquisitions, or even help listed companies protect themselves against hostile takeover bids.
- *Private banks* help wealthy people manage their assets.
- *Hedge funds* are companies that trade across numerous financial markets and get rewarded for their performance (as opposed to making money on transactions, as many banks do.)
- *Private equity funds* are partnerships that invest in illiquid assets such as startup companies, or take normally controlling interests in private companies, or in public companies, which they then privatize and reorganize.

As an individual seeking to benefit from future opportunities, you could either work in financial institutions, or you could invest in them, or invest through them. The latter is most common, so let's look at how it works.

———

I think rule number one about investing is simply to do it. American university professor and author Jeremy Siegel published a landmark paper in 1991, where he compared long-term returns if someone had invested $1 in each of a number of different asset classes in 1800 and held them for 190 years until 1990. During that time the consumer price index grew so much that you would need just over $11 simply to maintain the same purchasing power as in 1800. Here is what $1 invested in 1800 would be worth in 1990:

- If invested in gold: $19
- If invested in short-term government bonds: $3,570
- If invested in government bonds: $6,070
- If invested in equities: $1,030,000

Gold clearly wasn't that hot, but bonds were great and equities magnificent. For over $1 million in 1990, you could buy a whole lot more than you could for $1 in 1800. In 1990 you could buy a very nice villa in a good location from just the growth in value of that single dollar.

Now, past performance is no guarantee of future results, and between 1990—the end of the period Jeremy Siegel described—and the time that I write this, the American stock market has crashed no fewer than three times: in 1991, in 2000–2003, and in 2007–2009. What a disaster!

Hmmmhhh. Let me just check on my screen. Tap, tap, tap … OK, S&P 500 is trading at just over 1,000 right now … Sooo, ehh, what did it trade at the last day of 1990? Tap, tap, tap. Just under 330.

I hope you get the picture: In the very long run, say 30 years or more, it really does pay to be invested, even if you have to breeze through numerous wars, scares, recessions, and crashes before the day that you may need the money. Furthermore, it pays in particular to be invested in something volatile and risky. So, generally, being invested is one important rule.

Another one is that it reduces volatility a whole lot if one is diversified internationally and among different asset classes. The most important of these are the money market, bonds, equities, property, gold, commodities, collectibles, precious metals, and—if you are really exotic—perhaps timberland. Some of these may do well in times of rising inflation (commodities, precious metals, real estate, collectables), others do well when inflation is decreasing or low (equities, corporate bonds), and some thrive in crises (government bonds). What a prudent investor might do is to define a given asset allocation between these and stick to it forever. It might, for example, be:

- Money market: 5%
- Government bonds: 15%
- Corporate bonds: 10%
- Equities: 50%
- Listed property: 10%
- Gold, commodities, collectables, and precious metals: 10%

Of course, in order to do this one needs to rebalance from time to time—say, four times a year. That will mean that one ends up pushing more money into equities, when they have fallen a lot, which normally coincides with government bonds going too far up. Rebalancing will, in other words, force you to buy what's cheap and sell what's expensive. An addition to such a strategy could be to invest the same amount of new money into the portfolio every year, which means that you automatically end up buying more units when stuff is cheap. For small investors who pay retail-level trading commissions, rebalancing can get too expensive, so here it is better to only rebalance through new money that is committed. However, institutional investors can fairly easily rebalance. Finally, make the portfolio global, not local. This may by itself create some automatic rebalancing.

Such a combination of simple strategies is not at all bad. But let's look closer at the asset classes and how you actually invest in them.

We can start by looking at the simplest approach, which is to invest directly in money market accounts, bonds, or equities. The *money market* is enormous, since commercial companies, financial institutions, national wealth funds, central banks, and wealthy individuals use them constantly to place liquidity. So are *bond markets*, which are mainly used for financing government debt, mortgages, and corporate debt. With *equities* you own a part of a company, but the company doesn't have an obligation to pay you anything back (but it evidently normally will try hard, since shareholders elect the board, who elect the management).

––––––––––

The most liquid financial markets are the so-called "derivatives", which are primarily futures, options, and swaps. *Futures* are contracts to buy and sell an asset at a given day in the future. They are easy tools for hedging as well as speculating, and they can be used not only to make money when prices go up, but also when prices fall (if you sell a future you will make money if the price subsequently goes down). There exist futures for any "liquid" commodity such as copper, oil, or soy beans, as well as for bonds, equity indexes, and much more.

Options are like futures with a loss limitation attached. A call option gives you the right—but not the obligation—to buy a given asset at a given price and at a given date in the future, and a put option gives you the right to sell in a similar way. Since the risk is limited, there is a premium for an option, and speculators may sell (or "write") options to collect that premium (which makes their risk high or unlimited, however).

Swaps are contracts to exchange cash (flows) on or before a specified future date, based on the underlying value of currencies/exchange rates, interest rates, bonds, commodities, stocks, or other assets. By far the largest swap market is for foreign exchange.

The main categories of money market instruments, bonds, and equities

Money market

- *Time deposits* are bank accounts where one gets a premium interest against accepting a fixed maturity date.
- *Treasury bills* are government-issued "bonds" with 3 to 12 months' maturity.
- *Money funds* are pooled investments which buy money market securities.

Bonds

- *Government and agency* bonds. Agency bonds are issued by government-backed mortgage institutions.
- *Corporate bonds* are issued by corporate companies. If these are considered risky, the bonds are called "junk bonds" and will have a higher yield.
- *Municipal bonds* are issued by municipalities.
- *Mortgage-backed, asset-backed, and collateralized debt obligations* are all bonds backed by specific assets.

Equities

- *Financials.* These are banking, consumer finance, investment banking and brokerage, asset management, insurance and investment, and real estate.
- *Consumer discretionary.* This includes automobiles and components, consumer durables and apparel, hotels, restaurants and leisure, as well as media and retailing.
- *Information technology.* Software, hardware, IT services, and tele-communication.
- *Industrials.* Capital goods, commercial services and supplies, and transportation.
- *Resources.* Chemicals, construction materials, containers and packaging, metals and mining, paper and forest products.
- *Consumer staples.* Food, drugs, beverages, tobacco, and household and personal products.
- *Utilities.* Gas, electricity, and water.

Instead of trading directly in the money market, bonds, and equities, many invest in *mutual funds* (or "managed funds"), which use active managers to pick specific investments and perhaps increase or decrease exposure. Investors pay a management fee for this, and there are obviously also transaction costs involved in the buying and selling. The fees have annoyed investors for years, because the large majority of these funds have always underperformed their benchmark indices. For that reason there has evolved a huge variety of alternative funds called *ETFs*, which stands for "exchange-traded funds". When you buy an ETF, you participate in a given portfolio that doesn't change over time. Since ETFs are passive, their management is also cheap. Furthermore, they can be sold short, which gives sophisticated investors the opportunity to benefit from falling markets.

––––––––––

We have already seen that real estate typically constitutes a bit over 50% of all variable price wealth in society. There are five major approaches to investing in real estate. The first is *direct ownership*, which is what people often do when they want to use the property for their own purposes, whether it's private or commercial utilization. To directly own property for pure investment purposes may or may not be a good idea, but anyone who does so should consider the often enormous management task that goes with it. Some years ago I invested with friends in the purchase of approx. 45,000 m^2 of property in the center of Berlin. It has evolved well, but the only reason for that (apart from our fairly good timing) was the fact that we also bought a controlling interest in a local property management company, which could handle anything from daily routines to renovations, and so-called "privatizations", where apartments were converted from being rentals to being sold.

The second major investment form in property is *open-ended real estate funds*. These allow their investors to trade at net asset value, which is based on appraisals. This ensures a fair value, but will also force the funds to maintain a liquidity reserve so that they can handle redemptions.

The third approach is *REITs*, which stands for "Real Estate Investment Trusts". These are closed structures like normal equities, which means they can be traded, but not redeemed. Since they are a financial vehicle for another taxed investment class, they tend to be tax-exempt at the corporate level as long as they commit to pay out most (typically 85–100%) of their earnings as dividends. REITs are generally valued on so-called adjusted funds from operations (affo), which is rather similar to free cashflows. Reported earnings may be lower than affo if they write down their property, but that generally doesn't concern investors if they expect the property to appreciate over the long term.

The fourth is *listed property companies*, which I would divide into developers, trading companies, and holding companies. Developers are evidently companies that build and sell real estate. Trading companies buy property en bloc, but then improve them and sell them off either again in blocks or through individual privatizations. Finally, holding companies will predominantly manage a fairly static portfolio of real estate. An interesting aspect of listed property companies and REITs is that, like ETFs, they can be sold short, which makes it possible to gain from declining real estate prices.

The fifth and final category of important real estate investment vehicles is *private real estate funds*. They are mostly very opportunistic funds run as private partnerships. Their typical focus is to buy projects that are in trouble, or where they see a possibility to make large gains through value-added approaches. Some of the large investment banks run such funds in partnership with their largest clients.

Private equity belongs, together with hedge funds, to the least liquid part of financial markets. *Private equity* is investment funds that are not listed and which are only available to particularly solid and professional investors. There are two main categories: "venture capital", which is equity investment in startup companies, and "buyout", which involves the purchase of more mature and sometimes stock exchange–listed companies. Less frequent forms of private equity include

- Growth capital, which is normally given to mature companies that need to make investments.
- Distressed/special situations, where the fund takes over a construction project that ran out of money midway or where it buys up bonds issued by a company it thinks will go bust ("loan-to-own"). It will subsequently inject further capital and finish the construction project or reorganize the company.
- Mezzanine capital, which is somewhat similar to junk bonds and often given to risky companies that don't qualify to issue junk bonds. As risk compensation, the private equity fund will require a high yield and/or possibility to convert to equity at favorable rates. This was widely used to salvage financial institutions during the 2007–2009 crises.

Finally, there are other variations such as infrastructure, banking, energy, and even art funds that operate as private equity.

How does an investment in private equity work, and why are only professional investors with good reputations allowed in? Let's start with the mechanics. When you sign up as an investor in private equity, you will initially pay nothing. Signing up is a commitment to pay a defined amount in the future. This is why you need to be a professional with a good reputation: The fund needs to be absolutely certain that you have the money, when it wants it. And if you don't? They will most likely sue you and perhaps end up negotiating a deal where you can get off the hook by paying a part of your commitment while writing off what you already invested.

When an investor signs up for private equity, the recommended and normal strategy is to build up exposure gradually over approx. 8 years and then allocate more or less evenly over subsequent years ("vintages"). There is not much point in trying to time the commitments, as the fund managers try to do this themselves. After money-raising for a fund finishes, it will typically invest the committed amounts over a period of 3 years. It will then on average sit on each investment for around 7–8 years, which means that it typically takes 11–12 years before the fund is fully wound up. During that period, there will be a number of times where the fund asks its investors for more money (a "call") because it wants to invest, and others where it returns cash "distribution" because it has sold an investment.

How much should be committed to private equity?

There are three key terms anyone investing in private equity needs to know:

- *Committed capital* is the maximum investment amount you have signed up for.
- *Allocated capital* is the amount you actually desire to have invested.
- *Drawdown* is the difference between what is called and distributed.

Because each fund will return money continuously during its lifetime, drawdown in a given fund will rarely exceed 60% of committed capital. Furthermore, if you have a portfolio of funds committed over many vintages, the aggregate drawdown will most likely be even lower. This means that most investors choose to commit more than they wish to allocate.

This is not really a book about business ethics, but so many bad things are said about private equity—especially buyout funds—that I would like to just address a few of them. One frequent comment is that all they do is (1) buy a company, (2) load it up with debts, (3) fire a lot of people, and then (4) sell it gain at a profit while evading tax.

That can happen, but as a general observation it's simply incorrect. As for loading their target companies with debts, the critique is largely based on misconceptions. What normally happens is this: They borrow money to buy the company and then make a "pushdown" so that the acquired company assumes that debt. However, the typical target company of private equity is one that has very little leverage, and what private equity companies normally do is to bring leverage up to market standards. The debt is used to pay the seller of the company. However, after the transaction has taken place, the buyout fund will be on standby with more cash should that be needed and if the need arises urgently.

Does debt hurt a company? It can, but it can certainly also focus the management on profitability since they have to pay interest on the invested capital, as is normal. Another aspect of private equity business is that management typically co-invest with their own money so that they stand to gain if it goes well. But they could get in deep, personal trouble if it doesn't. That will certainly also focus management on the task.

The image of private equity companies as job destroyers is also wrong. Research from the U.S.A. has shown that private equity–owned companies have higher growth in employment, revenue, profits, and productivity than similar companies with other ownership structures.

The last common critique is that the funds try to avoid tax. However, those who sell their companies to private equity funds have to pay tax on their gains, and so do the companies they invest in, as well as the investors who fund them.

Hedge funds are funds that have very flexible strategies, including the possibilities to sell short to gain from falling prices. The main hedge fund strategies are

- CTA, or "Commodity Trading Advisor", hedge funds are global macro-funds that typically trade derivatives. CTAs are based on computer-trading strategies whereas global macro-funds are predominantly run by people.
- "Equity hedge" funds typically trade comparable equities, where they will go long the one they find cheaper and short the other. Or they may go long specific equities and short the index as a whole. Some

specialize in "value" shares, whereas others focus on "growth" stock. There is also a hybrid called GARP ("growth at a reasonable price").

- "Relative value" hedge funds take cheap short-term loans to buy long-duration bonds or currencies with high yield. These are called "carry trades".

- "Event-driven" hedge funds are typically investments in bonds issued by companies that are getting into trouble—they are similar to vulture funds. Pension funds are typically not allowed to own such bonds and may sell them at exceptional distress prices as they get de-rated from investment grade towards junk. Hedge funds may then buy them either hoping that the company makes it, or that if it doesn't they can take it over and engineer a turnaround. Another event-driven strategy is to trade on takeover attempts. A hedge fund may here employ lawyers to try and find out whether such a deal in reality will go through, and if so at what price. They can then make relative value trades between the shares of the buying company and the acquisition targets.

Fee structures versus talent in hedge funds and private equity

The fee structure for hedge funds and private equity is typically what you call "2 : 20". They charge a 2% annual management fee plus 20% of the net profit in a so-called "performance fee". In private equity, performance is calculated for the duration of a fund and in hedge funds, it's typically quarterly, but with a "watermark", which means that if the value of the fund goes down, then payment of the performance fees stops until it has surpassed its hitherto highest level, which is referred to as the watermark.

These fees can reach insanely high numbers, which is why many of the really talented people in finance end up working in hedge funds or private equity. However, such potential fees also attract people who aren't that smart. The simple rule for investing in such funds is that they should belong in the top quartile in terms of historical performance. Apart from that, you should seek a wide diversity of exposure over time, of course, and over different managers and investment styles, and then hope that, on average over the long run, they generate superior cashflows to compensate for their reduced liquidity.

The financial sector is special inasmuch as it is involved in almost everything consumers, governments, and commercial companies do.

Much of what you do in finance involves none of the friction that you experience in commercial business. Whereas, for instance, there is a mountain of paperwork involved in buying a house, a financial trader can swing around hundreds of millions of dollars with a few phone calls within a few minutes. This lack of friction makes it easy to make money if you are good, and quick to lose if you aren't (most people doing it aren't!).

But the lack of friction also tempts many to assume too much risk, when the going has been good for a while. In particular, this tends to happen when people trade with OPMs, which is short for "other people's money". As we saw with the subprime salami crises, many banks had assumed risks that were completely reckless, and which I think those responsible rarely would have taken with their own money. The driving force may have been groupthink plus the fact that stock options and bonuses only worked one way: they rewarded success, but didn't punish failure. Many thought that a sizable part of hedge funds would collapse in the crash, but that didn't happen for the simple reason that most hedge fund managers have their own money invested in their funds. They are very concerned about losses, and they know that losses will be blamed on them personally, not on a big institution where it will be difficult to pinpoint who did what afterwards.

––––––––

So, let's look at where the most powerful financial centers are. In terms of volume, the foreign exchange ("forex") market is by far the largest. According to a survey made by the Bank of International Settlements (a sort of central bank for central banks), approx. 24% of the global foreign exchange market was done through institutions in the U.K. The second biggest was the U.S. with 17%, followed by approx. 6% in each of Switzerland, Japan, and Singapore, respectively. Just over 4% was done through Hong Kong and Australia. India had only 0.9% and China 0.2% of global forex turnover.

When we look at market capitalization and trading volume of stock exchange–listed instruments, the four major blocks in the world are the U.S.A., Europe, China, and Japan. The table below gives an overview of market capitalization and trading volume in the major exchanges in these regions as of Q1, 2009. It shows that Europe had by far the largest market cap and the U.S.A. (due to NASDAQ) the largest trading volume.

Market capitalization and year-to-date total turnover at the end of May 2009 of major exchanges		
	Market value (U.S.$ trillion)	*Share turnover* (U.S.$ trillion)
U.S.A.	12,348	20,246
Europe	8,757	4,850
China	4,406	3,086
Japan	3,102	1,561
Source: Wikipedia entry: "stock exchange".		

There are several aspects of this that I find striking. First, whereas China was still tiny in terms of forex trading when these numbers were compiled (it has strict currency regulations), it was already very big in more traditional trading—actually not far behind Europe. Also, the *market cap of Shanghai was almost as large as that of the London Stock Exchange* (it actually surpassed London a few months after these numbers were recorded). Bear in mind here that the London Stock Exchange has existed since the 17th century and is thus more than 300 years old. Shanghai, on the other hand, opened in 1990.

As for the more creative parts of finance—hedge funds and private equity—the dominance is Western. The entrepreneur/venture capital–focused organization *Red Herring* gave awards in 2009 to whom they considered the 100 best venture capitalists in the world.[1] Their distribution by country was very uneven (as shown in the table overleaf).

By far the biggest block was the Anglo-Saxon world (English-speaking except India), which had two-thirds of the leading venture capital funds. But it was interesting that there already were eight Chinese top funds, the same as in France and Germany combined, and almost three times as many as in Japan. *So, China is now on the map in venture capital as well.*

The World Economic Forum annually publishes the so-called *Financial Development Report*, which ranks 55 of the world's leading financial systems and capital markets on over 120 variables. These rankings,

---

[1] Red Herring website.

Country	Number of Red Herring award winners, 2009
United States	59
China	8
U.K.	6
France	4
Germany	4
Japan	3
Canada	3
Israel	3
India	2
Australia	2
Singapore	1
Korea	1
Sweden	1
Denmark	1
Switzerland	1
Luxembourg	1
Total	100

which concern institutional and business environment, financial stability, financial services, and financial markets and access are not measures of size but of quality. In 2009 the rank was as follows:

Financial Development Report rankings

1. United Kingdom	6. Canada
2. Australia	7. Switzerland
3. United States	8. Netherlands
4. Singapore	9. Japan
5. Hong Kong	10. Denmark

What is noteworthy here is that the top six nations all are Anglo-Saxon—the U.K. and former British colonies.

So, where does all of this leave us? As for the more sophisticated parts of finance—hedge funds and private equity—the main locations are "former British Empire". France and, in particular, Germany have made serious attempts to challenge London within European finance, but with limited success: London has maintained its very clear lead. *I believe that within a few decades there will be two international power centers in global finance: Greater China and former British Empire.* Interestingly, India belongs to the latter and should begin to throw its weight around a couple of decades out. A third group of players will be Switzerland (wealth management) and the Gulf States (Islamic finance).

In summary, I think the finance sector will begin to expand again—and ultimately a lot. However, following the 2007–2009 fiasco, the sector will probably change in a number of ways. *The managed fund industry will increasingly be replaced by ETFs and other simple, low–transaction cost "plain vanilla" products,* which people can use for constructing robust asset allocation portfolios. *Hedge funds will recover* and continue to play a role in identifying and utilizing mispricing, and *private equity will thrive again,* as it fulfills its role in helping startup companies and adding knowhow and commonsense to mature companies that need it. *Banks will be more focused on servicing their clients well* and with *delivering simple products that clients can understand.* At the same time they will trade less for themselves (so-called proprietary trading, or "prop-trading"), since neither their clients nor society as a whole can live with banks that may not be safe, and they will scale back on very complex products. Finally, as financial partners for their clients, they will develop professional media products that work on the web as well as mobile devices.

In a sense, I think that what needs to happen and probably will happen is an increase in the separation of roles into three broad categories:

- *Financial utilities* that provide standard services such as deposits, transfers, e-banking, custody services, etc. These will largely be de facto IT companies, and their fee structures will typically be a percentage of the asset under management plus a fee for each transaction. Being clever online will be key; and it is more than likely that some purely IT companies will enter the field with great success. Google, Apple, Dell, and Microsoft spring to mind.
- *Financial marketing organizations* that take the client's point of view and help in setting up the right portfolio of solutions against fees, which may be high. These offerings will be based on an "open architecture",

which means that they may include products made by the financial institution as well as by its competitors. Insurance advisors, boutique banks, and corporate banking offering mergers and acquisition advice, etc. are examples.

- *Creative finance* that is rewarded by percentages of its market outperformance (if any). Hedge funds and private equity spring to mind, but I can imagine other forms of creative finance such as complete outsourcing of financial management for large funds.

In terms of location, finance has strong, entrenched network effects, and the two major power centers will (as already mentioned) be the English-speaking world plus greater China. In any case, for anybody doing business in the future, understanding finance is essential, because no business can exist without it, and much of the best business is done through it.

12

Real estate

I have a question:

"Were you around during the global economic crisis in 1973–1975?"

This was the first oil crisis, triggered by OPEC's decision to stop oil export to any nation that supported Israel during the Yom Kippur War. The crisis lasted until March 1974, but a lot of economies remained depressed up to 1995. These included Japan, where real estate markets fell during the crisis.

Now, let's imagine that you were a Japanese investor with a healthy contrarian mindset: you liked to buy property during recessions. We could say you came up with the equivalent of $1 million cash, and that you took out $2 million in mortgages, so that you could buy Japanese property for $3 million. Let's for simplicity assume also that rental income exactly covered all your expenses including interest on the mortgage, and that you didn't pay the mortgage down.

That would have been great, because after the first 10 years your property would have doubled in value to $6 million, so after deduction of your mortgage, you would be worth $4 million—a gain of 400%.

Pretty good! Inspired by this we can now imagine that you decided to stay with your investment for another 10 years. Would that be a good idea?

Oh, yes! If you had kept them for these extra 10 years, their value would have gone up another 300%, which would make your investment worth $18 million, or $16 million after deduction of your mortgage.

You would have made a 1,600% return on your original investment in 20 years.

Awesome!

More wants more. Let's assume that you decide to hold the same property exposure for yet another 10 years. Remember the adage: Third time lucky!

That would have been a disaster. During the third decade you would have lost almost everything, leaving you with a minimal return after a total of 30 years. The behavior of the Japanese market around those 30 years is illustrated below.

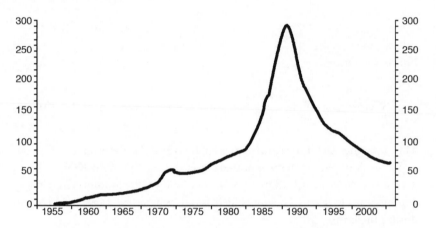

Japan Land Price Index: six big cities. *Source*: Thomson Datastream.

The reason I start my chapter about real estate with this story is to mention that whereas real estate surely is one of the leading wealth creators in society, it is also one of the leading wealth destroyers. It all depends on where, when, and how you buy, and equally on when you sell. In this chapter I will address some of that, plus of course the reasons why I think real estate qualifies as a supersector for the coming decades.

There are many kinds of real estate. There are, for instance, buildings for retail shopping (supermarkets, malls, etc.), as well as *office buildings* and *industrial buildings*. There are also *hotels and convention* buildings as well as warehouses, *parking lots* and *multistory car parks*. All of this is what we call "commercial property". However, most of what you see in daily life is probably *apartment buildings and houses*, or what we call "residential" real estate. The normal distribution of property in a developed country is, as I mentioned in an earlier chapter, approx. 75% residential and 25% commercial. Commercial property may constitute a higher proportion in some developing economies where many live in slum housing that has little value but work in real factories, whereas residential may be higher in places with many second homes or retirees.

There is also real estate that has yet to be developed: *forests*, *farmland*, and *construction land*. Personally I think of forests and farmland as more related to commodities than to the rest of the property market, so I will not cover them here, but construction land is clearly linked to other real estate in general.

I have already suggested some reasons why we are facing a boom in international building construction. Two obvious ones are massive population growth (+2 billion within 40 years) and wealth explosion (developed markets: +200–300%; emerging markets: +400–600% within 40 years). However, there is also urbanization (+3 billion), and aging (+1.6 billion retirees).

In Chapter 5, I showed a graph comparing expected population in rural and urban areas, but I will now show one that makes the point crystal-clear. The figure at the top of the next page shows likely development from 2010 to 2050.

The first time I saw these numbers (and made this graph) I was surprised, since I realized that we not only need to build houses and apartments for all the 2 billion additional people on Earth between 2010 and 2050, we also need to adapt to the net inflow of people from rural to urban areas. Essentially, even though the population will grow, there will be many rural houses that will be abandoned. So, we need to handle a population growth not of 2 billion, but of 3 billion. However, it doesn't stop there, because our family and age structures will change dramatically too. Because of modern lifestyle, aging, and lower fertility, there will be far more singles or couples without children, which means that we will need more units than when two or three generations of families brought up many children in the same building.

"What about slums?" one may ask. "Will many of those who move to big cities in emerging markets not end up in slums, which cannot be defined as 'buildings' in the commercial sense?" Unfortunately many will, just as many already do. According to U.N. Habitat, no fewer than a third of all urban residents in global emerging markets (810 million by 2008) lived in slums in 2008. However, if average incomes grow as expected, the proportion of people living in slums will decline, which

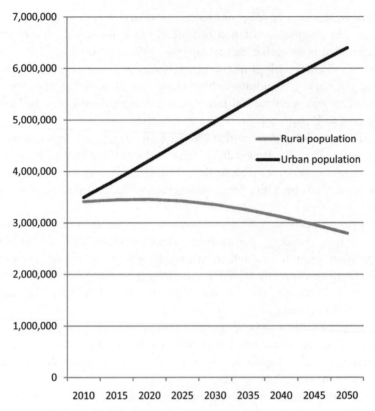

Global rural and urban population forecast 2010–2050 (thousands). *Source: Urbanization Prospects: The 2008 Revision*, U.N. Population Division, 2008.

means that new urban housing will not only come from the factors I just mentioned, but also from people moving out of slums. Finally, the middle and upper classes will increasingly acquire second homes. I think the reality is that we need to build net, new residential property for something like 100 million people a year on average over the next 40 years.

That number should actually be fairly stable through the entire period, apart from one or two temporary slumps during property cycle turns, because whereas population growth will level off, the migration from rural to urban areas will accelerate. So, this is a number we need to know: *between 2010 and 2050, average annual new housing construction needs to accommodate around 100 million new urban residents a year, or around 8 million a month.*

But this is only residential construction for net, new tenants and owners. We will build more than that. First, it is not as if there will be

---

The 10 new lifestyles

The demand for new residential real estate will not only come from population growth and wealth growth, but also from adaptation to new lifestyles such as these:

1. Fly: fun loving youth
2. Yuppie: young urban professional
3. Guppie: gay urban professional
4. Sinbad/singad: single income, no boyfriend (no girlfriend), absolutely desperate
5. Oink: one income, no kids
6. Dinky: dual income, no kids yet
7. Opf: one-parent family
8. Spear: senior people enjoying affluent retirements
9. Grampie: grown, active, moneyed people in excellent state
10. Yeepies: young, energetic older people into everything

---

no building construction in countries with stagnant or declining populations. Property will get replaced, changed, or upgraded all the time, even when populations are in freefall, as in Russia and Japan. According to an article in *The Economist* in 2008, whereas 78% of all houses in the U.S. had been resold, the equivalent number for Japan was just 13%. The reason? The Japanese often pull down buildings after around 30 years and replace them with new ones. Furthermore, if the world population on average gets a lot richer, then they will want bigger, better, and perhaps more property—think of the many holiday homes in Florida, Spain, Thailand, Dubai, or wherever.

Also, we shouldn't forget commercial property. Since emerging markets tend to have very high capital spending, it is likely that additional commercial property will exceed 25% of the value of all building construction there for a number of years.

Most of the property boom we can expect will naturally be low-cost units. While 70–90 million people will be lifted into the middle class every year, there will be much larger numbers lifted from utter despair to something just below middle class. These are the ones who use micro-financing and buy soap and toothpaste in extra small packages from Procter & Gamble. In either case, the typical trend in emerging markets is that people move from their homes in the countryside to small towns first. Later on, they move to bigger towns, or perhaps their children do,

Developing world urban slum populations—800 million live under slum conditions

In 2008 just over 800 million people—12% of the world's population—lived in slums. Many slum-dwellers don't own the land they build on, and their property has consequently little commercial value.

Developing world region	Slum population (million)	Percent of local urban population living in slums
Subsaharan Africa	166	62
South Asia	201	43
East Asia	215	37
Latin America + Caribbean	117	27
West Africa	31	24
North Africa	12	15

Source: U.N. Habitat, Global Urban Observatory, 2008.

and only in the third phase do they perhaps move to the really big cities. This means that many of the more successful property developers start by specializing in some smaller towns, where competition isn't too big, before later on maybe targeting large cities.

I believe that in order to succeed in the long term as a real estate investor, there are three crucial aspects that need to be really well understood: location, valuation, and timing. You don't want to invest in real estate located in an area that is going nowhere, you don't want to buy at inflated prices, and you don't want to buy close to the peak of the property cycle.

As for location, whereas emerging markets will clearly boom, we have already studied some of the demographics and seen reasons why property construction will decelerate in most developed markets: a smaller workforce, falling populations, and aging. One consequence of aging and falling populations is that the number of young people ready to buy property for the first time will decline in many places. The

OECD has investigated the age pyramid in its membership countries and found that the number of these young buyers was broadly stable in most of the countries from 1980 to 2000, but actually rose strongly in South Korea, Spain, Mexico, and Italy. The only country among the 14 member states where it fell during those 20 years was Japan. However, if we look at the OECD's projections from 2000 to 2050, the picture looks very different: the number of new entrants in these countries will gradually decline by 240 million to under 800 million, which is below the number for 1980. So, that is obviously a vital headwind for many property markets. The countries worst hit by this effect will be Korea and Spain, followed by many central European countries.

Other developed countries with better demographics—and thus better long-term growth prospects—include *the U.S., Canada, Australia, New Zealand, the U.K., France, the Netherlands, Ireland, Switzerland, and Scandinavia.* These countries have both historically encouraged skilled immigration and/or been good at assimilating new inhabitants, or they have relatively high birth rates.

When it comes to global urban expansion, the three big contributors will be the U.S.A., China, and India. The largest increases in urban population between 2010 and 2025 will be in India, which within those 15 years will add approx. 260 million urban dwellers. To get your head around that number, just consider that it is not much less than the entire population of the U.S.A. as of 2010 (approx. 305 million). So, let me restate it: *Urban expansion in India over 15 years will be almost as big as the entire population of the United States.*

The second largest urban expansion will be in China, which will grow by almost 200 million between 2010 and 2025. *China's urban growth over these 15 years will be three times the population of Germany.*

Together, India and China will provide a third of the global urban population expansion from 2010 to 2025. In the following 25 years—from 2025 to 2050—they will still represent a third of the global urban expansion, but India will now contribute twice as much as China.

Now, let's look a bit at so-called "megacities": those with over 10 million inhabitants. In 1950 there existed only two: New York and Tokyo. By 2010 there are around 20 (depending on how you define the border between each city and its suburbs). If we take the 20 with the highest expected growth between 2010 and 2025, then total additional population here should be approx. 82 million. Interestingly, of these 20 megacities there are only two in OECD countries: New York and Los Angeles, and these rank only 17th and 18th in growth, respectively. No fewer than 80 million new megacity inhabitants of the 82 million will

Six important facts about property cycles

- *Characteristics of property cycles*: There exists an inherent property cycle with an average duration of 18–20 years. After a property cycle peak, the property market starts to decline prior to the economy as a whole. These episodes will typically lead to serious and longer lasting recessions/depressions plus banking and perhaps currency crises.

- *Drivers of property cycles*: The inherent, 18–20 year (on average) property cycle is essentially driven by lags and thus instability in supply, whereas shorter and smaller property fluctuations during capital spending and inventory cycles are simply passive responses to changes in aggregate demand and credit conditions.

- *Why property cycles can be very dramatic*: There are three major impacts when property cycles turn down. First, the wealth effect, which is a GDP decline of around 4% of the wealth loss from falling property prices. Second, falling property prices and recession means declining building construction (building construction averages a little over 10% of GDP). Finally, many property cycle downturns lead to banking crises, and in some cases even exchange rate crises, which can amplify the overall negative impact.

- *Property during capital spending and inventory cycles*. If business cycles turn down because of a correction in inventory or capital spending, it will typically have a brief and limited effect on property, which may just stagnate or decline a bit. This effect will start some months after the economic cycle has turned down. A reason that the effect is so limited is that the falling interest rates associated with recessions support real estate.

- *Residential property is a business cycle kick-starter*. Residential property tends to lead the economy during revivals. This behavior of residential property can be very helpful for central bankers trying to restart an economy, since rising housing starts is often one of the first significant responses they get to easing.

- *Commercial property is a typically lagging indicator*. Whereas residential property amplifies the effect of central banking policies immediately, the commercial property market picks up at a later stage and acts thereby as a kind of "echo" to the initial, monetary stimulus. This revival of commercial property markets will often happen at a time when central bankers no longer wish to see additional, economic expansion.

live in emerging markets. A curious aspect is that some of these massive cities are fairly unknown to the public today. (Quick quiz: "In which countries are the megacities Kolkata, Kinshasa, Lahore, and Lagos located?" ... Come on, now!).

Big cities have big buildings. The McKinsey Global Institute predicted in 2008 that China will build 20,000–50,000 skyscrapers by 2025. At that time, China alone should have at least 4 megacities and around 220 cities with at least one million inhabitants.

Let me change to a completely different angle of property growth: tourism, the hotel industry, and holiday homes. Tourism is one of the world's great growth industries and creates many jobs. Even though travel companies rarely are particularly profitable and travel industry jobs for the same reason tend to have low pay, the industry is a significant economic driver through its effect on real estate markets. It may create considerable construction business and can also create enormous gains in land prices.

Tourism has on average grown approx. 25% faster than the world economy. However, it is volatile: normally, the growth of international tourism grows much faster than the world economy when global GDP growth exceeds 4%, but it grows slower than the world economy when GDP growth dips under 2%. International tourist arrivals worldwide have grown from 25 million in 1950, to 277 million in 1980, 438 million in 1990, 684 million in 2000, and then reaching 922 million in 2008. The World Tourist Organization forecast that this number will climb to 1.6 billion in 2020.

According to the same organization, only approx. 3.5% of the world's population traveled abroad in year 2000, and only 7% of those had the health and finance to reasonably do so. So, tourism will continue to grow and grow. Countries new to tourism find it tends to develop in three phases. The first is largely about packaged tours, where people want to see as many famous spots as possible and get their picture taken in front of them, or where they go to relax in an all-in resort that they never leave.

The second phase of tourism involves more focused traveling and more individually planned trips. Some will seek culture, other adventure or education. There will also be those who travel to visit family and friends; a group that insiders call VRFs (as in "visit relatives and friends"). Still others will go shopping, partying, or get cheap hip replacements or heart transplants. This phase of outbound tourism from the new emerging market middle class will have a massive effect on retail, hotel/convention property, and, in due course, on secondary

Populations and expected population growth in the 20 leading megacities by 2025, millions

2007–2025 growth ranking	Megacity	Population 2007	Population 2025 forecast	Growth forecast (million)
1	Dhaka, Bangla Desh	13.5	22.0	8.5
2	Lagos, Nigeria	8.0	15.8	7.8
3	Mumbai, India	19.0	26.4	7.4
4	Karachi, Pakistan	12.1	19.1	7.0
5	Kinshasa, Congo	10.1	16.8	6.7
6	Delhi, India	15.9	22.5	6.6
7	Kolkata, India	14.8	20.6	5.8
8	Shanghai, China	15.0	19.4	4.4
9	Jakarta, Indonesia	8.6	12.4	3.8
10	Manila, Philippines	11.1	14.8	3.7
11	Cairo, Egypt	11.9	15.6	3.7
12	Guangzhou, China	8.4	11.8	3.4
13	São Paulo, Brazil	18.8	21.4	2.6
14	Mexico City, Mexico	19.0	21.0	2.0
15	Istanbul, Turkey	10.1	12.1	2.0
16	Rio de Janeiro, Brazil	11.7	13.4	1.7
17	New York, U.S.A.	19.0	20.6	1.6
18	Los Angeles, U.S.A.	12.5	13.7	1.2
19	Buenos Aires, Argentina	12.8	13.8	1.0
20	Lahore, Pakistan	9.8	10.5	0.7

Source: *World Urbanization Prospects: The 2008 Revision*, U.N. Habitat; Wikipedia.

residential construction in many countries. Consider this: According to the World Tourism Organization, the Chinese will take approx. 100 million trips abroad in 2010. That is about as much as the total number of foreign arrivals in, say, the U.S.A., Mexico, and Germany combined in 2010. In addition, non-Chinese tourism will continue to rise; so, whereas the Chinese will only constitute 6% by 2020, their impact will clearly be felt wherever they go. Other emerging market tourists will obviously add to that.

And it will continue. When people move away from their farms to urban jobs, they often get something they have never had before: holidays. And when they move from subsistence to middle-class status, they get something else that is new: discretionary income. We have already seen that the global urban population will increase by approx. 75 million people a year, and that the global middle class will grow by 70 million to 90 million per year. There is no reason to think that the number of tourists traveling internationally won't grow by at least the same numbers annually.

Wealth growth will lead increasing numbers to the third phase of tourism, where people acquire several homes and shift between them. This has become far more doable for many white-collar workers with the advent of the internet, satellite, WiFi, and smartphones. For more and more people, it really doesn't matter where they work anymore. The reason the global yacht market started booming in the late 1990s was largely down to one thing: Improved satellite communications which enabled businessmen to communicate effectively when at sea.

All of this makes holiday homes a great growth market if not exactly a new one. I once read a book called *Gardens of the Roman World* which described not only, well … the Roman gardens, but also their numerous summer houses by the shores of Lake Como in Northern Italy, among many other places. These were built several thousand years ago. Later on, in the 17th and 18th century, the wealthy citizens of Amsterdam created summer homes on the banks of the River Vecht, while wealthy Englishmen built cottages for hunting parties, etc.

Construction of second homes took off in America during the so-called Gilded Age from 1865 to 1901, when business tycoons began constructing huge summer mansions in Greenwich, like the Marble House (completed in 1892 for Mr. and Mrs. William K. Vanderbilt), and The Breakers, a 70-room Italian Renaissance-style palazzo completed in 1895 for Cornelius Vanderbilt II. Many smaller summer residences were built in the early 1900s around Lake George, New York as well as in Santa Fe and Taos in New Mexico. Afterwards came the developments of The Valley of the Sun in Phoenix with its famous Scottsdale, Glendale, Mesa, and Tempe communities, which attracted not only American sunseekers, but also many middle-class investors from colder Canada. Cape Cod followed, and then, of course, Florida: Miami, Fort Lauderdale, Palm Beach, etc.—some of these developments were destined for the extremely rich, but some were accessible to the ever-growing middle class. Typically, people from northern states would go south whereas San Franciscans headed for Lake Tahoe and Bostonians for Cape Cod. However, as air transportation became cheaper and travel habits changed they all started looking abroad and began buying in Mexico, Costa Rica, Panama, and even as far away as Europe and Thailand.

Europeans followed a similar trend as people started buying homes in the South of France, and then in resorts along the Spanish coast, including the Costa del Sol, which went from largely deserted to massively overbuilt within 40 hectic years. Majorca and Ibiza followed, although with more moderation, together with Croatia, Turkey, etc.

It wasn't only beautiful lake districts and seafronts that attracted millions. In North America and Europe there was also the allure of skiing. It appears that skis have existed for almost 5,000 years, but the first known civilian ski race took place in Norway in 1843. The first ski club was founded 32 years later, also in Norway, and the first ski tour in the Alps that we know of took place in 1894, when Sir Arthur Conan Doyle—author of the *Sherlock Holmes* books—traversed from Davos to Arosa with two friends. The first resort-based ski school in the U.S. was opened in New Hampshire in 1929, and organized ski trains from Boston began running to the White Mountains of New Hampshire the same year. However, skiing did not evolve into a mass market until the 1960s, and now it's huge in both continents. As a result, European Alpine villages with a few dozen dirt-poor mountain farmers evolved in next to no time into high-power tourist hotspots, where land plots for single houses in Gstaadt, St. Moritz, and Verbier by 2010 were costing $30 million— some $40 million or even more. Similarly, Aspen, Vail, etc. have become magnets for private jetsetters in America.

There are around 3 million Frenchmen and 750,000 Brits who own second homes today. In the U.S. the sales of second homes as a proportion of total home sales peaked at around 40% in 2007, 12% of which were holiday homes (the rest were bought for investment). Holiday home sales slid from 12% to 9% of the total during the crises in 2008, reducing the number of transactions from 740,000 to 512,000 in that year.

Who buys holiday homes? It seems that buyers can be divided into three groups: (1) those who do it mainly for financial diversification and investment, (2) those whose children have moved away from home and who want to have more and better holidays, and (3) the growing number of spears ("senior people enjoying affluent retirements"), grampies (grown, active, moneyed people in excellent state), and other moneyed middle-aged or old people. Studies by NAR in the U.S. indicate that the average buyer is 52 years of age and has $82,800 in household income per year.

Global tourism is about to get a huge boost from new participants—from China in particular. According to the *China Outbound Travel Handbook*, the most popular travel destinations for the Chinese in 2000, 2005, and 2007 were:

Most popular travel destinations for the mainland Chinese			
Rank	*2000*	*2005*	*2007*
1/2	Hong Kong/Macao	Hong Kong/Macao	Hong Kong/Macao
3	Thailand	Japan	Japan
4	Russia	Vietnam	South Korea
5	Japan	South Korea	Vietnam
6	South Korea	Russia	Russia
7	U.S.A.	Thailand	Thailand
8	Singapore	U.S.A.	U.S.A.
9	North Korea	Singapore	Singapore
10	Australia	Malaysia	Malaysia
Source: *China Outbound Travel Handbook.*			

These were still really early years for Chinese tourism, so travelers must have gathered and shared valuable experiences along the way. Why, for instance, am I not surprised that North Korea dropped out of the list in 2005? Australia dropped out too, even though it is known as an attractive tourist destination, but its currency rose a lot against the greenback between 2000 and 2007, which might have been a factor. Anyway, these two countries were replaced by Malaysia (#10), and by Vietnam (#5), which has a huge stretch of coastland south of China and must be a great growth area for Chinese tourism. Thailand has lots to offer too, but it slipped over time against Japan.

There is another way of finding out which places the Chinese like: Ask them. In February 2007 Nielsen Online carried out an omnibus study and asked, among other things, which places people viewed as dream destinations. The most common answers were

1. Europe: 32%
2. China: 23%
3. Australia or New Zealand: 13%.

Europe and Australia/New Zealand are a long way from China, and expensive too; nevertheless, they seem to be the most desired foreign travel destinations. If one looks in detail at actual trips to Europe, Germany seems to be the most popular, followed by France, Italy, and Switzerland. This is actually interesting, because it doesn't fully reflect global tourist rankings, which put France, Spain, the U.S.A., China, Italy, the U.K., Germany, Ukraine, Turkey, and Mexico as the top 10, in that order (2007).

What stands out here is that the Chinese seem much less interested in Spain, the United States, and England than global tourists on average. Why, on the other hand, are Germany, France, Italy, and Switzerland the destinations of choice? I think it might have something to do with the culture of luxury: They are home to leading producers of luxury brands such as BMW, Mercedes, and Porsche (Germany); Louis Vuitton, Moet & Chandon, and Chanel (France); Ferrari, Versace, and Giorgio Armani (Italy); and Rolex, Patek Philippe, and Breguet (Switzerland). As we have seen, Asians have an exceptional fascination with European luxury and the culture that created it. However, as for where the Chinese will buy holiday homes abroad when it becomes possible can only be a guess—maybe Vietnam, Thailand, or Australia. They will come to Europe on holiday, but not many will want holiday homes that are so far away.

The Chinese are also getting seriously into skiing. As late as 1995 there were probably no more than 500 people in China who could ski, and these were all professional athletes. However, by 2005 the number had grown to 5 million and the *growth rate since has been about a million a year*. If you want a ski chalet and can afford it now, then perhaps you should buy it now—especially if it's close to China's population centers. Soon there won't be enough space.

From looking at what has happened in the West, I think we can make the following very rough, but useful conclusion: *when a country gets rich, and when its population starts to age, there comes a point where about 10% of all its real estate purchases are for vacation purposes and where around 5% of its population owns a holiday home.* So, let me see . . . 5% of 1.3 billion Chinese . . . that's 650,000 holiday homes. However, if China, India, and other emerging markets follow anything resembling the patterns we have seen in developed countries, then the waves of money will initially flow to the mass tourism and business travel industry, including hotels, conference centers, shopping centers, etc. However, at a later stage it will increasingly also benefit the leisure home construction industry. I believe that with the explosion in world wealth over the coming years, *there will be many limited space locations such as prime coastland, ski resorts, and central areas of cities with rich, genuine culture where tourist business may thrive and land prices appreciate considerably.*

There will be lots of people ready to enjoy such places. I mentioned before some of the new lifestyles that are growing across the Earth: first, there are all the types of young without children; the yuppies, guppies, sinbads, singads, oinks, and dinkys I listed earlier; they are people focused on careers, don't want or can't find a partner, are gay or simply choose to postpone children for as long as possible. I also mentioned spears (senior people enjoying affluent retirements), grampies (grown active moneyed people in excellent state), and yeepies (young energetic elderly people into everything). These people have money, time for leisure, are fully mobile and/or interested in second residences abroad. What many of these people have in common is that they are moneyed and mobile.

———

Another driver of economic growth, and thus of real estate markets, is *access to good transport.* Lots of cities have sprung up where planners decided to make a train stop 100 years ago, or where there were harbors, canals, rivers, or crossroads. Indeed, if you look at a long list of the historically most successful cities, they are almost all near navigable water. New York, Hong Kong, London, Shanghai, Singapore, Basel, etc. are all accessible to coastlines or rivers.

Economic growth, both in terms of GDP and wealth, largely occurs where taxes are low. Taxes were rarely high years ago, but now they typically are, and it is evidently practical for a company or an individual with large earnings potential to live in low-tax areas. Numerous smaller countries or counties have started from basically nothing but with the simple idea of having low taxes, and many of them have eventually evolved into global powerhouses. This idea is largely based on the so-called Laffer Curve, which is a generic way to describe what the optimum tax pressure is, if you want to maximize long-term tax revenues. The curve shows expected total tax revenues at given taxation levels, and is perhaps best described by noting that if your tax level is 0%, you get zero revenue, and if it is 100% you will also soon get nothing because everyone will leave. The optimum is somewhere inbetween. In the short term this optimum tax pressure may be fairly high, but the results of high taxes over the long term are a migration of talent, a reduction of entrepreneurship and ambition, and an increased culture of tax evasion. In a way, overtaxing is similar to overfishing the oceans: it gives you higher yield in the short term, but lower in the longer term. Why take risks, people will think, if the potential downside is all ours, while the government takes most if we succeed? And why work overtime if it just brings you into a punitive tax bracket? And finally, the cost of a complex tax system is probably 10–20% of the taxes paid. With flat tax, it gets a lot less.

It is pretty impossible to calculate where the optimum point is on the Laffer Curve, and because of that, it may be that those who try get biased by their own ideologies. A study from (left-leaning) Sweden showed that it was over 70%, whereas studies from (right-leaning) America have indicated that it was closer to 30%. A big difference, but Sweden and Denmark, which have been leading the world rankings in tax pressure for many years, have been slowly but steadily sliding down the global GDP per capita rankings. This is gradually eroding their tax base and thus long-term revenue potential.

Switzerland may be the world's most illustrative tax laboratory, since the majority of taxation here is done at the local level—in each canton and village/city district. Each area has different tax pressures and the differences can be big. The experience here shows that those who chose a low-tax strategy early have vastly outgrown the rest. The consequence was an increase in their tax base, which enabled them to cut tax rates further, even though Switzerland has a system where the richer cantons transfer part of their abnormal revenues to those with lower income. However, income is only part of the evidence, because with virtually permanent full employment, much of Switzerland's production is outsourced to other countries so that it doesn't contribute to Switzerland's GDP. The result, though, is that whereas Swiss GDP doesn't grow particularly fast, Swiss wealth apparently does. At least as far as the Swiss cantons go, the optimum marginal tax rate including social contributions seems to be below 30%, and the optimal corporate tax rate below 15%.

Another aspect of practicality is *the rule of law* and of course that the laws are reasonable. Places where assets may be confiscated randomly, or where you need to pay bribes to get things done, have been far less successful in the long term than those with a clear and clean system. I should add that an essential part of reasonable laws is that you can register the rights to what you own, so that it can be used as collateral for credit. It is exactly this that is often difficult or impossible to do in the world's poorest countries. The organization Transparency International annually conducts a series of surveys among businessmen and analysts, who are asked about their perception of corruption in countries they are familiar with. They subsequently aggregate all these numbers into a series of corruption indices. The result is shown in the map on the next page. The 10 "cleanest" countries in 2007 according to this measurement were Denmark, Finland, New Zealand, Singapore, Sweden, Iceland, the Netherlands, Switzerland, and Canada, with the first three countries sharing the top position. The most corrupt areas were in Africa and the Middle East. Somalia was the world's worst, followed by Myanmar, Iraq, Haiti, Uzbekistan, Tonga, Sudan, Chad, Afghanistan, and Laos.

There is a second group of theories about what creates growth and wealth: *natural resources*. It is certainly true that many of the richest countries in the world in the old days owed much of what they had to the presence of natural resources such as forests, good farmland, iron, or coal. Emerging market booms are now driving natural resource prices up—many wealthy oil-producing nations built their current success on little else. I believe that until we manage to get much further in our transition away from fossil fuels, and until global population growth decelerates much further, we may see natural resources as a major growth and wealth driver in many places. However, if natural resources are all a country has to offer, it is commonly the case that a sizable proportion of the wealth it generates seeps away. It seems that a considerable part of the wealth made in Latin America moves to Miami, for instance, and that much of the African, Middle Eastern, and Russian wealth ends up in Europe.

There is another natural resource, which is far more controversial: human intelligence. Dr. Richard Lynn has together with Tatu Vanhanen published comprehensive studies comparing intelligence and wealth in different countries and found very high correlation between GDP per capita and so-called general intelligence ("g"), which is unrelated to any specific education in, for instance, math or language. The highest average

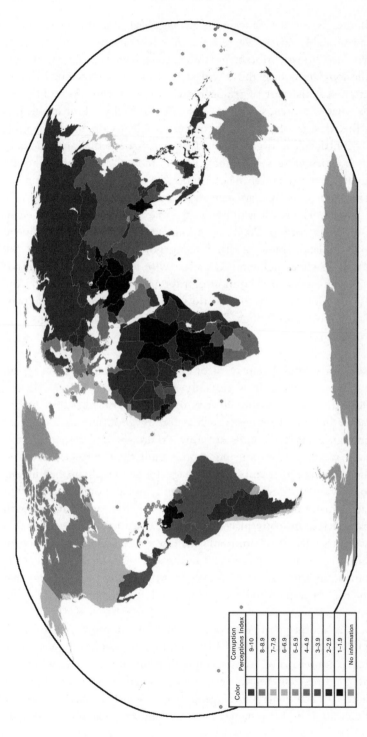

World map index of perception of corruption. The countries with least corruption are mainly in North and West Europe, North America, Australia, New Zealand, and Japan. *Source*: Wikipedia.

intelligence has been found in Ashkenazi Jews, the Jewish communities that descend from medieval societies in the Rhine Valley (in the west of Germany) and northern France. If you calibrate global IQ tests, so that the global average is 100, then the Ashkenazi are around 112–115 on average. To put that in perspective, you typically need to be around 105 to qualify for college. Below the Ashkenazis come a group of Asian countries with IQs ranging from 105 to 108. Most of North America, Europe, Australia, and New Zealand average around 100, with some differences between regions. Many developing and poor nations range lower—some much lower.

The Flynn Effect (rapidly rising IQ) seems to suggest that economic development has a very large effect on general intelligence ("g"), whether it is through nutrition, healthcare, or intellectual stimulation of children when each parent has less to take care of. However, some Asian countries with high IQs have in fact been dirt-poor very recently and are still economically very far behind—and yet they are slightly smarter than the European average. I would think that such Asian countries have enhanced economic growth potential for that reason.

———

Another angle at looking at future real estate growth markets is where people want to work. Creative thinking is the world's greatest renewable resource, but it is also totally mobile. Trying to herd talent is like herding cats, but you can *tempt* smart people to come to your country. American scientist Richard Florida has studied where creative people want to live. One of his findings was that *these people increasingly decided first where to live, and second where to work. This means it was less the people hunting the jobs than the jobs hunting the people.* Furthermore, since most creative people expect to keep each job for a limited period, say 3–4 years, they thought the location of their home was a more important fixpoint in their life than the name of their employer. Americans change job every 3.5 years on average; a frequency that has been increasing steadily. The U.S. Department of Labor estimates that the places Richard Florida spotted as most attractive had diverse cultures, an interesting social scene, authentic culture, and access to nature.

The movement of creative people with high earnings potential or high wealth has become more and more international over time, and these people will be looking for combinations of the factors listed above: great social and natural environments, rule of law, low taxes, etc. However, the profile may be a bit different if you are already wealthy. A consulting company with the somewhat scary name Scorpio Partnership creates a *Mobile Wealthy Residency Index* which every year tracks the best places to live for the world's ever-growing population of "mobile wealthy". The list rates different destinations for 11 factors that rich people care about, such as economic and legal stability, local law, depth of financial services, education opportunities for children, proximity to desired locations, culture/infrastructure, and employment and business opportunities. Their list in 2009 put Switzerland on top, followed by London, Singapore, New York, Hong Kong, Jersey, Cayman Islands, Isle of Man, Monaco, Dubai, and Guernsey, in that order. These are only partially overlapping with places that meet Richard Florida criteria for being attractive to creative workers; places like San Francisco, Boston, Seattle, Los Angeles, Dallas, Austin, San Diego, New York, London, Milan, Munich, Berlin, Copenhagen, or Paris.

One factor that might be forgotten in this is the languages spoken. I noticed not long ago that all passenger messages in an international French airport were given in French language only. I like the French a lot—the language, the people, the cheese and the wine—but given that only 2% of the world's population speak French, I thought it was an odd decision for an international airport.

The most spoken language in the world is Chinese, followed by English. However, the world's leading language in business, finance, and science is English—by a long margin. That goes for travel as well. What this means is that *there is a considerable preference among many of the world's creative and wealthy people to live in places where English is either the native language or at least common in most professional workplaces (and airports).* Interestingly, it seems that there may be more English speakers in China than in India. In fact, China may soon be the largest English-speaking nation on Earth.

Historically, the United States has attracted more talent than any other country. This is due to its excellent Ivy League–class universities, creative, multicultural environments, leading technology companies, low taxes, and typically great lifestyle. Other countries such as Switzerland and Singapore probably owe a lot of their success to an ability to attract foreign talent. Japan has pursued another solution by trying to use technology rather than immigration to deal with labor shortage. They have, for instance, pioneered the use of robots in factories and for healthcare.

It should perhaps be mentioned here that there are three emerging markets that actually have policies to encourage the opposite of immigration, which is emigration—people leaving to work elsewhere. These are Mexico, Morocco, and the Philippines. Two major motives are to solve

Rank	Language	Speakers (native, plus as second language) (million)	Percent of world's population
1	Mandarin Chinese	1,051	18
2	English	510	9
3	Hindi	490	8
4	Spanish	420	7
5	Russian	255	4
6	German	229	4
7	Arabic	230	4
8	Bengali	215	4
9	Portugese	213	4
10	French	130	2

Source: *Languages of the World*, Etnologue, 2005.

unemployment and receive the remittances the workers will send home from abroad, which are often far more than they could earn at home. Mind you, it's evidently not doctors and engineers they want to see leave—it is people with lower earnings potential.

The losers are either countries that are too poor to offer good education or exciting job opportunities; or countries which pursue punitive taxation, are nasty to live in due to corruption, crime, low cultural diversity, or have anti-business policies etc. Extreme cases of the latter, such as Zimbabwe, Cuba, or Venezuela, have actively prevented their best business talent from operating successfully at home.

While emerging markets probably mainly suffer under brain drain conditions, it may give them some advantages over time. First, emigrants often send home sizable remittances. Second, the emigrants may serve as local connection points for exports, and, third, they may return later in life with valuable business experience.

Examples of brain gain countries	Examples of brain drain countries
• U.S.A.	• Russia
• U.K.	• Baltic States
• Canada	• Poland
• Switzerland	• Hungary
• Australia	• India
• Norway	• Iran
• France	• Iraq
• New Zealand	• Cuba
• Israel	• Venezuela
• Singapore	• Pakistan
• Hong Kong	• Germany
• The Emirates	• Zimbabwe

There is a network effect in much of what I have described above. *Professional specialists are attracted to places where there is a lot of talent already.* If you are a biotech expert, for instance, you wish to work in a place where there is a large community of talented biotech people, irrespective of whether you are an entrepreneur or job-seeker. Furthermore, *high earners as well as wealthy people prefer to live where there are many other high earners.* There are two reasons for this: (1) communities with high average income can deliver good public services even with very low tax rates due to their superior tax base and reduced social needs, and (2) the rich will not stand out too much in such places. Tradition and reputation can also matter a lot. As we saw with luxury, *once an area has earned an international reputation from making first-rate luxury products of a given kind, people will expect such products to keep coming from that area.* Some communities or nations can for all these reasons develop local business powerhouses that start feeding on themselves while their tax base increases alongside falling tax rates.

Let's now move on from the question of location to valuation: Where is the value of property, and how do you measure it?

One important consideration about real estate is recognizing which parts may appreciate in value over time. I think that it is very rare for buildings to appreciate in value. They will, in fact, mostly decline in real value. Just think about it. If you build a house, will the faucets and the windows appreciate in value? The floor? The tiles on the roof? Hardly. If there is high inflation, then the replacement value of these items may indeed go up, but after a while much of what is in a house is actually replaced; as I mentioned earlier, in Japan they typically replace the whole thing every 30 years or so on average. Even for the parts you don't replace, the value increase (if any) isn't likely to exceed inflation.

However, land is another matter. *Whereas our population will grow 30% and our real income and wealth 400% from 2010 to 2050, the amount of land on Earth will not change.* We have increased the land available for construction, but often not as fast as the growth in demand, and there are many places where there just isn't any more available for construction. If you build your house in Siberia, the value of your land may not keep up with inflation if the local population keeps declining. However, if the land under your house is located in, say, an average location in central Germany where there is a stable population, then it may appreciate in line with the average nominal income growth in the area, which should beat inflation, if productivity rises. Imagine instead that it's located somewhere in Asia where there is (1) a limited amount of land, (2) rapid population growth, and (3) even faster average income growth. That will make your land a good, structural investment. The first criterion here—limited amount of land—wouldn't be so important if people tried to spread themselves evenly around all livable land, which they would if they all hated each other. But they don't—rather on the contrary.

The reality is that *land has network effects* very similar to the information technology world. Some teenagers start using Facebook and YouTube, then everybody wants to do the same. With land, many people want to locate themselves exacctly where there are many other people already, because that is where the jobs are. As mentioned, many rich people want to go to where there are many other rich people, because that is where the low taxes are. Many intelligent people want to go to where there are many other intelligent people, because that is where the great companies are. Many artists move to where many artists are because that is where they find inspiration and, for instance, art dealers. *More creates more, and the economics of land has, in other words, many self-reinforcing processes.*

———

I mentioned earlier that there are three crucial aspects of property markets that need to be really well understood: (1) location, (2) valuation, and (3) property cycles. You don't want to invest in real estate located in an area that is going nowhere, you don't want to buy at inflated prices, and you don't want to buy close to the peak of a property cycle.

I have already described some of the considerations regarding location, but how do you value properties? The most important financial benchmarks in the property business are known as "CAP rates" (capitalization rates). These are defined as the expected rate of return calculated as annual net operating income divided by the purchase price of the property. It is, in other words, the cashflow before financing costs, income tax, and percentage improvements in the purchase price. An example: A property is bought for U.S.$10 million and generates $0.6 million in net cashflow. So, the CAP rates are 6%. The rule of thumb is that CAP rates probably are acceptable if they are 1–1.5% higher than 10-year bond yields. If they are 3% higher than 10-year bond yields, then it looks like a clear buy, and if they are lower than bond yields you would need a very good specific reason to buy, such as the possibility to "privatize" (sell) rented apartments, make money by improving the property, or see values and rents rise because of an exceptional increase in demand.

Another important metric is DCR ("debt coverage ratio"): net operating income divided by debt-servicing costs, which are interest plus repayments of debt. It's viewed as a cause for concern if operating income doesn't provide 1.1–1.3 times debt-servicing costs.

To estimate whether residential real estate that is tenant-occupied is undervalued or overvalued, you will typically look at three key indicators:

1. Affordability, which is average monthly mortgage payments as a proportion of disposable income
2. Ratio of the average house price to employee compensation
3. Ratio of house prices to GDP (the two trends should roughly follow each other over the very long term). If house prices start pulling significantly ahead of GDP, it's a warning sign.

The third critical issue of successful property investment is timing. If property is bought near the peak of a cycle, there is a real risk that it will become difficult to rent out, impossible to sell, and that lenders will try to call in their loans—all at the same time. To master the timing of property investments, one needs to understand business cycles. I think the typical development of the property cycle can be described with the 30 steps I have listed below, starting at the bottom of a recession.

Stages 1–4: Recession

1. Money supply increases and short-term interest rates, including money rates, fall far below bond yields ("yield curve steepening"). This will typically begin something like 14 months before the trough in the recession.

2. Equity prices start increasing when the smartest investors note a change in "the second derivative" of economic decline, meaning that whereas the economy is still declining, *the decline is no longer accelerating*. This normally happens approx. 5 months before the low point in the economy and thus 6 months after bond prices turned up and interest rates down.

3. Building permits for new private-housing units, or what is normally called "housing starts", begin to rise. These are together with interest rates, bond prices, and equity prices among the best leading indicators for the economy. The rise in housing starts will, like the turn in equity prices, often happen 5–6 months before the low point in the economy. One reason for this is that lower interest rates are attractive for people who want to build.

4. Other leading indicators such as new orders, vendor performance, and initial unemployment claims turn, thus indicating that an economic turning point is near. The index of composite leading indicators typically turns 2–4 months before the low point in the economy. However, headlines in newspapers remain terrible during this phase, and people can't figure out why equity prices rise, when all is so bad.

This period provides the best opportunities to invest in existing real estate. When owners default on their loans, the property is seized by lenders' REO departments (real estate–owned), recovery teams, or owned real estate operations (OREOs). What one should bear in mind here is that one of the effects of recession is that people don't spend or invest—they save. This means that more and more money piles up in money market accounts, while companies bring down their inventories to next to nothing. This creates the conditions for the recovery, which may go as shown in the following phase.

Stages 5–14: Recovery

5. Companies find that their inventories now have reached a bare minimum, so they resume normal ordering, which is enough to kick-start the economy and even force an increase in ordering for inventories.
6. Consumer spending picks up.
7. The recession ends, even though this is only confirmed much later. This stage is what equity investors call "the sweet spot", because inflation and interest rates are still low or falling, while economic activity and corporate earnings grow rapidly. Equity prices may now already be higher than they were the day the recession began.
8. The combination of low or falling interest rates and reduced property prices has substantially improved the affordability of residential property. Prices of apartments, single-family houses, shops, and hotels start to rise, and people return to full service hotels, which have been rather empty during the recession.
9. Gross rents begin to climb, net rents rise even faster as costs are outpaced by income.
10. Professional developers hesitate to start new construction, as development costs have gone up, so they try to meet rising demand by renovating existing buildings.
11. The interest in office rentals picks up approx. one year after the return of demand for residential property.
12. This phase will also encourage white-collar business (particularly in the service sector) to look for good office space, while prices are still reasonable. "Good" means downtown, so downtown offices get filled up first, leading to rising prices there.
13. The economy grows steadily, prosperity spreads, and production capacity gets tight. Land prices are now beginning to advance strongly, as existing real estate inventory is sold out.
14. Consumers are doing much better now, and many can afford to move from apartments to single-family homes, which causes the latter to outpace the former.

The phase just described—stages 5–14—is an economic wonderland, but it doesn't last. There is something in human psychology that makes us move straight into the excessive boom phase.

Stages 15–27: Overheating

15. Consumers will often begin to overcommit at this stage, as they tend to underestimate the true costs of buying at higher prices, when inflation and interest rates are falling. Interest rates are, after all, low, because inflation is expected to be low for some years. Low interest rates make initial mortgages low too, but real mortgages (corrected for inflation) will not fall as quickly as when inflation was high. Investors are thus cannibalizing more on future spending power than they may realize.

16. Access to property financing is enhanced by the perception that investing in real estate is now safer, since prices have been rising steadily, and also because existing real estate can be used as collateral for more investments—in more real estate.

17. Automobile sales are brisk at this stage, and commercial parking lots do well.

18. Consumers have now drawn down a fair amount of their savings, but they are confident, so they keep spending. Residential land prices accelerate upwards on the heels of the residential property boom.

19. Industry, meanwhile, is struggling to keep up with demand, so it starts to build new capacity, which gives the economy a late boost. Capacity building means that prices of industrial properties (R&D flex and industrial warehouses) as well as industrial land rise smartly.

20. Office seekers are now forced to look outside the main centers, so suburban office spaces thrive, and land for office building picks up.

21. Inflation may have begun to rise during this phase, and hotels and commercial parking lots can raise prices continuously.

22. There are many subdivisions of plots now, and speculators buy for speculative purposes. Financing is getting easier still, and many developers can start projects using very little money of their own.

23. Meanwhile, the new building activity absorbs vacant land, which leads to windfall profits for landowners, and land speculation takes off as a response. This is the beginning of a speculative fever, where real estate promoters publish wildly optimistic forecasts for future growth rates using the most optimistic academic research (more conservative, scholarly projections are ignored). They also create marketing material showing future settlements on bare land. Aggressive sales methods abound.

24. The boom attracts the interest of local authorities, which wish to support the growth by re-zoning more land and constructing new

supporting infrastructure. This gives buyers of subdivided plots more confidence that further development is imminent, but it also makes the land useless for farming, should these expected urbanizations fail to materialize.

25. Stock prices stop rising and go into a multi-month phase of wild, trend-less churning. Large, professional players such as hedge funds and skilled speculators are here net sellers, whereas small investors are net buyers.
26. Composite leading indicators turn down.
27. Real estate prices remain firm, but trading volumes decline substantially.

The timelag from the point where leading indicators turn down until the economy keels over is normally 6–8 months, so the warning before an economic top is clearer than the warning before a bottom. This lead time might in theory give property investors time to get out, but reality may be different because (as mentioned in point 27 above) there aren't many buyers around anymore. Firm prices, but few transactions. And then the next phase.

Stages 28–30: Collapse

28. Consumers are maxed out, industrial capacity building has peaked, and the mere cost of rentals and construction begins to hurt the business community.
29. Equities crash. The economy goes into decline a few months later.
30. The demand for real estate levels off, as replacement sales outpace new demand. Rents decelerate, vacancy rates increase, and property prices go into decline, even as construction activity continues to expand perhaps one year after GDP has peaked.

I have to add here that all of this seems simpler, of course, when you read about it in a book, than when you have to navigate it in real life. But there are huge gains possible for those who get it roughly right, and huge losses for those who get it wrong.

The identification of location, valuation, and timing amounts to what investors some times called "beta". However, there is also an "alpha" in investment, which is the more active part. Within real estate, this can involve actively developing or redeveloping the assets. You can, for instance, buy a large tract of land, subdivide it, build on it, and sell it as single units. Or build apartment buildings, factories, office buildings, and whatnot. This can be very profitable if you don't do it too late in the property cycle.

It is also possible to buy existing property and improve it to extract more value. One may, for instance, buy apartment buildings, where the flats are rented out and then "privatize" them one by one, as people move out (or are paid to move out). Privatize means selling them one unit at a time, typically after they have been renovated.

There are still others who will convert buildings or even whole neighborhoods to accommodate changing business patterns and demographics. The classical example is to convert industrial property to apartments, or to upgrade whole areas for more affluent buyers. New park areas with trees and plants can be added, for instance, or common entertainment facilities, local shops and restaurants, tennis courts, a country club, 24-hour surveillance, or one can even gate the community. Many have also upgraded environmental standards through better insulation, etc., and thus vastly enhanced the property values.

There are also opportunistic financial strategies that can be extremely rewarding during crises. Listed property companies and REITs will often trade well below the realistic net asset value during crises, which makes it far more attractive to buy them than to buy properties outright. There are furthermore great opportunities to buy REO property ("real estate–owned": property that has been seized by lenders) at heavily discounted prices, or to buy at foreclosure auctions. Between these two, it is generally the directly negotiated REO purchase that works best.

A third group of opportunistic financial approaches involves investing in distressed property companies You can extend bridging loans or mezzanine loans to save the company, against getting a good slice of the upside. There is also the loan-to-own approach that I mentioned briefly in the previous chapter:

1. Find a developer in trouble and buy up its loans or bonds in the market (or from banks) at heavily discounted prices.
2. If the developer that owes you money doesn't go under, then you will receive a very high real yield and be happy with that. Let's say, for instance, that the interest on the loan is 6%, but that you bought the bonds at half price, which means that you actually get 12% interest.
3. If, on the other hand, it blows up (as it very well might do, given how discounted its loans were), you have work to do. Typically, the

shareholders will be wiped out in what follows, and the creditors (you) will end up owning the project or company. You will then need to come up with additional financing to finish the project and get it to a profitable stage.

Investments in distress are called vulture investment and, in spite of their name, I think they are generally good for society as well as for its investors, when done well.

––––––––––

I started this chapter by showing the historic bubble and real estate crash in Japan, where early investors may have generated something like a 1,600% return on their investments during the first 20 years. I would guess that many actually made a whole lot more, since people tend to mortgage their paper profits and add continuously to their exposure during such markets. What I know for sure is that a lot of them lost everything in the subsequent crash.

Personally I find it very likely that there will be great, fundamentally justified bull markets in many emerging property markets over the coming decades, and it wouldn't surprise me if some of these evolve into bubbles like we saw in Japan. The best hope for avoiding that lies in the lessons learned by policymakers during the Japanese meltdown and international subprime salami fiasco.

Bubbles or not, there is another development we can be very sure of: In the coming decades we will see a property construction boom in emerging markets that the world has never seen before, and may never see again. Property construction requires a lot of financing, as mentioned in the previous chapter. But it requires something else: A massive number of commodities such as metals and energy. This leads us directly to what the next chapter is about: The global demand for commodities.

Fifteen ideas for the buildings of the future

1. Moisture and strain sensors built into structures for early detection of potential problems.
2. Interior walls made of smartglass, which can turn milky by touching a button. Some of these should have e-zones, which work as computer/media displays operated by no-touch hand movements.
3. Solar energy–generating windows. Skylight glass with a dye coating that absorbs light with matching wavelengths and re-emits this to the edges of the glass for power generation.
4. Smartglass. Vertical windows contain a coating that automatically creates reflecting shade, when sunlight is strong.
5. Smart wallpaper. Entire walls or large parts of walls that can turn into displays for media updates or to set an ambience.
6. Entire roofs and walls made of photovoltaic cells.
7. Lock and secure your house with a single remote control click, like you do with a car.
8. Smart light control by photosensors in gardens, infrared sensors in hallways and other pass-through areas, or timers.
9. Ambience control. One click, easily programmable control of light, smartglass walls, and smart wallpaper in zones.
10. Wireless communication throughout.
11. Designer garages. Entrance halls in old houses were generally made to look nice—it was the first thing you saw. In modern life, the first thing is the garage, which is often directly connected to the interior. Make them look good.
12. Robots. Automated washing room, robotic vacuum cleaners, and lawnmowers.
13. Smart perimeter control, intrusion detection, and access control aided by artificial intelligence and connected to the web and your smartphone.
14. Secure standard locker for deposit of groceries ordered via the internet.
15. Remote control of house automation and surveillance systems via web and smartphone.

13

Commodities

On August 1, 1900 the *New York Times* ran the following little story:

United States Produced Last Year 10,702,209 Out of 26,841,755 Tons.

WASHINGTON, July 31.—Vice Consul Monoghan, at Chemnitz, Germany, has transmitted to the State Department an interesting statement concerning the steel production of the world. German authorities, he says, estimate the production last year at 26,841,755 tons, as against 23,866,308 tons in 1898. The cast-iron output is placed at 40,000,000 tons, against 36,000,000 tons in 1898. Seventy per cent. of the cast-iron production was used in the production of steel.

So, what this demonstrated to readers was that world steel production had grown by 4 million tons in 1898 to reach 27 million tons in 1899. The main driver was evidently the industrialization of America and Europe. However, while this was impressive, it was also a cause for concern, because it was difficult to see for how long America could continue its rapid depletion of its iron resources. In 1908 the governors at the White House convened a conference to discuss this problem. The following is how a newspaper covered some of this meeting:

GOVERNORS CHEER ROOSEVELT'S TALK

He Tells Them Conservation of All Natural Resources Needs One Coherent Plan.

PUTS JOHNSON IN CHAIR

Carnegie Pleads for More Careful Husbanding of Coal and Iron, Which He Says Are Being Wasted.

Special to The New York Times.

According to this article, President Roosevelt made the following alarming statement:

" The enormous stores of mineral oil and gas are largely gone. Our natural waterways are not gone, but they have been so injured by neglect, and by the division of responsibility and utter lack of system in dealing with them, that there is less navigation on them now than there was fifty years ago. We have so impoverished our soils by injudicious use and by failing to check erosion that their crop-producing power is diminishing instead of increasing.

Andrew Carnegie, one of the country's leading industrialists at the time (in fact of all time), followed up with this:

> " By 1938 about half of the original supply of iron ore will be gone, and only the lower grades of ore will remain, and all the ore now deemed workable will be used long before the end of the present century.
>
> ### Iron Ore Going.
>
> " I have for many years been impressed with the steady depletion of our iron ore supply. It is staggering to learn that our once supposed ample supply of rich ores can hardly outlast the generation now appearing, leaving only the leaner ores for the later years of the century.

In spite of these warnings, the production boom continued over the following five years, until it peaked in 1913, where global production reached 78 million tons. Then it declined, leveled, and picked up again, but with much slower growth.

However, it didn't run out, and the global expansion of iron production wasn't over. The next big production expansion came from 1950 to 1979. That was caused by the reconstruction of Europe plus the massive growth in Japan following World War II. When that peaked, production leveled off again and remained rather tame until around 2000. Meanwhile, most commodity prices failed to keep up with inflation, which meant that profits for producers remained under pressure. Many went bankrupt and others pulled out to spend their cash on something better, or to give it back to their shareholders. For instance, in copper, one of the biggest industrial metals, there weren't any major new mine openings after the early 1980s. Exxon, which had invested in the Disputada Copper Mine in Chile, chose during the global slowdown in 2003 to sell its interests to Anglo American.

But then something surprising happened: The demand for all metals exploded. It was 608 million tons in 2002 and grew to 720 million in 2003, and 802 million in 2004. In fact, *within the single decade from 2000 to 2010, global steel consumption managed to double to approx. 1,200 million tons; something it hadn't done for 110 years.* To be more specific: It grew by more than 600 million tons within 10 years—an increase that exceeded 20-fold total world production in 1900, when Carnegie expressed his concern about depletion of resources. And the same pattern was repeated for all other industrial metals.

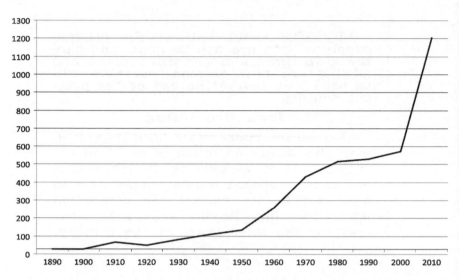

Global steel production 1890–2010 (forecast), million tons. *Source: Iron and Steel Statistics*, U.S. Geological Survey; *New York Times*, January 15, 1902.

So why did demand for metals suddenly go through the roof? Let's look at the basic numbers. The main industrial metals are aluminum, copper, zinc, lead, and nickel, in that order. The average citizen of the world consumes approx. 150 kg of steel, 4.5 kg of aluminum, 2 kg to 2.5 kg of copper, 1.5 kg of zinc and a bit over 1 kg of lead annually. Not that you walk into a shop and ask for it, of course, but its embedded in things we buy.

Let's start with aluminum. Approx. 40% of world aluminum production is used in transportation, since it is light. Another 18% or so goes into building construction, 16% is used in packaging (mainly cans), 9% in electrical equipment, and 9% in machinery/equipment. As for lead, approx. 76% goes into lead acid batteries (especially automobile batteries). A very large part of lead is fortunately recycled, as it is poisonous.

I mentioned aluminum and lead together because they have one thing in common: they are largely used in automobiles and transport equipment. This makes them very dependent on capital-spending cycles, and also on inventory cycles, since automobiles constitute a big part of world inventories. But this also means that demand for these metals may be driven by the explosive increase in automobile production that awaits us—I will come back to that.

The two other big industrial metals are copper and zinc, and these are largely related to building construction. Copper is an excellent conductor and is therefore primarily used for electrical applications, such as wire (50%), general and industrial engineering applications (20%), and architectural building and construction parts, such as roof tops, lighting fixtures, plumbing fixtures, and plumbing (15%). A smaller part is used in the transportation sector, where it goes into radiators and intercoolers/ heat exchangers, etc. (11%). A substantial part of the electrical applications mentioned are also part of building and construction—they are just not what is called "architectural". This means that *almost half of all copper consumption is tied to property construction* some way or the other. As for zinc, approx. 57% is used in construction, 23% in engineering applications, 20% in building and construction, 15% in transportation, and 11% in other applications.

We have already seen the forecasts that 70 million to 90 million people will move out of poverty into middle class every year over the coming decades, and approx. 75 million into urban environments. Unless my predictions in this book are way off, the commodity industry simply isn't ready for what we will face, even if they are surely fully aware of this by now. It takes 5–10 years to start up a new mine, and it can cost billions. You need to get agreements with politicians and then with labor unions. You need to train local people, hire skilled managers and persuade them to move to harsh locations in desert or jungles. You need to put massive infrastructure in place to transport the commodities from where they are found to harbors for shipping—and you may even have to build these harbors. Extracting commodities requires water, and many places don't have that nearby. In Chile they use desalination plants to remove salt from water before pumping it up to 4,000 m altitude, where some of the copper mines are.

Global copper production in 2010 is approx. 16 million tons. You may need around 6 million tons annually to move people out of poverty into middle class, but you will also need an ever-larger amount to move the world's middle class to increasingly higher income levels. So, demand should continue to increase, but traditionally there is a long timelag before mining operations can fully respond to such demand. I think prices of industrial metals will go up, and perhaps they will get very, very high at times, until a clear effect on demand materializes. Furthermore, as supply eventually does respond, it will often be from mines that are far more costly to manage than they were in the past. Even if this causes prices to rocket, there may only be a limited reaction in demand. After all, would you not build a new house because the price of a very small part of it—copper—has trebled? Or would you just pay up for that part?

In addition to the inflexibility of supply and demand to price changes, there may even be situations where higher prices *reduce* supply. When prices rise fast, some governments may come back and ask for renegotiation of previous contracts with the mining companies, and labor units may call strikes. Some mines may get nationalized and, if they do, then their production may decline. This happened in Zambia and the Congo, for instance, after the mines were nationalized. Ultimately much of metal mining may come from offshore sites, which means under seawater. That will not be cheap.

———

Metals are not the only resources that will be in high demand. With the world's population growing from 7 billion to 9 billion people, and with improving living standards, the demand for water will rise rapidly. Lack of clean water is probably the world's largest health problem. An estimated 3.5 million die annually because of problems with water—about 43% of those from diarrhea. This is so bad that, at any given time, half of the world's hospital beds are occupied by patients suffering from water-related diseases. It is generally estimated that humans need around 100 liters of clean water daily for drinking, washing, and personal hygiene. Almost 900 million people lack access to safe water supplies, and studies have shown that poor people living in slum areas often pay 5–10 times more per liter of water than wealthy people living in the same city.

And yet, it is only 8% of the world's water usage that goes to domestic supply. Almost three times as much—22%—is used for industrial purposes and *a whopping 70% of our water consumption goes to agriculture. It often takes around 1,000 tons of water to create one ton of food.* That may be no problem in countries with sufficient rainfall or large rivers, but it can evidently raise conflicts between urban developers and farmers in places where water is scarce. In and around Murcia in Spain, for instance, farmers have been denied access to some of the water they need for farming, as more and more of it is diverted to tourist developments along the coast, where it is used for tap water, golf courses, and swimming pools.

Global average precipitation on land is 30 cm per annum. Most human settlements have for good reasons been built close to freshwater, whether it be lakes or rivers. As their populations grow, more and more will need costly technical solutions to supply their water. Dams can contribute to it by leveling out freshwater flows in rivers, since rainfall is often concentrated in autumn months, whereas the melting of ice and snow happens in springs, while summers and winters may cause riverbeds to dry up. Other technical solutions include pumping up groundwater, moving freshwater through long-distance pipes, rerouting rivers, using roof collection systems, or desalinating seawater (which costs approx. 50 cents per m^3 and can be powered by solar panels)

Technology offers many ways to conserve and reuse water. Since farming uses most water, it is here that the biggest savings may be found. Drip irrigation in farming can cut water consumption by 30–70%, while increasing yields by a whopping 20–90%. Furthermore, it is possible to genetically engineer crops that use far less water. However, what all of this has in common is that it costs money, which means economic growth needs to match population growth.

A rapidly growing solution for countries short on freshwater is a combination of desalination plants in coastal areas, and so-called offshore farming (farming abroad). Desalination plants work fine, but they leave behind mountains of brine, which has to be removed. As for offshore farming, between 2000 and 2010, $20 billion to $30 billion worth of farmland in Ghana, Ethiopia, Mali, Tanzania, Kenya, and Sudan was purchased or leased on long-term contracts by China, South Korea, Saudi Arabia, Kuwait and other countries. This farmland exceeds the size of all farming areas in France, and these early land-grab cases, which are really water-grabs, may be the beginning of a long trend. Africa doesn't have a transcontinental highway system, and less than 20% of its roads are paved. However, if foreign countries wish to carry out efficient, large-scale farming there, this may stimulate improvements in its transportation infrastructure.

––––––––

People eat increasingly more. Between 1970 and 2000 the world's population grew 64%, and yet we managed to increase the daily calorie intake per capita from 2,411 calories in 1970 to 2,789 in 2000. That is a 16% increase in the amount of calorie intake per person within 30 years. Furthermore, per capita food consumption grew most in developing countries, where it increased by 26%, although hunger still periodically affected around 10% of the global population.

As for the demand side of this, the reasons for increased food intake are declining poverty, an increasing middle class, and increases in obesity, average human height, and muscle mass. Concerning the supply, some 80% of extra food production during this period came from improvements in farming productivity and only 20% from the development of new land. So, *by increasing farmland by approx. 20%, we managed to almost double food calorie output, while at the same time shifting towards more expensive and resource-intensive foods (people ate proportionally more meat), and while also diverting an increasing proportion of farming output to biofuel production.* Furthermore, this was done by an ever-smaller number of farmers. Denmark, a small, densely populated country with just over 5 million people, produced enough farm products to feed around 15 million in 2010. The total number of people working in farming and food processing responsible for this is only around 150,000, which means that each worker in the sector feeds 100 people. Annual Danish productivity increase in the food sector has been 6% since 1970.

Similar patterns have been seen in numerous other countries. During the 1970s European farmers became so efficient that the densely populated EU with its increasingly overweight population ended with huge surpluses of food and wine, which were stored in giant warehouses (e.g., the EU's "butter mountain" and "wine lake"), and the EU and US paid farmers massive amounts as compensation for *reducing* the amount of land they farmed, just to avoid even further food surplus buildups. This ever-increasing food productivity was so dramatic that real food prices (meaning prices adjusted for inflation) fell by approx. 90% between 1900 and 2000.

The FAO, the Food and Agriculture Organization of the United Nations, undertakes frequent studies and forecasts of world food production. In 2006 they published a revised version of their *World Agriculture: Towards 2030/2050*, where they predicted that per capita calorie intake would continue to grow. As populations also would grow, the gist of their predictions was that global food production would rise 40% from 2008 to 2030, but after that it would decelerate considerable due to a smaller increase in per capita consumption as well as continued deceleration in population growth. However, while global calorie intake is now passing its most intense growth phase, the transition towards more meat consumption will be pretty intense. Different organization have estimated an increase in meat production of 85% between 2010 and 2030 and a doubling by 2050.

I think that the core of the matter is that we have already passed the time when the most intense pressure was applied to the global food sector without it leading to structurally higher prices (they actually fell in real terms), and since we will have twice as long to meet the demand growth for the coming world population increase of 2 billion (as we did for the previous one), the future technical challenge seems very manageable—especially since the genomics revolution has really only just started. In summary, hunger and undernourishment in some parts of the world is not because of global inability to produce enough food, but rather due to local lack of money to pay for it, or local lack of skill to produce it. It's an economic problem; not a resource problem.

However, what is clear is that only countries with ample natural water supplies will be able to produce at competitive prices. As much of the expected population increase will happen in places like the Middle East, where water is scarce, this can lead to severe balance-of-payment problems for some of those nations. Furthermore, some may sense supply insecurity. During the brief commodity bubble in 2007, which also engulfed food prices, many nations with food exports slapped export taxes on their products, which meant that net importers felt particularly squeezed. When food prices rise dramatically in an emerging market, it tends to create riots and become a threat to the regime, and this may have added to a sense of urgency, further driving the trend of offshore farming, which would be unnecessary if people trusted in free, international food markets.

Considering, in particular, that the Middle Eastern population is expected to grow to 75% from 2010 to 2050, where it will reach 750 million people, it may turn out that the Middle East's dependence on foreign food and water gradually overtakes the world's dependence on Middle Eastern oil and gas.

And that brings me to the last big resource issue the world is confronting: energy. The primary source of energy in the universe is nuclear fusion. This is what makes the stars burn, including our own Sun. The Sun is a huge nuclear reactor which gives us sunshine that can be captured by solar panels and thus converted to electric or thermal energy. The energy radiating from the Sun is also the reason we have wind and waves, which again we may harvest energy from. The Earth is also a huge nuclear reactor, which is the main reason that its core is very hot. We can utilize this through geothermal energy (that is in fact how my family's house is heated).

The energy from the Sun does much more: it enables plants to capture carbon from the air and minerals from the ground and link these into huge protein structures, as well as sugar and fat. When we extract oil, gas, and coal today, we are really harvesting ancient energy stores that were made possible because of the Sun—and thus because of nuclear fusion.

Most of the coal, oil, and gas that we use today comes from the Carboniferous Period, which lasted from about 360 million to 286 million years ago. The name of this period, which had a warmer climate than today, is in fact derived from "carbon". During that period the land was largely covered with swamps and bogs filled with huge trees, ferns, and other large, leafy plants, and the sea was filled with single-celled organisms called protoplankton. There were numerous fish and land animals, which are no longer with us.

Over time, layer upon layer of these organisms died. Many quickly rotted and released much of their carbon to the air, but some, perhaps 1% or so, died in locations that didn't have enough oxygen or were too acidic to support a full rotting process. This was primarily in sedimentary basins, where the water was shallow. These basins could be large lagoons in the seas, or inland lakes or marshes surrounded by land. Sometimes the climate would change or the land shift, which made huge forests sink below water. This debris would then pile up layer upon layer, perhaps for thousands or millions of years in the same location and would at times get covered by mud, rock, and sand, which further reduced any access to oxygen. The remnants of bacteria, algae, and plankton would then degrade slowly into oil. What was left of plants and trees turned into humic acids and a spongy material called peat, which looks like coal and tastes and smells a bit like some Scottish single-malt whiskeys (for the simple reason that they are actually made using water from peat bogs—try Lagavulin, for instance!). Several, alternative developments now took place:

- More and more rock and other material piled up on top of a layer containing peat, which sank deeper into the ground. This was squeezed in the process, and also heated by geothermal forces. The water was squeezed and/or boiled out of it and some of it decomposed further into oil and gas, which escaped too. What was left was *coal*.
- The remnants of micro-organisms and perhaps some remains from large trees and plants turned into oil, which slowly worked its way upward through the Earth's crust, finally evaporating at the surface and leaving nothing in the ground.
- The deposits never sank deep enough to decompose into oil. Instead it turned into kerogen, which looks like rock, but can burn. This is called *oil shale* in the oil business, even though it contains neither oil nor shale. There are enormous deposits of it in the Rocky Mountains in the U.S.—about 1.5 trillion barrels equivalent, or probably more than all the conventional oil in the world.
- Oil and gas worked its way upward through the Earth's crust, but was stopped by an airtight geological layer, such as granite or marble. Such a "cap rock" sealed them like a cork on a bottle. It thus became a *traditional oilfield* of the kind we mostly use today.

- The oilfield was sealed by a cap rock. However, this sealing layer eroded over time, which exposed the oilfield at, or close to, the surface. The gas and the more volatile parts of the oil started to evaporate, but the heavier parts still remained when we found it. These are called *tar sands*—they have a fluid, but thick consistency. There are huge reserves of tar sands in Venezuela and Canada.

One could easily imagine that these processes only occurred in a few places. However, because it went on for millions of years, and because it is difficult to comprehend how much can happen in millions of years, we may not grasp the scale. First, the large majority of all oil and gas that was ever created has evaporated or rotted thousands or millions of years before we evolved. In fact, it is probably a fair estimate that virtually every corner of the Earth has been an oilfield or gasfield many times before. Apart from the coal, what we find today are those rare occurrences where liquid or gaseous fossil fuel couldn't evaporate because of a cap rock that has remained intact until today.

It is also difficult to grasp how much is still baking in the oven, so to speak. It is generally estimated that there exists a total mass of kerogen on Earth today of approx. 10,000,000 billion tons. Much of that comes from dead organisms. Your share of that existing kerogen, if we divided it evenly among all the people on Earth, would almost be 14 million tons, or 14,000,000,000 kg. All this kerogen is still being squeezed and baked in the ground, and much of it will become graphite, which we regard as rock. However, approx. 0.1% of it will eventually turn into coal. Your part of that coal would be 1,500 tons. The size of a decent hill, really, but you will be long gone before the coal is ready. A tiny fraction of it will also degrade into oil and gas.

———————

Approx. 62% of our current oil supply comes from the Middle East with Saudi Arabia supplying approx. 22%, Iran 11%, and Iraq 10%. About 60% of it is today used for transportation and it constitutes approx. 95% of all energy that goes into transportation. The underlying trend in oil demand grows approx. 2% annually.

Unexploited oil resources are divided into three categories, which are called P90, P50, and P10. P90 means that there is a 90% chance of recovering it, which makes it "proved reserves" in industry jargon. P50 is "probable" reserves since it is thought that there is 50% chance that it can be recovered, and P10 is "possible" reserves.

In discussing reserves, the oil and mining industry makes use of the so-called "Hubbert Peak" theory. Hubbert was a geophysicist at Shell and developed a rather simple model to predict when the extraction of a raw material would peak. According to him, the rate of petroleum extraction tends to follow a bell-shaped curve that peaks when half of all commercial resources have been recovered. The first time he published his theory, he purported that a gradual buildup of the nuclear power industry was necessary to prepare ourselves for the future oil deficit. This was in 1956.

It didn't take long after Hubbert published his theory until the global rate of oil discovery peaked. This happened in 1963 and gave the first warning that the peak in production might be in sight. The second warning came in 1980, when oil consumption overtook oil discovery for the first time.

A majority of the studies conducted throughout the past 10–20 years have estimated that the commercially accessible oil resources available amount to approximately 2 trillion barrels. Sometime between 2005 and 2015, we will have used half of that, which could indicate that we are very close to the time when oil extraction peaks. There are, however, a minority of models predicting that this will not happen until 2040.

Most Hubbert Peak models do not include oil extracted from shale oil, tar oils, and other unconventional oil sources. The development of these resources, however, requires considerable energy in the form of natural gas or nuclear power. When including these oil resources, we might be able to postpone the culmination of oil production to around 2060. But we cannot postpone the escalating production costs. I should add here by the way that the book *Limits to Growth* from 1974, which I mocked earlier, predicted in their most optimistic scenario that we would run out of oil in 2024, which we will definitely not.

The same book predicted that we would run completely out of natural gas in 2021. However, since then we have found more and more, and our known gas reserves have actually trebled from 1980 to 2010, so that we now seem to have enough until around 2080 at current consumption rates. The energy contained in these reserves is larger than that of our known oil reserves. I should mention here that these numbers do not include the natural gas that may be extracted from coal and oil shales, which again would take us well into the next century.

For delivery over land, gas is normally sent via pipelines. For overseas delivery, it is compressed into a fuel called liquefied natural gas and sent via specially designed ships that are easily recognizable with LNG in huge letters emblazoned on the side. Gas is a cleaner fuel than oil and coal, but it can also be converted to a liquid that doesn't need to be kept under pressure. This process is called GTS for "gas-to-liquid", and it can serve as a stopgap when we are short of liquid fuel. Indeed, as new discoveries of gas have soared lately, the use of this technology may increase rapidly. However, the process consumes the equivalent of 45% of the energy in the gas, so it is not a solution that would be pursued were oil prices low.

As far as we know, the biggest fossil fuel reserve is coal. The known world supply of this energy resource is absolutely massive, and it should last until somewhere around 2280(!) given current consumption rates (*Limits to Growth*: year 2122). Our great-grandchildren will be able to burn coal, although I think they would find the idea completely laughable, just as we would if we lit our houses by burning whale oil.

The largest coal deposits are in the U.S.A., Russia, and China, in that order. It is technically possible to convert coal to gasoline or gas. Nazi Germany actually did the former during World War II and South Africa started doing it during the boycott years. The biggest issue with coal is that it is highly polluting, but a number of initiatives are under way to create clean coal (or cleaner coal). These include chemically washing minerals and impurities from the coal, gasification, removing sulfur with steam, and capturing carbon from the exhaust. Another new technology that is currently being rolled out is the so-called "integrated gasification combined cycle" (IGCC), which turns coal into so-called "syngas"—synthetic gas. By capturing the carbon from smoke, it may be reused to create biofuel with bacteria or algae, or it may be sequestered below ground. The latter is not easy, though, because if you pump carbon into the ground, it may come back up unless there is a cap rock or a rock formation that can readily absorb it. However, as proposed in Al Gore's book *Our Choice*, instead of pumping carbon into the ground, we may turn it into charcoal and mix it with soil.

How do these fossil fuel sources compare pricewise? It all depends on where and how, but the table overleaf gives a fairly good idea of what we are talking about. What it shows are the so-called "breakeven prices" that define the salesprice necessary for you to start making money on any given activity.

Conventional oil (listed at the top of the table) is traditional oil in the sense that you stick a tube into the Earth and pump it up (I know it's more complicated than that, but I think you know what I mean). The cost starts as low as around $3 a barrel in the Saudi desert and goes up to $40 a barrel in more difficult places. Oil sands are more expensive but still not that bad. However, they are highly polluting. Next comes the enhanced oil recovery method, or "EOR", which comprises a number of methods for improving yield so that typically 30–60% of the oil is

Breakeven price for different oil resources. The minimum price required before exploration for the types of oil mentioned becomes profitable.

Energy source	Breakeven price of oil (U.S.$ per barrel)
Conventional oil	3–40
Oil sands	30–65
Enhanced oil recovery method	35–80
Deepwater and ultra-deepwater	38–65
Arctic	38–100
Gas-to-liquid conversion	40–110
Oil shales	50–110
Coal-to-liquid conversion	60–110

Sources: Credit Suisse; UBS.

recovered instead of the 20–40% one can expect with traditional methods. EOR involves the injection of gas, CO_2, chemicals, or microbes, or thermal heating to stimulate the oil flow, or even ultrasonic stimulation. It works, but it adds to the cost. Next on the price scale comes deepwater and ultra-deepwater drilling, where the most expensive sites have production costs that approach $70 a barrel. This is followed by Arctic, which may cost as much as $100 a barrel (or as little as $38).

The final three methods are gas–to-liquid conversion, oil shales, and coal–to-liquid conversion, all of which are expensive but also have huge production potential—especially the last two, which could supply us well into the next century.

I think that the numbers in the table tell us that, *with an oil price either above or between, say, $80 to $90 per barrel, it should become profitable to utilize new resources that are truly abundant.* However, what the table doesn't tell us is how long it would take to produce these resources in sufficient quantities or whether anyone would risk big money on it if they weren't sure that oil prices would stay high.

In terms of location, a number of emerging markets—besides Canada, Australia, Norway, and others—stand out regarding their natural resources, which may generate huge profits over the coming decades. When it comes to traditional fossil energy, the leading nations are predominantly some Middle Eastern countries, followed by Russia, the U.S.A., China, India, Canada, Venezuela, Brazil, South Africa, Nigeria, and others. As for unconventional oil, it's Canada, the U.S., and Venezuela that dominate.

———

I would like to move from the supply aspect of fossil energy to demand. Let's start with an example of what the issue is about: China's automobile market really only took off around 2000, but by 2010 there were still only around 56 million automobiles on its roads. This is nothing compared with, for instance, the 260 million in the U.S. in the same year. *If China had the same automobile density as America, they would have over 1,100 million vehicles.* But they don't. Since it is still early days for the development of China, their oil consumption per capita is just a tenth of what it is in the U.S. The Chinese automobile pool is expected to grow to approx. 400 million around 2030 and 500 million by 2050.

Someone will have to be really clever to solve this, and those who do so will make a lot of money in the process. Resources are a constraint to growth, but they are also an investment opportunity. However, there is a problem: the *speed* of the growth in populations and incomes. We may be sufficiently inventive to manage this task in the belief that our energy resources may just be ultimately unlimited, but we might find it difficult to handle the adjustment *quickly enough.*

Not that we are not making every effort to overcome it. Today, we use some of the world's heaviest machinery to excavate thick tar oil from the sands of Canada, and we look for conventional oil in seemingly impossible places. At the end of 2007, Petrobras in Brazil announced that they had discovered huge oil reserves. There was only one snag: the oil reservoir is 8 km below sea level in an area where the salt layer is about 2 km deep. In order to maintain production in this area, it will be necessary to pump gas through 2 km of water and 6 km of rock at enormous pressure.

There are three major problems associated with focusing too heavily on the extraction of oil and gas as energy resources. The first is the risk of global warming, which I have already addressed. The second is that democratic nations purchasing oil and gas transfer vast sums to dictatorships, which in some cases are even hostile towards their clients. Experience tells us that the abominable behavior of some of these states is directly proportional to the price of oil—the higher the oil price, the bigger the aggression. The third problem is that it may prove very difficult to comply with an ever-increasing demand for energy from developing countries fast enough, as exemplified by my calculation scenario with Chinese cars.

––––––––

I started this chapter with the story of how global steel production had evolved during the past. We looked at the manner in which it increased as first Europe and the U.S. got industrialized, and then Japan and Korea. We managed that fairly well. However, the issue for the coming decades is the sheer magnitude of what will happen. The combined population of Japan and Korea was approx. 125 million when their economies took off in 1960–1970. *The combined population in the BRIC countries today is 3.5 billion—almost 30 times as much.*

It is obvious that this will create pressure on all sorts of resources. As that happens numerous conferences will be held where people with PowerPoint presentations will show plans for saving the world, which is all very fine. There will also be mobs that will burn cars and smash shop windows to show their opinion, which is not. But the reality is that it tends to be more popular to talk about the need to get problems solved than to actually solve them.

However, at some point they will be solved by the many small armies of mostly ordinary people who work anonymously in the "machine rooms" of the world, so to speak. I am thinking about the investors, engineers, technicians, business planners, entrepreneurs, workers, etc., who will struggle every day to play their small part and who will often risk their own money and health to move things forward.

The field that will require most creativity here, and which happens to involve the biggest investments and the largest potential rewards, is alternative energy. This is the subject of the next chapter.

14

Alternative energy

The definition of alternative energy depends on who you ask. From an ecological standpoint it's anything that doesn't pollute (except perhaps when the equipment used to produce it is made). From an economical point of view it's perhaps anything that isn't used on a major scale yet, or which could be expanded massively. To me it is a combination of the two.

Much is said and written about alternative energy, and a lot of it seems to ignore the realities on the ground. One of these realities is cost. The table overleaf is a pricelist. It gives estimates of the breakeven points for all the important alternative energy sources when compared with oil prices. It is thus similar to the breakeven table for conventional energy that we saw in the last chapter.

I have sorted these in descending order so that those that may (may!) be cheapest are at the top. However, these price ranges are not all static. Since there is a lot of innovation going on in most areas, many breakeven prices will come down over time. I think *the prime candidates for falling prices are solar photovoltaic (which is power generation from solar power), solar thermal, and biofuels.*

Another comment: Nuclear appears at the top of the list partly because its lowest breakeven price is just $10 a barrel. This is a bit unfair, since it can only apply to an existing nuclear plant that has been written off. But if you close such a nuclear plant, that may be what you say goodbye to: $10 a barrel oil-equivalent that doesn't pollute the air. I wouldn't.

Now, if we look at the pricelist then we see that many of these energy forms can actually compete within realistic oil price levels. That goes not

Breakeven price for different oil resources. The minimum price required before exploration for the types of oil mentioned becomes profitable.

Energy source	Breakeven price of oil (U.S.$ per barrel)
Nuclear	10–125
Hydro	35–140
Wind onshore	35–80
Sugar-based ethanol (as in Brazil)	40–50
Cellulosic biofuels	40–70
Geothermal	40–110
Wind offshore	45–125
Solar thermal	55–180
Tidal and wave	60–140
Algal/bacterial fuel	90–120
Biodiesel	125–140
Solar photovoltaic	150+

Source: Credit Suisse, UBS.

only for nuclear, but also for hydro, wind, sugar-based ethanol, cellulosic biofuel, geothermal, and solar for thermal heating (such as heating swimming pools and tap water by means of solar panels on the roof in sunny climates). But they can only do so under their own individual special conditions.

Due to naturally occurring nuclear reactions, the temperatures in the Earth's interior are very high. In fact, 99% of the planet is hotter than 1,000°C, and only 0.1% is cooler than 100°C. We can harness this as geothermal energy, which is brilliant in some places like Iceland, the Philippines, Turkey, and Northern Italy. In some of these places all you need do is stick a tube into the ground, pump cold water down, and get steaming hot water (or simply steam) back up. At other places you have to dig deeper, and what you get back may be lukewarm and need to be heated more by means of electric power (using a sort of inverse refrigerator). I already mentioned that this is actually what we have in our home in Switzerland, where it is widespread and cheaper than oil in some parts. The typical geothermal installation for a single home in a building block has tubes that penetrate 150 m to 500 m into the ground. However, there are now numerous research projects that plan to go much deeper ("enhanced geothermal systems", "hot dry rock technology"), where efforts are focused on reaching a depth of around 5,000 m and using geothermal energy to produce electricity and heat. Geothermal energy is most economic close to tectonic plate boundaries, which are typically around mountains. Almost the entire west coast of North and Latin America is such an area, for instance, as are the Alpine areas of Europe, East Africa, Japan, the Philippines and the Himalayas.

Waste burning is another important alternative energy source. The incinerators used provide three benefits in a single process:

- Reduce the volume of the original waste by 95–96%
- Generate energy for heating or electricity
- Destroy hazardous waste that contains pathogens and toxins.

I mentioned in the previous chapter that nuclear energy is the primary source of all energy on Earth, and indeed in the universe. The nuclear energy produced by nuclear reactors can be ramped up massively within a reasonable timespan without emitting carbon dioxide to the atmosphere. It is the potential clean-air "heavy lifter" in the international energy landscape. There are approx. 440 nuclear reactors operating in the world delivering approx. 7% of all the energy currently used and approx. 17% of all electric power. To understand how this is possible, just consider that 1 kg of uranium contains as much energy as 3,000,000 kg of coal.

The reactors in use today are predominantly second-generation. They have been expensive, largely because they were all essentially one-off designs. However, several third-generation designs have been developed, including new pebble bed reactors. These are based on putting pebbles of uranium oxide on top of a large tank and taking them out from the bottom, making the whole thing appear like gumballs in a gumball machine. Each of the pebbles in such a design contains thousands of kernels of uranium oxide, which are all encased in silicon carbide and a pyrolytic coating, and then further into a graphite shell. You then send helium through the reactor which results in the helium getting hot—helium has the advantage of not becoming radioactive. In this way you can use a flow process instead of a batch process. Furthermore, these reactors cannot melt down and the fuel is very difficult to convert for use in nuclear bombs.

Historically—even including the Chernobyl accident, which released more than 100 times as much radiation as the atomic bombs dropped on Nagasaki and Hiroshima—nuclear has been far safer than coal without even considering the potential global warming coal brings. The coal industry used to kill approx. 70,000 people a year in coal-mining accidents in the 1970s, and it still kills at least 10,000 annually. As for how many fatalities Chernobyl will ultimately claim, we shall not know for another generation. The highest estimates are 4,000 deaths, but as of 2010 the fallout has brought about approx. 4,000 additional cases of thyroid cancer (which is generally treatable) and 57 deaths. It has not been possible to observe the increase in rates of other cancers among the 800,000 who suffered radiation exposure. While this is terrible, coal is clearly orders of magnitude more dangerous, especially considering that new nuclear reactors (or even old Western ones) are built in such a way that accidents like Chernobyl are consigned to history.

The nuclear reaction that takes place to produce nuclear energy today is based on fission, which means splitting atoms. The fuel used is uranium, but the reactors are only capable of using approx. 7% of the energy potential in it. However, there exist so-called breeder reactors that reuse the spent fuel from traditional nuclear reactors and extract further energy from it. *It is generally estimated that currently identified uranium resources in mines will last 280 years at current rates of consumption.* If we take a further step and add breeding reactors then there should be enough for a few thousand years. And if we start extracting uranium from ocean waters then we should have enough for *several hundred thousand years*. Nuclear fission is truly an abundant resource.

Nuclear fusion is something else and would be on a completely different scale. With fusion we would actually directly simulate what happens in the Sun, albeit it on a very minor scale. Experiments to create nuclear fusion have been going on for generations and there is an old saying that nuclear fusion is 40 years away and will always be. But progress is being made, and we are closing in on the point where a fusion reactor—albeit briefly—can generate more energy than is put into it. If nuclear fusion ever gets to work commercially, we will have solved the majority of our energy problems. The fuel for this process is tiny pellets of deuterium and tritium, which can be extracted from the sea. *Nuclear fusion would produce no radioactive waste, and we have enough reserves of deuterium and tritium to keep us supplied with electric energy for several million years.*

———————

Methane hydrates have the potential to be the second largest form of alternative energy. It is estimated that there is at least 100 times more methane hydrate than natural gas, and utilizing even a small fraction of it could keep us going for centuries. However, methane hydrates release carbon dioxide into the air when they are burned, so they cannot be called clean. Even if we never use them, they are considered a potential threat since most are trapped in the frozen ground in Siberia. However, if that heats up, some of its carbon hydrates will evaporate and subsequently be broken down into carbon dioxide and water, with the former contributing to global warming. There exists so far no commercially viable method to extract methane hydrates.

An alternative energy form that—in contrast to methane—is attracting very serious money and political support, is ethanol, which is particularly widespread in Brazil and the U.S. Brazilian production is based on sugarcane and has become highly competitive against oil. Furthermore, it is easy to deal with. All one needs is a simple modification to automobile carburettors and then they can run just as well on ethanol as on gasoline. However, great as this is, Brazilian ethanol production is equal to just 0.3% of world oil production.

The Americans produce more, but their climate is less suitable than Brazil's, which means that they mainly use corn instead of sugarcane. American ethanol production consumes almost as much energy as it creates, which makes it seem like an enormous pilot project. This is based on so-called first-generation technology, where the fruits of the plants are fermented, but not the cellulose, hemicellulose, and lignin. Actually, plants have evolved these materials exactly to avoid being broken down easily by bacteria, fungi, and insects.

However, the American ethanol business may turn out to make sense in the long run, because *there are numerous projects underway to create so-called cellulosic ethanol, where not only the fruit of the plants but also structural material, which comprises much of the mass of plants, can be used.* This requires more extensive processing but, apart from giving a higher yield, it also has the advantages that offal from farming and forestry can be used. Some of the resources that are being tested include corn stover, poplars, hybrid willows, sycamores, sweetgums, *Eucalyptus*, *Miscanthus*, and woodchips. However, one may really use virtually any sort of tree, grass, and bush. This technology is evidently renewable; what is more it is carbon-neutral, as the carbon is absorbed from the air when the plants grow and then released back when the fuel is burned. Apart from ethanol it is also possible to make biodiesel from vegetable oils, animal fats, recycled grease, and methanol.

Interestingly, ethanol can also be made with switch grass, which doesn't require irrigation, fertilizers, cultivation, or replanting, as these plants are perennials and can grow on land that fails to reach the standard for traditional farming. There are places where the optimum strategy is to rotate between food crops and biofuel crops. *Second-generation biofuel will provide two to three times as much fuel per land unit as first-generation and will clearly be net energy–positive.* Some of the technologies that can accelerate its adoption are genetic modification of plants and creation of enzymes (perhaps also through genetics) that can break down cellulose, hemicellulose, and lignin.

However, even as the second generation is under development, there are now many teams working on the so-called third-generation of biofuels. These are made using genetically modified algae or bacteria, which are kept in water tanks naturally heated by the Sun. This involves far higher capital investments than the two other forms of biofuels, but algae and bacteria grow between 20 and 30 times faster than the fastest plants, and *yields should be 15–300 times higher per unit area than conventional crops.* Furthermore, since genomics has now become an information technology, one might suspect that efficiency might enter an exponential growth curve. Indeed, Craig Venter has spoken of making bacteria that are 1,000 or even 1,000,000 times as efficient at this process as they are today, perhaps by computer-designing them from scratch. As an aside, it should be mentioned that it would be perfectly possible to create bacteria with an extremely high metabolism to capture carbon and turn it into sugar, building materials, and numerous other substances.

The growth tanks needed for third-generation biofuels can be placed in areas that are not suitable for established crops, such as deserts, arid land, or land with excessively saline soil. The U.S. Department of Energy estimates that for algal fuel to replace all the petroleum fuel in the U.S. an area of approx. $40,000 \, km^2$, equal to one-seventh of the area currently used for corn farming, would be required. For Europe to do the same an area approximately the size of Belgium would be required. However, perhaps radical bioengineering could reduce the size of this drastically.

Wind power has been one of the most successful recent forms of renewable energy. The bigger windmills are, the more efficient they become, and one of the most promising ways to deliver meaningful power from them is through large offshore windfarms. However, while this technology will continue to expand, it does raise environmental issues inasmuch as they can be unesthetic, annoying, and kill birds. Furthermore, even more than solar power, they can be unreliable inasmuch as they depend on the presence of wind. In Denmark, which has installed considerable wind capacity, they don't run when there is no wind, and when there is too much wind many of them have to be shut down because the network cannot absorb their power.

A technology area that probably has much larger potential in the long term is solar power. Global solar influx is approx. 7,000 times as large as world energy consumption. By covering just 2.6% of the Sahara Desert with solar panels, we could generate energy equal to the global energy supply annum 2010. Solar energy can be divided into two main categories: solar thermal and PV (photovoltaic). Solar thermal heats up a liquid, the steam from which then perhaps drives a turbine that generates electricity. In its simplest version, the liquid is simply water that goes directly to a utility water tank or to heat a swimming pool. PV, on the other hand, creates electricity directly. PV has seen a cost decline of 20% each time its installed base doubled, which suggests that it is a hybrid between an industrial technology and an information technology. There is also a new kind of thin film cell, which costs a lot less, but also produces less power. PV might become extremely interesting over time, as its production cost may continue to decline rapidly while the devices in which it is used get more elegant. Instead of being a device you stick onto a building, which can be ugly and impractical, the great promise is to make solar panels the surface material of buildings as well as, for instance, roofs on automobiles, ships, etc.

––––––––––

The last, but perhaps the most economical and accessible energy resource of all is energy conservation. To show how effective this can be, two places—California and Denmark—have been able to increase GDP vastly without increasing electricity consumption at all. The large majority of the energy mankind uses is wasted, and much of this waste can be fairly easily reduced. The average coal-based and oil-based electricity plant wastes 60–65% of its energy (and even that is a great improvement over what was the norm a few decades ago). Furthermore, of the 30–35% energy remaining, 10% is typically lost in the grid. About 95% of the energy that is sent through a light bulb is wasted as heat. So, let's just go through this again:

- If we burn 100 liters of oil in a power plant, we get back 35 liters worth of electric energy.
- About 10% of this is lost during transmission through the grid, which brings us down to 32 liters.
- This is then sent through light bulbs, where just 5% actually creates light.

That's 0.6 liters of oil actually being put to use out of the 100 we started with—more than 99% was lost in the process! It doesn't look much better in automobiles. About 87% of the energy is wasted in the engine, idling, transmission, etc. The remaining 13% goes in roll resistance, aerodynamic drag, and roll resistance; much of this could be saved if automobiles were lighter, more aerodynamic, and could recuperate some of the braking power, as hybrid cars can. Indeed, why build automobile chassis of anything as heavy as metal? The best sportscars are already made of carbon fiber, and perhaps biodegradable carbon is the future basic material of automobiles.

There are many ways to save energy. The most modern power plants may have higher burn temperatures, which ensures increased efficiency. Another approach is cogeneration, or "combined heat and power", which reuses the heat generated in a power station to heat buildings.

The grid that moves power to its destinations can also be managed better and contain lower resistance. Much of this is good, solid engineering combined with lots of experience. The same goes for much of what might be done in houses, like providing better insulation or exchanging traditional light bulbs for fluorescent light bulbs or LEDs, which last much longer and use only a fraction of the power. Color rendering has been an issue in these (the lamps made everything look cold) but this has been improved on.

There are lots of processes that can be improved in manufacturing industries. One of the biggest areas is to use new enzymes to speed up chemical reactions, or to use bioengineered microbes to create desired products. Much can be saved by replacing old, large-scale, electric motors with newer ones.

Finally, transportation burns a large part of our energy, and much can be achieved through technologies such as cylinder deactivation, turbocharging, hybrids/plug-in hybrids, reducing roll resistance in tires, and utilizing lightweight materials such as aluminum, titanium, ceramics, and carbon fiber.

A whole group of technologies relate to saving energy by means of information technology. IT can be used for videoconferencing of such a quality that people greatly reduce traveling for face time. IT can also remove the need for lots of physical stuff such as printed books, CDs, DVDs, many shops, etc., and it can prevent people driving inefficiently. Furthermore, clever software and good location planning can ensure better management of the world's ever-growing computer parks, which by now consume as much energy as a midsize nation. One way forward is to locate server parks where there is abundant, cheap renewable energy, such as close to hydropower stations (e.g., where Google has placed server parks in the U.S.), or close to wind power stations (as in Texas), cheap geothermal stations (Iceland), or solar power stations (Southern Spain). Another important area is so-called virtualization software which organizes tasks between many computers and may, for instance, ensure that as many as possible go into sleep mode when not used, while only those actually required are running.

Smart metering of power is closely related to this. It is a concept in which the production price of power is calculated in real time and trans-mitted to users so that their electric devices—such as washing machines, swimming pool filters, and in particular tomorrow's electric cars—auto-matically go into recharge mode at night, when power consumption is low and the power production price therefore cheap. Not only does this save resources at power stations, but it also provides a way to absorb exces-sive power from wind and solar at times when the weather is particularly favorable for these. The concept of a supergrid with real-time power metering and where everyone has a right to sell as well as buy power is sometimes referred to as an "electranet". If this makes you think about the internet, it's exactly what they want you to think. If such nets existed, and if everyone knew that fossil fuels would remain expensive, then the sum of all human creativity would probably develop a very wide range of diverse energy forms and businesses, which would make us completely independent of fossil fuel within a few generations.

A fairly common misconception is that we should build "the hydrogen economy" to solve our problems. The good news is that 90% of all atoms in the universe are hydrogen, so if that's what we want there's plenty of it. Furthermore, when you burn it, the waste product is water—nothing else.

However, that is where the good news ends. Hydrogen is an extremely reactive atom, and you never find it isolated in nature—it is always bound to other atoms, so these have to be separated first, which requires energy. That energy will always exceed what you gain when the hydrogen is subsequently burned—typically by 30–40%. This means that *hydrogen is not an energy resource at all, but instead a costly way to transport energy.*

I think it is an extremely impractical way. Hydrogen is a very volatile and light gas, which is why it was used in zeppelins such as the Hindenburg. However, the fact that hydrogen is light means that it is not dense, which again means that the potential energy per volume unit is tiny. If you want to use it in a car you will need to compress it to a fluid to get any noticeable power from it, and that can be done by cooling it to $-253°C$ and then keeping it at that temperature thereafter. That sounds very energy-consuming and dangerous, so the alternative would be to compress it massively. Unfortunately, hydrogen under pressure tends to pass slowly through metal at a rate of 1–5% daily, so while you are on holiday the tank will gradually empty and the garage fill with hydrogen. Hydrogen is invisible and has no smell, so if you light a cigarette in such a garage, it might explode. So might your car in an accident, and in this case rather violently since the hydrogen would be compressed. So might the trucks that would transport compressed hydrogen to filling stations. There are possible workarounds for all of these problems, but it seems to me that there are far better overall approaches to our energy challenges.

––––––––––

Here is a question: Since there exist such a broad variety of ways to save and generate energy, couldn't we go full speed on all of them and thereby get the necessary transition of our energy structure done with? Why, in fact, hasn't it happened already?

There are many reasons for that. The first is that it needs to be profitable or subsidized before it happens, and the second is that you need to have some level of confidence in future prices before you invest in new energy forms, as such projects often will only start to generate income 5–10 years after you start. As for subsidizing, most developed economies have no realistic opportunity to increase public budgets, since raising taxes would erode the tax base and since most of these economies are running deficits already.

As for profitability, one problem with alternative energy projects is that they are capital-intensive, and that their payback time is frequently fairly long. There are three business rules of thumb that should be borne in mind here. The first one is π, which I would call "the empirical factor of time and money". Mathematical π is around 3.14. Here is how it goes: *You sit down and make a logical calculation of how much time and money is required for a project, and once you are finished, you simply multiply both numbers by π.*

I have done this many times and found that it really does make things a lot more realistic. Often, when academics who haven't worked with a real, large-scale project make estimates for how to save the world, what I think you need to do is multiply their cost and time estimates by π.

The second important number is 7%, *which is the typical cost reduction every time you double annual production of a mechanical/industrial product.*

The third number is *15%, which is the internal rate of return that most investors would expect from a risky project.* This is the benchmark people expect from well-run hedge funds and private equity, for instance. If the project is less risky, their expectation may go down towards the current cap rates of property, or towards equity earnings yields or even long-term bond yields—typically 3–7% if inflation is low. The World Bank typically uses 8–10%.

The Stern Review and the discount rate

The British Government commissioned the *Stern Review* to examine the economic consequences of global warming. As for the *cost* of warming mitigation, the report took the midpoint of IPPC's cost range and divided it roughly by 2 (personally I would have multiplied it by π).

Regarding the *benefits* it took numbers substantially higher than any of the possible scenarios provided by the IPCC, inflating some by as much as eight times.

And then it wrote economic history by using a discount rate of approx. 1.4%, which doesn't come close to anything I have ever seen in the real world.

I have already mentioned that, whereas the cost of traditional fossil fuels is likely to go up, the cost of many forms of alternative energy will decline, at least in real terms, due to innovation and increasing scale economies. However, if we take wind and solar power as examples, it becomes clear why the convention toward moving away from fossil fuels will take time. Of the world's energy consumption in 2010, approx. 33% comes from oil, 25% from coal, 20% from natural gas, and 7% from nuclear. The rest, approx. 15%, is "renewable", but the vast majority of that is hydroelectric, which cannot be increased very much. However, solar and wind power supply less than 1% of global energy consumption combined. Just think about it: *Together, wind and solar supply less than 1% of global energy consumption, which has a trend growth of approx. 2% per year.*

This means that *the annual growth in energy demand is twice what we get from the entire installed base of solar panels and windmills in 2010.*

The reality is that all of these technologies will take a long time to install in quantity and that, apart from nuclear, each of them only makes sense under specific circumstances. For solar power you need reasonable amounts of Sun, and for wind power evidently lots of reasonably stable wind, and for the other forms of power you need cheap land, ample water, geothermal heat, etc. One way to get a handle on what is realistic is to look at the Desertec program, which was signed on October 30, 2009 by 12 founding companies, including heavyweights such as ABB, Deutsche Bank, E.ON, Munich Re, and Siemens. The purpose of this was to create an environmentalist's dream (and mine too): a European/ North African/Arab power grid connecting solar plants (mainly in Africa/Arab areas, of course), geothermal (Iceland, Italy, Spain, etc.), windpower (mainly Europe's northwestern coastlines), biomass (mainly Europe), and hydropower (mountain areas). Through this combination, it will be easier to smooth out power production over the day and the seasons of the year, and it will be possible to export solar-based power from desert areas to power-hungry Europe. The budget is approx. €400 billion (€400,000 million) and the project should provide approx. 15% of Europe's power supply by 2050, despite a transportation loss across the Mediterranean of approx. 10–15%. The average power price is expected to be below what it is today, when corrected for inflation. This is a splendid project in all ways, but my point is that €400 billion is a staggering amount and 15% of the power supply in 2050 isn't that much.

The best way to stimulate alternative energy is probably to use high, flexible taxes on fossil fuel energy combined with the promise that the consumer oil price will never go under a given level, or even that this floor level will be adjusted upwards a bit every year. However, as I write this, the reality is that Europe has high energy taxes (but no credible floor price), and the U.S. has far too low energy taxes and many emerging markets *subsidize* energy consumption, which is about as stupid as it can get. But alternative energy will come, and it will be one of the world's biggest growth industries.

It will happen in waves. The first focus will be the upgrading of power grids plus implementation of energy savings that have a very short payback time. Also, in the short term there will be massive commissioning of new coal and power plants, which are not "clean" (especially coal), but which will be much cleaner than previous generations. This may be largely based on very high–temperature technologies or syngas. There will also be major projects to extract shale gas and to refine tar oil.

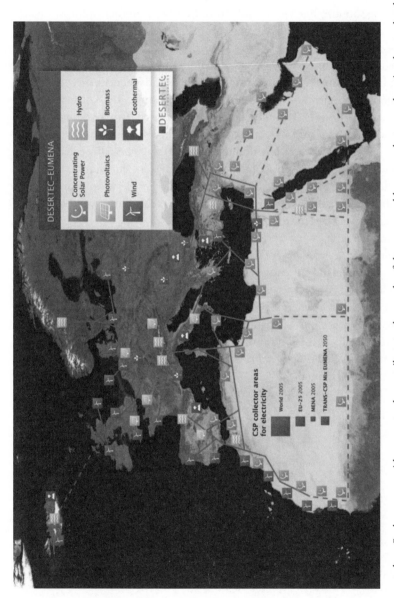

Desertec concept plans. Such a power grid may not only contribute to the supply of clean, renewable energy, but may also stimulate trade relations, etc. between the nations involved. *Courtesy:* Desertec Foundation.

These will enable a gradual switch toward electric cars, which will provide large-scale-buffer battery capacity for excess power production during parts of the day. Sportscars will remain driven by liquid fuel forever (you need the sound!), but will be able to run on both biofuel and fossil fuel.

From approx. 2020 we will probably witness the introduction of large-scale second-, third-, and fourth-generation biofuels based on genetically modified bacteria, algae, and plants, and by 2025 there may well be a commercial roadmap to making us independent of coal and oil altogether within 20–30 years. At the same time, PV solar will have become so cheap that it will be commonly used as a building surface. Furthermore, we will see very large-scale thermal solar plants in warm areas. Finally, before the middle of the century we shall probably have resolved the technical challenges of nuclear fusion, enabling us to roll it out during the following decades. This would enable us to dismantle the windmills and remove solar panels and thereby improve the esthetic appearance of our environment.

In summary, what I believe is this: *The world will not be saved until there is money in it.* Fortunately, increasingly there will be. The main reason for this is that demand for energy will explode and that, as human knowledge doubles every 8–9 years or so, we will come up with some incredibly smart solutions to energy problems. By 2050 human knowledge will be approx. 45 times greater than it was in 2010. Within that knowledge will be a complete set of solutions to energy problems. All will be based on information technology, expressed in the form of nuclear science, genomics and biotechnology.

The last two are the subjects of the next chapter.

15

Genomics and biotechnology

When my father worked as a scientist, he used to apply for research grants from time to time. This was typically for amounts anywhere from U.S.$20,000 to U.S.$500,000. At these levels, as long as the applications made sense, there was a fair chance of getting the grants. But sometimes his applications were rejected and he would then get in a bad mood and complain about the grant committees, who didn't understand the importance of his team's work. I gradually developed an image of a grant board as being a bunch of evil, alcoholic politicians, who didn't understand anything.

Now here is a wild fantasy about a grant committee.

It is a gray winter's day in 1989. A grant committee has assembled to go through a number of applications. We are already one hour into the meeting, and most applications have been rejected. The chairman now opens a folder and says:

"Here is application number 9. It is a very large project, so I have asked a representative from the science team behind it to come and explain what it is."

He walks to the door, opens it, and invites a bearded scientist in a suit and tennis shoes in. They both sit down.

"Good morning, gentlemen," says the scientist, "I would like to present ..."

"How big is the application?" interrupts an alcoholic Congressman with a loud, rusty voice.

"Ehh, it is for, eeehhhh, $3 billion. To be spread out over 13 years."

"Million or billion?"

"Billion."

The Congressman is stunned and starts thinking about whiskey. The chairman now turns to the scientist and says "Perhaps you can explain to us what the purpose of this is?"

"Well, what we are going to investigate is the structure of a molecule that is very important for the understanding of . . ."

"Why does it cost 3 friggin' billion?" interrupts the Congressman, who has recovered from his first shock.

"Well, you see, the molecule is very, very long. Really long, actually."

"How long?" asks the chairman gently.

"Two meters. Or just under seven feet."

The Congressman feels his blood pressure rise and starts thinking. Three billion friggin' greenbacks for two meters? That's ehh, $1.5 million per millimeter. Insane! His thoughts drift to whiskey again.

"Can you put those two meters into perspective for us, please?" says the chairman.

"I can try. The molecule consists primarily of two strings of bases, called adenine, thymine, cytosine, and guanine. Sometimes we call these letters. As each of these letters is always paired with another, we talk about 3.2 billion base pairs."

The Congressman is now discreetly sending SMSs to his secret girlfriend, but the scientist doesn't notice and continues his explanation: "Imagine that we printed out this string of letters with one character from the alphabet for each of the base pairs. I mean printed it out with a normal printer, but in a way so that it came out in a long string. OK, so we put this string at the curb of a highway and then we start driving at the beginning of the printout and keep driving until we reach the end, because we want to see how long it is."

The Congressman gets interested. He loves automobiles.

"So, accelerate the car and go up to the speed limit. Let's say you go 75 miles, or 120 kilometers, per hour. And then you keep going at that speed while the little string of printout letters passes by on the curb."

"So, how long will it take until you reach the end of the printout?" asks the chairman.

"If you drive non-stop at the speed limit it would take two days and two nights. In other words about 50 hours until you reach the end of the printout."

"OK . . ." says the Congressman, "We get that this is big. But what makes it important enough to justify spending $3 billion?"

The scientist looks at him for a while without answering. Then he says, "That molecule holds the secret of life."

I am sure that nothing even remotely similar to the meeting I just described ever happened (although some scientists do wear tennis shoes with suits. I have seen it!). However, there really existed a project in 1989 to spend $3 billion and 13 years to describe a molecule. It was called the "Human Genome Project", and it did get its funding. The work commenced in 1990.

The human genome is the code that is contained in the DNA molecule, which is exactly as long and complex as in my story above. There is a copy of our DNA in every single cell in our body except the blood cells, and there are similar DNA strains in cells of all other life—animals, plants, bacteria, fungi.

Long before the Human Genome Project began, researchers had known that genetic instructions of human life were hidden in these DNA molecules, and that each living human being was the result of one, unbroken, 3-billion-year-old chain of predecessors, who all had in common that they were reproductive (the last approx. 200,000 years of that as *Homo sapiens*). In other words, we contain all the instructions from the dead humans before us, as well as instructions that were created in earlier, more primitive lifeforms such as bacteria.

I want to put the size of the code, the 3.2 billion base pairs, in the genome into perspective. In computers, the length of a code is described by the number of lines—this is called source lines of code (SLOC). The world's largest software programs contain approximately 300,000 lines of instructions with perhaps an average of 20 characters per line (many lines contain a very short instruction or only a number). That is, around 6 million characters. This equals 0.2% of the human genome, which means that our genetic code is approximately 500 times as long as the largest software programs in the world.

How much of this genetic code actually serves a purpose is another business. Approximately 80% of it is suitable for generating proteins, but there is much to indicate that only around 2–5% actually has a function. The rest is called "non-coding DNA" or "junk DNA". For instance, there is a code called ALU which consists of 300 letters and which is repeated 300,000 times in our DNA. What's that good for? Nothing, we think. It seems to be junk.

Actually, we know for certain that lots of junk DNA exists, because we have tried to remove what we expect to be junk from animals without this making any obvious difference, and furthermore, there are other indications of this from other species. The Japanese puffer fish *Takifugu rubripes*, for instance, has DNA that is one-tenth the length of human DNA, even though the number of genes is more or less the same. On the other hand, there are bacteria and worms that have much more DNA than we have. A massive portion of this must be junk. The one-celled amoeba *Amoeba dubia* has DNA chains that are 200 times as long as ours. No one can convince me that they are so sophisticated that they need that. So, yes, there is junk, and if we subtract that, the length of our useful DNA equals the size of large software programs.

Since this is replicated in each and every one of the cells in our body, except in our blood cells, we have 100 trillion (100,000,000,000,000) copies of our DNA. If we put all these DNA strings together end to end, they would reach the Sun and back over 600 times.

When I started programming, I stored my computer code on punch cards. Later, I could copy it to a disk. It is not that easy with DNA. You cannot just look into a microscope and see how the DNA chain is made. Instead you have to find that out through a number of chemical reactions. This is time-consuming, although the principle is not that difficult. Initially, the model has been to use enzymes to cut the DNA strands at defined places. Then they are placed in bacteria, which are reproduced in order to obtain much larger quantities of the individual strands. Subsequently, the process of gel electrophoresis is applied to study the contents of the individual strand. I have worked with this myself at the university. The problem arises when the molecule you have to analyze is so ... insanely ... madly ... unbelievably ... long.

Human beings have around 23,000 genes. Each of these is a part of the total genome (i.e., in the overall DNA chain), which stands for a specific, chemical function, or sometimes several. Small sequences in the DNA interact with so-called "RNA", which again constitutes matrices for very long proteins that fold and react with each other in an extremely complex process.

Our 3.2 billion base pairs were written over more than approximately 4.4 billion years or so, which means the addition of a new base pair every 17 months. This may sound impressive, but we should bear in mind that most are actually junk, which means that it has taken 30–60 years for each useful, single-atom change to occur.

Also, whereas human generations may have averaged 15–20 years, the large majority of life has been single-celled organisms that divide within days or hours. Nature's computer code is changed regularly by millions of small mutations—typically 100 at every human birth, for instance. These do not only happen in a linear chain from father to son. They occur in parallel in thousands, millions, billions, or, as for single-celled organisms, countless trillions of individuals of the same species, the strongest of which have the best chance of surviving and reproducing. So, evolution is supermassive parallel computing, driven by the simple algorithm that the most fit have the highest chance of reproducing.

Not all our genes are equally susceptible to mutations. A few, such as those coding for the eyes, are described in the genes in a manner that is somewhat more robust than other parts. Most mutations, when they do happen, are very small—typically only one atom, which has been knocked out of place due to oxidation, Sun exposure, cosmic rays, or radioactivity. Or it can be a very short sequence that has been copied several times, added, or fallen out. But it could also be a long chain representing a coherent genetic instruction, randomly being carried from one organism to another by a virus, or, in rarer cases, by bacteria. In this process, one individual or organism can receive a long, coherent string of program code from another one, who might not even be of the same species. By far the majority of such mutations are harmful, but some of them turn out to be improvements, which provide the next generation with a competitive advantage, and this is what created evolution and biodiversity.

———

The Human Genome Project progressed extremely slowly during the first years, and there were surely many who doubted that it would ever finish within the allotted 13 years. However, in 1998—eight years into the project—one of the scientists involved, Craig Venter, created a private company called Celera Corporation. He claimed that through an innovative new technology he could finish the genome project faster than all the publicly funded university teams combined. Mr. Venter's approach was called "shotgun sequencing", and it involved the use of 600 computers which made more than 1,000 billion calculations per second. To begin with, the people working on the Human Genome Project were very skeptical toward Venter, but eventually concluded that his method was better. The two projects reached their goals almost at the same time in 2002—one year ahead of schedule. Venter spent U.S.$300 million (i.e., one-tenth of the original Human Genome Project budget), although it must be added that he got free access to the data already compiled by the public project.

Since then, Venter's team has collected DNA from more than 10,000 human beings and has started to map the differences between these people's genes. He also sent his yacht around the Earth, collecting genomes from millions of bacteria, algae, and viruses, which have also been decoded by his people. His teams have now found numerous new forms of life and described more than 10 million genes in a database that grows by the day. As a minor subproject, he has also decoded and published his own, complete genome—a project that originally would have cost U.S.$13 billion.

This is truly revolutionary. Throughout the past 300 years, biologists all over the world have systematically studied vast numbers of living species and described how they live, die, breed, eat, and fight. Now we are investigating all the same species one more time, but this time we are looking at the underlying *mathematics* (i.e., ascertaining the "source code", as it would be called in IT, of human beings, animals, plants, bacteria, fungi, and viruses). This is an enormous amount of work—there are between 3.5 million and 100 million species on Earth, of which 1.5 million to 1.8 million have been described.

One of the methods applied to understand the genes of mammals is by experimenting with so-called "knock-in and knock-out mice", where a specific gene is either implanted or deactivated to see the effect. By this means we have discovered, for example, that if a given gene is deactivated in a mouse the animal will contract colon cancer, which naturally indicates where we should focus our human colon cancer research and treatments. *The quest to understand precisely how pieces of DNA act with RNA and proteins and their effect on functions in living organisms is among the most important discovery processes in the history of mankind*—perhaps the most important of all. And it is very new.

Research and innovation in genomics is accelerating and will do so even more in the coming decades. Some companies are now capable of analyzing hundreds of thousands of base pairs ("letters") *daily*. Today, it is possible to decode a human gene for approximately U.S.$50,000, and the price is likely to drop to U.S.$1,000 within a few years. In April 2008, I read in the *MIT Technology Review* that two U.S.-based companies were working on a new technology that might make it possible to decode a human gene for around $100. In 1990, it would have cost *$3 billion* and take *13 years*. Now people are saying it can

be done for *$100*? Oh, did I mention how long it would take?—*eight hours*
. . .

Once a gene has been decoded, the next step is to analyze the proteins
it creates. This is extremely complicated, because proteins fold into 3D
spaghetti and the way in which they fold is decisive for how they work.
However, one thing we do know: a protein will always fold in a way
that minimizes its internal tensions. This is why large computer systems
are applied to all known information about chemical bindings in order to
simulate how the strand in a give protein will behave. Based on this it is
possible to simulate the chemical reactions the protein is likely to produce.

Gene technologists apply a number of different working methods.
The most frequent is genetic analysis and diagnosis. This includes DNA
decoding, or "sequencing", as it is called. In 2002 the gene technologist
Richard Davis from Oxford University calculated that the price for
sequencing a DNA base pair halves every 27 months, but since then it has
declined faster. One of the reasons is the use of so-called DNA chips,
which hold DNA sequences on a microscopic grid. Specific parts of the
grid attract specific parts of a DNA sequence and, when this happens, the
sequence can be viewed through fluorescent molecular tags that light up
when a complementary strand binds to a particular spot. In this way, it is
possible today to perform amniotic fluid analysis to test 450 potential
genetic defects at a very low price. Similar methods can be used to
identify, for instance, rapists and murderers (or to free those who have
been unjustly jailed).

Another methodology in genomics is synthesizing, where a pure
combination of atoms and molecules are glued together in DNA chains
according to a specific recipe. Some years ago, the company Dupont
modified *E. coli* bacteria so that they could produce 1,3-propanediol, a
material that can be used as a textile. Their managing director even wore
a suit made by this *E. coli*–produced material. Monsanto and other
companies have long been working with products based on gene modification. The insulin industry keeps approximately 4 million people going
via medicine created by bacteria that have human genes inserted. It is also
possible to insert a gene in a cow, which will then excrete a desired
substance in its milk, a method known as "pharming".

An additional area of genomic synthesis is the development of
medicines to attack diseases more accurately than today. This can be done
if we have a better understanding of precisely what triggers the diseases
in humans and if we succeed in making drugs that have the ability to

target the disease and nothing else. We are well on the way to getting vaccines against asthma, multiple sclerosis, leukemia, arthritis, malaria, high blood pressure, rheumatoid arthritis, *Salmonella* infection, and substance addiction, etc. Furthermore, we will find that success in combating one kind of disease often prevents another from taking hold. Cancer may often be caused by a virus, for instance, so vaccinating against the latter may prevent the former. Arthritis may be caused by general inflammations, so preventing these may keep the blood vessels more healthy. Another interesting field is to identify and then silence faulty genes by blocking their expression.

A field of particular interest is perhaps the artificial development of antibodies. When a new bacterium or virus is identified, it is possible to have its DNA (or RNA for certain viruses) analyzed, following which an artificial intelligence software program may suggest an antibody. This can then immediately be synthesized and mass-produced by using genetically modified bacteria and algae in order to obtain a rapid defense against new diseases such as Spanish flu, a virus that was said to have killed between 2.5% and 5.0% of the world's population in 1918–1919. Scientists from Columbia University warn there will be many such new diseases.

Furthermore, we will be able to tailor medicine to one specific person or to the specific mutated bacteria that may have infected just one patient. Such medicine may assist or destroy specific cells, or it may silence some unfortunate genes. Also, we know that all standard medication has side-effects, but that most of these only appear in a very small fraction of patients. With cheap gene-testing, we will be able to discover precisely which medicine suits each individual best. Among the end-goals are to replace today's terrible chemotherapy with a pill or injection stopping the cancer and otherwise leaving the rest of the body alone and perfectly healthy. Numerous clinics and even homes will have simple devices to analyze our blood, urine, and breath and give an instant diagnosis as to whether we have cancer or countless other diseases.

As with many other new ideas, gene manipulation is viewed with suspicion and is indeed potentially dangerous. Imagine a situation where the qualities of a carrot are changed so that it contains a gene from a nut. A person who is allergic to nuts eats the carrot, suffers an allergic reaction, and dies.

So, yes, it can be dangerous. However, if human beings are experimenting with genes, we are not alone, because nature does it all the time. Bacteria mutate constantly. Every time a living cell divides, be it in an animal or in a micro-organism, somewhere between one in a million and one in 10 billion divisions turn out to be defective. Most of these divisions will damage the cell, but some make them stronger and help them adapt. This is how bacteria, for instance, have developed antibiotics resistance.

When a woman conceives a child an average of around 100 spontaneous gene mutations take place (i.e., 100 atoms have changed at random in her DNA). The majority of these changes may be of no significance at all, very few may give extraordinary advantages, and others may lead to small faults or inconsistencies that are easy to live with. A few types may lead to disability, miscarriage, or early death.

Incidentally, numerous changes in each of our cells take place after we are born. It is estimated that the average cell in our body has around 10,000 atoms kicked out of place in its DNA *every day*—mostly from oxidation. Luckily, a healthy body will be able to repair 9,997 of them, but this still leaves the cells with 3 genetic defects which are not corrected, and as we age they add up. Of course 3 out of 2.3 billion in a day isn't much, but you never know if these 3 will cause a disaster, a minor problem, or have no effect at all. It might even be beneficial.

One of the problems when we grow older is that cells that have started to function poorly due to these accumulated changes often stay alive. They may subsequently emit substances that bother other cells and, as this accumulates over the years, the body is generally weakened. Another problem, which is far more serious, is of course when a mutated cell starts to multiply uncontrollably. This is what we call "cancer".

However, we should not forget that we have actually manipulated nature's genes for thousands of years. Before we knew anything about DNA, people were engaged in creating life that would match our objectives, but we did it through selective reproduction. We selected and cross-bred plants intentionally so that they got to look totally different from the original species found in nature. Farming was introduced shortly after the last Ice Age approximately 11,000 years ago, and through targeted selection we have developed many of nature's plants to a stage where they have very little resemblance to their "ancestors". Many garden plants including orchids and roses are also manmade.

We have done the same with animals. It was probably around 12,000 years ago that man started to live with gray wolves, and since then we have bred them into the more than 160 different dog races of today. Grandma's cute little Fifi no longer has the looks of a gray wolf, because Fifi has been created by man and would in no way have even a remote chance of survival in the wild. But she is in a sense still a gray wolf and could breed with one. In the U.S. today there are approximately

50 million of these manmade dogs compared with a mere 30,000–40,000 wolves. In other words, more than a thousand "artificial" wolves for each "natural" wolf. Similarly, we have created horses, pigs, and cows, which have very little in common with their natural ancestors, but if we had not done this we could never have fed the world's present population. Similarly, grain has been made to better withstand stormy weather, yield larger crops, and grow faster, and today's fruits are much bigger, less perishable, and often more juicy than nature's original specimens.

The ability to analyze and synthesize genes has changed biotech from a predominantly analogue industry to a truly digital one, which is increasingly similar to the software industry. In the synthesizing process, a person may in principle sit in Singapore and using a computer model come to a decision about creating a specific DNA gene which, according to the model, might have some useful effects. He could then email the code to a laboratory in the U.S., which will have it made within a few hours, put it into an empty bacteria cell, and "boot" it up the same way as installing a new operating system in a computer. Within a few hours, the bacteria will then change and do what its new DNA orders. It's virtually a new species. If we take this a little further, we might be able one day to communicate with a civilization living 70 light-years away. We may then send them a few DNA sequences via radio waves, following which they will recreate exactly these species on their own planet.

A third working method is to try and *improve functionality* in a genome. I have already mentioned that genomes have many superfluous sequences and can be very messy. It sounds a bit like when my computer has been used extensively and suddenly starts to slow down. I can then "defrag" it in my Windows software, and the system will start to organize data in a more orderly and efficient way. After this my computer runs smoothly again. There are companies specializing in improving functionality in one particular gene. They produce a huge number of slightly modified variants of this gene to see if some of them function better than those prevalent in nature. Often this process proves successful. We can think of this as a sort of "gene-tuning".

The fourth important discipline in gene technology is *metabolic engineering*. Often you may come across a bacterium in nature which naturally produces a chemical substance that is useful—but it does it very slowly. By applying metabolic engineering some genes are transferred from another bacterium which grows faster to speed up the process. Alternatively, genes that are responsible for production of the requested material can be transferred to a rapidly growing variant of a bacterium such as *E. coli*. As improving the functionality of genes is called "gene-tuning", then a good name for metabolic engineering would be "genome-tuning".

————

I think it is only a question of time before we decide to make a kind of Noah's Ark in the form of a computer server, where complete DNA sequences for all known species are stored. If one becomes extinct, it will be possible to reproduce its DNA, place it into an empty cell, and breed a new generation. If the DNA of the extinct species is too different from anything alive, the process can be carried out in different stages. The first stage is to take the nearest existing species and then make a fraction—say, one-fourth—of the changes required to recreate the extinct species. In the offspring, the same procedure is followed with the next fourth, etc. After four generations, that extinct species has been recreated.

It will even, albeit to a limited extent, be possible to go back in history and recreate species that became extinct long ago, although it will hardly ever be as far back as in the book (and the movie) *Jurassic Park*. When this movie was shown in 1993, various scientists were asked if this scenario was possible, and they typically answered that the principles of the movie were logical enough, but could never be carried out in practice (the idea was that mosquitoes in amber would have dinosaur blood in their stomachs and that the DNA of the dinosaur blood could then be inserted into birds' eggs).

Now, let's fast-forward. In 2008, 15 years after the *Jurassic Park* movie was released, scientists reported that they believed they could recreate the mammoth—for around U.S.$10 million. It has been discovered that frozen mammoths in Siberia have relatively well-preserved DNA in their hair, and by analyzing a sufficient number of genomes from the same animal (which is no longer prohibitively expensive), it is possible to put the actual sequence together. According to researchers, it might even be possible—perhaps even fairly easy—to recreate Neanderthal man, although this is hardly an option since the most suitable breeding animal would have to be human beings.

————

Personally, I do not believe that it stops there. Daryl Macer from the Eubios Ethics Institute in Japan conducted a survey in 1993 on international attitudes towards using genetic manipulation and screening with the purpose of preventing genetic diseases in children. He found that in Asia, in particular, there was a large majority of supporters.

Four methods of genetic backup

Genetic backup works automatically in a healthy, ecological system. However, as a safeguard it can be subdivided into four possible backup systems:

- Natural breeding in a self-regulating ecosystem
- Zoological/botanical gardens, where living species are nursed by humans
- Cooled or frozen cell samples/seed grain
- Computer disk with genetic sequence.

The first method is of course what we want, but the others may provide backup for disaster recovery.

These people were also specifically asked if they would be interested in applying gene manipulation and screening to improve the physical and mental abilities of children. The number of proponents shrank a bit, but the indication was that, particularly in Asia, there was still a majority in favor of the idea. On the next page I have given some of the answers to the question that starts with "How do you feel about scientists changing the genetic makeup of human cells to . . ." and finishes with various alternatives.

The table shows that *an overwhelming majority in each country approved changes to genes if the purpose was to avoid disease. When it came to gene manipulation with the aim to increase child intelligence, there was overwhelming support in India (70%) and Thailand (72%), whereas approval was far weaker in Australia, Japan, and Russia. The U.S. took a middle position with 44% approving.*

I am quite certain that human gene manipulation will gain ground. Today, we can see how far people have already come in their efforts to improve themselves and their lives. We have invented medical science, which has altered natural mortality and fertility; on the one hand, contributing to the population explosion and, on the other, controlling it through the pill. People get more fillings in their teeth, have hip and knee replacement surgery, heart transplants, artificial hearing, artificial retinas, contact lenses, pacemakers, liposuction, hair transplants or permanent hair removal, plastic surgery, and botox. Some of these things I find rather repulsive, others positive, but the overwhelming fact is that it's very popular.

We also produce huge numbers of in vitro babies. The first child conceived in this way was Louise Brown, who was born in 1978, and at

Answers to selected questions regarding the ethics of changing the genes of unborn children

		Australia	Japan	India	Thailand	Russia	U.S.A.
"… reduce the risk of developing fatal disease later in life?"	"Strongly approve"	47	35	48	50	46	39
	"Somewhat approve"	34	40	35	32	33	38
	Total approval	81	75	83	82	79	77
"… prevent children from inheriting a non–fatal disease such as diabetes?"	"Strongly approve"	50	25	42	63	45	41
	"Somewhat approve"	29	37	31	28	26	36
	Total approval	79	62	73	91	71	77
"… improve the intelligence level that children inherit?"	"Strongly approve"	15	13	41	48	18	18
	"Somewhat approve"	12	13	29	26	17	26
	Total approval	27	26	70	72	35	44

I have excluded the results from two additional nations in the survey: Israel and New Zealand. *Total approval* lines have been added by me even though they include "Somewhat approve".

Source: Macer, J., J. Azariah, & P. Srinives: International attitudes to biotechnology in Asia, *International Journal of Biotechnology*, Vol. 2, No. 4, 2000.

the time there were critics maintaining that such children would become psychological monsters. Since then, almost 500,000 children have been conceived in vitro, and there is nothing to indicate that they are mentally or physically different from everybody else. In fact, this first reaction towards in vitro children was more or less the same as people's attitude toward having children delivered in a hospital. One hundred years ago, this was considered odd. Today, most people believe it to be an unnecessary risk for the child *not* to be delivered in a hospital.

We have already seen the first gene transplants in people with serious genetic diseases. This is normally done by infecting the patient with a virus which has the correct version of the defective gene. The virus then invades the body's cells and will in many instances correct the problem by adding a healthy copy of the gene. This is called somatic therapy. One of the diseases subjected to this type of treatment is cystic fibrosis, which clogs up the lungs with sticky excess mucus production, leading to severe suffering and a shortened lifespan. The patient is treated by breathing vapor infused with the relevant virus, which is then supposed to infect the affected lung tissue. There are other approaches to gene therapy, including injection of naked DNA into muscles, or even growing whole cells outside the body and then inserting them. However, from a technical perspective, it is much easier to correct genetic defects *prior to conception* (i.e., by analyzing the genes in eggs and sperm cells and then correcting any defects, following which conception is made in vitro).

It seems likely to me that humanity—as the first species ever—will start to reconstruct itself genetically. One of the reasons is that our genome is increasingly mismatched to modern life. The human software that we contain in our genes evolved almost entirely during the Stone Age. It tells the body to store fat as an insurance, in case we are unable to find food, or if the ground snows over for longer than usual in the winter. Furthermore, the body seems to lose much interest in self-preservation after we stop having children, even though technically we could live much longer, and that our accumulated knowledge from a lifetime is largely lost when we die. Our genome makes us prone to hysteria and panics. It doesn't give us the intelligence we need to comprehend the technologies we have made.

Another reason for genetic engineering is that most people want to live a longer, healthier life. In 1999 biologists at Princeton University added a gene to mice which made them (the mice) much cleverer; and that same year researchers in Milan deactivated a gene in mice, following which they lived on (again, the mice) with no change in energy—30% longer in fact. In 1985 researchers discovered that the bacterium

Caenorhabditis elegans lived more than twice as long if a single gene was altered; and in 1999 other biologists prolonged the life of a certain bacterium by 50% by implanting genes to create two antioxidants. The sequence of steps toward human self-modification could be something like this:

1. The first step is amniocentesis, where a small amount of amniotic fluid containing fetal tissue is extracted from the amniotic sac surrounding a developing fetus, and the fetal DNA is examined for genetic abnormalities. This is already very common. Fetuses carrying serious defects are aborted.
2. The second step is embryo screening, where an embryo is screened for genetic defects before implantation. This is sometimes also done on female egg cells prior to fertilization. This is also fairly normal today.
3. The third could be that people start to clone their beloved dogs and cats. This has already begun, but is rare.
4. Then maybe somebody would use gene manipulation to develop, for instance, dogs with a particularly high intelligence and long life expectancy. People would now buy and breed these dogs and thus get used to the thought that gene manipulation of animals isn't inherently very different from selective breeding.
5. The next step could be that couples who cannot have children and therefore plan in vitro children instead ask to have a number of egg cells and sperm cells screened for around 4,000 different genetic diseases and then choose the best.
6. At a later stage, it may become possible to choose to have a few modifications made, in which details from genes that are known to give higher intelligence, better health, or longer life, are copied. In other words a human "app store" along the lines of Apple's iPhone. I can envision a situation where someone at a birth clinic asks a couple whether they would like their child to have a natural pitch (the ability to remember a specific tone is known to be reflected in the location of a few atoms in a gene). If the answer is yes, some of the atoms are switched around. It might even be possible to choose between three variants: (1) some changes that are not automatically passed on to the grandchildren, (2) others that only work on the condition that the individual on becoming an adult starts to take a pill activating the atoms, and (3) others that may be permanent. Technically, this can already be done. Those using it would perhaps be people who are not themselves very gifted, but who choose to give their children a better

chance, whereby the gap between the more and less privileged is reduced.

7. After this, one could imagine some genes being taken from other organisms such as plants and placed in the human genome. For instance, a gene that protects our cells from decay by discharging antioxidants, whereby the aging process is perhaps slowed down by 50%, enabling a 150-year yet healthy lifespan.

8. An extreme development would be for human beings to be given an extra chromosome in which to place the new genes.

If this happens (and personally I think that most of it will), I believe that phases 3 and 4 may develop rapidly and be widespread. Phase 5 (the screening of alternative in vitro children) will create an uproar in many countries, but will become popular in the U.S. and Asia. The next phases (implantation of improved genes) will face strong opposition especially in Europe, Latin America, and the Arab world. Instead it will originate in Asia, where the attitude towards such thoughts is very positive. Perhaps China will lead the way. After all, the Chinese are only allowed one child per family, and so their wish for this child to do well may be particularly pronounced.

————

While gene technology may be key to enhancing human health and ability, the more important near-term consequences of these technologies lie in solving environmental and resource problems, particularly in the agricultural sector. Between now and 2050 we may want to increase our agricultural production by 100%. The way we can do this is either by (1) replacing much more of the world's remaining wilderness with farm-land, (2) letting millions and millions of people die, or (3) using, among other things, precision agriculture (based on exact, real-time measurements to optimize seeding, irrigation, etc.) and gene technology to raise crop yields drastically.

Most people regard agriculture in a favorable light and indeed are grateful to the farmers of the world, without whom they would be unable to feed themselves daily. However, while a corn field can be very beautiful, it is anything but natural. Modern agriculture has taken plants from one part of the world and cultivated them elsewhere. Furthermore, as I mentioned earlier, we have manipulated them so that they bear little resemblance to their natural ancestor. When we cultivate them, we spray against infections and insects. When we plough we unwittingly create conditions that could lead to serious erosion of the soil, and if we use natural manure instead of artificial nitrate for fertilizing purposes, we end up destroying the habitat of wildlife in nearby streams.

Furthermore, much of the food we produce via agriculture is in fact extremely unhealthy. In fact, many natural plants would fail to be approved as food today if tested by the same criteria used for genetically manipulated food. Many nuts, for instance, can cause allergies that are sometimes fatal. Nuts would immediately be banned if they were something we had created through genomics. The same would most likely go for wheat and corn, which often contain small quantities of very strong toxic substances from plant diseases. Or how about food containing fat leading to atherosclerosis (plaque building up inside the artery walls)? Such food would not stand a chance. Nevertheless, people eat these foods every day and drop like flies as a consequence. Actually, now that I mention it, we could actually fix these problems through genomics. Allergy-free nuts, anyone?

The downside of farming is that we have cleared enormous natural areas to make way for agriculture and by doing so we have removed the natural habitat of wild animals and plants. In total, what we use for farming is about equal to the total landmass of South America.

Ecofarming will not solve the problem of loss of natural habitats. On the contrary, ecofarming requires much more land to obtain a given yield. If we were confined to ecofarming, we would either have a global famine or have practically no wildlife left. Widespread use of ecofarming would have been possible had we numbered fewer than 1 billion, but we are currently 7 billion and soon will be 9 billion. However, biotechnology can help us make farming more compact and intelligent, in much the same way as we managed to zoom computers down from something weighing many tons to something you carry in your pocket. The aim should be to minimize the amount of land we use for farming in order to maximize the natural areas that are left.

Gene manipulation in farming was originally carried out at the University of California and Stanford University, and it started with very primitive techniques, such as breaking down cell walls in various plants and then mixing their genes to see what would happen, or speeding up random gene mutation using X-rays to see whether such random high-speed mutation could bring something new and better. Later on, the processes involved changing specific genes in a few plant cells and then generating entirely new plants from them through "tissue culture", which, by the way, turned out to be pretty difficult in most cases.

Gradually, the process became more elegant. Some researchers noted that when the bacterium *Agrobacterium tumefaciens* infected a plant, the plant grew some odd nodules, which could be cut off and grown individually. The reason these nodules appeared was, apparently, that the bacterium in addition to its normal DNA had a loose gene strand, which invaded a plant's cells and changed their function. Scientists inserted this DNA strand into other plants and the same effect was seen. Studies were later conducted on the soil-dwelling bacterium *Bacillus thuringiensis* (or "Bt"), which the Japanese had used as a pesticide since 1901. They then got the idea that they could find those gene sequences in the bacterium that were ultimately responsible for killing larvae and insects and incorporate them into the genome of the plant—thus avoiding the need to be sprayed. For this purpose, the gene needed to be modified somewhat, because plants "read" their genes a little differently from the way bacteria do. However, after numerous attempts the experiment finally succeeded, and a generation of plants that could defend themselves against larvae and insects were created.

Later on, another idea surfaced. In the 1970s the U.S. company Monsanto introduced the weedkiller Roundup, which was revolutionary when compared with other weedkillers on the market. Normally weed-killing agents were rather selective and had immediate effect, which furthermore persisted for many weeks or even months. However, Roundup had no visible effect the first week, and when the effect finally set in it killed *all* plants, and then quickly degraded. This soon became popular for spraying roadsides and gaps between flagstones. Farmers used it instead of ploughing, as the latter could cause soil erosion and was very energy-consuming. The idea was to turn the normal way of thinking upside down: to identify genes that protected utility plants against Roundup. If this could be done, it would become possible to spray the field so that everything other than the desired utility plants died. After many years of intense work, the scientists' efforts were rewarded, and a seed grain with this Roundup-resistant modification was marketed as RoundupReady. The result was that *farmers did not have to plough and their need to spray was reduced.* Trials in Mississippi and Alabama showed, for instance, that farmers went from spraying an average of 8 times a season to only 1.5 times, after having gone over to RoundupReady. All in all there was a fourfold environmental gain—less energy consumption, reduction in loss of yield per acre, less soil erosion, and fewer herbicides in food.

In 2008, 8% of all cultivated land in the world was planted with GM crops and the technology was evolving rapidly. In 2009 Monsanto launched Genuity Smartstaxx corn, which has 5–10% higher yields than before, and RoundupReady 2 Yield Soybeans, which seem to improve yields 7–11% over the original RoundupReady soybeans.

There is evidently something interesting going on here. Seed companies used to be "analogue" enterprises, which would examine plants and choose the best as the basis for next year's seeds—a process which on average improved yields by 1% annually. However, *farming is now clearly an information technology, and this will accelerate productivity gains dramatically.* Monsanto is now using a so-called "seed-chipping machine", which picks a seed and rotates it to a position where a tiny part can be chipped off without destroying the seed's ability to grow. Afterwards they examine the genome in the chip to find clues as to the characteristics of the final plant. By using this to select seeds, they can speed up the selection/breeding cycle dramatically. As a result, they expect to increase annual productivity growth to over 3.5%, thus *doubling* the yield between 2010 and 2030. If this works out, it will be vitally important because *the world population will increase approx. 20% from 2010 to 2030. So, crop yields growing by 100% over the same period as a result of using genomics means we are easily winning the race to feed the world and at the same time expand the production of biofuels.* In fact, even if there is a reluctance of much of farming to use genetically modified plants, *we may very well be in a position to start giving some of our farmland back to nature before 2050.*

Furthermore, there will be a drift toward so-called functional foods, which have been genetically engineered to produce omega-3 or to have other health benefits, such as more vitamins, fiber, or protein. For instance, the fat in a plant can be made to include the healthy omega-3 fatty acid by incorporating some genes from algae. In developing countries it will be possible to reduce hunger and malnutrition, which would otherwise lead to millions of children becoming mentally disabled, blind, sick, or dying.

The thought of meddling directly with genes in our food scares many, particularly in Europe, but research continues, and over the coming years we will see many new crops providing a higher yield per acre, requiring less water, being more resistant to wind and frost, and needing less fertilizer or perhaps none at all. Unfortunately, when Europeans ban the import of genetically modified farm products from Africa and other poor regions, they effectively prevent GM crops from being used there and are therefore indirectly forcing the poor to pay for the rich's scare.

———————

Whereas the biochemical development of plants may be the single most important thing to save our environment and livelihood, the development of bacteria may also prove an essential part of bringing this about.

The first 2 billion years of life on this planet consisted of single-celled organisms. Then came the first multi-celled beings that evolved into the large organisms we see today: trees, cattle, people, etc. However, many researchers estimate that the total weight of bacteria today actually equals the weight of all plants, including the algae in the sea and the trees in the woods. And since we keep on finding bacteria in the most bizarre places, such as 3 km under the surface of the Earth, many researchers now believe that bacteria constitute more than half of the total biomass of the world.

Some bacteria live in organic material; others eat sulfur or stones, or get their energy from geothermal heat or photosynthesis. Some need oxygen, others would rather live without it. Some can withstand heavy radioactivity or superheated water at the bottom of the sea; others can only live in milk at a very specific temperature.

Some prefer to live in our body. It is estimated that man is the carrier of more bacteria than there are cells in his body. However, the cells of bacteria are on average much smaller than our own and therefore these organisms "only" constitute approximately 10% of our total dry weight, which, however, tells me that we are indeed walking ecosystems.

I mentioned earlier that in 2006 Craig Venter sailed around the world in his yacht and collected water samples to catch millions of bacteria, algae, and viruses. He sent the samples back to his laboratory, where his decoding machines chewed their way through the material and isolated millions of new genes. This process, which will no doubt be copied by many others, has given his firm an enormous database which can be searched to find genes with known characteristics. Such work may create the basis for the development of numerous new variants. What if, for instance, it becomes possible to create a bacterium that mass-produces the material spider webs are made of? It would then be possible to weave very thin, bullet-proof shirts for the military or police. Or bacteria that are modified to make all kinds of medicine? Such bacteria are in fact already widely in use.

However, third- and fourth-generation biofuels may be the most interesting application of all: bacteria or algae photosynthesizing, sucking up carbon dioxide from the air, and transforming it into oil. *Voilà!* With such a bacterium we would stop the accumulation of carbon dioxide in the air and have a sustainable energy source that could be used by airplanes, automobiles, and boats without having to modify the transport infrastructure the least little bit. There are now several companies in the U.S. working hard to get there first by developing such bacteria, and the most likely outcome is that within a very short time such bacteria will be available on the market, where they will compete with genetically modified algae to create third-generation biofuels. When this algae-produced or bacteria-produced oil technology is optimized through gene-tuning, genome-tuning, and modification, we will have to build a number of "oil breweries" or some such name. A good place to start would be the chimneys of coal-fired power plants. The effect of such technologies would be to create a fluid fuel that fits easily into our current transportation infrastructure and is renewable, compact, and carbon-neutral.

This, like much else in genomics, has the potential to become a massive business. Apart from providing elegant solutions to many of our environmental and resource challenges, it will help us tremendously in dealing with our healthcare challenge as the number of elderly is expected to grow by no fewer than 1.6 billion in the next 40 years.

So far the main players in this industry are located in the U.S., Switzerland, Singapore, Denmark, and a number of emerging markets, led by Brazil, China, Egypt, India, Israel, South Africa, and South Korea. Genomics does not have the same massive network effects as IT, which reduces the possibility of creating insanely profitable companies within relatively short timespans. However, the lack of network effects opens up the area to more new players.

———

DNA—and the 20 amino acids in proteins—is the greatest open-computing platform that will conceivably ever exist, and what nature has done with it defies imagination. Almost everything that one could possibly imagine has been tried by nature and tens if not hundreds of millions of species have lived on Earth. Scientists believe that approx. 99% of all life that ever existed has been eradicated—most of it long before the first humans appeared, but over the long term the number of species has generally trended upward.

And yet, there is one aspect of genomics that is truly striking. While it's an open platform and the expressions it creates are limitless, the actual coding behind different species is amazingly similar, where just minor changes often have major effects. Think about how monkeys think and talk. Various studies have been conducted on getting a meaningful dialogue with monkeys, where they were able to communicate with us

---

Similarities between IT ecosystems and natural ecosystems

Biological ecosystems have existed for millions of years, but it is only very recently that we have started to map the mathematical logic behind them. However, as we do, it seems striking how much they resemble what we are creating artificially in our IT world. In the biological as well as the electronic world there is often a gigantic software architecture with layers upon layers of logic which all build on very basic code, which in computers is chip architecture and machine code, and in biology DNA sequences.

Other similarities: electronic machinery as well as biological individuals use electric power to send information, although nerve cells are made of different material in the two worlds. Furthermore, both the electronic and the biological world have error codes, object-oriented codes, etc., and both can be replicated.

Electronic devices—the combination of software and hardware—are increasingly more reminiscent of primitive animals. There are computers today that can see, hear, smell, orientate themselves, and speak.

It does not end there. In the computer world we make backups (hopefully) of our software. Nature has its own backup system in that DNA is double-stranded. In the IT industry, we have managed to make a direct connection from software design to physical production by means of CAD/CAM and this is exactly what life does in genetics, where the software produces its own hardware from chemicals collected from the surroundings.

---

by pressing buttons that meant certain words. This resulted in sentences such as

> *"Nim eat. Nim eat. Drink eat me Nim. Nim gum me gum. You me banana me banana you."*

Nim is the monkey here, if you didn't guess, and what he says doesn't sound too bright to me. At least not when we compare it with what humans sometimes might say. Things like

> *"If we apply a Hadamard gate to the first qubit in a quantum computer, the effect is to produce a new description for the quantum computer with numbers $t_1, t_2, \ldots$ given by $t_1 = (s_1 + s_{2n}/2 + 1)/\sqrt{2}$."*

Or even

"I could dance with you until the cows come home. On second thought I'd rather dance with the cows until you come home."

The first of these two human quotes, which I think are very bright, is by Michael Nielsen, a scientist, and the second by Groucho Marx, a comedian. Who would have thought that when we compare the DNA of monkeys—such as Nim—with people like these two talented humans, base pair by base pair, the difference is only around 4%? Not only is my own DNA almost identical to that of a monkey, but it is not that different from many bacteria. This is what I mean by the world's greatest open-computing platform. By the way, according to Professor Steve Jones of University College in London, we share 50% of our DNA with bananas (this may explain how I feel some Sunday mornings).

But enough about biotech and genomics—we shall now move on to so-called "information technology", which is our bad term for what people do with computers.

16

Information technology

If you have normal eyesight, then it is possible to see a single human hair. A hair is about 50 μm or 50,000 nm wide (50,000 billionths of a meter). This is about five times the size that a human eye can resolve (the smallest we can see is 0.01 mm). Let me give an example to put that into perspective. San Francisco Bay is 20 km across at its widest part. Or, if you stand in Copenhagen in Denmark and look across the sound to Sweden, the widest part is approximately the same. Now, let's magnify everything 400 million times. If we do that, then the width of a hair becomes the distance across San Francisco Bay, or between Copenhagen and the shores of Sweden. In this world, the smallest object visible to a human being would be a fifth of that, or 4 km wide.

I know it's weird to imagine a hair that is 20 km wide, but please try for a moment, because it leads us to something extraordinary. In this reference frame, a nanometer would be 0.4 m, and a typical bacteria cell would be around 10 m in diameter. As we stand a safe distance from this 10 m long bacteria, we would be able to see a number of hydrogen atoms connected to other atoms. Each of these hydrogen atoms would be approximately 4 cm in diameter, so roughly the size of large pebbles. An electron would be something in the region of 0.00000000000001 cm, and a quark would be around 0.000000000000004 cm, so even in this absurdly magnified world, you wouldn't be able to see either.

On that scale, what would a really compact computer chip look like? Here is a clue: In 1959, the Nobel Prize Winner Richard P. Feynman presented his views on the amount of data that could be compressed into a chip in the future. He said that if it was possible to build a computer where the physical representation of each bit was only 100 atoms, or

10 nm, it would be possible to store the full text of all the books that had ever been written (at the time 24 million books) in one computer chip of $100,000 \times 100,000$ nm or 1×10^{-8} m^2 in each direction. So, in our magnified world, what he talked about was representing 1 bit—a "1" or a "0"—within a space the size of 100 large pebbles, or 4 m.

But again, what would a computer chip look like in our reference frame? If the distance between Denmark and Sweden (20 km) was the width of a hair (50,000 nm), Feynman's entire chip would be 40 km in each direction or twice the distance I mentioned earlier across San Francisco Bay. In the real world, it would be twice the width of a hair. A tiny grain, really.

So, what he described was 24 million books within a speck of dust. If all of these books were printed on paper they would weigh something like 800,000 tons. If you were able to lay them end to end, they would cover the distance between London and New York. Of course, Feynman just hypothesized about it in 1959. We shall later see how realistic he was.

In order to do what Feynman described, you need to use an invention called a transistor. In fact, you would need an absolutely astronomical amount of very small transistors.

Transistors are, in my opinion, one of the two greatest inventions in the history of mankind—the other one is the wheel. There exists a special case of wheels which we call cogwheels. If you take a complicated, mechanical watch and wind it up, there will be an incredible number of small and bigger cogwheels interacting with each other to convert the simple, mechanical energy from your process of winding up the watch to complex information. Perhaps it shows dates, hours, minutes, seconds, time zones, Moon phases, and more. All of it from simple rules upon more simple rules, expressed in the relative sizes and connections of all those cogwheels. The minute cogwheel turns 60 times, which makes the hour cogwheel turn once. The hour cogwheel turns 24 times, which makes the day change. Stuff like that.

Now, if you write software, you also have simple rules. One of the most common is called an "if ... then ... else" statement. To explain what that means, let's say that you drive your automobile towards a stoplight:

If the light is green, *then* continue, *else* stop.

A transistor is a physical device that expresses this simple rule. It was first patented in Canada in 1925, and any attempts to make computers before that (and there had been some) had actually been based on cog-wheels, just like in watches. With the transistor you could replace one of our two greatest inventions with the other.

Amazingly, after mankind had made this invention, over the next 22 years, no one used it for anything meaningful. In fact, virtually no one had ever heard about it. It wasn't until 1947 that the first technical breakthrough for the transistor came, as engineers at Bell Labs found that you could make a transistor by applying electric current to a crystal of germanium. Without power, the crystal was a very bad electric conductor, but with it, electricity could easily flow through. Germanium could, in this way, become an on/off switch to control current flow through the device:

If power field is on, *then* it's conductive, *else* it's not.

One of the most common applications for the use of the transistor is as an amplifier. For instance, hearing aids use transistors as such, by letting the sound that is captured by a tiny microphone drive the control current (or "base") and then use a battery to let a stronger power pass through the transistor and drive a tiny loudspeaker.

Because germanium can conduct if it has current applied to its base (and can't without it), it is called a "semiconductor", as in "sometimes-

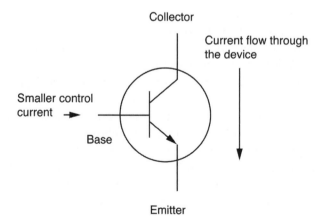

Transistor schematic drawing. The basic principle of operation is that the current passing through the device, from the "collector" to the "emitter", is controlled by a much smaller control current at what is called the "base". It's a bit more complicated than a wheel, but not much. Actually, a wheel with ball bearings seems in principle more complex than a transistor. *Source*: Marcus Nebeling, Fiber Network Engineering Co.

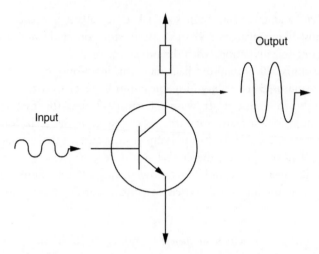

The transistor as an amplifier. Small variations in the input signal control larger fluctuations in a more powerful current. *Source*: Marcus Nebeling, Fiber Network Engineering Co.

but-not-always" conductor. If you interconnect many transistors with each other, you will have an array of switches that will support a myriad of functions. In a way this is similar to a watch, where numerous cog-wheels create a whole lot of complication. However, there is one huge difference. The transistors in a computer chip operate extremely fast, capable of turning on and off *several billion times a second*. One reason for this incredible speed is that electric signals move very fast (not the actual electrons, because they move rather slowly, but the electric field). Actually, the fields move at close to the speed of light, which is equal to traveling 7.5 times around Earth at the Equator. Not per day, hour, or minute, but per second.

The first transistors were big, but they soon got smaller, and the germanium was eventually exchanged with silicon and other materials, which like germanium could work as semiconductors, if you treated them with small impurities such as arsenic, phosphorus, antimony, boron, gallium, or aluminum (a process known as "doping"). This was a great idea, because silicon was cheaper and easier to work with than germanium.

Next idea: Make the transistors so small that many of them could sit on a little chip the size of a fingernail. Shortly after that innovation was conceived and shown to actually work, some engineers started making cal-culations for how it would function if you simply zoomed everything down in scale; smaller units, less power, etc.—*everything*. Perhaps to their surprise they found that it should work just fine, and that it would be much faster on top. Given an identical layout, it wouldn't even create more heat per surface unit, since the necessary power decreased because of lower-capacitance interconnects. So, they began downscaling everything, and once they had made the chips smaller they made them smaller still, and so on.

To produce these chips you take a so-called "wafer", which is made of nearly defect-free, single-crystalline silicone. This clean material is then cut with a diamond-edged metal to get a completely smooth surface. Next follows a whole series of processes, where one of the most important is addition of so-called "photoresist" fluid. After this has been applied, you put a template over the wafer, which has a pattern similar to what you want for electric current flows and transistors within the chip.

This is in a way similar to putting a template on a surface before you paint-spray a logo onto it, for instance. However, the "paint-spray" in chip production is actually neither paint, nor spray—it is light. So, you paint-spray the wafer (the photoresist on it) with a complex pattern of light, which creates chemical reactions. These patterns are thereby burned onto the wafer, while the rest of the photoresist can be washed away. The resulting product is called an integrated circuit. In order to save time and money, production is done simultaneously for many circuits— one wafer contains numerous integrated circuit patterns, which you cut out at the end as "dice" before finally attaching external wiring and other stuff on them. Finally, before selling them, you test each, and the percentage that have no errors are called "yield", whereas the rest are wasted.

I have previously mentioned Moore's Law, which states that the number of transistors that can be placed inexpensively on a chip (or integrated circuit) doubles approximately every two years. That law is evidently not one, like Newton's laws, that will last forever. However, when Gordon Moore first described it in a paper in 1965, he tracked it back to 1959, and almost 50 years later it is still working, which is quite amazing. Indeed, the observation has been so captivating that it actually became partially self-fulfilling—it became such a mantra in the industry that, since your competitor kept up with Moore's Law, you better do a bit better than that. In the 1970s there were periods where capacity actually doubled every 12 months.

How could they keep doing it? There were many drivers of this relentless progress. The sizes of the wafers were increased, for instance, and everything in the chips went to smaller and smaller geometries, while different means to better utilize space were devised. Furthermore, parts of the circuits were made with several different layers superimposed on top of each other. By 2000, chips typically contained more than 50 different chemical elements, all of which played a vital role in improving speed and reliability. Another method to improve the ability to manufacture smaller and smaller geometries was to shift to light with shorter and shorter wavelengths, since light with a long wavelength eventually couldn't create patterns that were fine enough. This in turn created huge challenges for the creation of new variations of photoresist that would work at these shorter wavelengths; a task that has been so complex that chemists basically needed to start working on such a project 10 years ahead of the time before the given wavelength was taken into production. After all, the photoresist had not only to be sensitive to the specific wavelengths of light applied, it also had to provide high contrast and sharp edges. Furthermore, it also needed to be able to stick to the wafer and not get removed during the washing processes.

The challenges didn't end there. The engineers had to develop optics that were more exact than those used in the Hubble Space Telescope, with lasers that could create the shorter and shorter wavelengths needed. There was also the problem of avoiding so-called tunneling, where electrons spontaneously jump between transistors or wires when they are extremely close to each other. To this purpose they developed isolation material, which could be applied in spaces that were only a few atoms wide. To use the earlier analogy, if a hair was 20 km wide, then you would need to efficiently isolate spaces that were perhaps about a 0.5 m wide, and you would have to do this for millions of such spaces without a single error or omission anywhere.

There was also the issue of clock rate. Let's say that you want to do a series of calculations. So, you send in electrical signals and consequently electric field changes rush around close to 300,000 km per second, and within an instant it's all done. Then what? Then you want to make the next series of calculations, which may build on the results from the previous ones. So, you send new impulses in. How, by the way? You use crystals that have a given inherent frequency, like when you let your hand glide over the wet edge of a crystal wineglass, and it starts to emit a tone. When a computer chip is started, a circuit around the crystal applies a random noise to it, which will inevitably include the natural vibration frequency of the crystal. This will now start to oscillate, and that movement amplifies electric signals coming out of the crystal. The interval between these impulses is called the "clock rate". The first commercial PC, the Altair 8800 used an Intel 8080 CPU with a clock rate of 2 million cycles per second (2 MHz). By 1995 we had reached rates of 100 million, and around five years later we broke the billion-per-second barrier. By 2010 the norm is that a chip does over 3 billion (3 GHz).

To get there has not been easy. After each clock pulse, the connections in the transistors need time to settle to their new state. If the next clock pulse comes before that, you get corrupted signals. Also, when running so fast, data processing creates more heat, which could damage the integrated circuit. Since heat generation is such a serious issue—it has been one of the key areas where Moore's Law is challenged—the chip designers have not been able to accommodate the current heat loads in these faster chips; consequently, they have needed to go to having multiple cores to address thermal loading.

As long as Moore's Law works, it means that the increase in computer capacity in the next two years, whenever you read this, will be as large as the overall increase since the world's first real computer was launched in 1943. So, let's say its 2010 and the law will uphold until 2012. This means that *performance growth over those two years will equal performance growth in all the previous 67 years.*

For how long will the law function? The experts don't know, because they can only see as far as their current ideas reach into the future, but as at 2010 most say that they see fairly clearly that they can keep it going until 2020 or even 2025. Can it work after that? Maybe, maybe not, they will typically say. "We don't know what will be invented before it's invented."

One thing we do know, however: If the logic gates in integrated circuits are smaller than 5 nm, the electrons may leap over, even if the "door" is closed (This minimum distance by the way is half the minimum distance that Feynman assumed in his article in 1959!). Since we saw that a nanometer equals the width of 10 hydrogen atoms, the distance of approximately 50 hydrogen atoms is about the smallest unit that an electron in a chip cannot spontaneously and unintentionally conquer. So, that is exactly where we will go with the current concept of computer chips.

Imagine again that we are down in the insanely magnified world that I described earlier, where a hair was 20 km wide. It's 2020 and we are looking at a computer chip. There will perhaps be 15 to 20 billion transistors on it, and the smallest gates in it are now down to only five hydrogen atoms wide, meaning just 20 cm. It contains 625 cores and the clock frequency is 73 GHz which means that 73,000 million times per second it sends electromagnetic pulses racing through the maze of interconnected transistors at a speed of almost 120,000 billion km per second

Prototype of IBM 3D water-cooled chip. The photo shows a complete view of a single-interlayer, 3D, cooling prototype before assembly. The active cooling area, the structured area in the center of the prototype, measures 1×1 cm, has a height of 100 µm, and contains up to 10,0000 vertical interconnections. *Photo*: Charlotte Bolliger. *Image courtesy of* IBM Research—Zürich.

(when the dimensions are amplified, the speed is too). That's roughly where we are headed with the current concept of integrated circuits.

However, there are already strong indications of what may happen after we reach that final level of compression around 2020. I could imagine that 3D design could keep Moore's Law going for another decade or two after 2020, so perhaps until between 2030 and 2040.

———

I mentioned earlier the wheel as one of the world's two greatest innovations. If you have an automobile and a bicycle, you own six wheels right there, but there are also small wheels in modern drawers, under office chairs and numerous other places. If we add the cogwheels you own, we probably get to at least hundreds and more likely thousands. After all, they are embedded in your automobile and bicycle, as well as in watches, electric and mechanical engines, etc.

But then take transistors. The production of transistors in 2010 will come close to 10,000,000,000,000,000,000, which means somewhere between 10 to 100 times bigger than the global population of ants. We will also produce more transistors than grains of rice every year. In fact, annual transistor production by 2010 is so high that if we distributed it

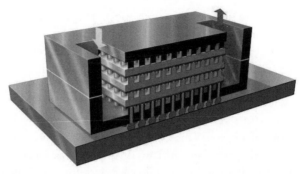

Schematic of IBM 3D water-cooled chip. The image shows the interlayer water-cooling technique in which the cooling structures are integrated directly into the chip stack. Using a special assembly technique, developed by IBM researchers in cooperation with the Fraunhofer Institute IZM, the layers can be connected in a high-precision and robust way that allows water to be pumped through the 3D stack embedded in a cooling container. Water (20°C) is pumped in at one side, flows through the individual layers of the stack, and exits at the other side. *Courtesy:* IBM Research—Zürich.

evenly among all people in the world, they would probably get around *1.4 billion transistors each*. If you were a family of four you would get 6 billion. If you are a geek, your personal allotment for this year would probably be closer to 100 billion of these things. Mankind is simply producing a vastly higher number of these transistors than we do of any other product component, and we keep doubling the production every 18 months.

By 2020 a standard computer should be about 30 times as powerful as in 2010, and if Moore's Law holds up until 2030, it will be around 1,000 times as powerful. But transistor production will grow much faster, because whereas each chip will contain more transistors, each household and factory will have more chips.

However, when you buy a computer or a smartphone, it's evidently not transistors you want, but the data handling and what that can do. Data-processing capacity is normally calculated in so-called "MIPS" (i.e., "million instructions per second"). In 1972, IBM developed its "system/370 model 158-3", which had a capacity of 1 MIPS and people were flabbergasted. One million instructions per second! One *million!* And IBM even promised that it wouldn't end there.

So, many began to ask themselves what you actually could do with one or several MIPS capacity. The American robot specialist Hans Moravec has described it in terms of what a robot with that capacity in its brain would do, which is fairly easy to relate to: One MIPS, for instance, will be enough for a robot to point out or follow something very simple (e.g., a white line or a coloured spot). This was the capacity of an IBM mainframe in 1972.

Let's multiply by 10. A capacity of 10 MIPS equals finding or following gray-tone objects such as a smartbomb might do. (In 1987, Motorola launched a chip with this capacity. During the first Gulf War in 1990–1991, we saw the precision of smartbombs.)

Next step: With 100 MIPS, an automobile can slowly find its way through a natural terrain. This could, for instance, be done with Intel Pentium Pro, which was launched in 1996. Four years later we reached 1,000 MIPS, enough to guide mobile utility robots through unfamiliar surroundings.

We multiply by 100. With 10,000 MIPS, the vision becomes three-dimensional and the robot can find and grab objects. By 2005 we had come this far, and in 2008 Intel launched the Intel Core i7 Extreme 965EE with 76,000 MIPS. The target everyone now have their eyes on is 100,000,000 MIPS capacity, because that is what the human brain is believed to have.

The rate of growth we have seen and expect to continue to see makes innovation of new applications evolve at amazing speeds. Let me give an example: Try to take an iPod or iPhone annum 2010 in your hand and take a good look at it. It is fantastic, but a thing like that was completely impossible to make when the IT bubble burst in 2000. And yet, in 2010, 10 years later, many hundred million of these devices are in daily use.

The increase in computer performance is not only about MIPS, but also about memory, data storage, bandwidth, and, for portable devices, battery life. Bell Labs announced in the spring of 2009 a new world speed record for fiber-optic transport. By transmitting 155 simultaneous wavelengths of light over a single 7,000 km long fiber, it managed to achieve a speed of 100 petabits per second per kilometer, equal to a payload of 15.5 terabits (trillion bits) per second. This was enough capacity to carry 10,430 simultaneous uncompressed HD video signals.

As all these technologies continue to evolve exponentially, it is a given that 10 years ahead, there will be new, incredible IT products sold in hundreds of millions that you can hardly imagine today. Maybe a small device with an enormous collection of movies.

Actually, some of the technologies for this scenario are already well on their way. Scientists at the University of California have demonstrated how it would be possible to store the equivalent of 250 DVDs on a device the size of a small coin, and a new "5D" technology developed at the Center of Micro-Photonics at Swinburne University of Technology uses a color filter plus polarization to add two dimensions of data represen-

---

The 10 top IT gadgets in the future

1. *The transparent smartphone.* Mobile phone which enables you to look at the real world through a transparent screen and get the world in front of you explained/conceptualized.
2. *The digital paper.* A soft, bendable e-reader that can download and display any media.
3. *The home movie server.* A compact server that can contain thousands of searchable and annotated movies.
4. *The media wall.* Entire walls that look like monochrome shiny surfaces or mirrors, but can turn into media screens at the touch of a finger.
5. *Widescreen PC display.* A several meter wide, single, flat screen, where some areas can be turned transparent, if not used for work.
6. *Car entertainment system.* Back seat and passenger seat online entertainment with movies, television, internet, etc.
7. *Wireless monitors.* Small devices that monitor everything you own and let you see it anywhere you are.
8. *Composable computing.* The ability to easily project content from any intelligent device to any screen near you (e.g., from a smartphone to a media wall).
9. *Automatic house cleaner.* Cleans floors and surfaces while you are away. Recharges itself at wall socket.
10. *Non-steal items.* Once an object is reported stolen, it transmits its geographical position to the police, who can then track it. If automobiles are stolen, police can remotely stop them, or block them if they are already stopped.

---

tation to the three that DVDs already have. The result should be a DVD with 2,000 times the normal capacity, which in my opinion would cover all movies ever made that are worth seeing. Let's guess that we, with that capacity, could store 2,500 movies (ranging from classics, which have little data to more data-consuming, high-definition movies). If you are a complete movie freak, and yet you do go out from time to time and on holidays, then you might see 250 movies a year. So, *one disk would keep you going for 10 years*, and by the time you were finished, you could probably just start over again.

Some of the new IT solutions will not be related to massive computing power, but to the efficiency of small sensors. In the future there will be three main methods to check where stuff is: RFIDs, GPS, and mobile phones. As I write this chapter I have just come home from skiing. Whenever I approached a ski-lift, it would automatically let me pass without showing my ticket. In the biggest lifts it would even show a photo of my face to the control guy. This is possible because the credit card–sized season card for the lifts that I carry in my pocket has glued on to it a tiny "radio-frequency identification tag", or "RFID" tag. This is a very small, very inexpensive chip that contains a grain-sized integrated circuit surrounded by a flat, printed metal antenna. All of it glued onto my plastic card and barely noticeable.

How does this RFID work? When I approach the gates of a lift, there is a little sensor that transmits a radio signal towards me. This signal creates an electromagnetic field in the antenna of my RFID, and the power from that field enables the integrated circuit to send a return signal back. This return signal contains my personal subscription code, which is cleared with the lift systems' computers before the gate opens and I can enter the lift. Furthermore, the computers bring up a stored photo of me so that the lift guard can check that my card is not stolen (except that I am impossible to recognize due to my goggles, helmet, and blue nose). RFIDs do much the same as bar codes, but as my ski example shows, you don't need to expose them directly to a scanner—just being close to one will do. They are getting cheaper and cheaper, and they can be made so tiny that you can glue them onto live ants. (In fact, some scientists who wanted to know about ant movement patterns already have. I kid you not.) Today RFIDs are being placed on countless consumer products, on containers, parcels, parking tickets, and even stuck to the ears of pigs and cows. They are also used for toll roads (automobiles with a valid RFID can pass; others not), on museum pieces, etc.

In the future there will be RFIDs on almost every product, for several reasons. The first is that it will enable you to load up with goods in a supermarket and then just pass the exit gate. The RFIDs will reveal themselves to an automated reader and you will just have to click "accept" on the detailed shopping list and the bill pops up on a screen. By doing so, it will bill your RFID-equipped payment card, if not your mobile phone. Another reason that we will see an explosion in RFIDs is that they can not only identify a product, but also trigger the launch of its "story". Point your smartphone towards it and you may read, see or hear everything the supplier has to tell you on a screen big enough to read (remember: there will be lots of old people unable to read small print on a package). Perhaps even what other people have to say about the same product, like consensus ratings. *The combination of RFIDs, corporate product stories, and ratings will be big.* Ratings, by the way, will be of everything:

corporate ethics and sustainability, holiday resorts, restaurants, automobiles, people, and this book. It has come pretty far already. If you want a corporate rating of transparancy and ethics, check the ISO 2600 standard. Wine? *Parkers Wineguide* (and many others). Books: Try Amazon.com. Investment opportunities? Ask your bank. Holiday resorts? tripadvisor. com. Here is a third killer app for RFIDs: washing instructions. The reason the robot in your future washing room will not wash your black socks with your white shirts is that it will check the RFIDs and understand what doesn't go together.

The second location technology is GPS, or the global positioning system. This is based on a fleet of satellites orbiting the Earth which each transmit time signals. A GPS receiver reads signals from several of these satellites and uses a combination of these to locate itself to a typical accuracy of 5 m (less, if the weather is terrible). The satellites broadcast their signals but do not receive any feedback from all the gazillion GPS receivers that people have in their boats, automobiles, or smartphones, etc. So, these types of satellites cannot "track people", as you sometimes hear, but if a GPS receiver is connected to a transmitter (such as a mobile phone it may be embedded in), then this transmitter might evidently send out coordinates of where it is.

In fact, as soon as you turn on your mobile phone, you reveal to the networks roughly where you are, since they can read your signal strengths at various mobile phone antennas, and this makes phones the third critical location technology. If they read you from just one antenna then they will have a very rough idea of where you might be, but if there are three antennas reading you, then they can triangulate and pinpoint your location very accurately. This has frequently been used for catching criminals and terrorists, and it has another extremely useful function: It reveals where there are traffic jams. Since most people have their mobiles turned on as they drive, it is easy to track statistically how many automobiles there are on any major road such as a highway, and how fast they are driving. Through this information it is thus possible to not only discover traffic jams instantly, but also to predict when and where they may appear. This information can then be fed back to the drivers via radio broadcasts, and the GPS systems in the automobiles can automatically alert the drivers and reroute them.

The creative possibilities coming from the combination of RFIDs, GPS, and mobile phones are countless, and so are the derived business opportunities. How about that you just click for "taxi" on your smartphone, and the phone sends your coordinates to the taxi, which finds you? This would be extra smart if in fact the taxi is robotic. Or how about stuff that calls either its owner or the police if it is removed from its expected location (like your expensive camera), or you, if it deviates from its expected route (your child coming home from school, or your senile parent). You just type in for them what their max authorized travel distance is (for your stereo: 10 m), or show it all authorized routes. Indeed, your child may carry a tracker which sends a message upon arrival at the school, tennis club, or wherever. Here is more: GPS-controlled lawn mowers. Car radios that inform you of upcoming events in the places you are approaching. Food that transmits an alert when it's about to expire (stick your smartphone into your fridge and get a list of what you need to eat soon).

Basic innovation in IT will also continue to change electronic media. People will want to be informed and entertained on their mobile devices, in real time and at any time. Perhaps there will be two of those mobile gadgets: the smartphone, which fits into a pocket and has two modes (transparent screen and normal screen), and the tablet computer/e-reader, which also has two displays (one with a backlight for indoor use and another with a liquid e-reader interface for outdoor viewing). Another change will be the increased growth in popularity of online games, and in particular massively multiplayer games, where millions of people simultaneously play against each other or in some cases against real-time challenges playing out in the real world, such as a live automobile race. As the latter begin to resemble high-definition movie quality, such games can become natural, seamless extensions of movies. You see an adventure movie, and the moment you are finished, you go back to your favorite scene and start playing in it. Perhaps these will be called "moviegames".

Furthermore, news and debates on television may morph into video conferences, and thousands or millions of such special interest programs take market share from large, standard TV packages. For instance, there may be 20,000 premium subscribers to a television channel; and the users will be able to "be there" and join in during question rounds, just as in any other video conference. "TV conferences" may be a good term.

If we assume for a moment that Moore's Law remains valid until 2020, single-chip computers will then handle approx. 4 million MIPS, or 4 "TIPS", for "trillion instructions per second". Since the human brain is assumed to have approximately 100 TIPS, we shall have reached approx. 4% of brain capacity by 2020. We shall also have surpassed Feynman's vision of 24 million books in a tiny grain. However, if the doubling every 24 months continues after that, chips will reach human capacity just after 2030. However, 2030 is not the time where the biggest computers will surpass the human brain. *That will actually happen around 2020.*

How is that? If we go back to 1997, an IBM computer called Deep Blue won a chess game against the ruling champion Gary Kasparov. Deep Blue had a capacity of approximately 3,000,000 MIPS (or 3 TIPS), since it had 256 state-of-the-art chips, which enabled it to make 200 chess move simulations per second. This means that Kasparov was beaten in chess by a computer that only had 3% of his own data capacity, but that was possible because Deep Blue did nothing else than play chess. The computer was simply capable of calculating all possible moves and counter-moves 14 steps ahead. This was enough to overwhelm the grandmaster, and the result was so impressive that he suspected the computer was being fed personally by another grandmaster. In fact, he said that he sometimes saw deep *personality* in Deep Blue's behavior—something original, creative, and brilliant. Simple functions may create complex and elegant outcomes.

However, the point here is that Deep Blue was massively powerful for its time because it combined the power of 256 chips. Such *multichip/multicore* computers will be on par with humans by 2020, if not considerably more powerful. Such technologies are in fact already par for the course; also for PCs. If one chip annum 2020 does 4 TIPS and the human brain does 100, you might need to put 25 chips into the computer to match a brain. OK, more chips or cores cooperating with their combined horsepower is generally not as efficient as a single one, but multi-chip computers can nevertheless be extremely powerful. But if the combination of many chips doesn't fully add up efficiently, you put in more. As I mentioned, Deep Blue had 256 chips. One way or the other, we are closing in on the brain.

A 3D chip is in a sense the most efficient form of multicore chips, and such chips could again be networked into multiple 3D chips, to create more oomph. But that will not be the last paradigm. For instance, you could replace or complement electric current with light. Or combine sensitive, ultra-high performance, fault-tolerant chips with safer traditional chips. Maybe the ultimate solution will be something combining quick, precise and fault-tolerant chips in silicon with others based on optics and nano-tubes that may have a larger risk of bit errors, but on the other hand have enormous parallel computing capacity.

There are also researchers working on using DNA to perform some computer functions. DNA is an extremely compact method to store information, since it uses 32 atoms to represent a bit of data. This is many orders of magnitude less than what we can do with today's chip architecture, even when it reaches its ultimate incarnation. An example of how we can utilize DNA is this: Calculate the shortest route between King Ling Road and Tai Chung Kiu Road in Hong Kong. Here is the method:

- We make a DNA strand for each road stretch between street corners in the area and give it a recognizable base sequence plus a length proportional to the stretch in question.
- We now use bacteria to propagate thousands of copies of each of these sequences and then mix them all together. They will now glue together in strands of various lengths.
- We screen the result and separate the strands with one end representing King Ling Road and the other Tai Chung Kiu Road.
- By using gel electrophoresis, we find the shortest of the strands and then read its sequence. This will give us the shortest route.

Actually, the GPS in many automobiles can do the same thing within a few seconds, which tells me that DNA computers are either in their infancy or perhaps don't have particularly high potential.

The ultimate solution might just come from so-called quantum computing, which applies some esoteric principles found in nuclear physics, where a particle may be in several different states and places at the same time and be symmetrically linked with another particle far away. The particles to represent bits here are electrons, which of course are much smaller than atoms, and almost infinitely smaller than the smallest way we could possible represent a bit in a silicon-based computer. In quantum computing, a single one of these electrons should then be able to represent four alternative conditions because an electron can spin in four different ways.

You could compare a quantum computer with today's best main-frames, but it is like comparing a container ship with a rubber duck or a spaceship with a paper airplane. Actually, even that would be an under-statement. If we took all the atoms in all the galaxies and placed them in an astronomic computer based on today's best technology and then asked them to solve a task that required many billion years of calculating, a small, compact quantum computer would be able to do the same in a frac-tion of a second. This is how much difference there would be. However, it should be added that it is not for all types of problems that quantum computers have such an advantage. Where they will do best is in some special sorts of query problems where random guesses are involved.

And what would this small computer look like? Well, to begin with, the few people working with quantum computation thought that the easiest starting point was to use a quantity of fluid for the calculations.

Several of them specifically suggested that the computer could be built in a cup of coffee! One thing we do know is that three people actually built a quantum computer in 1998. They were Isaac Chuang from Los Alamos National Laboratory, Neil Gershenfeld from Massachusetts's Institute of Technology (MIT), and Mark Kubinec from the University of California. We also know which calculations they got the computer to make. It added $1 + 1$ and got the correct result . . . 2. Later, in 2009, researchers succeeded in building a quantum computer on solid matter, so we might be on our way.

Such a computer could in principle have much higher data-processing capacity than all the human beings and computers put together have in 2010. However, it would be extremely sensitive to cosmic rays—the minute particles that reach the Earth from outer space at nearly the speed of light. There are on average two of these passing through the head of any person on Earth per second, which evidently doesn't hurt, but often creates some genetic damage. Since having such a particle passing through a quantum computer chip easily could knock an electron out of space (out of the computer, in fact) and thus mess up the representation of a bit, it would be necessary to isolate a quantum computer from the surrounding environment, while still finding a way to communicate with it. One might, for instance, place it in a dedicated room, perhaps lined with eight meters of lead on all sides, but also with some kind of access. Alternatively, the machine could remain more exposed to cosmic rays, but perform each calculation many times and deselect those that deviated from the majority.

———

Have you ever thought about how big an ant's brain is? The reason I ask is that ants have a highly organized type of society, which has been so successful that the overall biomass of all ants is more or less equal to the biomass of the human race. These tiny insects succeed in building their nests, collecting food, navigating around in complex surroundings, fighting, reproducing, etc. However, the head of an ant is so small that one can hardly see it. Compared with theirs, the human brain is enormous. Still, many people make an absolute mess of their lives, because something is wrong with their "software". What this shows is that a gigantic piece of hardware such as our brain is no guarantee of success. Success comes when this hardware is fitted with good programming. And this brings me to the following question: How do we write software for a computer whose hardware is much more powerful than our own? Since the biggest computers will surpass the human brain in performance within a fairly short time, it's really worth thinking about. How do you make instructions for intelligence that exceed your own?

This, of course, depends on what it is to be used for. If it is supposed to produce tables of logarithms and calculate prime numbers, we can use the computers and software we already had 50 years ago. However, for some of the more complex and intuitive tasks, programmers have developed programs performing so-called "artificial intelligence" or "AI".

The inventor and scientist Astro Teller has described artificial intelligence as "the attempt to make computers do what they do in the movies." Scientists and engineers have been working intensely with artificial intelligence for 30–40 years, and in many cases it has been a frustrating and disappointing experience. However, within the past 10–15 years, we have seen a number of breakthroughs, primarily because investment banks and hedge funds have invested large sums in the development of systems that could recognize patterns in economic and financial markets in the hope of earning money accordingly. However, they are not the only ones that have had some successes. One of the most intriguing AI systems has been "TD-Gammon", a piece of software that could play backgammon. The only information it was given was (1) the rules, (2) the position of the pieces, and (3) the name of the winner, when playing. Evidently, in the beginning it played like a complete idiot. But then it got better, and after a while it had taught itself over time to become an extremely apt backgammon player.

There are other smart programs doing things that are close to human intelligence. For instance, the Natural Language Processing Group at Columbia University in collaboration with Mitra Corporation developed the program bio-Gen, which is capable of reading news from a massive amount of sources and then generate a daily news coverage which looks as if it were written by a journalist.

In the perhaps less useful category of artificial intelligence, we find programs such as BRUTUS writing short stories that appear as if they were written by a competent writer. And then there is the EMI program composing music. EMI can listen to a portion of music from a given composer and then compose something new that sounds as if it came from that same hand. Douglas Hofstadter, an American professor of cognitive science, was so surprised by the way EMI worked that he invited the teachers from one of the U.S.'s leading music institutes to listen to a relatively unknown composition of Chopin and a Chopin-inspired composition made by the EMI program. He then asked the teachers if they could identify the real Chopin among the two, and the majority pointed to the one the EMI had written. Software beats artist!

Other programs draw artistic paintings (the most well-known is AARON), recognize handwriting, analyze fingerprints, discover signs that a person in an airport is nervous, etc. One of the major applications is translation, but here this has actually turned out to be incredibly difficult. Some years ago, the search engine Alta Vista had an automatic translation function. If you entered the expression: "The spirit is willing, but the flesh is weak" and had it translated to Spanish and back from Spanish to English, the result was: "The alcohol is arranged, but the meat is weak." Translation is not only a question of knowing the meaning of the words. It is also a question of semantics, context, style, and perhaps humor (I should say, though, that Google now handles cross-translation of the mentioned quote perfectly. Just checked.)

There is a wide variety of other human-like programs. For instance, scientists have made software that searches the mathematical world for interesting theories and phenomena and have set up models to explain them. My favorite is the program ELIZA, which was written for fun to simulate the questioning technique of a psychologist. If, for instance, you say, "My mother-in-law does not like me," it will answer something like this: "Why do you think your mother-in-law does not like you?" Rather surprisingly it turned out that people who exchanged information with the program believed that it was a live person and thanked the system profusely for helping ("you are like a father to me").

A particularly funny situation occurred when a vice president of a U.S. firm sat in a room at MIT (Massachusetts Institute of Technology) one Sunday morning to use a computer. He found a note on the teletype that read: "Type all messages into this teletype, and end them with a period." Before starting, however, he wanted to write to an employee called Bobrow and ask if it was OK. What he did not know was that the keyboard he was going to use was not intended for communication with Bobrow, but with ELIZA. The following dialogue took place:

Vice president: Do you think that I can use the computer this morning?
ELIZA: Why do you ask?
Vice president: I might be able to make some additional telcom sales.
ELIZA: Why aren't you so sure?
Vice president: My prospective customers have never seen a demonstration of the system.
ELIZA: Does this mean very much to you?
Vice president: Of course it does.
ELIZA: You seem very positive about that.
Vice president: This is ridiculous.

ELIZA: What do you mean, this is ridiculous?
Vice president: Is there any reason why I can't use the computer now?
ELIZA: Tell me more about your prospective customers.
Vice president: Please dial me up on 491-1850

As you might notice, the VP forgot to put a period sign after his last sentence, so ELIZA didn't answer him. He now waited for Bobrow to call him, but of course this did not happen either, because Bobrow was in fact sleeping. This so infuriated the VP, who thought Bobrow was playing games with him, that he called him up, woke him from his deep sleep, and said: "Why are you being so snotty to me?" Bobrow answered: "What do you mean why am I being so snotty to you?" Once the truth finally dawned on the two, they both had a good laugh.

I mentioned earlier in the book that the world publishes approx. 80,000 mass-market periodicals, 40,000 scholarly journals, 40,000 newsletters, and 25,000 newspapers. These are growing mountains of information that no human could ever keep track of. This is where so-called "data mining" can become immensely valuable. Whereas traditional miners look for commodities, the stuff data-miners look for is information.

A good way to explain this is perhaps to think of this book. It took me approx. 2 months of book reading plus 5 months of writing, editing, seeking reproduction permissions, etc. to produce it, so 7 months, or 28 weeks in total. I previously claimed that my productivity in such a process is approx. 10 times higher now than in it was in 1985 (which meant that earlier books had a more narrow scope). The question is if it would be possible to increase such productivity by a factor 10 for the next 25 years through IT? In 2035, will it be possible to write a book, for instance, about "Theories of Economic Growth" in less than 3 weeks?

I can imagine that it actually might. Let's say we have a software program called SpeedWriter that continuously scans the web plus e-books etc, as search engines already do now. However, SpeedWriter is different, because it has the capability to make sense of things. It can, for example, scan all research ever made about the health effects of eating red meat and then produce a meta-study that ventures an overall conclusion on the basis of all this research, which may include thousands of separate studies.

OK, so it's 2035. In order to write my book, I start by asking SpeedWriter to list the most quoted thinkers on growth theory. A few seconds later it gives me a list of the 25 leading writers in the area, listed in order of relevance. It found these by checking how frequently famous authors quoted other growth theory authors ("famous" is determined by how many articles they had published in the leading science publications plus how often each author is quoted by other authors, etc.).

As the next step I ask SpeedWriter to visually show me when these writers lived and when each of them published their most important work. SpeedWriter shows me this in a diagram. I ask it to divide the authors into schools of thought, which it does. I think for a while, and then I type:

- "Write 150-page book on theories about economic growth
- Primary structure: chronological; secondary structure: schools of thought
- Style: academic
- 20–40 technical illustrations, 5–10 author photos
- Flesch–Kincaid readability index: 25–30
- Full sources with online links."

The computer delivers the manuscript after a few minutes and I scan over it. I realize it is much, much too dry, so I ask SpeedWriter to find all anecdotes that involve at least two of the quoted authors and include them at appropriate places in the timeline. Furthermore, I ask it to change the style to "popular science" and the readability index to "50". The results appear soon after and it's much better. "Add 10–15 summary boxes," I type, and it does.

"Getting close," I think, but then I get an idea. I type: "Create 5–10 different 30–300-second movies with authors explaining their most important contributions. Include one where two of the authors who were active in the field at the same time argue a point."

The computer finds photos of some of the authors and renders animated characters that look like them, which it uses in the movie snippets. "OK, we are almost done," I think. All I need now is some interaction, so I write: "Add multiple choice exam and tutorial." It does. I upload the result to my digital e-reader and go out in the garden to study it. It's been an hour now, and I have a full draft of my interactive multimedia book. But I have set aside 3 weeks for the task, so I will use these to refine the draft. No sweat.

Data mining can be used for countless tasks. It can check if a person knows anyone who has ever been involved in crime, and even if any of these people know anyone who has. In fact, it could even be that it would automatically rate and profile people based on ethics, social network, academic achievements, and many other variables. The whole concept of rating will in itself grow. People are already rating consumer products, restaurants, books, etc. online, and the future world may be one where almost all things are rated by users and/or electronic expert systems, where even the raters are rated.

Data-mining systems can map traffic congestion (by checking where mobile phones are) and use this for suggested route planning for automobiles. It can scan blogs to check what people are interested in, and much, much more. It can evidently also use such techniques to create a daily newspaper and suggest a weekend entertainment plan that is completely tailored to the likely interests of any given person it serves.

In addition to artificial intelligence there are many other ways for software to help us understand our surroundings. One, which is called "expert systems" is based on collecting knowledge about how human experts make decisions. An example of that is MYCIN, a program for disease diagnostics that functions well, which is based on manually gathered input from a lot of doctors. Another category of smart software is "neural networks", which is meant to simulate how the brain works.

However, the brain actually doesn't seem to work remotely like any software mankind has yet made. It consists of around 150,000–175,000 *kilometers* of nerve fibers entangled in the most complicated hairball imaginable, through which billions of electrical impulses pass every second (remember, the brain can do 100 trillion instructions per second). Furthermore, its shape isn't fixed. The nerves keep changing shape and forming and dropping interconnections. All of this is in fact so intense that it takes up around 20% of the body's total energy consumption, even though the brain only accounts for a few percent of a grown person's body weight and doesn't visibly move.

Given this complication, it is not surprising that it has been really difficult for mankind to figure out what goes on in our own brains. Furthermore, no person can sense the mechanics of his own thinking, because if he could then it would constantly distract him. However, we have learned a great deal about the human brain lately. We know for sure that human intelligence—what makes us so much smarter than animals—is predominantly located in the so-called neocortex, which consist of six layers on the outer edge of the brain. The neocortex is only 2–4 mm thick, but since our brain is full of wrinkles and grooves, it has a very large surface—approximately two-thirds of it is hidden in the folds, and its total surface measures something along the lines of an unfolded serviette. In fact, it appears that the reason our brain has these strange folds is exactly to increase the surface so that the neocortex can be as big as it now is.

Inside this serviette are something like 30 billion neurons. That is a lot. I can illustrate it with the spot below, which is 1 × 1 cm:

Size of an area of the neocortex containing 10 million neurons.

If that spot was a piece that we had cut out of the neocortex, then we would expect to find something like 10 million neurons entangled into each other within it.

However, complexity does not stop here. The three upper horizontal layers in the neocortex mainly receive nerve impulses from the lower layers and particularly from the fourth layer, when viewed from above. If you imagine that impulses from the optic nerve enter layer 4 (from above), these impulses will generate cascades of derived signals in layers 3, 2, and 1. If you look at it through a microscope, you will see that the nerve fibers in the outer layer—layer 1—predominantly follow the surface of the neocortex, whereas all the deeper layers extend from the inside out and from the outside in.

If you take a closer look at each neuron you will find that it does not look like a thread or a wire—it looks more like a bush. They all have a number of branches (axons) which are connected to other neurons. In fact, on average each of them is connected to as many as 5,000 or even 10,000 others. So, let us take our square centimeter one more time and think of how many nerve connections it contains. The answer is that, whereas there are 10 million neurons, there are around 50,000,000,000 to 100,000,000,000 (50–100 billion) nerve *connections* inside this area:

Size of an area of the neocortex containing 50–100 billion nerve connections.

Nobody can relate to figures of this magnitude, so here is another way of looking at it. Let us take a section of the neocortex the size of a full stop:

↓

.

I hope you can see my full stop under the vertical arrow. A cylinder of neocortex of this diameter will contain approx. 140–280 million nerve connections. As for an ant's brain, by the way, it contains approx. 250,000 cells, which probably have 1,250–2,500 million nerve connections, so about 10 times as many as my full stop sign on the previous page.

Such numbers are still difficult to relate to, so we could go down to the smallest object an eye can see, which is 0.01 mm—a fifth of the breadth of a hair. Such a slice of human neocortex would contain approx. 40,000–80,000 nerve connections. That's how compact our brain is, and that also explains how insects with brains so small that they are barely visible can navigate their surroundings at high speed.

By the way, since a brain is so compact, how can we think a computer chip, or a small assembly of computer chips could ever match it? It seems like the entire neocortex has 150–300 trillion nerve connections. If a computer chip in 2020 has 15–20 billion (not trillion!), it is heavily outmatched, which also seems intuitive, since it is far smaller (the brain, after all, is a 3.5 kg 3D chip). Even a computer tasked with competing with the human brain in 2020 would only have 150–200 billion transistors, which is still about a factor of 1,000 less than the nerve connections in the brain. However, the transistors in computers depend on the on–off speed of semiconductors combined with electromagnetic fields, whereas nerve cells in brains depend on chemical reactions. The former—the computer hardware—works approx. 100,000 times faster than the neurons. If indeed we can simulate a brain, we can probably do it with something that is far smaller than the biological brain.

But what is it that is going on in all the neurons of the brain? Quite a few years ago, researchers concluded that if the signals from the optic nerve entered the four layers, they would send signals up through layer 3, then layer 2, and finally layer 1. All this suggested that layer 4 was receiving raw data from the nerves in the body, and that in the next two layers these data were transformed into some kind of pattern recognition. Eventually when reaching layer 1 with its many horizontal connections, the data were connected to a variety of information stores from other parts of the brain, whereby it was possible to get a meaning out of them.

The neurons in the neocortex have the same structure and more or less the same thickness all the way through, and the nerve fibers look pretty much the same everywhere in it. Similarly, viewed under a microscope, the neocortex is a uniform structure, although it handles various functions. This concurs with our knowledge that if part of the neocortex is damaged, another part can take over its work, and that if nerve input from a sense organ is moved from one part of the neocortex to another it will still function after a while.

Also, we know that the brain can easily learn functions that have never existed before. Having evolved over several hundred thousand years, when there were no automobiles, pianos, and computers, the brain can easily learn to drive an automobile, play the piano, or read and write. In other words, the neocortex is coded to receive sense impressions and send motoric instructions, but the actual purpose of these instructions is of no interest to the neocortex—apparently, it uses more or less the same principles to solve *all* problems. But what are these principles?

The brain uses no mathematical formulas or logical algorithms that in the least way resemble the workings of computers. It seems like the brain is actually more like a movie server. Such a server contains numerous movies that are compressed in, for instance, MPEG or AVI format. More and more scientists believe that the function of the neocortex is primarily to store a wealth of sense impressions from our life, which it replays when we experience something similar.

Let us first take a look at how data enter the system: If we see a face, the neocortex receives lots of raw pixels, but then they are translated by the higher layers of the cortex to a number of patterns, whose relative proportions are memorized in compressed, stylized, and conceptualized form. This turns into patterns and phenomena that are stored primarily in the outer layers of the cortex, where they can be classified, recombined, and related to other memories. An example: When we see a cockerel, to begin with the brain receives the raw sense impression which it perceives as pure sound and image and perhaps smell. But in the next layers of the cortex, this impression is transformed into an impression of a slightly arrogant and sometimes silly animal—which always reminds me of the way Picasso sometimes drew them. And in the outer layers of the cortex, the connections are then made to the word "cockerel" in all the languages we know and to "bird" and perhaps "dawn", or even "coq au vin" (cockerel in red wine).

> Incidentally, *coq au vin* makes me think of a holiday we spent in Provence where we had exactly this course . . . We then lived in a vineyard where they also had some very fresh fruit . . . which we brought with us to the beach . . . here, we bathed a lot, and . . .

. . . and now I am surfing around related memories in the top layer of my neocortex, and as I do that my brain uses massive parallel computing. The "movies" I have stored are compressed down to proportions, relative distances, ideas, symbols, and concepts. In other words, we compress, and while much information is lost because of that, we gain the advantage of speed, memory space, and, perhaps most importantly, the ability to recognize things that are similar, but not the same. We can, for instance, recognize a person although we see him/her in a different light and from another angle than before. If we hear a piece of music, the neocortex will store the distance of time and the tone between each detail of sound. If we walk down the street, the neocortex stores the relevant combination of motoric/somatic instructions given to the muscles and senses received from our feet, etc.

Impressive images

Picasso is labeled a post-impressionist, but what he painted was the impression things made on him, not their optical image, and this makes his work so captivating. It seems that the brain also transforms what it senses into symbols and impressions.

And in this way we arrive at how information flows back to the system. When we have to do something, the neocortex plays some movies forecasting what will happen in a short while. If we walk along the street, it will play a film that tells us how we should use our muscles, the sensations we can expect in our feet when they touch the ground, the way it should sound, etc. This movie makes us walk, and if everything goes as predicted by the movie in our neocortex, we need not be conscious about it. It plays automatically. I know it very well from myself. I often drive across Switzerland, and sometimes my wife calls me en route and asks how far I have come. I don't know. "Did you pass Berne?" she may then ask. I don't know that either, because I do not think about my driving at all. It is just a film running in one part of my brain while the rest of it is thinking about other things.

I can think of another good example you probably know from yourself: I am sure that many times you have tried to walk up an escalator that did not work. It is a strange feeling, because even though you can see beforehand that it does not work, you almost fall over your legs when taking the first step, because instinctively, the brain has prepared itself for a moving escalator—for that feeling of the foot being pulled forward as soon as the first step is taken. What actually happens doesn't match the movie it is playing; it simply consists of movie snippets. And this explains why there are approx. 10 times as many nerve connections pointing away from the brain than toward it from sensory nerve cells.

Here is a third example. Try to see if you can read this:

"I cnduo't bvleiee taht I culod aulaclty uesdtannrd waht I was rdnaieg. Unisg the icndeblire pweor of the hmuan mnid, aocdcrnig to rseecrah at Cmabrigde Uinervtisy, it dseno't mttaer in waht oderr the lteretes in a wrod are, the olny irpoamtnt tihng is taht the frsit and lsat ltteer be in the rhgit pclae. The rset can be a taotl mses and you can sitll raed it whoutit a pboerlm. Tihs is bucseae the huamn mnid deos not raed ervey ltteer by istlef, but the wrod as a wlohe. Aaznmig, huh? Yaeh and I awlyas tghhuot slelinpg was ipmorantt! See if yuor fdreins can raed tihs too."

The letters are incredibly garbled, but the sentence actually makes sense, and therefore the neocortex will guess the words and the sentence. I have tried this on children as young as 9 years, and they did it well. When a computer can read that without being trained for it, we will have arrived.

The conclusion is that while a computer uses mathematics, the brain does something quite different. For instance, it does not try to calculate where the tennis ball will land during a match or how you should move your body when swinging on skis in powder snow. It simply recalls previous experiences when you hit the ball correctly, or swung around elegantly in the snow on your skis. And it recalls these previous experiences in the same sequence as before. You remember the alphabet, but not backwards, and definitely not all at once. You remember it as a film. You might be able to sing Frank Sinatra's *My Way*—but not backwards. If you recall walking down a street in Paris, you will memorize it as bits and pieces—you cannot recall all of it in a single instant, just like you could not recall an entire James Bond movie simultaneously.

Since the brain apparently functions that way, you understand why it is futile to fantasize about instaling chips inside it with instructions of how to speak French or do integral mathematics, because the brain wouldn't be able to interpret them. But there is something else we *should* be able to do. We should be able to add new senses. I believe it would be possible to equip us with radar which is connected to a chip with metal arms sticking into the brain mass. The brain would probably after a while recognize the pattern in the signals and learn to see in the dark. Incidentally, something very similar has already been done. In the U.S. a blind man had a chip connected to a camera transplanted into his tongue. The tongue's nerves now caught the signals from the camera and sent them to the brain and (hold on now) ... after a while he could see with his tongue. Not very well, mind you, but still: He saw with his tongue.

As computers close in on the human brain, it is worth asking how they will compare and compete with us. I think we can divide human intellectual activity into different forms of (1) gathering data, (2) interpreting the world, and (3) expressing talent. Evidently the reality is a fluent combination of all three. Just as the neocortex plays back movies while gathering information, we constantly and continuously combine mental skillsets in our performance of different tasks. The ability to do that is in fact what makes us street-wise and able to succeed in a complex world.

On the next spread of pages I show a set of tables that present what I believe to be the 12 key skillsets of human intelligence. I have indicated with gray the areas where computers routinely beat humans. Light gray means that they in some cases beat humans and dark gray means that they are often vastly superior.

The tables on the left page show the situation in 2010, and those on the right page show how I think it might be in 2030, when computers exceed the human brain in firepower and where we master neocortex simulation.

As indicated by the two sets of tables, I do not expect computers to have any emotions by 2030, but I do think that they will be pretty good at faking them. Furthermore, they will have made vast improvements in terms of data gathering, where they will routinely beat humans in terms of discovering what goes on and flagging events that warrant attention. Being immensely fast and tireless, combined with a vastly improved ability of detecting important correlations, will do the trick.

In terms of expressing talent, they will be able to make artistic paintings and music, and to write literature, design houses, and do countless other creative tasks that we consider exclusive to the human domain today. They will also be able to do more formal and well-defined work at a speed and scope that will often be hard to match for any human. They will, for instance, perform many military tasks with far higher efficiency than men, and will be able to instantly detect connected data on the internet and create structured presentations of it at lightning speed. They will also be able to have factual conversations with humans such as in technical helpdesks or as tutors.

So, they will be immensely smart. The chess game between Gary Kasparov and Big Blue was the first of many contests between men and computers. We know that computers already have cheated people, who mistook them for other humans. The question is when will we see a computer do an amazing score in an IQ test that it hasn't been specifically trained for, whether a computer will one day qualify for a Nobel Prize or Pulitzer Prize. If so, to whom do we give the money? Or will we let a computer win a prize originally intended for people?

––––––––––

The reality is that there are already numerous activities in the IT world today that approach what the neocortex does and give a taste of what the future will bring. Just think about the whole concept of "prosumers" and interactive content. A prosumer is a consumer who contributes to the creation of his own product by supplying specific or indicative information to the producer. You may, for instance, select specifications of an automobile online, or provide hints to your suppliers through internet-browsing habits. In interactive media, a journalist, publisher, or manufacturer may publish information which immediately meets a tenfold larger response from consumers. This is very similar to the behavior of the neocortex where the information coming in is met with a tenfold larger flow of information expressing expectations. It is very efficient in the brain as well as in the market place.

I believe Google for all practical purposes is beginning to emulate parts of neocortex functionality. When you make a search that is misspelled or doesn't exactly make sense, the program will typically respond by asking "did you mean . . ." followed by a suggestion that is spelled correctly or makes sense. This is building on its empirical experience. It is, in a sense, "playing back movies" of what to expect in a given situation, like the neocortex, and these are based on what it has seen before. It is using people as tutors, and then playing tutor for people.

Computer versus man annum 2010		
Gathering data		
	Informal	*Formal*
Ad hoc	Investigation	Inspection
Continuous	Control	Surveillance
Interpreting the world		
	Informal	*Formal*
Factual	Synthesize	Analyze
Emotional	Empathize	Moralize
Expressing talent		
	Informal	*Formal*
Factual	Conversation News reporting	Physical movement control Logic/scientific writing Precision work
Emotional	Art, design, and music Social people skills	Writing literature People skills for corporate and service business

Computer versus man, annum 2010. Computers can be good at gathering data, analyzing them according to predetermined criteria, controlling some physical movements such as in cars and airplanes, and doing logical and precise calculations. However, when it comes to informal and emotional tasks, they are generally very weak.

Google has several hundred thousand custom-built servers and keeps adding thousands every week. These servers are divided into clusters, which are each coordinated by proprietary software running on open-source software. On these servers it maintains a copy of the entire internet, which it continually updates through use of "spider software" that automatically crawls from link to link in the web and copies everything it finds. It also updates digital copies of books, scientific magazine articles,

Computer versus man annum 2030		
Gathering data		
	Informal	*Formal*
Ad hoc	Investigation	Inspection
Continuous	Control	Surveillance
Interpreting the world		
	Informal	*Formal*
Factual	Synthesize	Analyze
Emotional	Empathize	Moralize
Expressing talent		
	Informal	*Formal*
Factual	Conversation News reporting	Physical movement control Logic/scientific writing Precision work
Emotional	Art, design, and music Social people skills	Writing literature People skills for corporate and service business

Computer versus man, annum 2030. Computers will now have learned to distill information from a diverse range of sources, which they each judge qualitatively. They will also be able to perform normal conversation as tutors, help desks, order takers, etc., and they will excel at many creative/artistic tasks, as well as professional writing such as news summaries, manuals, software documentation, etc.

etc., and uses a set of mathematical algorithms to index and rank every page and every other source it finds in connection with different search words and terms. For this task it also looks at how people search and tries to learn from that—in other words, the software uses people as tools, which is sort of new and upside-down.

So, now I want to do a search. I type in: "When will oil production peak?" After 0.11 seconds it brings me rated links to approx. 52,000 links related to that question. How on Earth did it do that in ... 0.11 s? It uses massive parallel computing. When I type in a query, the Google software routes that simultaneously to each of its server clusters, where its software distributes the query further to the individual servers. This means that for 0.11 s, I have thousands of computers, perhaps hundreds of thousands, working for me. These are then transmitting all their results upstream through a reverse cascade of clusters, and then finally to where the highest level of ranking and aggregations happens—and finally to me.

This, I think, is very similar to some of what the neocortex does. It plays back memories, and that is why, as I mentioned before, whenever there is incoming data to the brain, it matches it with a far bigger flow of outgoing data which is a simulation of what will probably happen next.

Internet search is still in its infancy. The search engine WolframAlpha renders it possible to ask simple questions such as "How long is a Gulfstream 150?", and the answer pops up immediately. Not as a reference to countless websites, but as a figure: 18.97 m (the factory actually claims it is 17 m and 25 cm). I don't have a Gulfstream, so I can't check who is right, but we're moving forward.

During the next 20 years, we will perhaps manage to build a computer that really can copy what our neocortex does. The Allen Institute for Brain Science, a non-profit organization that was established in 2003 with a $100m seed donation from Microsoft co-founder Paul Allen, has since been working on mapping spines and brains. It uses robotic methods to cut brains into hundreds of thousands of tiny, almost transparent slices, which are then photographed digitally and bar-coded. A small brain like that of a mouse will, for instance, be cut into approx. 250,000 slices, which are each so thin that, when you see one on a piece of glass, it looks no thicker than a fingerprint. Once these slices have each been mounted on glass, they are immersed in solutions with different strands of RNA that can only attach to specific gene strings. After this has been done, the slices are washed again with chemicals and specific antibodies that will stick to the RNA to make it visible, thus showing the scientists which genes are expressed in each part of the brain.

If we do manage to make a realistic simulation of the neocortex, then it will not copy our feelings or our consciousness, because they do not exist in the neocortex. And why would we? Simulating feelings would be asking for trouble. What if a computer feels anxiety or aggressiveness? The computer HAL 9000 did so in the film (and the book) *2001: A Space Odyssey*, and the outcome wasn't good.

One of the companies that have already experimented with brain simulation is IBM, which in 1995 launched Blue Brain. The aim of this project was exactly that: To build a simulation of the human brain on a supercomputer. In 2008 they succeeded in simulating a fraction of the neo-cortex in a rat's brain that had 10,000 neurons, with about 30 million synaptic connections, which is an insignificant number compared with the neurons and nerve fibers in the human brain. But just wait and see: Projects like the one mentioned will be expanded over time. IBM estimates to have data capacity to simulate a human brain before 2020.

———————

I would not be surprised if one day you will be able to gather all books, all music, and all films ever published in a relatively cheap and compact server. That we are able to reach so much more is evidenced by the fact of how far we have already come. Since the 1950s computer capacity has grown more than ... hold on ... 10,000,000,000,000 times. Yes, 10,000 billion times. Therefore, it is not so strange that information technology is still evolving dramatically and that there are thousands of fantastic products underway.

When I was a child, people predominantly used central computers with passive slave screens, sometimes referred to as *master–slave*. The first of these masters was even dumber than an ant. After centralized computers came the so-called *client–server*. These were big, central computers connected to many intelligent terminals such as personal computers.

The next level was *network-based* computing, where millions of computers—big and small—were connected to each other via the internet and began to exchange knowledge and resources. This development had a massive social impact as it mobilized communities in a way that hadn't existed before. Anyone trying to manipulate people would immediately be opposed by blog-writers and self-made publishers on the internet. Patients with chronic diseases would find each other online, discuss their experiences, and often end up telling doctors how they should be treated, instead of the other way around. This is where we are now. So, where do we go from here?

I think there are two ways of looking at it: from a technology perspective and from a user perspective. As for the former, I think we are moving at accelerating speed though an evolution, comprising seven or eight phases:

(1) *Master–slave computing.* Central computers which can only be operated by highly specialized experts.
(2) *Client–server computing.* Large, central servers connected to decentralized computers that are fairly easy to use.

(3) *Networked computing.* Millions of user-friendly computers connected over the internet.

(4) *Ubiquitous computing.* Computers appear everywhere in the environment, often embedded and invisible, or mobile and handheld. Anyone can use them.

(5) *Autonomous computing.* Software can learn and perform intuitive and sophisticated analytical tasks such as service functions, research, data mining, and scanning of environments.

(6) *Virtual computing.* Networks of computers work in swarms where the demanding part of the computation is done by utilities that are online in real time to both stationary and mobile computers.

(7) *Self-modifying computing.* Software can identify the need for new software and does the coding itself. An explosion of software diversity follows.

(8) *Conscious computing.* Software realizes that it exists.

The fourth phase is exploding right now, with computers popping up everywhere, often hidden and integrated into other systems. "Ubiquitous computing" or "pervasive computing" are the more professional terms. Today, we all have very strong computers in our digital cameras, automobiles, mobile phones, and all kinds of places.

A recent example of ubiquity is e-readers, like Amazon's "Kindle", which is a product for reading books and magazines from a screen instead of from paper. Kindle does not require special light conditions; it is like looking at a piece of paper and, as opposed to normal electronic screens, this one is actually the easiest to use in direct sunlight. The display is made of microscopic balls that are white on one side and black on the other and are controlled magnetically. I believe that future e-readers will be bendable, have built-in video clips, weblinks, and be updated regularly, whereby the downloading of a book or a magazine means access to a vivid multimedia document.

I mentioned conscious computing for the eighth phase, but I don't know whether it will really ever happen. How could one know? If you start doing budget revision on your computer one day and it suddenly shuts down your spreadsheet and tells you that it prefers to play games today, I guess you would know.

Anyway, this was the technical perspective. From a user's point of view, I think the coming decades will be dominated by the following combination of trends in IT and digital media:

- *More unbundled.* When stuff gets digital, it is no longer bound to a physical container. Music is no longer bound to a physical CD, and

Plastic Logic's QUE™ proReader was launched on the American market on January 7, 2010 at CES in Las Vegas. E-readers will most likely replace much of what we today print as magazines, etc.

therefore you might download one track at a time instead of buying the whole CD. With online news, you can repackage as you want so that you only see the parts you want.

- *More atomized.* The popularity of Twitter shows that many people like text media in a form that resembles single sentences in a conversation. Similarly, you may want to use a given piece of software or have real-time access to a given stock exchange only a few times a year.
- *More instant.* Increasingly people expect to get information a few seconds after they realize that they need it. Google and Wikipedia are examples of great resources to that end. Business people and investors expect a constant beam of targeted information that supports them in real time.
- *More mobile.* Access to any IT or digital media for different screen types wherever you are and whenever you need it.
- *More conceptualizing.* Computing will be able to draw on external resources in real time to show you what the meaning and context of anything you come across might be.
- *More autonomous.* IT systems are not only answering question, they can make intuitive decisions and be creative.
- *More virtualization.* Use IT to make physical stuff redundant.
- *More real time.* IT will give us information about the world as it happens, and will seamlessly integrate models and games with live events in the physical world.

So, there are eight application trends, plus the seven or eight technical phases that I mentioned before. However, there will be a third aspect: A separation of the industry into three clearly defined roles:

- *Information utility companies.* To provide standard services such as data processing and storage.

- *Information marketing organizations.* To look at the client's point of view and help him with setting up the right portfolio of IT products against fees, which may be high. These offerings will be based on "open architecture", which means that they may include products made by the IT company as well as by its competitors.
- *Creative IT companies.* Such as development houses, startup companies, consulting companies, etc.

So, these are the principle drivers I can imagine for the IT world over the coming decades. However, perhaps we should get a bit more concrete and look at some of the products that the IT sector might launch in the future. We might as well begin with what they mostly show in science fiction movies: robots.

───────

From time to time, as I sit at home, office, and work, I have to lift my legs to give space to a little guy called "Roomba". This is a robotic vacuum cleaner. As of 2010 more than 2.5 million of them have been sold. The cat thinks it is funny. I think it is interesting, because it's the robot industry's first real mass-market success.

I guess a robot can be defined as a computer-controlled, unmanned object peddling around in the real world. It is to the robot industry what Pac-man was to computer games: The first big hit. But it is not any wiser than a woodlouse. The best known robots today are probably the charming *Star Wars* characters C3PO and R2D2, who remind us of a jumpy gay man and a super-gifted Nilfisk vacuum cleaner, respectively. Both of them show great courage (especially R2D2), and you become fond of them as you go along. However, they do not exist in real life.

Automobiles and airplanes, on the other hand, do. Some modern automobiles have more computer capacity than the first spaceships had. They have anti-lock brakes, a brake assist system, and a traction control system, which make a large number of calculations (25 times per second or faster) to identify danger signals. Furthermore, they use satellites for navigation guidance, radio for online road condition reports, radar-guided parking distance control, and distronic distance control systems. They are, in other words, constantly reading feedback from wheels and engines plus radio signals, satellite signals, and radar return signals to inform, assist, and guide the driver. They are not yet robots, but they are bloody smart.

Photos transmitted by the robotic probe *Opportunity* from Mars November 2009 (left) and by its sister vehicle *Spirit* in 2004 (right). The robots landed in 2003, and it was planned that they would function for just 3 months. However, they have continued to function perfectly until *Spirit* got stuck in soft sand on May 1, 2009. *Opportunity*, on the other hand, was still operating flawlessly at the end of 2009. *Courtesy*: NASA/JPL-Caltech.

In the space industry, self-running probes, which are more or less self-driven vehicles, were launched a long time ago. They have been very successful on Mars. The two robot vehicles *Spirit* and *Opportunity* landed on Mars in 2003; engineers had predicted that they would last 90 days. But they just kept going. So, after the initial mission was completed (cost: U.S.$820m), another four were commissioned, one after the other, while new software was uploaded to the robot vehicles on Mars from time to time. The cost of mission 4 dropped to $104m, and mission 5 is expected to cost just over $20m. By the end of 2009, *Spirit* had a problem with a wheel after driving into soft sand and getting stuck, but *Opportunity* was still happily moving around in its seventh year, with 11 km on the odometer.

Water has been found on the Moon, and *I can imagine that we shall see a permanent base there around 2025–2030.* This is partly because it will be a more practical space observation post than an orbiting satellite, since many things get easier when there is a bit of gravity around. Second, there are considerable reserves of helium-3 on the Moon, which could be ideal as a second-generation fuel for nuclear fusion. The Sun produces it all the time and blows it out as solar wind, but there is very little of this on Earth since our magnetic field deflects it. However, the Moon is full of this great fuel.

Closer to Earth, the latest Learjets are 100% "fly-by-wire", which means that there are two computers controlling the aircraft. When the engine is started, each of these two computer systems diagnoses all the aircraft's systems, and it is not possible to take off, unless both computers produce identical status reports. If they do, one of the computers will take over flying. These technologies are not robots as per the definition, because Learjets are manned, but they do some of the work you might expect from an advanced robot. However, military drones are unmanned, and so are numerous other military vehicles that are either in use or in various stages of testing. Some of these require remote control, but others can operate autonomously (e.g., surveillance vehicles).

Computer chips surpassed the brain level of flies in 1995, and today we have absolutely no problem in making robots that are as clever as flies. A fly has approximately 100 MIPS supplied by approximately 100,000 neurons, and it flies well enough to be almost impossible for us to catch in flight. But it is virtually incapable of learning anything new. If it sits on my arm and I try to swat it, it will fly away. But shortly after, it will perhaps fly back and sit on the exact same spot. How dumb can it be? I try to swat it one more time, and this will be repeated a third time. It has learned absolutely nothing.

The next stage is something on the level of lizards charging around sticks and stones without banging their heads too many times. This we can also handle today. An example is the annual DARPA Grand Challenge. The first one was held in 2004 when a number of robot vehicles made by different universities were programmed to drive through 240 km of desert. Out of the 15 finalists, not one finished the race. The most successful vehicle only managed to drive around 12 km—approximately 5% of the stretch. The year after, the race was repeated with 23 finalists and this time they all succeeded in getting farther than 12 km—in fact, five of them crossed the line. In 2007 the DARPA Urban Challenge was held with 11 finalists who were to navigate 96 km through a city environment without colliding with other automobiles or violating traffic laws. Six of the 11 teams completed the race. This is a very fast rate of progress.

There is a rule in technology that it takes approx. 25 years from the time that an attractive technology concept works at the experimental/laboratory scale until it is widely adopted (although some IT products sell much faster). Given that the technologies for robotic vehicles are largely in place by 2010, it would not be unreasonable to expect that they may be widely used around 2035. One way to start may be by robotic trucks for highways. A truck going from Italy to Poland may, for instance, be towed to an Italian highway by a driver, who then puts it on autopilot. The truck will then automatically drive to Poland without any human driver and will park at a roadside parking lot upon arrival, where

Image of autonomous robot from the Second Grand Challenge. *Source*: User Spaceape on en.wikipedia.

a Polish driver will pick it up and take it to its final destination. Regulations may well stipulate that it has to park during rush hours and only drive at night. If it needs refueling or battery repowering on its way, it may automatically go to a suitable gas station and either plug itself in for electric power, or perhaps wait to be served by a human or robot.

There is another obvious mass application for robots: shopping. Personally I would divide shopping into four kinds:

- *Pleasure shopping*. Shopping for luxury, art, or fashion as a pleasant experience.
- *Laser shopping*. The specific replacement/purchase of a well-defined item.
- *Explorative shopping*. Searching for a gift or decoration item, but you don't know what it should be.
- *Refill shopping*. The routine purchase of standard household goods.

I think the first is best done the old-fashioned way (since it's nice), and the next two often online (where selection is broader and search faster). However, most shopping falls in the fourth category, which is utterly boring and very time-consuming. Robots should pick your stuff up at the warehouse and dump it at the local gas station or in your home. All gas stations should be acquired by supermarkets for that reason (and because automobiles will go electric). They are perfect pickup places.

The next stage will be robots with a considerable learning ability. In other words, robots that will study their surroundings in real time, react to changes, and to some extent predict the reaction to them by the surroundings. I am thinking about something like a cat.

The computer industry is likely to use two principal solutions for teaching such sophisticated robots. One is "top-down" where attempts are made to program a number of rules. Mankind has already developed software and hardware that are capable of simulating almost everything we do ourselves. We have cameras that can see (also in two dimensions), microphones for listening (in stereo), sensors that are capable of feeling and even smelling. We also have GPS telling us where we are and how we can reach our destination. Furthermore, we have software speaking several languages, understanding what others are saying (such as Dragon, NaturallySpeaking, and IBM ViaVoice), translating and communicating with a service-minded attitude (such as the internet systems Haptek and Oddcast). We also have programs that can read out loud, calculate, write, search for information, and many other things. We have automobile parking assistance control software to avoid collisions and other software recognizing and interpreting images and objects. If we glue all this together, we must have the wherewithal to make a smart robot function? Maybe. But if we try to combine it all, we could end up with software of enormous complexity.

The alternative approach is the neocortex way; to teach robots from the "bottom-up", where the robot can do almost nothing to begin with, like the backgammon software I described earlier. Here, we start with a few algorithms enabling the robot to learn from his errors and to appreciate rewards when doing something right.

How does nature do it? The brains of insects and shellfish are predominantly hard-coded, meaning that almost all instructions related to their abilities are predetermined in their genes. They only have a few hundred million base pairs in their DNA, but they are enough to identify how the brain cells need to be connected. The 3.2 billion base pairs of human beings, however, are not enough to specify how all the 30 billion neurons in our brains should be connected.

But humans are different. What is so characteristic of our species is the ability to adjust and learn, so our brain cells only specify how only a very small number of brain cells need to be connected, and what they should do. This is why newborn babies are completely helpless, even though they have an enormous brain. All of a child brain's enormous quantity of nerve fibers starts to form patterns as a result of learning, although this is colored by their genes. When a person develops into an expert within a specific professional sphere, it is estimated that in general the individual has between 50,000 and 100,000 lumps of information and experience on the subject in question. Obviously, each of those lumps consists of a massive number of nerve connections.

I believe the top-down approach will mainly be used in cases where the robots might become dangerous, especially when used as automobiles or aircraft. Bottom-up may be preferable to almost anything else. However, many systems may end up having some of both. After all, humans, who are overwhelmingly self-taught, do have numerous hard-coded functions as well. Reflexes, automated breathing, heartbeat, etc. Perhaps robots will be based on 5% top-down hard-coded instructions and 95% bottom-up neocortex simulation.

Ten tasks for computers that predominantly simulate a neocortex

1. *Drive our automobiles.* Today, there are approximately 800 million automobiles, and in 20 years there will be 1.3 billion. People get bored in their automobiles, bump into each other, end up in long traffic jams they could have avoided, get lost, and drive them uneconomically. Computers could do it much better and leave us to work, read, talk on the phone, sleep, surf the internet, or watch TV while driving. We might still drive automobiles (especially sportsters) manually at times, but only if we think it is fun.

2. *Create personal media.* An intelligent computer could set up a detailed profile of our interests and then regularly go through all sources on the internet and other media to find exactly what we want. It could then write a personal newspaper, and make a personal radio program and/or a personal TV program with exactly everything we find interesting.

3. *Private tutors.* At some point during their school time, most children experience falling behind in a subject, and a computer could then work as their private teacher outside normal school hours. The same phenomenon could also be used by adults for new learning and supplementary training.

4. *Safety.* An intelligent computer could use smell sensors similar to those of a bloodhound, infrared sensors, and eyes recognizing people and interpreting them as "belonging" or "not belonging" in order to carry out surveillance on private homes, office buildings, harbors, parking lots, airports, railway stations, factories, etc.

5. *Sorting*. Computers could perform very precise garbage sorting for recycling and would at the same time be immune to the toxic substances that are sometimes involved. It could also walk along roadsides, on beaches, etc. and pick up litter.

6. *Laundry*. It could also sort laundry in private homes, wash it, iron it and hang it out to dry.

7. *Dish washing*. Nobody likes washing dishes, but almost every home and all restaurants do it every day. This is done within a limited physical area, so it must be possible to make a dishwasher which can fill and empty itself.

8. *Diagnosis*. When a doctor talks to a patient, an intelligent computer could monitor the consultation. Just before the patient leaves, the know-all computer could tell the doctor if there was anything he had not thought of or perhaps done wrong.

9. *Peer reviews*. When scientists publish research results in scientific publications, these are often followed by critical reviews by other scientists. Intelligent computers could be involved in this work and would have the advantage of larger background knowledge than any single scientist.

10. *Military functions*. Computer-controlled automobiles, airplanes, and camouflaged "listening stations" could take over a large part of military reconnaissance functions. In certain instances, they could also take over combat functions and control fighters—but with a human monitor taking part via telecommunications. And, finally, they could see through "the fog of war", as Carl von Clausewitz called it, and see what must be done next amid chaos and confusion.

Please note that not all these 10 ideas involve physical navigation in the surrounding world and that those that do will have very little physical resemblance to a human being. The body in a robot-controlled vehicle is simply the automobile. In a robot-controlled airplane the body is the aircraft, and in a robot-controlled safety system, the sensors and cameras represent the essential part.

Almost everybody I talk to about robots say immediately and almost instinctively that they will never be like us—that we are "special". We certainly are, and we are, from a technical point of view, absolutely amazing. Our brain is still far more powerful than any computer, and yet very compact. Our body is largely able to repair its own damage, and we can replicate ourselves. We have incredibly accurate touch and temperature sensors across our surface and within the body, and we can see, hear, and smell with amazing accuracy. Tell an engineer to match that with a machine, and he would faint.

But now think about what robots can do that we can't. The first concerns the physical location of the brain. *The brain of robots does not have to dwell within their body.* Instead, they may have a wireless connection to a large, stationary computer controlling them, as military drones already do today. Some of these fly missions controlled via satellite by a pilot sitting on the other side of the globe. Today, we can make robots in which simple "instinctive" controls such as collision control are placed in the body, but in which the more demanding parts of the brain are located at a distance. In fact, not only can they draw on other computers' intelligence via electromagnetic waves, they can also *combine many computers' data power very precisely and simultaneously into one gigantic, virtual computer.* This phenomenon is used in the SETI project, which stands for "Search for Extra-Terrestrial Intelligence". Through SETI@home, in 2010 there are approximately 300,000 personal computers interconnected, which voluntarily make their idle data-processing capacity available to the SETI project when not otherwise in use.

Another advantage of robots is that—unlike human beings—they are capable of *turning off their brain without losing data.* Therefore, it will be possible to send them on year-long, monotonous space odysseys to distant planets, where people would never even dream of going, or where they would go mad from boredom during the journey.

Then there is the issue of data copying. What I learn will not be inherited by my children; not even if I am cloned. I may leave something as a contribution to my society's culture and knowledge inheritance, but my children (or my clone) will not be *born* with my knowledge; the only learned things passed on are the epigenomes, which are little related to intelligence or knowledge. However, what the TD-Gammon learns can be cloned to 1,000 similar TD-Gammons, and if they then learn even more, then they can be cloned, and so on. The evolution of AI will be many orders of magnitude faster than biological learning. It takes at least 30 years to teach a newborn what an adult professional knows, and much of it will be forgotten again down the line. However, *a computer can copy an absolutely massive amount of knowledge within a few hours or even less.*

In addition to this, you can use the computers that have been best at learning and then compress the result and put it into smaller and cheaper computers, which can be replicated. And, unlike humans, *computers forget nothing.* They can remember billions of information items without missing out a single detail, and a given computer not only searches through its own knowledge in a fraction of a second, *it can also search the full knowledge of thousands of other computers.* Unlike us, it can read minds. It does this much faster than any individual can achieve, simply because electronic transistors are many million times faster than the neurons in our brain.

Computers and thus robots have even more advantages over human beings. Admittedly, they need to be maintained and updated, but in many ways, they are *easier to deal with* than human beings. For instance, they need no rest, sleep, popcorn, vitamins, sex, or football on TV, and they *feel neither anxiety nor pain*, for which reason they are capable of assuming tasks that we ourselves cannot or will not carry out. Examples of this could be cleaning sewers, looking out for stolen license plates, working in mines, and performing military reconnaissance, etc.

So, in comparing robots with humans, I would say that robots do have some formidable advantages. In summary: *robots will have more brainpower than us, will be able to learn several thousand times faster, will have an extremely fast evolutionary cycle, will read each other's minds and forget nothing, and will need no sleep and have no fear.* Touché!

Computer and robot intelligence: 10 advantages over humans

1. Their brains do not have to sit on top of their body.
2. They can disseminate precise and wireless communication in real time across many thousands of kilometers.
3. Many computers are able to combine their "mental" powers to solve particularly demanding tasks.
4. Their know-how can be cloned in a few seconds.
5. They forget nothing.
6. They can search through all their knowledge in fractions of seconds.
7. They can search through the knowledge of other computers without missing anything.
8. They need neither rest nor sleep.
9. You can turn them off without them losing any data.
10. They feel no anxiety or pain.

Robots fall into phase 5 of the development phases of IT that I described earlier: autonomous computing. Among other products that could undergo dramatic development in that area are intelligent surveillance systems that recognize people and interpret what they are doing. Already, there is a system where a camera mounted onto a police car reads all license plates and checks whether they belong to a stolen automobile or to an automobile other than the one they are placed on. Other systems scan people at airports for signs of nervousness or fever and still others (like the one known as "Hyperactive Bob") can monitor each employee's productivity in a restaurant. These are systems that take over routine work that was previously carried out by human beings. Personally, I think they eventually could do much of the work associated with running a budget hotel. Everything from the check-in counter to delivery of room service might in principle be run by computers and robots. It wouldn't be very charming, but probably cheap.

Visual search got a new dimension with Google Earth, where you can see all places on Earth through high-resolution satellite photos on a computer or mobile phone and where people can upload their pictures, but in the future millions of webcams might make it possible to see an abundance of places in real time via the internet and on mobile devices.

However, there will also be large market potential in automatic searches in which one's computer receives dedicated instructions, following which it screens the entire internet and delivers relevant reports when something new appears within one's field of interest. It will be easy to make a personal website with live videos from places of interest (including your summerhouse, if you have one), what your friends are doing, where your cat is, how your stocks are doing, and when some of your favorite musicians are giving a concert in your area or publishing new music. In fact, all the technologies for this are available today, but they remain yet to be standardized, integrated, and thereby widespread. This, I think, will show us a combination of autonomous and ubiquitous computing with mobile, unbundled, and atomized media experiences.

Telecommunications are also charging ahead. In the future, as I drive, I will be able to see pictures from locations as I pass by, traffic jams, and bad weather; and I may click on commercials for restaurants, museums, etc. nearby. When I arrive at a railway station or an airport, I will be able to run my ticket through a barcode scan, following which my telephone will show me which way to go. In a city, I may type the name of a shop or brand into my phone, and it will show me how to get there by displaying a map made up of roads and arrows to guide me through the city. And, finally, teleconferencing will really start to work when the screens get bigger, the resolution higher, and the voices are delivered through surround sound.

Teaching will also become far more effective. In Switzerland, my children already use laptops for all their teaching, which is more or less paperless. The teacher can at any time bring a student's screen up on the

The intelligent eye

Today, a typical quality camera can handle 20 megapixels and a video camera 60 images per second. This is impressive, except when you compare it with the human eye, which can handle approximately 175 megapixels and perceive 220 images per second. Furthermore, the eye transmits its data (the image) in real time to the brain for interpretation, while the camera doesn't. However, in the future we may have devices that act much more like brain-connected eyes.

A Japanese web designer named Mac Funamizu has described some pretty bold ideas on what future mobile phones might look like, so that they not only record what you hear or see, but conceptualize it. He imagines them to be transparent in order for you to hold them up in front of something and look through them. Using the internet the telephone will retrieve data on the object.

Maybe it will tell you which building in New York you are looking at, or it will look at the bottle of red wine you are holding, recognize the label, tell you that should not drink this wine for three years, and that the wine received 94 points in *Parker's Wineguide*. Or you could show it a meal, and it would tell you how many calories or how much sugar it's likely to contain.

Maybe you can hold the phone over a text in a book and point to a word, following which the telephone will collect related information from Wikipedia. Or you hold it up in front of a man speaking a foreign language, only to receive subtitles in real-time translation. The interesting thing here is that where data-processing capacity will appear limited due to its size, it will via a broadband connection be able to work with much bigger computers in the internet to provide real-time assistance.

Source: http://petitinvention.wordpress.com/

board for everyone to see, and the students can write and draw to illustrate their thoughts. Exams are downloaded to their computers and uploaded in a completed version to the teacher before they leave the room. When they work in groups, virtual work teams are established so they can sit back at home or anywhere with WiFi and work at the same time on the same document.

Ubiquitous computing is especially great at solving two desires: mobility and situational awareness through conceptualizing computing. We want to be mobile because it is obviously no fun to be chained to an office chair all the time, and we want situational awareness because it makes us spend our time much better and avoid mistakes.

Information technology is also increasingly enabling virtualization of the physical world. Many things can never get virtualized, of course (e.g., a cup of coffee or a swim in the ocean). But stuff that has to do with information can. Today we have virtual tickets, for instance, and virtual books, letters, catalogues, money, CDs, DVDs, X-rays, 3D models, meetings, and seminars. This brings about a reduction in how much physical stuff we need. Is there a need for libraries, if all books are virtual? For shops, if you can shop online? Bank branches if you can do e-banking? Offices? Business trips? Companies are even beginning to test launch products in virtual worlds to gauge the demand before deciding to make them.

I think we do need physical locations when they serve a social purpose, and many will probably much prefer to buy a luxury item in a gorgeous high street shop than ordering it from the internet. But if dealing with information is just something you have to overcome, it's much better to do it virtually. In our family we order many of our groceries via the internet and save lots of time and hassle in that way. We transfer money electronically, buy electronic books online, download music, etc. This saves huge physical and environmental resources, it saves time, and it's cheaper too. It's win, win, win.

Interestingly, the IT sector is also virtualizing itself. Every businessman knows that it takes a lot of time and money to run and constantly upgrade an IT infrastructure. However, just as the financial world is breaking down into massive utility companies that carry out business within largely IT-based infrastructure (such as retail banks and online brokers) and others that do creative thinking (like hedge funds and private equity), the IT world is also building mega-utilities with enormous computer and server parks that are made available to thousands of clients.

Virtualization and resource conservation

Innovation in information technology is helping us replace physical products and services by resource-saving virtual ones. Some examples:

- Video conferencing and mobile phones replace travel
- Video downloads replace video rental shops
- Telecommunication replaces offices and daily transport
- Downloads replace DVDs and CDs
- E-readers replace print publications, book shops, and libraries
- Email replaces lettermail
- Online directories replace physical directories
- The internet replaces catalogues and brochures
- Internet shopping replaces shops
- Wireless and optical data communication replaces copper wires

---

This has created two highly successful phenomena: "cloud computing" and "as-a-service" models.

A "cloud" is a computer park that is available to many different clients. Is this outsourcing, then? No, because in outsourcing you pay an organization to take care of your hardware and software. What cloud computing offers is like an IT hotel, where the clients rent a room, but don't own it. This is called a "multi-tenant system". However, it's an odd hotel, because there may be strangers sharing your bed: in cloud computing you access a number of anonymous computers, and it may very well be that these are each capable of supporting different clients simultaneously from the same software and hardware, without the clients ever noticing it. As I write this, there are already several thousand companies offering clouds, with Apple, Google, and Microsoft in the lead and companies such as Oracle, SAP, Deutsche Telekom, IBM, HP, Amazon, and EMC not far behind. Cloud computing has fostered three popular as-a-service business models:

- Infrastructure-as-a-Service (IaaS)
- Platform-as-a-Service (PaaS)
- Software-as-a-Service (SaaS)

All three are about having access to IT support (hardware and/or software) without owning any of it. Amazon offers, for instance, its

Simple Storage Solution for digital data storage, its Simple Queue Service for exchanging digital messages between different software applications, and its Elastic Computer Cloud, or EC2, which lets clients run their software on Amazon's computers. You may be using a part of a single computer, for instance, which three other clients are also using each for its own purposes. While the return to centralized server parks may appear to go against the trend towards decentralization, it fulfills (1) separation of the creative aspects of IT from the utility aspects, (2) atomizing the access to software and hardware, and (3) instantaneous access to new capacity.

Here is what the cloud/as-a-service future may feel like: You want to create an online service, so you open a web browser where there are icons representing what you need. It shows you servers, firewalls, routers, cables, databases, software packages, etc. By dragging and dropping with your mouse, you indicate how you want it all connected. At the bottom of your screen you will all the time see a price indication of your fixed monthly IT cost, given that configuration. It will also include a variable part, depending on your data storage and traffic estimate.

Once you feel sure that you have the right configuration, you send it to your digital shopping basket and move on to the next issue: the hardware you actually need in your office. You take out subscriptions to different printers and "thin clients" (small computers) plus a few powerful ones for the staff that do the most creative work. These computers will thus be automatically exchanged with newer ones from the provider from time to time. You move this to your shopping basket too.

Even though e-readers are gradually replacing print, you still want a couple of printers for legal documents and stuff, so you take out subscriptions to those too. The print paper that comes with them will stand on a set of scales, which automatically signals the supplier when they need to send you more. And the printers will of course order their own toner, when they begin to run low.

For your website you decide to run some ads, so you drag an ad service logo in. This will give you clickthrough-based revenues. Even though it will be a revenue generator, it goes to the shopping basket as well. The deal is that the revenues from this will be offset against your costs. Finally, you want to enable your clients to shop online from your service website. You order a complete virtual credit card clearing solution for that, and you are ready. You go to the shopping basket, review what you have listed one more time, and then you click "confirm". You are in business.

The 10 top challenges for future computers

In the future I think there are ten areas that will be particularly demanding of powerful hardware and ingenious software:

1. *Data mining.* Constantly scanning and analyzing digital data and the real world and making sense of it. This can be used continuously for informal observation or studies, or *ad hoc* for stricter and more formalized surveillance and analysis.

2. *Creating meta-studies.* Automatically summarizing all known information about a given subject into easily read reports.

3. *Biotech simulation.* Simulating how a protein is created and folds in 3D or what goes on within a whole cell, or even inside a whole organism. Using this as a basis to create new medical treatments and production methods. Eventually it may become feasible to avoid most live trials of new medical treatments and simply replace them with credible simulations.

4. *Robots.* Teaching and controlling mechanical devices that navigate autonomously in the physical environment.

5. *Situational awareness.* Enhance our real-time knowledge about where we are, what goes on around us, what we are looking at, where we should go, or if there are any security risks or opportunities anywhere that should concern us.

6. *Software creation.* Software that identifies tasks and writes more software to handle these tasks.

7. *Portable smart-eyes.* Transparent, portable computers/phones that tell you about what you are looking at by uploading its image and location to the web for interpretation.

8. *Massively multiplayer games.* Internet games in high definition where millions of people simultaneously play against each other in virtual worlds.

9. *Real/virtual gaming.* The ability to play games appearing in the real-time world, such as racing virtual automobiles against real automobiles in Formula 1.

10. *Reverse engineering of old media.* Reconstruct old movies and music so that they appear to have been recorded in high-definition/high fidelity, surround sound, color, etc.

Time to summarize. I listed IT as one of the seven most interesting sectors for the coming decades because, while it has already had a great run, it's nothing compared with what we are going to see. The computer world will increasingly resemble an ecological system, and computers will even begin to write their own software and perhaps wake up to the fact that they exist.

Computers will reach and then surpass human intelligence, and the robots will come into their own. We will have media walls, portable smart-eyes, self-driving automobiles, personalized news, and answers to almost any question readily presented within seconds.

People will stop thinking about having "a" collection of books, music, or movies, and will instead own "the" collection: Everyone will be able to own a copy of all the best stuff that was ever made.

As for where the greatest businesses are, it's the U.S. that dominates in the more complex chip business (e.g., Intel in Oregon). A number of software companies—mainly American—have established network effects that are so powerful that they will be extremely difficult to challenge seriously for decades. Apple, Google, Amazon, eBay, Bloomberg, and Skype are examples. The creative and commercial centers for software are mainly in Seattle and California, but there are lots of smaller concentrations in places like Boulder, Austin, Boston, and Los Angeles, etc. In Europe, software development is widespread throughout northern and central Europe. India has a clear lead among emerging markets. As for artificial intelligence and robotics, the Pittsburg and Massachusetts areas are leading-edge, whereas Japan leads when it comes to actual mass-production of small, commercial robots.

17

Luxury

Some people need silence when they work—so much so that they tiptoe around in protective slippers. I am here thinking about the famous watchmaker Patek Philippe's workshops in Switzerland. A watchmaker tolerates little noise as he polishes the protective cover over the sapphire crystal caseback of an officer's watch. The final user of the watch will open this cover with a flick of the thumb and index finger, and the sound when he does that and when he closes it again has to be very special.

I'm not kidding. It does. And therefore the watchmaker polishes and polishes, and then he tries to open and close the cover—and listens. If it doesn't have that perfect sound yet, then he goes back to polishing another few fractions of millimeters here and there. Then he tries again, and then he polishes some more. Sometimes this goes on for days. It has to be perfect.

The car designers working at Rolls-Royce will also need silence from time to time, because when they design new models, they need to test how it sounds when you close the car's door. Does it give that fat, opulent sound that a Roller should?

At Ferrari, they don't do silence, really, but they are very particular about their noise. When a Ferrari accelerates up past 4,000 revs per minute and pulls out to overtake, it has to make a characteristic, high-pitched, devilish Ferrari roar. This has to be so special that the driver of the car that was just overtaken, who didn't get to see what just flew past him, will know from the sound what it was. "A Ferrari!" he will think. There must be no doubt.

This is all about luxury, and for this exclusive market segment the devil really is in the detail.

———

Luxury is not a big market: Watches and jewelry is an approximately $40 billion market (annual turnover), ready-to-wear plus leather $35 billion, spirits and champagne $30 billion, still wine $50 billion, watches $10 billion, jewelry $30 billion, fragrances and cosmetics $30 billion, and ocean-going yachts $15 billion. Add those up and we get to just under $200bn. On top of that comes aircraft, luxury cars, and ultra-high-end audio equipment. How much of that is for pleasure and can be called luxury is hard to define, but I wouldn't expect the global luxury market to exceed $500bn in 2010, equal to approximately 0.8% of global GDP.

However, luxury is an extremely profitable market and one that grows much faster than our economies. Consider this: In 1977 Louis Vuitton was a small family business with two shops and fewer than $10 million in turnover. In 2009 the company Interbrand estimated the commercial value of Louis Vuitton at $21 *billion*. Each year, Interbrand analyzes a very large number of brands to estimate their commercial value. This is not a measure of how attractive these brands are, but of how much discounted future cash generation they will create. The table on the facing page shows how the biggest luxury brands ranked in 2009.

From Interbrand's top-100 list I did not include American Express, which have luxury offerings (platinum and millennium cards), but are mainly for the mid-range and mainly a practicality. I also didn't include Goldman Sachs and Morgan Stanley, which cater entirely to wealthy people (and successful companies), but which I do not consider being in the luxury business. Other brands I excluded from among the top-100 list were Toyota, Honda, Ford, BlackBerry, Nokia, Disney, Nike, Sony, Budweiser, Adidas, Smirnoff, Nivea, Starbucks, and Puma. These are life-style brands, but they don't make much if anything that qualifies as true luxury. However, I did include Apple and Nescafe, even though some would dispute their luxury status. I think they qualify since they charge far more for some of their products than the competition, and they have a huge fan base.

Despite ignoring so many consumer brands, we still end up with no fewer than *22 of the top-100 money-making brands in the world that are mainly or purely luxury-related. This is impressive for a business area that represents less than 1% of world GDP.*

But what is luxury? Overpriced crap that rich people buy to show off? It can be, but I think there is a whole lot more to it. First, luxury is

Luxury businesses among the world's top-100 most commercially valuable brands		
Global brand ranking	*Brand*	*Estimated brand value* (U.S.$ billion)
12	Mercedes Benz	24
15	BMW	22
16	Louis Vuitton	21
20	Apple	15
25	Nescafe	13
41	Gucci	8
50	Zara	7
59	Chanel	6
65	Audi	5
68	Rolex	5
70	Hermes	5
74	Porsche	5
76	Tiffany & Co.	4
77	Cartier	4
78	GAP	4
82	Moet & Chandon	4
87	Prada	4
88	Ferrari	4
89	Giorgio Armani	4
91	Lancôme	3
98	Burburry	3
99	Polo Ralph Laurent	3

Source: Interbrand, 2009.

fairly closely associated with fashion and art, but there are also important differences:

- Luxury is mainly bought for oneself and might often increase in value or at least be timeless, so that the owner can keep using it without appearing out of touch. It is product-centric and is about admiration for the craftsman who made it and identification with the broader culture it represents.
- Fashion is for others and loses value quickly. I tend to regard fashion as a sort of storytelling—a collective theater, where everyone is allowed to play. It offsets the negative element of urbanization—which is that we all become anonymous, spend so much time indoors, and lose contact with the great outdoors—and replaces it with fashion seasons.
- Art can be a fad, or it can be timeless. It is emotional expression for the pure sake of it. It may be beautiful and esthetic, but may also express any other emotion. Blues music is traditionally sad, for instance (or at least the words of the songs are).

The clearest intersection between all three has been *haute couture*, which I think is luxury, fashion, and art wrapped into one. This used to be associated entirely with the fashion industry, but has largely vanished there. However, it is now being pursued with gusto by other luxury sectors such as the watch and car industries with their limited edition complication watches or supercars.

Designer jewelry also intersects the three, as does some interior design and architecture. Perhaps there are even overlaps that most people do not quite see as such. When sports car manufacturers explain why their street-cars couldn't have electric windows or air-conditioning, because it would slice a second off their lap times, many people have surely thought of it as ridiculous. But perhaps it's actually a pretty cool happening, as in performance art—with the difference being that the people doing it here are not professional artists trying to be provocative or interesting. No, they just want a fast car, even if that means sweating in an uncomfortable seat.

True luxury (like art) can never be designed through consumer research. It has to come from a small team or a single person with a passion, a dream, and an idea. Furthermore, again like art, it may also take some time for a consumer to learn to appreciate it.

Luxury has something else in common with art and fashion: It should make an emotional impact. When people see a true luxury car parked in the street or a beautiful luxury boat in a harbor, they stop and take pictures of it, because it takes their breath away and they want to remem-

Luxury has always been a way for society to signal what it can do when it does its best. There is a strong desire among many people to connect with that. This desire seems to be particularly strong in emerging markets.

ber that sensation and share it with others. The English psychologist David Moxon once ran a test on 40 randomly selected men and women between 22 and 61, in which he swiped their mouths to test for testosterone in their saliva (a measure of sexual arousal) before letting each of them listen to the sound of a Maserati, Lamborghini, Ferrari, and a Volkswagen Polo in random order. After each of these tests, he checked their testosterone levels again. The results were clear: testosterone went up when they heard a sports car, and amazingly down, after they had listened to a Polo. The strongest effect was recorded when the women in the test listened to the Maserati. All of the 20 women in the study got elevated testosterone levels from this car, even though some of them afterwards said in interviews that they were not interested in cars. The thing is: *They were emotionally influenced by these products, whether they knew it or not. And therefore, the sports cars were luxury products.*

Also, like art, *a true luxury product doesn't compare itself with other products—ever.* When Lexus was launched in the U.S., its first commercials compared it directly with Mercedes and suggested that you could get more for your money with a Lexus. That is not a luxury strategy, it's a premium strategy. A luxury product can't be compared, because it's unique. It's like a piece of art—you wouldn't compare a Rembrandt with a Picasso. You wouldn't say, for instance, that one costs less per square meter than the other, or that one uses more red color than the other.

Because luxury is unique, it doesn't want to be advertised next to other products (thus the frequent magazine double-spreads) and it doesn't want to be sold next to other products (hence dedicated stores or areas within department stores). Nissan may build a car that is faster than a Lamborghini, but the two could never be compared.

There is another criterion for a luxury brand: It has to be international. People who buy luxury normally travel a lot, and they expect the product to be so good that it is coveted globally. If that isn't the case, then it can't be luxury.

One of the most important aspects of luxury is tradition. *A luxury product has to have a long history or at least come from a community that has a long history for luxury production in the given product area.* In perfume, Guerlain was started at the end of the 19th century, and many of the leading watch manufacturers are centuries old. If we look at the list of the most profitable luxury brands in the world on p. 367, it is striking that 20 out of the 22 come from Europe and two (Tiffani and Ralph Lauren Polo) are American. If we include leading brands that are not in Interbrand's top-100 list, (yachts, aircraft, wine, audio equipment), it's entirely European-dominated for yachts and wine, and it is European or American for audio equipment and aircraft. In other words, Europe dominates completely in anything old, and Europe and America share leadership in objects that were only invented after America became a great nation. It is actually possible for new luxury brands to come up fairly quickly, but only if they clearly evolve from these traditions. Regarding watches, for instance, F.P. Journe, Frank Muller, and Daniel Roth are examples of this, but they all came from the Swiss watch industry. Had they lived in Sweden, it wouldn't have worked.

All of this does not mean that Swedes couldn't make good watches or that Japan, China, India, or other countries cannot or do not produce products of extremely high quality—it is just that they haven't done it for long enough to gain international recognition, or they do not wrap it up into a total experience that feels like luxury. *When you buy luxury, the purchase process must itself be very special.* Many luxury shops have an appearance reminiscent of an art exhibition in which each object is displayed with lots of space around. *No one will try to sell you a true luxury product—* the product is above the client and it should be felt that way. It is the client that seeks the product and not the other way around, or else it isn't luxury.

The uniqueness of luxury products may come from many aspects—the look, smell, feel, and sound. It may come from the way the products age. Buyers of luxury will often feel that they connect with a refined culture and craftsmanship that they admire—perhaps even with the people who designed and manufactured the products. *A luxury product may increase in value over time.* Old Louis Vuitton suitcases, old Patek Philippe watches, or old Bugatti cars may, for instance, sell for more than their first owner paid, corrected for inflation, because they are testimony to the finest a culture could offer during a given *époque*. In addition to this, the patina that develops as they age adds value, unless its excessive. A veteran car that looks too new will fetch less at an auction than one that looks its age in a well-kept manner. Similarly, the most expensive luxury chalets are today built of old, worn wood, which cost four times as much as new wood. Patina may not come cheap, but it really can provide an essential part of the luxury feel.

Another aspect: The more people have paid for luxury, the more they value it. It is not just a product that has a price—*in luxury the price is a part of the product.*

There is another aspect. For a musician, it's not just the money you want, it's the applause. If you give people money as a gift, it's like saying that you don't know them or don't care about them. If, on the other hand, you give them luxury, you send them a message: "I think this beautiful perfume is you" or "I think this designer handbag suits you". *By giving luxury, you make a personal statement.*

Of course, it all depends on the sense of style. Everyone except those who do it think spendthrifts are vulgar, but those who invest well in beautifully crafted objects are often admired for it. This mostly applies perhaps to art, but can be the case with fashion and wine, etc. In 1991 Bernard Dubois and Patric Duquesne made a study of European luxury buyers and found that whereas luxury consumption had a strong correlation with income levels, it was about equally correlated with openness to cultural change. Culturally open people were far more likely to buy luxury than people with closed minds, and that was the case within all income classes.

The part of the luxury culture that perhaps best defines its attraction is to see how people treat luxury as a result of personal economic ups and downs. The typical consumer will only start to buy luxury when her income rises to a given level, which suggests that luxury belongs at the top of Maslow's pyramid of needs. However, when that person unexpectedly sees a decline in income, it is not unusual for her to desperately hold on to her luxury items while cutting expenditure on basic goods to the bone, like the *nouveau pauvre* who stays in the castle but can't afford to heat it. *After a while, it's not only that you possess your luxury items—they also possess you.*

So, all this defines a market that is small but highly lucrative, and is subject to rules that do not apply to other markets. When it really works it creates one of the most remarkable effects in marketing: The brand effect.

The world's leading luxury brands

An interesting subject to discuss is which luxury brands lead globally in the sense of desirability and mind space, but here is my suggestion (the absolute top brands in italics):

- Private jets: *Gulfstream*, Bombardier Challenger/Global, Learjet, Falcon
- Pleasure motor yachts: *Feadship*, *Lurssen*, *Amels*, Aberking & Rasmussen, Benetti, CRN, Heesen
- Sailing yachts: *Perini Navi*, *Royal Huisman*, Wally, Swan
- Sportscars: *Ferrari*, *Lamborghini*, *Bugatti*, *Aston-Martin*, *McLaren*, Porsche, Lotus, Shelby
- Limousines: *Bentley*, *Rolls Royce*, *Bugatti*, Mercedes, Maybach, Audi, BMW, Cadillac
- Champagne: *Krug*, *Dom Perignon*, *Roederer*, *Cristal*, Lanson, Laurent-Piper, Moët & Chandon, Taittinger, Veuve Clicquot-Ponsardin
- Wine: *Château d'Yquem*, *Château Mouton-Rothschild*, *Château Lafite Rothschild*, *Château Margaux*, *Château Latour*, *Château Cheval Blanc*, *Petrus*, Château Haut-Brion, Pingus, Opus One, Vega-Sicilia, Sassicaia, Tignanello
- Cosmetics: *Guerlain*, Chanel, La Prairie, La Mer, Lancôme, Valmont, Clinique, Dior, Estée Lauder, Sisley
- Fragrance: *Guerlain*, *Chanel*, Bulgari, Dior, Dulce, Cabanne, Calvin Klein, Gucci, Marc Jacobs, Hermès
- Whisky: *Lagavulin*, *Highland Park*, Talisker, Springbank, Macallan, Gragganmore, Ardberg
- Cognac: *Hennessy*, *Courvoisier*, *Louis Royer*, *Moyet*, *Bache-Gabrielsen*, *Hine*, Rémy Martin, Camus, Frapin, Martell, Larsen, Otard, M. Ragnaud
- Leather goods: *Hermès*, *Louis Vuitton*, Bottega Venetta, Fendi, Prada, Gucci, Chanel
- Women's ready-to-wear: *Chanel*, *Valentino*, *Dior*, Giorgio Armani,

Gucci, Christian Halston, Missoni, Prada, Marc Jacobs, Dolce & Gabbana, Oscar de la Renta.
- Women's shoes: Chimmy Choo, Manolo Blahnik, Christian Louboutin, A Laia, Todds, Ferragamo.
- Men's suits: *Brioni, Kiton, Canali, Zegna*, Giorgio Armani, Versace.
- Jewelry: *Van Cleef & Arpels, Tiffany*, Harry Winston, David Yurman, Cartier, Graff, Bulgari, Chopard
- Audio equipment: *Krell, Pass Lab, Wilson Audio*, Magico, Audio Research, Mark Levinson, McIntosh, Martin Logan, Sonus Faber, Bang & Olufsen
- Watches: *Patek Phillippe*, A. Lange & Söhne, Bréguet, Ulysse Nardin, Frank Muller, Audemar Piquet, Piaget, Vacheron Constantin, Jaeger LeCoultre, Rolex, Cartier, Omega
- Furs: *Birger Christensen, Fendi,* J. Mendel, Christian Dior, Copenhagen Fur, Great Greenland, Saga Furs of Scandinavia

The only luxury market with limited branding is jewelry, where approx. two-thirds of the world market is dominated by local family jewelers instead of global brands. Finally, diamonds have no branding at all. They are, unlike any other luxury, actually classified by a technical description (clarity, color, carat, and cut). Even semiprecious stones are defined not only by the country they come from but often also from the mine, such as "aquamarines from Santa Maria". But diamonds are not.

I would like to write a few pages on the amazing properties of international brands, because it is only after fully grasping the potential magnetism of brands that it becomes clear why the tiny luxury business can be so profitable.

So, how can we fully grasp it? One way would be to isolate it from everything else, like scientists try to do when they study something. In other words, we need to find some magnificent brands that don't relate to products or services. Brands for brands' sakes, so to speak. That sounds difficult. Paris Hilton being famous for being famous might work, but how do we value her brand? No, we need something that really sells— one unit at a time.

Come to think of it, there is perhaps an area where we may find just this: contemporary art. I subscribe to different art catalogs and magazines, including some from Christie's. One day in 2006 I saw a description of a painting from Yves Klein which was simply blue. Nothing else, just completely uniform blue all over. Fine by me; Klein had painted 11 of these identical paintings, and had exhibited them together, and I could imagine that it could look cool in some places. It so happened that I had a painter working in my house, so I showed him the catalog and said that I thought he charged too little for his work. He laughed hysterically, but the point here is that while he could also make monochrome blue paintings, no one would pay him a lot for it—he wasn't a brand. Anyway, Christie's catalogue described these blue paintings as follows:

> "These works allowed the viewers to bathe in the infinite, in the luminous spiritual realm of the Blue. Influenced by his experiences of Judo, his interest in Rosicrucianism, his fascination with the age of the atomic, Klein had created paintings that have no frames and therefore no edges, and are thus windows into the eternal and endless spiritual realm."

Whatever. But what I found odd was that the specific one I read about in the catalog had just sold for £994,000, or something like U.S.$1.8 million, which meant that all 11 should be worth something like $20 million. That's branding!

Apart from isolating the object that they study, scientists have another way of proving the effect of something—longitudinal studies. These involve following something over time to see how a variable can change it. I know of many episodes in the contemporary art world that we can use here, but there is one that stands out. Before I get to it I need to introduce the main character: Damien Hirst. Hirst has a long and rich (as in wealthy) history in the art world and is probably best known for describing the 9/11 mass murder as "kind of like an artwork in its own right" and saying to his shame that "So on one level they kind of need congratulating ...". But he is also known for the tale of the stuffed sharks.

It appears that the idea to put a dead shark on display in a vitrine came from the famous advertising and branding mogul Charles Saatchi, who also happened to be one of the world's leading contemporary art collectors. Saatchi had discovered Hirst some years before and seemed determined to build up the artist's fame by investing in him. He asked Hirst, or so the story goes, to find a shark and put it on permanent display. Hirst agreed, placed ads for dead sharks in Australia, and received a response from a fisherman named Vic Hislov. Hislov had a tiger shark, which Hirst bought for £6,000. Another £2,000 was paid for freezing and shipping which meant a landed cost of around £8,000. Hirst had the poor creature preserved in formaldehyde, mounted in a glass show case, and gloriously named *The Story of the Physical Impossibility of Death in the Mind of Someone Living.* He then sold it on to Saatchi for £50,000, a price that the *Sun* newspaper found so laughable that they ran a story about it called "50,000 for fish without chips".

Unfortunately, the shark started to decay badly during the following years. The skin got wrinkled and greenish, one fin fell off, and the surrounding liquid turned muddy—it all looked like a bad joke. However, Saatchi got the last laugh. In 2004 he asked the world's most famous art dealer Larry Gagosian to find a buyer. It soon became known that Nicolas Serota from the famous Tate Modern museum had offered $2 million for it, which Gagosian declined. For a good reason, apparently, because after a while he sold it instead to Steve Cohen, an American hedge fund manager, who clearly had money to spare. The price he paid was reputed to be $12 million, which is really not that much if you manage $11 billion. Perhaps it also helped that the object had been created by one of the world's most branded artists (Hirst), subsequently owned by one of its most branded collectors (Saatchi), then offered for sale by its most branded dealer (Gagosian), who had rejected an offer from one of the most branded museums (Tate). Brands, brands, brands.

The story could have ended there, but a part of the agreement was that Hirst would replace the decomposing animal with a new and better preserved one, so he called Vic Hislov the fisherman and asked him to send him three more tiger sharks plus a great white for good measure. Hislov agreed and sent in fact five—the four requested plus another he threw in for free. All was now fine except for one thing: People began speculating whether Hirst would make more sharks and thus undermine the collector value of the first. I shall come to that later. The real reason I introduced Hirst was actually to describe a longitudinal study, which in this case is about a painting of Stalin that a writer for the *London Sunday Times* had bought for £200. The writer's name was Gill and he decided to get rid of the painting, which was by an unknown artist, and asked Christie's if they would sell it for him. "No thanks," they answered, because they did not sell Hitler and Stalin objects. So, Gill asked if they would sell it if it had been made by Hirst or Warhol. They would.

Gill then called Hirst and asked if he would paint a red nose on the Stalin and sign below (the painting had no previous signature). Hirst complied and with the signature in place Gill went back to Christie's who now accepted it and put a price of £8,000–£12,000 on it. It sold for £140,000. That to me is branding in its purest form.

I can think of another way to establish the power of branding—the time-honored placebo effect. There have been various examples of that. In 1964 newsmen from Sweden's *Göteborgs-Tidningen* hung some paintings in a gallery and claimed that they were by the *avant-garde* artist Pierre Brassau. The paintings soon drew acclaim, and one critic wrote:

> "Brassau paints with powerful strokes, but also with clear determination. His brush strokes twist with furious fastidiousness. Pierre is an artist who performs with the delicacy of a ballet dancer."

Little did this critic know that the paintings were actually done by a 4-year-old chimpanzee from the Boras Zoo called Peter.

A similar case was when the director of the State Art Museum in Moritzburg, was shown an abstract painting and suggested that it was by Ernst Wilhelm Nay, a famous painter who had won the coveted Guggenheim Prize for his work. However, the painting in this case was by Banghi, another chimpanzee artist. Banghi, by the way, worked under difficult conditions since her mate Satscho often destroyed her paintings before they could be saved for the contemporary art community. This is all anecdotal evidence, of course, but there is a very powerful, statistical placebo effect in the fact that around 40% of all top-class art sold is expected to be fake.

Stuff like that won't stop. Hirst employs large teams of assistants pumping out his products, which include paintings created by pouring paint over a spinning wheel. And people keep buying. As for the extra sharks in the freezer, he launched in early 2006 *The Death of God*, which was the shark his fisherman friend had thrown in for free. It was sold (again without chips) to the Leeum Samsung Museum in Seoul, South Korea. In September 2008 there followed *The Kingdom*, a tiger shark, which was sold by Sotheby's for £9.6 million.

So, yes, people do indeed keep buying. They also buy like mad (literally) from other mass-producing artists such as Andy Warhol, most of whose work was also created by teams of technicians. His *Green Car Crashing*, which is simply a silkscreen reproduction of a photo of an accident scene that had appeared in *Newsweek* in 1963, changed hands for $71.7 million.

I should mention that the authentication process for modern art factories is not without its problems. If most of Warhol's work was created by assistants, were they actually Warhols at all? Was he, for instance, present in the room at some point during their creation—at least for five minutes or so? One issue that art mass-producers clearly want to avoid is that a single assistant made a piece, because in that case, it was her, not the artist, who did it, and that really messes up the branding. So, when assistants make the art, it is important that they do it collectively so that each has no importance.

People also pay hundreds of thousands of dollars for On Kawara, who simply paints dates on a canvas, apparently never spending more than two hours on a painting (Christie's: "an existing statement, a proof of art") or U.S.$690,000 for Jim Hofges' *No-One ever Really Leaves*, which is a leather jacket tossed in a corner ..., or for that matter a pile of white and blue candles, which Sotheby's sold in November 2000 for U.S.$456,000. It's all branding, branding, branding. Branding of artists, collector–owners, dealers, auction houses, and art fairs. Unless you become a brand in art you become nothing. But if you do, then "They'll buy what you fucking give them," as Hirst once famously explained.

Personally I love great brands (when there is substance behind them), and so do most people. The state of Abu Dhabi paid $525 million for the right to use the name "Louvre" locally, $40 million for renovation at the Louvre itself in Paris, as well as $675 million for art loans, special exhibitions, and advice on art acquisitions. The future will be branded.

Sorry for this little detour, but I think it's important to emphasize the amazing power of brands. Since a luxury brand has to be international to be real, there are lots of fixed costs involved, but once the business passes a given economic threshold, it can become a virtual money machine. However, this requires that things are done right. The first rule is about how price is communicated. It is very rare for luxury brands to advertise their product prices since, as you know, if you have to ask you probably can't afford it. However, if indeed they do, then they will not talk about how cheap the products are, but about how expensive. After an art auction, what the auction house advertises is how high the hammer price was on the most expensive objects. About half of all objects that fail to sell at the reserve price (secret minimum price) are typically sold in private sales after the auction, but these disappointing prices are not public. In the rare cases where prices of true luxury are shown in advertising or mentioned in PR, it will be the most expensive configurations for the most expensive of their product lines. This is not only to communicate to potential buyers what unique stuff this is, but also to let everyone else know that people who have these objects paid a lot for it.

There is something else about luxury prices (and art prices): *Prices may never go down.* If it seems like the price of an artist's work will fall, then his dealer would much rather drop him than tell his clients that they can now get the same cheaper than before. For the same reason real luxury doesn't do sales. It costs what it costs, and if you wait it will cost more. Your choice, really.

There is another distinct aspect of luxury brand marketing. Since the brand has to be kept above the client, it is important to make it at least a bit difficult to get. People wait forever, for instance, for their Hermès, Kelly, and Birkin bags, and Japanese women are only half-joking when they talk about putting their newborn daughters on the waiting lists straight away. And after all, it's all right to wait, because luxury is not a necessity, and just like it takes time for trees to grow and whiskey to mature in the barrel, the sense should be that however long the production time is: That is the time it should take.

In the art market you can be put on a list to buy the next work by a given living artist, but only if you have been a good client of the dealer in the past and have not, for instance, flipped any of your purchases by reselling them quickly in auctions. In luxury the manufacturers will aim to always produce slightly less than popular demand, and there will be special sub-brands and limited editions that only the very best clients ever will be allowed to get, and often after long waits. As for the dealers, there will often be a relationship that evolves slowly as you buy more and more.

The final stage may be where the dealer simply tells the client what he needs for his collection and gets it for him. This may be an art dealer managing the client's collection, or a wine dealer taking care of his cellar. Every time an artist's work is displayed by a major museum, mentioned in an art magazine, etc. its price goes up. A single display at a major, branded museum may in fact double its value, and if a leading, branded art dealer takes an artist into his stable, then the prices for that artist's work will typically appreciate immediately by 300% to 400%. Equally, every time a classic sports car participates in a race or gets portrayed in the press, its value goes up too. Furthermore, when judgment of the true value of a product is difficult, the price it trades for creates a signal. The satisfaction the buyer has with the product is a combination of the product itself, the community it allows her to join, the buying experience, and simply knowledge of how much its perceived value is.

The main markets and players

Luxury is likely to remain dominated by Europe. If asked to summarize what different countries mainly stand for regarding luxury, then it could be argued that Italy stands for luxury with a strong artistic bent, France mainly for pleasure, Germany for quality, England for tradition, Switzerland for precision, and America for technology. But that, of course, is a gross simplification.

Italy may be called the world's leading luxury producer. It is completely dominant in fashion with its Armani, Gucci, Prada, Valentino, Dolce & Gabbana, Ermenegildo Zegna, Max Mara, Salvatore Ferragamo, and Versace brands, and its automotive industry stands out for its world-famous Ferrari, Lamborghini, and Maserati automobiles. Furthermore, Italian yacht manufacturers produce more than half of the world's superyachts (over 30 meters), as measured by meters built. Italian furniture and apparel brands are also leading edge, and some Italian wines are among the world's best.

France may be called the second greatest luxury nation. Whereas the Italians clearly lead on textiles, it's the French who dominate in leather goods. France is home to some of the real megabrands such as Chanel, Hermès, Louis Vuitton, and Dior. And then, of course, there is its unbeatable wine industry, Dassault aircraft manufacturing, and Bugatti, which is spite of its Italian name and German ownership is manufactured in France, where Ettore Bugatti made the original vehicles.

The third-tier nations in luxury are Germany (mainly automobiles, but also some fashion and yachts), England (fashion, automobiles, aircraft, diamond trading, and yachts), Switzerland (watches), the U.S. (aircraft, yachts, diamond cutting, and fashion), Holland (yachts), Belgium (diamond trading and cutting), and Denmark (furs).

Some of the leading companies operating in the luxury space are LVMH, Pernod Richard, Estee Lauder, Richmond, L'Oreal, Chanel, PRP, Gucci, Bacardi, Rolex, Fortune Brands, Tiffany, Valentino, Hermès, Burburry, Swatch, Volkswagen, Daimler, BMW, Volkswagen/Porsche, Westport, CRN, Lurssen, Benetti, Azimut, Ferretti Group, Bombardier, Sunseeker, Embraer, Dassault, Raython, Perini Navi, Royal Huisman, Wally, and Swan.

Apart from the automobile manufacturers, the three giants in the industry are:

- LVMH in France (Louis Vuitton, Fendi, Loewe, Givenchy, Berluti, Dom Perignon, Moët et Chandon, Veuve Clicquot, Hennessy, etc).

- Richemont in Switzerland (Cartier, Van Cleef & Arpels, Vacheron Constantin, Baume & Mercier, Jaeger LeCoutre, Lange & Söhne, Officine Panerai, IWC, Piaget, Montblanc, Dunhill, etc.).
- PRP Gucci in Italy (Gucci, Ave Saint Laurent, Bottega Veneta, Boucheron, etc.).

———————

I previously described how luxury thrived in ancient Egypt, China, Rome, and other major empires, but from approx. 1450 to the beginning of the 19th century, it was predominantly a European phenomenon, which then spread to America. After the end of World War II it leveled off for some years until the Japanese economy revived strongly in the 1970s. From that moment on, Japanese consumers embraced luxury to a degree that no one could have predicted, and this has continued ever since so that no fewer than 94% of Japanese women today own at least one Louis Vuitton piece, and 92% have something that is Gucci. Since shops such as Louis Vuitton in Paris have one-item-per-customer policies, the Japanese organize paid trips for retirees to Europe on the condition that they bring back luxury goods. The Japanese lust for luxury is in fact so enormous that they buy around 40% of many of the leading luxury brands' global sales. Japan does not have the space for many large houses or multivehicle households, which might explain why so much money flows into luxury.

The mania has spread far beyond Japan's borders. Hong Kong is today sometimes referred to as one giant shopping mall, and luxury is visible everywhere. Saudis and Russians have been among the world's largest buyers of superyachts.

And then there is China. Luxury sales in China have grown more than twice as fast as GDP and there seems to be no end in sight to that. This might seem a bit surprising, I guess, because over the past 1,000 years China has had three dominant philosophies: Confucianism, Taoism, and Buddhism, all of which emphasize the principle of modesty. Most recently, they have had Maoism/Communism which has preached for years that, again, everybody should be modest and for that matter completely equal. This ideology has evidently faded, but nevertheless in 2005 the Communist Party issued an eight-point moral code for the country's inhabitants, the last one of which said: "Live simply, work hard, and do not throw yourself into luxury and pleasure." I think this message was pretty clear, and maybe this was the concept behind the following quotation from the book *Elite China* from 2009:

"The flying lady logo seems to be too much for China's superrich, symbolizing extreme power as exercised by the like of emperors and kings: In China nobody wants to be seen challenging the rule of the communist party. The comparative discretion and modesty of the Bentley is more suited to the mentality of China's superrich."

Modest indeed. The reality, however, is that the Rolls Royces for sale in China are normally sold on their first day in Chinese automobile exhibitions, in line with the Bentleys and Ferraris. To this should be added that 600,000 people came to the Shanghai Motor Show in 2009. Today, China is the largest market in the world for the watch conglomerate Swatch, the fourth largest market for Louis Vuitton, the third largest for Mont Blanc, and the fifth largest for Gucci. If you start to look at who is queuing to buy an exorbitantly expensive handbag at Louis Vuitton at Champs-Elysées 101, you will find that while the majority still may be Japanese, around 20% of those waiting are now Chinese from either China, Hong Kong, Taiwan, or Singapore. In an interview survey, 70% of the Chinese indicated that "earning a great deal of money and buying luxury goods is an important goal in life."

So, how does all of this gel with "do not throw yourself into luxury and pleasure"? There are probably several explanations here. We have already discussed China's extremely sophisticated culture in the past, where people bought enameled porcelain, gold, jewelry, paintings, pearls, silver, ivory, and where it was common for normal people to write poems and collect books. If there had been Bentleys in those days, the Chinese would have bought them. Rolls Royces too, I guess.

I believe that the mindset that created this sophistication still exists. However, there may be many other motives behind the lust for luxury. One could be to break away from paternalistic state and family patterns, which may be seen as increasingly irrelevant. By indulging in luxury, you show that you have broken out. It can also be an understandable way of showing the outside world that the Chinese are no longer suppressed and weak, as they were under Mao and under previous Western and Japanese influence. "Look, we are back!" Being wealthy can also be perceived as glorious not only for the person that possesses wealth, but also for her family. In business, showing wealth means showing that you know your stuff and are definitely not in trouble, which makes you a more credible business partner. And then, finally, there is simply the fact that the Chinese have a strong tradition for giving presents at festivities and birthdays, etc. If people know that your business is going well, then they would expect you to give good presents. Good as in Gucci, for instance.

The first affluent and superrich in China emerged in Guangzhou, which perhaps now looks mainly to Europe, Hong Kong, Macao, Taiwan, and South East Asia for cultural inspiration. However, it spread rapidly farther north, such that China's luxury users mostly live in Beijing, Shanghai, Guangzhou, Chengdu, Hangzhou, Dalian, Xi'an, and other growth centers in coastal areas. However, of all these places it is Shanghai that has become the epicenter of Chinese luxury lifestyle. This is because the really wealthy from other regions typically own houses or companies in Shanghai, or at least have regular business meetings there, and when they come to Shanghai they see China's culture at its most vibrant. Shanghai, after all, is home to the most magnificent luxury shops, incredible restaurants, and on average one fashion show daily.

What is happening in China is also happening in many other emerging markets. *The new middle classes and upper classes in Russia, the Middle East, Latin America, and the rest of emerging Asia show the same appetite for the best of the best.* The majority of these new luxury consumers have one thing in common: They made their own money. The Forbes list of India's 40 richest, for instance, shows that half are entirely self-made, almost equally from information technology and pharmaceutical industries. In many other countries, such as Russia, China, Poland, etc., becoming rich was simply illegal until a few decades ago, which means that all wealth is new. In Arab countries it's much the same; there were very few truly wealthy until the first great oil price hikes in 1974–1975.

Even luxury spending from mature economies is increasingly coming from new money. Whereas it often took generations to build a profitable business in older times, many of the greatest businesses are now built in a decade or less. *The wall of wealth that will hit luxury stores across the globe will overwhelmingly be new money.*

New money doesn't behave the same way as old. People who inherit their money will often be very discreet about their spending, simply because other people look down at them as they didn't make the money themselves. Owners of new money, on the other hand, feel they deserve the right to spend, and since they are business people they can also find the signal value in conspicuous spending good for their personal business brand.

We have already seen what is on the cards for China: The country's GDP as measured in Western currency will increase fivefold over the next 20 years, and during the same period between 300 million and 500 million Chinese will move from land to city. What do you think the impact on demand for luxury goods will be then?

I think it will go ballistic. As an increasing proportion of earnings is spent on luxury as wealth increases, Chinese demand for many luxury goods might increase at least fivefold over the next 20 years and possibly a lot more. If we add to this the growth in demand from countries in the Middle East, India, Brazil, Russia, etc.—countries where middle- and upper-class citizens do not hesitate to spend on luxury—*the demand for luxury will most likely explode.*

What about supply? Technically, emerging markets might produce many luxury items themselves, but there is every indication that they think like everybody else: Luxury is associated with (1) a well-known brand, which (2) has a long story, (3) comes from an area with a long tradition for making it, (4) enjoys international fame, and (5) is absolutely sublime. In other words, they want the same brands as everyone else. So, in real terms, supply is restricted to whatever existing brands decide to produce and, not sensing competition, each of these brands will typically pursue a strategy of modest undersupply.

———

As I argued in Chapter 8, which dealt with power and empires, I don't think luxury is just an unnecessary waste for the spoilt rich. Just like sports competitions, concerts, and art museums, it showcases what the most skilled and motivated people can do, when given the chance. It's about the best craftsmen, artists, and engineers in a civilization working together to deliver the finest product that this civilization can muster. We apparently spend 0.8% of GDP on it, but it makes people proud and think "humans did this!", or "our community made that". It sets benchmarks that everyone can measure themselves against, and it inspires a will to do even better, perhaps not just for the end result, but also for the joy of creation. Jeremy Clarkson, the co-host of the British automobile show *Top Gear*, once wrote:

> "I don't really want a Lamborghini Gallardo. But I don't want to live in a world where it doesn't exist."

I think that pretty much says it. At least the second part.

18

Lifestyles

I would like to end this part about supersectors by looking at lifestyles in the future. Private lifestyles affect all business sectors and influence everything from politics to macro-economics as well. Of course, it works the other way too: business and technology can change lifestyles.

It's now a long time ago that the use of primitive tools started to change our lives. Then we developed farming—and got plants and animals to work for us. We also began using yeast and bacteria to make cheese, beer, and wine from our farm products. Then we developed ships, money, and trade. Then factory machines, trains, and cars. Mathematics and statistics. Chemistry. Intellectual copyright and mass copying. Nuclear power. Computers. Satellite TV. The internet. These inventions have given us more leverage, power, income, knowledge, and wealth, and each has created new jobs and destroyed others. Machines, for instance, eliminated the need for extremely hard physical work and computers removed many ultra-boring, repetitive jobs.

But that is the past. In the next decades, billions will be lifted from poverty into middle class, and hundreds of millions will become rich. This will move jobs away from anything that is hard, manual, or boring to something more rewarding, and it will change lifestyles from rural to urban.

However, something else will happen to our lifestyles: Robots and neocortex simulation will radically change life for anyone who is no longer dirt-poor. In 2004 the U.N. Economic Commission for Europe (UNECE), in cooperation with the International Federation of Robotics (IFR), published a study on the increasing role of robots. It contained some revealing numbers (shown in the graph overleaf): A comparison between nominal and quality-adjusted unit prices of robots with the average labor cost (both in the U.S.A.). The graph shows indexed data from 1990 to 2003.

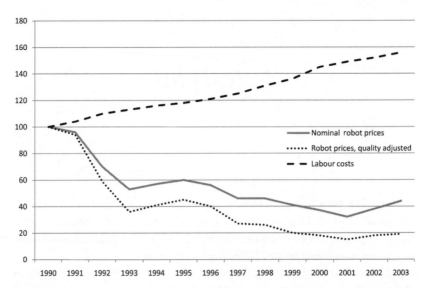

Indexation of the cost of labor versus robots, 1990–2003. The two graph lines representing robot costs show nominal robot prices and quality-adjusted prices, but it is the latter that really matter. These have fallen 80% at a time when labor costs have risen more than 50%. *Source: World Robotics 2004: Statistics, Market Analysis, Forecasts, Case Studies and Profitability of Robot Investment*, United Nations Publications, 2004.

The American university professor Richard Florida has written a number of interesting books and studies about different work sectors. Florida and his co-workers divide workforces into three broad categories, (1) manufacturing, (2) service, and (3) creative. We all know that manufacturing jobs (which includes farming) have continuously been substituted with machines, which is understandable when one considers that machines tend to become around 7% cheaper in real terms every time we double their annual output (and robots apparently 11–12% cheaper every year), whereas salaries go up. In America the working class peaked at approx. 40% of the labor force between 1920 and 1950, when it began to slide. The IT revolution has accelerated this decline, since IT machine productivity doubles every 24 months, while the working class continues to fall constituting less than 25% of the American labor force today.

Many manual labor jobs were replaced by the service sector, which grew from 16% of the workforce in 1900 to 45% in 1980. However, IT is now competing with large parts of the service industry as well. Service jobs that are purely routine and where the client has no real interest in whether it's done by a person or a computer/robot, will increasingly be done by the latter. We will surely prefer that a waiter or hairdresser is a person, but if changing tires on my car or border control was done by robots, I'd be fine with that.

The third sector—creative jobs—is where the recent growth has come from. To be creative means that you have to make complex decisions about how to handle your job, or think up stuff that is completely new. New technologies and styles are produced faster and faster, and this is the reason the need for creative thought increases. The creative sector comprises scientists, engineers, artists, musicians, designers, and knowledge-based professionals. The biggest industries for creative people are R&D of any kind, media, design, the arts, advertising, architecture, crafts, games, and fashion. The "creative core", according to Richard Florida, comprises people who create things from scratch, such as scientists, engineers, professors, poets, novelists, artists, entertainers, designers, analysts, and architects. A second tier comprises "creative professionals" who may work within more defined boundaries, but who must never-theless make numerous discretionary decisions about how to get from A to B. They could be lawyers, investment bankers, doctors, marketing directors, etc. This distinction is of course blurry—I have even heard of creative accounting!

The creative sector is red hot; in the U.S. it grew from around 3 million people in 1900 to 38 million by 2002. Furthermore, it doubled from 1980 to 2002; a process that I would personally think has a lot to do with globalization and the IT revolution—the drivers behind our deflationary boom. *Creative work now comprises around a third of all jobs and half of all personal income in the U.S., and both proportions are growing rapidly.* America is evidently not alone in going creative. Europe is heading that way as well, and China has launched a major initiative to change the mindset from "made in China" to "created in China", meaning that the Chinese should stop just making products invented elsewhere and start creating their own.

Since technology continues to replace manufacturing jobs and is increasingly also replacing service jobs, will an ever-larger part of the population end up in creative work? I am not totally convinced of that, because as we manage to simulate the neocortex with hardware and software, *computers will also get creative.*

As computers learn to simulate what happens in cells and organisms, they will come up with their own ideas for medicine and nutrition, and as they read anything that is published on the internet they will tell us about combinations of data that point to trends, opportunities, or threats. They will be able to create music and design buildings.

How can a computer be creative? Imagine this: You have a plot of land and want to build a house. You upload the land drawings to your computer, which automatically matches them with local building laws and illustrates visually for you where you may build on the plot as well as some scenarios of volume and height combinations. It then shows you a requirement specification tick box, where you check all the requirements you have: Three bedrooms, playroom, open kitchen, garage for two automobiles, and whatever. Next, the computer brings up a list of style guides, and you select a main style type you prefer. Click, and it brings photos of a large number of houses built within that style, and you tick off the ones you like most.

When you are done, you click "create", and a few minutes later the computer presents you with five alternative 3D renderings of houses that meet all your criteria plus local building regulations. Each comes with a computer-generated estimate of time and cost. You select one and email it to three construction companies, who can each give an offer for its construction. Perhaps a computer wouldn't come up with ingenious new things like the best architects could, but it would give you the advantage of being able to poke around and review large numbers of proposals before choosing. It could do creative work for you.

This example is just one idea, but there will be countless areas where computers may enter creative sectors—not eliminating creativity itself, but eliminating some creative human jobs.

However, computers cannot replace humans in the simple task of being humans. If you prefer that a bartender or a hairdresser is a person rather than a computer, I think it will remain a person now, next year, and forever, and for that reason it may very well be that the trend toward creative jobs stops and a new balance between service and creative is found—perhaps one where service eventually claws back some share of the job market.

———————

Richard Florida and his team made numerous statistical studies as well as focus group interviews and personal interviews to find out how people with creative jobs decided where to live and work. Here are some of the things they were looking for:

- Smart people everywhere
- Late night eating restaurants
- Good clubs and jazz/blues bars
- Access to places for individual sport
- Authentic, slightly chaotic architecture
- Repurposed old factories and warehouses
- A very diverse mix of people of different ethnic backgrounds
- Offices, residential, and shops in all shapes and forms mixed together
- Many different and highly visual lifestyles—metro, sporty, intellectual, yuppie, etc.

Clearly, it's about authenticity, freedom, diversity, and charm. Many creative workers emphasize that they like to see gay people around, even if they aren't gay themselves; they think a gay scene is a sign of freedom and tolerance. Furthermore, some women like to live in gay districts because they feel "safe" there.

Creative people need to be very focused when they work, so that they get into a "flow". If they get disturbed in that flow, it takes 20–30 minutes to pick up where they were. However, you can only do this for limited spans of time, and then you need to do something completely different, like lifting weights, go on a mountain bike, or blow your mind with heavy metal music for an hour. And then you can get back to your flow. Creative workers might listen to acid jazz, play drums at evenings in a local bar, do marathons, and brew beer in the cellar. They work a lot from home, but being around interesting people is essential, and they also need the social presence of their co-workers some of the time that they work. They work a lot more hours than people on an hourly salary, but it isn't "nine to five". They work in the day, night, weekends, and holidays, but need to mix their work frequently during the day with leisure, which for that reason has to be available in great variety where they live. Apple workers have been seen with T-shirts that said "90 hours a week and loving it".

Many creative workers frontload their life in the sense that they work incredibly hard in their young years to make their mark. Once they have succeeded the first time, they might very well shift to a completely new professional area, just for the fun of it. Meanwhile, they keep themselves fit because if they plan to have five different careers they had better be, because they aren't married yet, and because it's seen by potential business partners and employers as a sign of determination and stamina. They may like adventure sport, and also to venture out at the fringes of technology.

The idea that to attract talent it may be more useful to nourish a good social scene than to build science parks is perhaps surprising, but the evidence suggests that many of the greatest developments of regional power centers have happened where the smart people were in the first place, not where the smart buildings were erected to attract them. A recipe can be to take an old town long on charm, but short of business, and create a first-class university there. When young people come to study, they inspire the development of a good social scene. Some will now decide to start their own companies, and businesses will move offices to where the talent now is.

Future generations will be predominantly wealthy, and people will have tons of material possessions. *They will predominantly have jobs that are social, creative, or artistic,* because that is where they can still compete against computers and machines, and that is most fun anyway. In the long term, the socially minded service job sector may end up the biggest, because this is where computers or machines can never replace us.

As for their free time, I do not believe for a second that people will become any less materialistic than they are now. However, as more and more material demands are actually met through increased wealth and productivity, *there will be a relative tilt towards spending time and money on leisure instead of on ever more tangible possessions.* Given the choice between a new sofa and a great holiday, for instance, you will choose the holiday, if you already have three sofas. Furthermore, within leisure, it's the *experience* dimension that will dominate. The idea of a holiday as simply a break from your hard work, where you lie on the beach and do nothing, is already on the retreat. This will increasingly be replaced by more exciting experiences, such as sport, adventure, cultural exploration, training courses, or assisting workers in an exotic field like grape picking at a premium vineyard, truffle hunting, or biological surveying in a nattional park.

The experience dimension will also support a continued drive toward products that are not just functional, but also tell a story—or perhaps mainly the latter. *The fashion, art, and luxury sectors will outgrow economies as a whole,* and what people will seek in them will be not just the tangible product, but fascinating stories. *The future economy will also be a storyteller economy.*

An interesting case of how stories may be added to products is what has happened to the IT industry since the mid-1990s. Before that time, most people thought of computer technology as fairly dull stuff that would only interest geeks and nerds. But that changed when you saw students starting companies in their parents' garages and taking them public for billions soon after, and when the nerds became the organizers of the vibrant, virtual community.

From that point on, people got hired for IT jobs even if they showed up for interviews in Bermuda shorts or with rings in their noses, as long as they could write code. In fact, if they were really good, you almost *expected* them to look weird. A whole new language evolved in the industry where you started as a "newbie" (beginner) and advanced step by step to "user", "expert", "hacker", "guru", and "wizard", etc., as if you were working yourself up the ranks of Hell's Angels. Standard language got replaced by geek-speak and of course software code. For a newbie, it could take a while to discover that the answer to a funny email might be ⟨ROFLMAOSHIMFO⟩ ("rolling on floor laughing my ass off so hard it might fall off"), or, if the person at the other end was more conservative, simply ⟨VBSEG⟩, which meant "very big shit-eating grin". Nor would you know that "g2g" meant "got to go", or "hand" stood for "have a nice day".

All of this was a story that evolved around IT which made IT workers into the hippest social tribe on the planet. Code was now written by cool dudes.

In a society focused on creativity, artistry, and social activities, people will be free and independent, and those who have skill and courage can embark on adventures like the Vikings or cowboys did: Move into the unknown and perhaps bring a few like-minded with you. There will be tribes like there always has, but *in a modern society you are free to choose which tribes you want to join*—whether you want to be a biker, hippie, plane-spotter, tree-hugger, goth, suit, nerd, or a cool dude writing code is really up to yourself. Of course, if you aren't macho, the Bandidos may not want you, and if you can't write code, you can't. But then there is probably another tribe where you will fit, and in any case you are free to create your own new movement and see if someone will join. Such a movement may become a counterculture for a while, but if what you started is hip, then it will soon be engulfed by the mainstream and commercialized—hence, the artificially worn jeans and hippie chick designer rags which mainstream luxury brands now sell.

This enormous cultural diversity will have implications for fashion, because in a society with hundreds of vastly different lifestyles and tribes, there isn't any way you can get everyone to "wear orange this spring". People will be less inclined to follow single fashions and to copy each other from season to season. Instead, they will be more likely to unbundle what is offered, to pick, choose, and remix, so that everyone dresses in their own way and often in a highly creative way—a process similar to what we have seen in media, where CDs are unbundled into single tracks and newspapers into single online stories.

The experience economy will not only be about taking in experiences, but also about *sharing* and *creating* them. Most people have a fundamental urge to network continuously during the day, and as family and friends get scattered more around, and as they are more often on the move, they will seek electronic networking to bond and to tell stories of what they see, think, experience, are. If you walk around with a smartphone, you will be able to receive information about which of your friends are physically close to you, and they will be able to see where you are, if you let them. People might also use mobile networking tools to find potential friends and partners close to wherever they are. Furthermore, anyone with a middle-class income can afford a high-definition camcorder and computer movie-editing tool, which makes it possible for the individual to create media that is technically indistinguishable from professional Hollywood movies. This is interesting and can be great fun, but there are evidently also countless youngsters who publish data on the internet that they will regret as they grow up. Furthermore, even if you don't make yourself appear stupid, others might publish digital photos from a party that won't be helpful when you, 20 years later, try to become a CEO, high-court judge, or politician. The obvious response will probably be that people begin to accept that youngsters are what they are.

It is not only the young and middle-aged who expect experiences. New old people expect to have fun and are prepared to blow their money on the goodies of life. I have twice by chance run into a big Harley Davidson event—once in Puerto Banús in Southern Spain and once in St. Tropez in France. What struck me was how incredibly old the average hog-driver was. Many seemed 70 or older. Old people of our times go to rock concerts where they listen to equally old musicians rocking away. Who would have thought in the 1960s that the Rolling Stones, David Gilmore, Elton John, Eric Clapton, John Mayall, or the Allman Brothers would still give concerts far into the next millennium?

Growing individualism will also be reflected in the way people buy luxury and travel. The first phase of luxury spending is often to acquire it as a symbol of success to be seen by others ("baby, I have arrived!"). At this stage you may try as much as you can to upscale everything you wear and use, to show the new standard at any place and all times. In the second phase you learn to adapt and scale so that you, for instance, may wear relaxed clothes at some occasions, sporty at others, and more formal at still others. In the third phase, you stop caring about what others think and wear and use whatever you personally like, in whatever combinations you prefer. You become creative and autonomous. Your style becomes intelligent.

In your early stages of leisure travel, you will put high priority on going to many places, where you can have your photo taken in front of monuments, etc ("been there, done that!"). You may see Europe in a week by rushing from place to place, for instance. In later phases you start preferring to stay longer in single places to get them under your skin, and you may look more for profound emotional experiences or adventure. In the third phase you get a second home(s) so that your life oscillates between several locations, which all feel like, well . . ., home.

I already mentioned the trend towards storytelling. This will apply to the corporate world as well. In a storytelling economy, many successful companies in numerous industries will run professional media services. I mentioned earlier some of the trends in IT/electronic media: More unbundled, atomized, instant, mobile, and real-time media offerings, for instance. If a company has an interesting story, it will hire professional media people to ensure that this reaches the public in compelling ways in any format, at any time, on any device, and in any place.

There are four industries which must utilize this storytelling opportunity to the utmost: Sport, food/health, luxury, and finance. Why these four? Because that's what people are most interested in—perhaps even fascinated by. Check a range of newspapers and you will see that they dedicate lots of space to these four business areas.

The sports industry already knows how to do it. They follow their stars live and through backgrounders, on stage and off stage, in victory and failure. Whether their stars win or loose, the fans empathize with them because they understand through the media coverage how hard they try. However, the health, luxury, and finance industries have untapped potential that they will begin to use in the future.

For instance, the luxury business has great stories to tell, and its profitability depends on telling them well. Imagine that its 2024 and the grapes of the Graves wine district in Bordeaux seem very promising after a very warm and dry end to the summer. Perhaps this makes a classic vintage of Château d'Yquem possible? The aficionados will want to know. One morning they receive a video message from Château d'Yquem's chief oenologist:

> "Today, this morning, we decided that the conditions are perfect for harvesting the first part of the grapes, which I think are just perfect right now. They are ripe, and about a third of them have a mild

infection of botrytis which will give it perfect taste. We expect to pick approx. 15% today. Each grape will be chosen by hand, as you know. I will let you know when we go for some of the rest."

The d'Yquem fans may then want to watch some of the hand-selection of grapes from the head cam of a wine picker. And as the wine goes through fermentation, etc. they will want to be online from time to time with the oenologist, who tells them how and why he makes his vital decisions through the production process.

Château d'Yquem is well-established luxury, but lots of more common products can get elevated from commodity to premium, and then perhaps from premium to luxury. When I was small a cup of coffee was just that. Now, there is a huge variety, and they are sold with stories. The Nespresso I had this morning was called "Rosabaya de Colombia", and the package had the following description:

"This blend of fine, individually roasted Colombian Arabicas, develops a subtle acidity, with typical red fruit and winey notes, Intensity 6."

I chose to prepare it as a cappuccino, and the experience was very good. In the future I could imagine the coffee machine recognizing the color of each Nespresso coffee capsule and displaying information about the product on a screen—this time with video from where the coffee was grown, maps, more descriptions, etc. In fact, any product could have a little RFID tag that can trigger an electronic story being told on a screen near me. How about this: I point my smartphone at a product and click "story", and it tells me what I want to know.

The health/food industry has already come a long way. The thought of food as a part of managing your body ties in with an increasing interest in health, wellness, and healing. As people realize that there is a very real opportunity to live a fruitful and active life after the children have moved away from home and after retirement begins, they get increasingly interested in staying in shape and just being healthy. Furthermore, with modern clothes becoming increasingly revealing, they also give more thought to looking fit. However, there is also food that is focused on the enjoyment of the taste and smell. In the future, food will be divided into four main classes:

- *Fast food* that can be bought at drive-ins, etc. or can be prepared at home in 10 minutes.

- *Luxury food*, which is created under extreme care, handpicked, and presented in exclusive packaging and with a story about the craftsmanship behind it. This is about pleasure, admiration for a culture, and slow eating.
- *Ecological food*, which is presented with a back-to-nature/retro story plus environmentalism. The story here is about your body, the nature and the wholeness of everything, as in Taoism.
- *Functional food*, which has been genetically engineered to be particularly healthy (replacing saturated fat with unsaturated containing vital minerals and vitamins, for instance), and further segmented to suit different age groups, lifestyles, etc. (some for active sports people, and some for older people, children, obese, etc.). What it does to your body, will be the key message.

Of these four, it's the latter that will grow most. However, a common theme for all of them is storytelling. People want to know what they get, and if there is a good story, and if it is told well, they will listen.

As for storytelling in finance, the reason that the press covers it so vigorously is partly its never ending drama (as in the subprime salami meltdown), and partly that people's wealth depends on it. But why is it that investors are far more likely to use Yahoo as the home page when they go online, than their bank's webpage? Let me guess ... ehhh ... hmmmhh ... because the staff at Yahoo! knows more about finance than a large bank? Although some of what we saw during the subprime salami flop might have left that impression, I doubt it. I think that people prefer Yahoo!'s website and smartphone data over their banks' because the bank knows less about media aggregation than the staff at Yahoo! *Financial institutions have a unique chance to create live media which their clients can constantly access any place, any time, anywhere. When well executed, this will be so compelling and addictive that clients will never leave the media-savvy bank, once using its media has become a habit.* Such services could include interviews with analysts, live transmissions from morning briefs, live price tickers, charts, ratings, news, etc. Instead of only showing a polished surface, the smartest banks will open the hood and show the difficult market decision-making process they go through, their internal discussions, and this will humanize them and create a bond with their clients. What should not be forgotten here is that while most media can and will be pirated, live media is an exception. Live media tends to be proprietary.

I believe this growth in compelling, addictive, corporate multimedia is unavoidable, as it will be a part of a trend towards decentralization of media so that whereas some electronic media will always be created by large, professional media organizations (content is king), an increasing part will be generated by consumers (consumers are king) and companies (companies are king)—the latter mainly in the sport, food/health, luxury, and finance businesses. Furthermore, since the leading companies in finance, luxury, and some other industries are the ultimate experts in their fields, they can communicate what things mean far better than anyone else (context is king). Where will the role for trained journalists be in all this? I think there will be fewer jobs at newspapers, but more at companies needing to perfect their storytelling to a fine art.

Storytelling is not only about consumers, news, markets, and products, of course. The greatest stories in most people's minds are spiritual or religious. However, since non-affiliation seems to be growing rapidly, one might think that spirituality is declining.

I would doubt that. My impression is that while many may cease to show up at prayers, they will often still believe that there is a God and an afterlife. They just don't believe the doctrines of the formal religions, or trust the established religious institutions. They may not believe, for instance, that dressing in a special way, or fasting, avoiding certain foods and drinks that actually seem healthy, or making specific rituals brings them closer to salvation. But they do believe "there is something", and because of that, they create their own, private version of spirituality. A study by the PEW Forum showed that the majority of Americans mixed elements from different religions, and also mixed religion with other spirituality. For instance, among self-declared Christians, 23% believed in spiritual energy in trees, etc., 23% in astrology, 22% in reincarnation, 21% in yoga as a spiritual exercise, and 17% in evil eyes, etc.

Increasing numbers also seem to embrace various versions of pantheism, which is the belief that the universe is divine, and the Earth is sacred. By putting nature at the spiritual core, Pantheism embraces environmentalism. This has many forms and flavors. A recent example combining science with mythical undertones was the *Gaia Hypothesis* (named after the Greek goddess of Earth) written by the scientist James Lovelock. This described Earth as a feedback system where the biosphere and the physical components of the Earth are closely integrated and interdependent. Pantheism may also intersect with an obsession with human health ("my body is my temple") as expressed in yoga, healing, alternative medicine, and meditation. This is increasingly getting out of hand. More and more suffer from orthorexia nervosa, an eating disorder where you gradually exclude yourself from eating this and then that and soon almost anything. Typical cutouts are meat, dairy products, fat, or anything containing preservatives or coming from a factory, etc. Other radical forms of ritual cleansings include anorexia and physical overtraining—both serving to purge the body of any traces of fat.

I don't want this to morph into a nutrition guide, but the body actually needs fat, since it regulates the hormone system, provides a vital buffer during disease, and constitutes a big part of the liver, the brain, and the nervous system. Furthermore, a diet without fat means exclusion of vitamins A, D, E, and K which can only be distributed within fatty food. But what I am aiming at is that this stuff is not rational, and the consequences range from tiredness, reduced sex drive, osteoporosis, osteoarthritis, hair loss, depression, to premature death (it may also make you look weird). It all seems to be about ritual cleansing or lack of real purpose in life.

So, to summarize, *there will be a continued trend toward freedom, which will enable people to either be totally original, or to seek membership of any of thousands of lifestyle tribes—or even to try to create new tribes themselves.* The result of that will be increased diversity and a *focus on creativity, individuality, authenticity, and charm. Because this will make products and lifestyles far more interesting, storytelling by companies and consumers will become a major part of the future.*

In terms of occupations, *the trend will be toward creative and social work where the human touch is vital, and toward storytelling.* It will be away from anything repetitive. Computers are on their way to match us—and then beat us—in data gathering, in factual information interpretation, and even in many forms of expressions of talent that we may today regard as exclusively human domain, such as art, design, and sophisticated motion control. *Where humans will excel is in being emotional and ethical humans as such, in controlling information technology successfully, and in telling stories.*

Spending will move toward leisure, and the travel, media, fashion, art, and luxury business sectors will be among those growing much faster than economies as a whole. Experiences plus products and services with good stories will be sought after and command premium prices.

I would like to conclude this chapter with some remarks about how communities can attract growth. Some will pursue what we could call a "seed" strategy: Try to attract and nurse young talent in the hope that they will eventually stay, work, and make lots of money. Typical approaches will here be to establish world-leading universities close to attractive, creative communities. The main drivers for success include

---

Geographic growth drivers

The following is a list of factors that can drive growth and wealth:

- Fossil energy and metals
- Proximity to desired locations
- Fresh water
- Use of English language
- Temperate or subtropical climate
- Flexible immigration regulation
- Natural beauty
- Esthetic culture
- Creative culture
- Technological culture
- Educational institutions
- Artistic culture
- Entrenched network effects
- Economic and legal stability
- Transport/access
- Education opportunities for children
- Legal environment
- Low crime
- Low taxes
- Availability of quality housing
- Depth of financial services
- Sea access
- Cultural diversity
- High-tech culture
- Great nightlife

---

insuring the presence of a creative and artistic culture, reasonable immigration regulation, and availability of low-cost housing.

The second approach will be the "harvest" strategy, which means to attract existing companies and people who already have money and large incomes. The key factors here include economic and legal stability, education opportunities for children, low crime, low taxes and depth of financial services may in particular appeal to the wealthy.

Of course each one of these two models can lead to the other. When rich people move to tax havens, they often start new ventures there. After all, they probably got rich because they have that talent, and if you are an entrepreneurial person, you typically can't stop.

When it comes to human resources, North East Asia (Greater China plus North Korea, and Vietnam) stand out. This is clearly a geographical area where people have the ambition and ability to move forward at full thrust. However, this is also true of North America and Europe, which have created flourishing creative hubs that are ideal for fostering new and radical ideas. I would assume that most leading edge entrepreneurship within IT, genomics/biotech, and alternative energy largely will continue to come from Europe and North America.

Part V

Superbrains

- Progress is essentially the application of intelligence.
- The direction of all intelligence is toward more cooperative, decentralized, and creative levels. That goes for civilization as well. Totalitarian systems are uncompetitive in the long run and will always lose out.
- During history, one industry after another has shifted from being manual or industrial to being predominantly based on information technology. The chemical, pharmaceutical, and financial industries were among the first to make that transition, and farming is now following. Alternative energy should be next in line. Information technologies evolve orders of magnitude faster than manual or industrial industries.
- The development of all intelligence is by nature hyper-exponential, and the intelligence of human civilization as well as humans themselves will accelerate over the coming decades due to IT, genomics, globalization, and self-modification.
- Human happiness depends predominantly on the degree of freedom—especially economic freedom—and also on income and wealth.
- The long-term destination of our societies seems to be toward more freedom, more creativity, more experiences, more harmony, and more happiness.

For more information:
www.superbrains.com

19

Intelligence and happiness

Imagine that you had been at a dinner in 1970 and someone had made a speech, with the following forecast:

"40 years from now, in 2010, communism, which dominates much of the world today, will be almost gone. The Soviet empire will have disintegrated from within, Eastern Europe will be ultra-capitalist, and China will have a thriving free market economy, driven by millions of private enterprises.

Furthermore, automobiles will be connected to satellites and radio signals, which will enable them to navigate with complete precision, even through inner cities, and they will have radar and massive onboard computers. Telephones will not need wires, and most people will have them in their pockets, when on the move. There will be hundreds of non-stop TV programs available from a huge armada of satellites to any household.

We will know how to recreate extinct species, and we will have changed plants so that they don't need pesticides and grow much faster. We will use bacteria containing some human genes to brew human insulin and other medicine. There will be several billion more people on the planet, but fewer will starve. In fact, there will be more people that are overweight than people that go hungry.

Most houses will have computers, some of which will be so small that you can easily carry them with you. These will be much more powerful than our best mainframes today, by the way. You will also be able to store the music from a thousand LPs in your pocket. And it will be possible to scan almost all print information ever published about a given subject in a fraction of a second—for free.

Our known natural resources will be vastly bigger than today and despite a massive growth in population and wealth, we will have less pollution of air and water, better nutrition, and much longer life expectancies than today. The richest countries will be the cleanest, and they will have stable or declining populations.

The level of warfare over the next 40 years will have fallen dramatically compared with the last 40. While different tribes and countries in Eastern Europe, the Middle East, and elsewhere will have tried to conquer other people's land, these attempts will mostly have failed, with huge costs to the aggressors.

However, some of the areas we fantasize most about now will not have progressed much. Even though we landed the first men on the Moon and the first probe on Venus last year, 40 years from now, surprisingly few new milestones will have been met. Indeed, the recent Moon walks will not have been surpassed. Airplanes will look much the same as today and will barely outshine our 747 Jumbo Jet or Concorde."

To most, this would have sounded idiotic. Communism gone? Automobiles with satellite navigation and radar? Recreating species? A thousand LPs in your pocket? Come on!

However, I am sure that no one said all of that. No one could have. Looking 40 years ahead with any such precision was simply impossible then and, when people tried, they mostly got it very wrong. In this book, I am surely getting lots wrong as well. However, perhaps we can learn a bit from previous failures to forecast well. I believe the past has taught us four major lessons about technology:

- I have already mentioned that *developments in virtual or microscopic technologies follow very aggressive progression curves* (perhaps doubling performance every 18–24 months), whereas *physical/industrial technologies typically only improve around 7% each time annual output doubles*. This is one reason people in the past vastly underestimated or even ignored progress in genomics and IT, whereas they overestimated what would happen with aircraft and spacecraft.

- *Whenever a human problem or demand can be met through information technology or molecular technology (which is also information technology), it is extremely likely that solutions will evolve much faster than demand develops, which leads to falling prices and abundant supply.* Failure to see this explains why environmentalists and growth skeptics continuously have completely underestimated human ability to overcome challenges.

- *Beyond a threshold, economic growth, new technology, and wealth cease to be part of the causes of environmental problems, and become instead part of the solutions.* This is through the development of clean technologies, investments in recycling, etc. and population stabilization.

- *Political showcase developments that don't make economic sense will slow down or stop sooner rather than later.* The dominant motive for the manned space explorations in the late 1960s was rivalry between free and communist areas. The first man to set foot on the Moon did so in 1969, and the last just 4 years later—serving no major purpose except propaganda. As for the planned manned mission to Mars, it would be a monumental waste of money in itself and when compared with other priorities such as those listed by the Copenhagen Consensus teams. It will probably be postponed indefinitely.

I think there is also an important lesson regarding war, power, and empires. *The era of military land conquest is over, as are battles between two uniformed armies.* Battles in the future will either be civil wars in poor countries, or wars of attrition between insurgents and terrorists on one side and mainly robots on the other. None will be able to successfully conquer other people's land except in totally failed nations. The U.S.A. lost the Vietnam War, but after approx. 20 years the communist regime decided to pursue free markets and open up to the world. You can't win over people with violence anymore—and trying is massively costly—but you clearly can by the inspiration, visible success, and attractiveness of your ideas, even if it may take decades.

Finally, I think there is an important lesson to be learned regarding the leadership and politics of societies. Personally, I got the first taste of what the future might bring through movies and TV series when I was younger. Many of them fell into two categories. The first was what you might call "the cold, uniform world" along the lines of *1984* (published 1949) or *2001: A Space Odyssey* (1968). People were here dressed largely the same; the walls were made of metal, the furniture of plastic, there were huge computers everywhere, and you didn't see anything of the natural world. Furthermore, we seemed in these movies to be controlled by a nasty psychopathic big brother or self-aware mega-computer with personality disorders. I suppose the assumption behind these scenarios was that society simply gets ever more structured, and if that continues we will all end up as puppets living in an overregulated, computer-driven hell.

The other group of films depicted a post-apocalyptic world, where civilization had collapsed, perhaps because of some catastrophic event, and where warlords fought each other constantly in the anarchy that reigned. *The Road Warrior* (1981) and *Blade Runner* (1982) are examples.

Today we are way past 1984 and 2001 and are thus actually living well within—or very close to—the future that some of these books and movies imagined (the movie *Blade Runner* from 1982 takes place in 2019). Hence it is relevant to ask how close the political world actually is to what they portrayed, and also to ask what we may learn from that.

I think it's fair to say that post-apocalyptic worlds such as imagined in some movies really do exist today—they are even abundant. Afghanistan, for instance, has been a chaotic battlefield between local tribes for generations. The same with parts of Somalia, Yemen, Sudan, and Congo—countries where self-appointed warlords roam around killing, and where some even send out terrorists to kill innocent civilians abroad. Does that make the apocalypse movies realistic portrayals of the future? I think not. The chaos and terror in some communities today is not happening because these places have entered the future. It's because they haven't. These countries live like Europeans lived several hundred years ago, where numerous different armies roamed around and plundered, raped, and killed, often as a means of living.

How about the other extreme scenario from the movies—"the cold, uniform world"? Some communist countries such as East Germany actually came close but, with the current exception of North Korea, these all collapsed because such a model simply doesn't work (and nor does it in North Korea—it will collapse eventually).

What actually *does* work—the model that made tribes and countries rich, and which most emerging markets are now emulating—is very different from what almost anyone had predicted. The modern world is extremely diverse and fluid. We have more choices and more lifestyles to adopt than ever. Modern schools are more focused on creativity and individual thinking than the old ones, and today people can choose to travel, move, communicate, and change work in ways that were never possible before. We have radios, television, and the internet, but we still read books and magazines. And it's a free world, and one of enormous choice. None of the science fiction movies I saw as a child predicted that, but that is the trend: *The world moves toward diversity, not uniformity, and it moves toward freedom, not tyranny.*

But why? *Why* doesn't a more developed world become more centralized as shown in many science fiction movies? I think it has to do with a phenomenon that only occurred to me some years ago when reflecting about the similarities between genomics and IT. It's about some very basic characteristics of intelligence.

Let me first define intelligence: It is *the sustained capacity to acquire and apply knowledge.* I think the two basic sets of primary intelligent systems are quantum physics and math/statistics. These existed before the Big Bang, or were created by it, and they are the natural basis for everything. Between them they spawned—beginning within a fraction of a second— chemistry with its 117 elements, which again created the first genomics/ biochemistry about 1 million years after the Earth took its current shape. From that followed brains, civilization, and information technology. And those three intelligent systems have now created thousands, if not millions of intelligent subsystems, ranging from all our biological species to music with its notes, chess, countless software platforms, law, etc.

Intelligence of any kind, whether it is in computers, cells, brains, civilizations, or ecological systems, requires some common core principles (rules) to be obeyed before it can progress. If we understand them, then we shall see why it would have been really odd had civilization evolved toward either central control or chaos.

Rule number 1 is that *intelligence needs a written language.* By this I mean a way to write down the results of new discoveries. Intelligence of any kind uses a language that can enable it to acquire and apply knowledge. The code of life is based on DNA's four letters—A, T, C, and G—and in proteins it's based on just 20 different amino acids. Chemistry uses 117 elements. A seed of a tree is essentially a set of mathematical instructions that describe how to make a tree from the surrounding chemical elements. In computing, the most basic level of code comprises two characters—0 and 1 (which in a transistor means flow of current or no flow of current). The code in economics is largely written with our 10 basic numbers, but also with letters. The same goes for civilization. In the brain it's the organic transistors (if I may call them that) of brain cells—flow of current or no flow of current.

What is needed next—and this is rule number 2—are some *change agents.* In genetics, the necessary change arises from mutations caused by

- Random chemical reactions
- Sun exposure
- Radioactive exposure
- Cosmic rays

- Oxygenation
- Gene insertion/change through viral and bacterial infections.

Personally none of us wants too much of this stuff, but for a species trying to evolve, it's essential. In the human brain, change arises when we move through the landscape physically, socially, intellectually, and geographically. As concerns civilization, I have already mentioned a term for such change instigators: "meta-ideas".

Historically speaking, one of the essential meta-ideas has been to travel. The development of human civilization has been characterized by emigrants, travelers, and conquerors such as the Roman Empire, and in recent times primarily by researchers and entrepreneurs. All meta-technologies are change agents, but the two biggest in our times have probably been satellite TV and the internet.

Rule number 3: Further progress in intelligence requires *division of labor*. One of Adam Smith's best known theses was that economic growth is largely created by such a division of labor, as this contributes to specialization and increased productivity. One single cell, one single person, one single computer, or an isolated civilization may develop in a positive direction, but real progress and success starts when a wider division of labor emerges. In the human body, we have approximately 200 different cell types and numerous organs and structures which together create something that is much more effective than a giant lump of jelly containing 75 kg of identical, one-celled organisms.

Interconnection with networks creates network effects, where each unit gets more and more effective as the network grows. A large and complex ecosystem is more robust and effective than a small, homogeneous, restricted one, even though our instinct may be that isolation is protection. A large and open free trade area is also more effective than a number of small, self-supplying economies. A global network of internet users creates more innovation and new thinking than a number of isolated individuals.

Rule number 4: In order to thrive, *intelligence needs open standards*. An open standard is an immediately accessible foundation on which everything can be built and shared. Such a standard enables division of labor and network effects. The internet is such a standard, as GSM is to mobile phones and MPEG and JPG are to coding of video and images. In international communication, the English language has similarly become the *de facto* standard and, in commerce, free trade agreements between nations in the WTO, EU, and NAFTA serve the same function. In nature, this standard is DNA—whose similarity in most living beings is noteworthy.

I have already mentioned that in genetic terms a chimpanzee only deviates approximately 2% from a human being. In fact, there is an 85% overlap between the genes of a mouse and a human being, and a 50% overlap between the genes of a human being and a fruit fly.

Finally, rule number 5: *There has to be a way to copy what has been written.* RNA and (probably later) DNA play this role in life. Within IT, this function is of course handled by mathematical code in software, source code, and chip architecture, all of which is easily copied (and pirated). In the development of civilization, it is predominantly the written word of laws and literature, notes of music, works of art, and durable buildings that pass on knowledge from person to person and from generation to generation. In our brain, the synapses, etc. store everything we have learned.

These five rules for intelligence seem universal, as my examples hopefully illustrate. This is somehow interesting. However, what is equally interesting is that *the path of progress for all intelligence seems to be similar*. It reaches eight levels of sophistication through three major stages, which we can call "single-unit", "co-operative", and "creative". Stage 2 evolves faster than stage 1, and stage 3 faster than stage 2. *The progress of intelligence is always exponential.* Furthermore, *each form of intelligence creates new forms*. And finally, *different forms of intelligence can reinforce each other*.

Take life on Earth. It presumably started 2.5–4.5 billion years ago. Then came the self-contained cells organized by numerous, sophisticated combinations of derived rules (there is very strong evidence that these were the so-called prokaryotes). What followed was a split of prokaryotes into bacteria and Archaea, and then development of the first multi-cellular organisms, where each cell type complemented the others. We were now in the co-operative phase. Life produced oxygen, which for a while threatened to become a show-stopper, until oxygen-consuming organisms evolved to save the day. A mutually interdependent ecosystem was thereby established.

This ecosystem got more and more complex, and organisms such as plankton and jellyfish developed "brains" consisting of little more than a few nerve cells connected to light sensors—DNA-based intelligence spawning nerve-based intelligence. Sophisticated creatures like cats and dogs, which came much later, have billions of brain cells that are grouped together in regions that handle different tasks, but which are massively interconnected. Human beings are creative and self-aware; they deliberately train their brains through education, general information seeking, and skills training to enhance its function. Furthermore, as I have described, scientists are now trying to make artificial brains and to understand how our own brain really works. And, finally, for the first time in history, we are now able to actually design artificial intelligence.

A very similar development has been seen in computers. The first commercial computers where this was combined were single-unit ("master–slave computing"). These were followed by multi-cell ("client–server computing"), and multi-unit ("networked" and "ubiquitous computing"). We have now reached "creative computing", where software can also handle autonomous tasks, such as navigating a robot car, and where swarms of computers combine to solve complex tasks while drawing on each other's power. The next step, which has already begun, is software that writes software that is creative. We do not know whether software will eventually develop consciousness, but it will have the necessary technical firepower in TIPS and memory to do so soon.

As for civilization, it seems that the most primitive ones are small groups of people centered on a dominant figure. Extended families, in other words, or a few families co-habiting. When these families accidentally run into another such group, war typically breaks out and blood flows. However, over time these groupings merge into tribes, and then the tribes merge into nations. Then the nations form communities like the U.S. or the EU, which again start co-operating, and, before we know it, it's a global village co-ordinated by institutions such as the U.N. Developed and high-growth emerging nations are well into this creative phase of civilization now.

In summary, *all intelligence evolves through three similar stages*. The first is the single-unit stage starting with basic rules and matter, then comes the single-cell stage, and finally the multi-cell stage. The second main phase is *co-operative*, where we have multiple interdependent units that evolve into complex ecosystems. And the third phase is *creative*, where intelligence can exhibit autonomous behavior, can draw on other intelligence, become conscious of its own existence, and can start deliberately modifying itself. I think this is the natural, almost unavoidable sequence for intelligence.

Another conclusion is that *intelligence evolves faster and faster*. The first life on Earth was followed by ecosystems, human brains, human civilization, economic systems, and IT, etc. We are now using each of these forms of intelligence to enhance the others; IT to enhance genomics, perhaps genomics to create IT (DNA computers) and chemicals, and soon both to enhance our brains, etc.

A part of this process is that intelligence not only spawns new forms of intelligence, but also invades one area after another. In business, one industry after another will naturally morph from being predominantly manual or industrial to being information technology–driven. For instance, this happened with the chemical industry, which moved from being alchemy-based to science-based, and to the pharmaceutical industry, which shifted from snake oil, superstition, and "healing" to analogue experimentation and then to being built on exact knowledge. It has also been seen in finance, which is now largely a computer industry; and it has begun to happen in farming, which is well on the way to becoming genetic engineering–based. Energy should be next in line. And, finally, whatever tasks robots start doing.

Are there any rules about how fast intelligence evolves? There are. Since intelligence is the capacity to acquire and apply knowledge, it almost goes without saying that *it will mostly advance over time*. We have seen in biology or civilization that intelligence can move backwards for a while (or parts of it can be destroyed). But only for a time—then it picks up and moves to new highs.

Let me mention a form of intelligence that almost didn't make the cut: chemistry. This met four of my criteria for evolving, but the fifth— the ability to copy what was written—generally didn't work. The creation of one molecule would normally not lead to automatic copying. There were just two exceptions to this: The formation of crystals and carbon-based structures. While crystals represented a dead-end, carbon structures could create such a dizzying range of combinations that it was only a question of time before we found some that could self-replicate (RNA and DNA). In other words: Chemistry, which was initially a very simplistic intelligent system, spawned another—biochemistry—which was far more complex. Intelligence is a chain reaction in new systems and, since these are progressively more complex, it is also a cascade.

This also means that if we roll back time, we get to a very tiny starting point. Just think about how we observed the expanding universe and concluded that it must have come from a single point and thus a single event—the so-called Big Bang. It's the same thing. The start point for any intelligence must have been a freak, little event. A possible example: We do not know how the first, simple cells on Earth developed, but it could be that a string of RNA was randomly formed that could grab

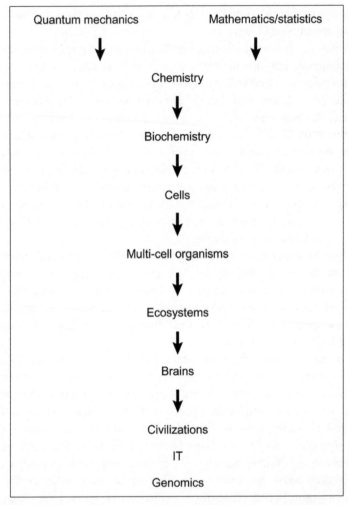

The cascade of intelligence. Each new incarnation of intelligence will provide feedback to the previous, and vice versa. To start with, everything was simply basic rules and chemical elements. Natural ecosystems and our brains are intelligent systems that primarily use the atoms in the first half of the periodical table, such as carbon, oxygen, helium, sulfur, phosphorus, and nitrogen. From this we evolved our electronic information technology, which is based more on atoms in the other half of the table, such as iron, gold, silver, and silicon.

amino acids from the surrounding soup and assemble them into identical strings (we know that this is possible, since we can replicate it in laboratories). So, where is the intelligence in this? It's (1) knowledge about how to assemble these strings, which is (2) applied when they are created, and when this knowledge is duplicated by self-replication, it is (3) sustained.

Another possible example: It may be that the first hints of civilization among hominids came from a random mutation that created a slightly improved capability to sense the intentions of other members of the flock, or from having opposable thumbs that enabled us to manipulate things precisely, or from the FOXP2 gene that plays a major role in enabling us to speak. It could also have been from all three combined, but each of them was very simple. As a fraction of our genome, we are probably talking about less than a 1‰ difference to enable us to create civilization.

In summary, due to the cascade of new intelligences, and the feedback between them all, *the natural progression of intelligence is hyper-exponential*.

Where am I going with this? Well, I want to draw some parallels to what happens to civilizations and economies, given that they are forms of intelligence. The *advanced form of human civilization has to be a creative, de-centralized, co-operative, constantly evolving, global ecosystem*. Why? Because "creative" intelligence, and all that comes with it, is the most efficient form of intelligence and thus the one that eventually wins in a competition. And this is why future visions of a sterile, centrally controlled nightmare have not come true, and never will. It is also the reason that chaos is a stage we go through, but not a destination.

We have come far. Economic systems have evolved from being local and isolated to being global and open. There have been numerous and at times formidable attacks on this model—fascism, nazism, socialism, communism, and religious fundamentalism. Each of these has offered the overall advantage of single-mindedness, often driven by widespread brainwashing—something that pluralistic societies cannot match or even muster. Some totalitarian societies appeared formidable for a while, because they mobilized all people in their community to march in one direction. But sooner or later they fell behind, as their institutional framework didn't encourage or incentivize individual creativity and innovation. In fact, after progress fizzled, what followed was often absolute decline, since personal initiative in such societies generally went into corruption, crime, or violence instead and, as this is refined and better organized over time, everything else breaks down.

From an economic point of view, socialism and communism are the most inefficient of these systems because they attempt to freeze developments at the centrally controlled stage (comparable with the mainframe stage in computing). Furthermore, the associated protectionism, chauvin-

The rules of intelligence

Definition: Intelligence is the sustained ability to acquire and apply knowledge. For intelligence of any sort to evolve, five elements are required:

- A written language
- Change instigators
- Division of labor
- Open standards.
- A method for copying what is written

If these are present, it will evolve through the following stages:

(1) Single-unit
   o Written rules
   o Single-cell
   o Multi-cell
(2) Co-operative
   o Multi-species
   o Complex ecosystem
(3) Creative
   o Autonomous
   o Conscious
   o Designed
   o Self-modifying.

Any form of intelligence starts with a very minor event. The subsequent developments are driven by random events combined with competition and thus survival of the fittest. When you move from single-cell to multi-cell, it allows division of labor, which accelerates the rate of progress. At a later stage, when multiple species begin to fill an ecosystem, the competition heats up. This accelerates natural selection and thus evolution even further. Once stage 3 is reached, progress itself becomes consciously managed and accelerates yet again.

The natural trajectory for intelligence is hyper-exponential, for the following reasons:

- Each form of intelligence creates new forms of intelligence.
- Different forms of intelligence will draw upon each other to progress, thus creating complex, positive feedback.
- Creative intelligence leads to conscious self-modification, which is orders of magnitude faster than natural modification.

ism, and nationalism are attempts to prevent the move from single-cell to multi-cell levels of economic intelligence, let alone to creativity. North Korea and Cuba have socialism and have thus prohibited emigration, mobile phones, global internet search, unauthorized satellite disks, and entrepreneurial activity—in other words, anything that might give inspiration, international work sharing, change, and network synergies. This is not a choice—for socialism to work (albeit badly), you need to censor information that would inspire people to lead different lives or revolt, and you need to close the borders to prevent the most dynamic and creative from leaving. North Korea, which in addition to socialism endorses self-sufficiency, currently has a GDP per capita which is just 6–7% that of neighboring South Korea. Average monthly salaries in Cuba are approx. $15, or equal to half a dollar a day. That is less than a third of what I earned cleaning toilets in Denmark—*per hour*—in 1974! It won't last.

So, I believe we are moving towards freedom and creativity, but what about happiness? This is actually a very interesting question. Thousands of research studies have been made on this subject, which falls under so-called "positive psychology" (studies of strengths and virtues that enable individuals and communities to thrive.) There exist magazines about happiness studies, happiness research institutes, and a scientific reference manual about personal ability to get happy (*Character Strengths and Virtues: A Handbook and Classification*, also called "CSV"). The world's leading scientist in happiness research is Rooth Veenhoven, who founded the World Database of Happiness in 1984. This aggregates, indexes, classifies, and compares the results of all scientific happiness studies made anywhere in the world. It's a continuous meta-study.

I don't think you need to read CSV to know that some people seem generally happier than others, irrespective of what happens to them. Others suffer from depressions, even though their life should be good. So, a part of it is genetic.

However, other parts clearly aren't, because there are substantial differences between how happy different populations are, and average happiness in a given country can change a lot over time. We know this, because these numbers are tracked in the World Database of Happiness. The scale that is used in these happiness studies goes from 0 to 10, where 10 is most happy. China scores a happiness index of 6.4 on that scale; India 5.5, the U.S.A. 7.4, Indonesia 6.1, Brazil 7.5, Pakistan 5.4, and Japan 6.2. The global, unweighted average is 5.8 but—since

mega-states like China, the U.S.A., Indonesia, and Brazil are higher—
I would think the global average is something like 6, which is pretty
much OK.

However, there are enormous differences from country to country.
The 20 happiest nations ranged from 8.5 to 7.4 on this scale, which is
way into the happy chappy zone. Based on averaging out all studies
made between 2000 and 2009, the 20 happiest countries in the world are
given in the table opposite.

So, these are all European and Latin American countries, or countries
that have largely been populated though European migration (U.S.A.,
Canada, Australia, and New Zealand), and most of them are among the
richest on Earth.

If we go to the opposite end of the scale and study the least happy
nations, they scored between 4.3 and 2.6. When you are below 5, you
are really not very happy and, if you are below 4, life generally sucks.
As the table at the top of p. 418 shows, these are predominantly African
and extremely poor. In fact, there is not a single wealthy nation among
them.

The database also shows whether a nation's happiness changes over
time. There are only a few developed nations that have enough data
points to reach a reliable conclusion in that respect. Tracking long-term
data t2ends—typically from 1973 to 2008—for 14 nations showed that
happiness had increased in 9 countries, was virtually unchanged in 3, and
had declined in 2. It had increased by 0.35 points in America and 0.28 in
EU9. So, among wealthy nations, *the happiness trend was slowly rising*.

But why? What makes people happy, and what has made them
happier over the years? Happiness, it seems, comes in three different forms:

- *Pleasant life*. Tell jokes. Do sport. Get a massage. Watch a good movie.
  Eat popcorn. Go to an Italian restaurant. Swim in the blue sea. Buy a
  Gucci bag. Load your iPod. Drive a cool car. Collect wine. Play a great
  computer game.
- *Engaged life*. Be totally into art or music. Run a blog on the internet.
  Join a professional society. Learn Spanish. Fall in love. Get children.
  Set a goal in sports and meet it. Climb Kilimanjaro. Learn to windsurf.
  Train a dog. Have lunch with your sister. Play cards with your
  friends.
- *Meaningful life*. Help people in need. Bring up your children to your
  best abilities. Start a company. Invent new technologies. Create
  lasting beauty. Be religious. Make people laugh. Defend the weak.
  Leave something behind.

The 20 happiest nations on Earth, average 2000–2009		
Rank	*Country*	*Happiness score*
1	Costa Rica	8.5
2	Denmark	8.3
3	Iceland	8.2
4	Canada	8.0
5	Switzerland	8.0
6	Finland	7.9
7	Mexico	7.9
8	Norway	7.9
9	Panama	7.8
10	Sweden	7.8
11	Australia	7.7
12	Austria	7.7
13	Colombia	7.7
14	Luxembourg	7.7
15	Dominican Republic	7.6
16	Ireland	7.6
17	Netherlands	7.6
18	Brazil	7.5
19	New Zealand	7.5
20	U.S.A.	7.4

Veenhoven, R.: *Average Happiness in 148 Nations 2000–2009*, World Database of Happiness, Rankreport Average Happiness, Version 10/09. Online at *http://worlddatabaseofhappiness. eur.nl/index.html*

The 20 least happy nations on Earth, average 2000–2009

Rank	Country	Happiness score
129	Congo (Kinshasa)	4.4
130	Angola	4.3
131	Georgia	4.3
132	Liberia	4.3
133	Rwanda	4.3
134	Ethiopia	4.2
135	Afghanistan	4.1
136	Cameroon	3.9
137	Haiti	3.9
138	Mozambique	3.8
139	Niger	3.8
140	Congo (Brazzaville)	3.7
141	Madagascar	3.7
142	Sierra Leone	3.6
143	Kenya	3.4
144	Benin	3.0
145	Burundi	2.9
146	Zimbabwe	2.8
147	Tanzania	2.6
148	Togo	2.6

Veenhoven, R.: *Average Happiness in 148 Nations 2000–2009*, World Database of Happiness, Rankreport Average Happiness, Version 10/09. Online at *http://worlddatabaseofhappiness. eur.nl/index.html*

The headings to these three happiness categories come from the psychologist Martin E. P. Seligman, whereas the examples are mine. In addition to listing the possible components of happiness, we should also note the importance of not feeling unhappy. For chemical reasons, the brain can only feel euphoria for limited stretches of time. However, it has no natural limitations to how long it can feel depressed. Avoiding pain, anger, boredom, sorrow, and anguish is therefore important. I think people in rich countries have particularly good opportunities to avoid massive misery.

According to Rooth Veenhoven (the founder of World Database of Happiness), the most important drivers of happiness are income and freedom, and all that these bring. For income, it doesn't seem to matter how big income distribution in a country is, as long as most people are at least at OK levels. In 2003 Veenhoven wrote a paper with co-author Michael Hagerty entitled "Wealth and happiness revisited: Growing wealth of nations does go with greater happiness". They found, as the title of their paper suggested, that there was a strong, statistical correlation between happiness and income.

However, whereas for income the effect starts to level off somewhat after a given threshold is met (below U.S.$15,000), the correlation with freedom is persistent: *The more freedom you get, the more happiness.* If you are free to choose your education, job, sexual orientation, lifestyle, spouse, faith, and place to live, then you will be far happier than if these choices are imposed on you. And if you can also choose to divorce, change job, move again, or whatever, then so much the better.

Among the different types of freedom, *it is economic freedom that has the largest effect on happiness*, whereas political and religious freedoms are somewhat less important. Immigrants who relocate from states with dictatorships to democracies move on average 2 points up the happiness scale, which is a lot.

Our global civilization is progressing like an airplane with no pilot, and what happens will be driven mainly by natural forces and urges that for the most part cannot be stopped. Typically, about one-third of the population will be against most change and one-third indifferent, as long as it doesn't hurt them personally. The last third will be eager for change. However, irrespective of who wants it and who doesn't, when things are possible, they do tend to happen, and during the 40 years from 2010 to 2050, I think we will see amazing change. Computers will surpass the human brain in processing power, and we will get to understand how our minds work. The period will also witness the first time a living species starts to manipulate its own genes (this has in fact already begun). We will also take major strides toward ridding ourselves of our addiction to fossil fuels.

Human wealth and intelligence will increase markedly, poverty will decline, and most people will dedicate a growing part of their time to creative work, leisure, art, and culture. Furthermore, we will increasingly seek products with "a story", and more and more of what we buy will be of premium or luxury standard, or will be experiences.

Asia, Eastern Europe, some of Latin America, and parts of China will reach Western levels of development. Meanwhile, the U.S.A., Japan, and some other developed nations will struggle with debt problems, which some will overcome, while others may not. The Islamic world will be divided into those that modernize quickly, and others that continue to decline or even disintegrate completely in orgies of terror, civil war, corruption, and crime.

The world will age, and the workforce in many developed countries as well as in China will shrink. This problem, however, will be largely offset by increased use of computers, robots, and genetic innovation.

The climate will probably heat up, but we will get a handle on how this can be stopped. There will be increased use of electric cars. Solar energy as well as second- and third-generation biofuels will go mainstream. Nuclear fusion power may be launched on a commercial scale.

The average person will own tens of thousands of books, movies, and music tracks, which will all be stored digitally on small servers and handheld devices.

About 80% of the world population will steam ahead, but the bottom billion will witness frequent chaos and an average of approx. 14 civil wars between 2010 and 2050, with 2–3 new ones starting each year. We will also go through roughly 1–3 global major property meltdowns followed by banking crises, 3–5 capital-spending collapses, 8–10 inventory cycles, 12–18 bubbles and crashes, and 12–18 scares.

However, for all the messiness there really is a destination. I concluded earlier that the overall direction of society seems to be toward a free and creative economy with more emphasis on experiences, and also toward greater harmony between peoples and the environment. If we assume that lots of people will be lifted out of poverty as well and if we believe that wealth and freedom make people far more happy, then I can summarize it all by saying the following:

In spite of all the turbulence and all the setbacks world history is full of, I think the outlook for human happiness is promising. *Assuming that (1) average incomes rise massively over the coming 40 years and in particular in emerging markets, and (2) the overall trend toward more freedom continues, I think it is safe to expect a considerable increase in average human happiness.*

However, we need to be wary as history has shown that advanced civilizations may go into structural decline that can continue for centuries if not millennia. This is definitely not my forecast, because billions of people will get up in the morning to make something that takes us forward. We still have lots to do to get to our destination but, fortunately, it will be done and most of it will be highly interesting, if not great fun.

20

Postscript: Looking back to now

A hundred years from now, what will people think of our times?

They will regard it with mixed feelings, I would imagine. They will probably think of it as a dirty, over-crowded, and messy period, burgeoning with terrorists, civil wars, pirates, pollution, overcrowding, and ugly cement buildings. They may also describe it as a time when the average human IQ was appallingly low. In fact, by their standards they will probably regard us all as imbeciles, including yours truly.

They may also wonder in horror at how people died of terrible diseases such as cancer, malaria, and AIDS; at a time when many were suppressed and brainwashed and when, incredibly, countless lived in slums and went to bed hungry. Perhaps they will have museums showing what a slum was like.

However, they may nevertheless call the period from 1980 to 2080 "the Second 100-Year Boom". Here is what they might say:

> "The First 100-Year Boom year lasted from 1800 to 1913 and was driven by industrialization and the first wave of globalization. However, only 15% of the world population achieved a decent standard of living because of this boom."

And they may add:

> "In the Second 100-Year Boom, lasting from 1980 to 2080, this number rose to 80%. The drivers behind this were a new wave of globalization combined with the development of information technology and genomics."

However, at the time they say that, they may already have entered "the Third 100-Year Boom", which may be driven by five major break-throughs: Global rollout of nuclear fusion, human super-intelligence, autonomous robots, quantum computing, and fourth-generation farming providing food and biofuel from massively gene-tuned plants, bacteria, and algae.

In this third mega-boom, starting just 20 years after the previous one faded, the main effort may no longer be on quantity, but on quality. "Freedom, not fear", will be a part of the mindset. "Harmony, not hatred." "Fun, not fuss."

The virtually unlimited resources available at that time may largely be used to clean up traces of pollution left over from previous ages. Furthermore, farmland may be given back to nature, and ugly houses pulled down and replaced by some with style and charm. The *belle époque* of the 22nd century will have begun.

Or so I hope.

Appendix A

The 100 most dramatic events, 2010–2050

VOLATILITY

1. Between 2010 and 2050 there will be 12–18 financial bubbles and crashes.
2. ... and 12–18 general scares.
3. ... plus 1–3 global major property meltdowns, each followed by banking crises.
4. ... 3–5 capital-spending collapses.
5. ... and 8–10 inventory cycles.

DEMOGRAPHICS

6. Global population growth is decelerating, but it will still increase by approx. 2 billion before peaking at approx. 9 million around 2050.
7. The largest growth will be in Africa (+93%) and the Middle East plus Turkey (+60%).
8. Somewhat slower growth will be seen in India (+33%), North America (+28%), and Latin America (+24%).
9. Western Europe and China will have roughly unchanged populations by 2050.
10. Eastern Europe (including Russia) and Japan will see their populations decline by approx. 18% to 20%.
11. Approx. 80% of the increase in world population until 2050 will be of people over 60. This increase in elderly equals approx. 1.6 times the

entire population of all developed nations today. Approx. 90% of this "graying" will be in emerging-market countries.

12. Global urban population will grow by 3 billion between 2010 and 2050.

13. Meanwhile, global rural population will decline by 1 billion, and many villages and country dwellings will become deserted as a consequence.

14. Global life expectancy will grow approx. 2.5 years per decade (i.e., a total of 10 years between 2010 and 2050). In Europe and North America, life expectancy will probably rise by around 6–7 years during the period, whereas it will be around 10 years in Asia, and in some poorer countries it will be much more.

15. However, towards the end of 2050, life expectancy will start to accelerate in some countries, as age prevention becomes an information technology through the use of advanced biotech and genomics. This may eventually take the average lifespan towards perhaps 150 years or longer in the coming century.

MACRO-ECONOMICS

16. Economic growth will generally be strongest in areas with low income, low taxes, free trade, English or Chinese language mastery, tolerant/ creative cultures, sea access, authentic and rich culture, and temperate or subtropical temperature.

17. Global GDP will grow approx. 400% in real terms from 2010 to 2050, with average real income per capita in developed countries typically rising 200% to 300% against a whopping 400% to 600% in developing countries such as China, India, Brazil, Russia, and the "N-11". Economic *expansion* in emerging markets will exceed the *total* current size of the six largest economies by 2030.

18. By 2050 the majority of current, emerging-market citizens will enjoy living standards similar to—or higher than—average OECD lifestyles today. The world will be very rich.

19. As part of this transition, the global middle class will increase by 70 million to 90 million people a year.

20. Furthermore, by 2050 the differences in income levels between countries will on average be much smaller than they are today. A significant international economic leveling lies ahead.

21. China will initially be the world's growth engine. It will also become the largest economy globally before 2040, but from around that time India will take over as the biggest contributor to global economic expansion, due to its superior demographics.

22. However, there are today approx. 1 billion people within 50–60 nations (the so-called "bottom billion") who missed the boat on globalization. The economies of many of these poor nations will continue to stagnate or even contract economically. These are predominantly located in Africa and the Middle East.

23. Many developed countries will lack the funds to pay for retirement booms. Several may go through acute debt crises.

WAR AND CONFLICT

24. There will be approx. 100 new wars between 2010 and 2050, almost all originating in the bottom billion countries. Most of these will be civil wars.

25. The bottom billion countries will also originate approx. 5,000 acts of terror, kidnapping, and piracy until 2050.

26. War between two uniformed armies will become very rare.

27. Robotic warfare between armies and insurgents, on the other hand, will become increasingly common.

28. Military functions will increasingly be outsourced to private military forces.

29. We will get an international legal environment for terror, as already exists for human rights abuses, crime, and war.

30. Large economic powers will sponsor dictators in return for access to resources.

31. The U.S.A. will remain the world's dominant military power by a considerable margin.

32. The great empires by 2050 will not be defined clearly by national boundaries, because they will be virtual, and they will grow organically. By 2050 there will be two such virtual empires: One will be predominantly Chinese, and the other Latin/Germanic/Anglo-Saxon. Many people will feel attachment to both.

KNOWLEDGE AND SCIENCE

33. Human knowledge will double every 8–9 years and will grow approx. 4,500%—or 45 times—from 2010 to 2050.

34. One main contributor will be the effect of Moore's Law, whereby computer chip performance doubles approx. every 24 months. Until approx. 2030, this will be sustained through ever-smaller geometries in

chip architecture, culminating just after 2020. Water-cooled 3D chips and multicore chip designs will be used to further sustain performance improvements beyond that.

35. Before 2050 we will also see optical computing and quantum computing. The latter, in particular, will enable a massive further increase in computing power.

36. The best computers will by 2020 rival the human brain in terms of data-processing capacity.

37. By 2020 computers will also be fairly good at simulating the way the neocortex of the human brain works. This will enable them to be creative and intuitive. Indeed, computers will begin to rival, if not surpass, the best scientists and artists in creativity. However, neocortex simulation will not give them emotions, although it may enable them to simulate emotions extremely well.

38. Another major driver of human knowledge will be the genetics revolution, which will sustain productivity growth equal to what we have seen in IT. This will enable us to understand all life right down to its core—the biggest intellectual endeavor in the history of mankind.

39. Furthermore, humans shall continue to develop "meta-ideas"—ideas about how to create and spread ideas—which will accelerate knowledge generation. One of the main future meta-ideas will be computers that tirelessly and at frantic speeds automatically "mine" digital data (read and comprehend it) and draw conclusions from it. Some of these conclusions and recommendations will be truly creative, and their sheer scale wil be far beyond what humans could ever have achieved.

40. Furthermore, telecommunication bandwidth and digital storage technology will also continue to grow exponentially.

41. Whereas computers in many ways will overtake human intelligence, the number of people with tertiary education will double every 15 years.

42. As this happens, women will on average become better educated than men.

43. Global average human IQ will increase approx. 12% from 2010 to 2050—mainly due to cross-breeding, better health and nutrition, and better upbringing. However, towards the end of the period it will start to rise much faster, as some communities will start modifying human genes to obtain even greater intelligence. This will be the start of a process leading to the creation of "superhumans" in the second half of the century, and their intelligence will be almost beyond (current) comprehension.

44. A permanent base on the Moon will be established around 2025—2030.

45. We will identify dark matter and discover the smallest particles in the universe before 2030.
46. We will have reached a consensus "theory of everything" before 2040.

RESOURCES AND ENVIRONMENT

47. Pollution will generally decline, in particular towards the end of the period. This will partly be as a function of increased wealth and decelerating population growth, but mainly because of an abundance of new technologies such as robotic recycling, metabolic engineering for higher farm yields with less or no need for tilling and pesticide spraying, third- and fourth-generation biofuels, solar and fusion power, etc.
48. However, carbon emissions will take several decades to get under control, and the planet as a consequence may heat 1°C to 2°C more than it would naturally. Sea levels may also rise modestly, but with limited impact.
49. In terms of resources, we will not run out of any commodities. The most successful sector here will be farming, which is rapidly becoming an information technology with productivity gains that will vastly exceed demand growth—even as an increasing proportion of land is used for biofuel.
50. This productivity growth will enable us to free up land for wildlife while doubling agricultural output.
51. The supply of freshwater will remain largely an economic problem, which will haunt the bottom billion countries, but will be more easily dealt with by wealthy nations.
52. There will be temporary shortages of energy and industrial metals.

THE SEVEN SUPERSECTORS

53. Seven business sectors will be particularly profitable during the coming decades. The growth in emerging markets in particular will drive the (1) *finance*, (2) *real estate*, (3) *commodities*, (4) *alternative energy*, and (5) *luxury* sectors. Furthermore, the (6) *IT* business sector will continue to flourish due to its massive innovation rate, and so will (7) *biotech/ genomics* for the same reason and especially as its outcomes will be desperately needed to solve healthcare problems for the exploding population of elderly, as well as to solve environmental and resource challenges.

54. The finance sector will benefit as emerging markets, which today have largely cash-based economies, develop credit cultures. Furthermore, the sector will finance a quadrupling of the world economy, including the construction of real estate, the funding of innovative startups and growth companies, in particular within the other supersectors.

55. The real estate market will have to construct net, new, residential property for 75 million people annually, as well as commercial property, etc. enabling a massive expansion of the world economy. Furthermore, land prices in the most desirable areas will grow very fast.

56. There will be periods when we will struggle to ramp up the output of industrial metals and energy fast enough to meet demand. This will lead to repeated, violent price spikes in these sectors, making commodities an interesting investment area.

57. In order to bridge the short-term growth in energy demand, the first general focus will be on upgrading power grids, energy saving, and more efficient coal burning. Next come deep-sea drilling, increased use of sophisticated recovery methods, gas-to-liquid technology, large-scale extraction of shale gas, and refining of tar oil. Shale oil, of which we have huge resources, may also be taken into use.

58. From approx. 2020 we will probably see large-scale, second-, third-, and fourth-generation biofuels based on new enzymes and genetically modified bacteria, algae, and plants—including some with extremely high "gene-tuned" metabolisms.

59. At the same time, PV solar will have become so cheap that it will be commonly used as a building surface. Furthermore, we will see very large–scale solar plants in sunny areas.

60. Finally, in solving the energy challenge, fusion energy will begin to work at the experimental stage around 2040 and will get rolled out commercially between 2050 and 2100. This will enable us to dismantle windmills and remove solar panels where they are deemed blots on the landscape. Energy will then become extremely cheap.

61. The demand for luxury will grow 5–10 times, and as more people seek products from established leading brands, these will be able to control prices and supply, and thus maintain very high pricing and profits.

62. Computers, electronic identity tags, electronic sensors, and robots will surround us everywhere. They will handle tasks such as driving our cars, creating personal media, provididng personalized tutoring, handling safety, sorting garbage, doing our laundry and dishwashing, carrying out scientific meta-studies and peer reviews, managing and executing military operations, and enabling us to take part in massive multiplayer games in lifelike virtual environments. Furthermore, they will assist

people like doctors to carry out their expert functions, by listening in when they work and discreetly correcting errors and oversights.

63. Robots will use a combination of (1) hard-coded software to handle basic "instincts" like collision avoidance, and (2) neocortex simulation for learning by doing. In terms of overall capability, the latter will be by far the most important. While this learning will take time, it may—unlike the case with biological life—easily be cloned to other robots once it works.

64. Software will get extremely good at writing software and at identifying threats and opportunities hidden in our combined knowledge as well as in our physical environment.

65. Computers will also help us decode life and support the forthcoming genomics revolution, largely through an ability to first simulate entire cells and then whole organisms. By doing so they will be able to come up with their own ideas for medicine, nutrition, and biochemical production methods. This will massively speed up the discovery and approval processes for all types of new biochemistry.

66. We will get vaccines against asthma, multiple sclerosis, leukemia, arthritis, malaria, high blood pressure, rheumatoid arthritis, salmonella infection, and substance addiction, etc.

67. General health checkups will make huge advances and will become fast and cheap.

68. We will have easy access to personalized medicine with fewer or no side-effects. Cancer may, for instance, be effectively targeted without seriously inconveniencing the patient.

69. We will start to re-create extinct species through "reverse-engineering" and create a global Noah's Ark of genetic information.

70. We will build massive fuel farms with genetically modified algae and bacteria that turn CO_2 into fuel. The first ones will be located beside coal-powered plants, where they will utilize CO_2 in the outlets.

71. We will begin to change our own genomes for reduced risk of disease, longer lifespan, and higher intelligence, etc.

PROFIT MODELS AND ASSET PRICES

72. Global real wealth will, like global real GDP, grow approx. 400% from 2010 to 2050, adding approx. $800 trillion in variable-price assets. The overwhelming majority of this wealth growth will come from developing markets.

73. Due to accelerating innovation speeds, an increasing proportion of new

wealth will be created by individuals and companies who can anticipate the future ahead of the crowd, move extremely quickly, and manage the ensuing network effects.

74. Furthermore, as the amounts of money available for spending and investing quadruple, the possession/acquisition of limited supply assets or products will often be a winning strategy. Energy, industrial metals, leading luxury brands, limited supply collectibles, or premium land may do very well for that reason.

CONSUMER PRODUCTS

75. Houses will have interior walls made of "smartglass", which can turn milky by the touch of a button. Some of these will have e-zones, which work as computer/media displays operated by no-touch hand movements. These may be called "media walls".

76. They will also have smart wallpaper: entire walls or large parts of walls that can be turned into displays for media or to set up a desired mood or ambience.

77. We will get private media servers containing every good movie, book, and piece of music ever made.

78. The back seat and passenger seats in most cars will get online entertainment, which we will have plenty of time to enjoy when cars learn to drive by themselves.

79. Our most valued possessions will call the police if they are stolen, and the police will then be able to track their location and/or disable them.

80. Entire roofs and walls will be made of photovoltaic cells—which will often look cool.

81. Computer "brains" (CPUs), keyboards, and screens will become unbundled such that, for instance, any handheld computer will be able to display its content on any screen that happens to be nearby.

82. The concept of books will remain with us, but these will mainly be read on electronic screens and will often contain animations, movies, and links.

83. Massively multiplayer games will get high resolution and surround sound and will become extremely popular.

84. We will get transparent mobile phones with web-based annotation of the real world. In fact, this may become one of the most compelling consumer products of all times.

85. Video conferencing will finally reach mass use as latency problems are

resolved and wider screens/multiple loudspeakers enable users to distinguish who says what.

86. Many niche TV programs will morph into e "TV conferences".
87. Old media will get reverse-engineered so that it looks or sounds new.
88. We will be offered diets tailored to our personal genetic makeup.
89. Food will get divided into four main categories: (1) fast, (2) luxury, (3) ecological, and (4) functional. The latter—food that has been tailored to meet specific nutritional needs or desires—will be the fastest growing segment.
90. We will get electric cars which charge their batteries when power prices are cheapest—typically at night. These may even sell back unneeded power at a higher price to the grid .
91. We will stop making automobile chassis of metal. They will instead be made of biodegradable fiber, which is stronger and lighter.
92. Cars that are mainly used for long-distance travel will have fully reclinable seats, like in first-class sections of passenger planes.

LIFE

93. People from open cultures will continue to blend and unite. Racism and nationalism will decline.
94. Most new jobs will be in creative, service, or storytelling sectors.
95. In terms of lifestyles, there will be a trend towards creativity, individuality, and authentic charm.
96. The market for luxury, experiences, and storytelling will grow faster than the market for basic products.
97. People will increasingly feel free to define themselves, their spirituality, and their way of life individually.
98. People will remain materialistic, but will gradually shift their consumption mix towards experiences rather than products, and to quality rather than quantity.
99. Consumers will want to tell stories through electronic media and will seek products and companies with great stories. Leading companies will thus hire media professionals to create or tell their stories. This will be particularly popular in (1) sports, (2) finance, (3) luxury, and (4) food/health.
100. As we get richer and get increased freedom—in economic and other ways—people will on average get happier.

Appendix B

Sources

There is an online source list (and other stuff) on *www.supertrends.com*, and most of this can be clicked for direct access to the actual content.

However, I would like here to comment on a few of the numerous books I have enjoyed, each of which in its own way relates to the subjects of this book. These are the ones among many that I would recommend to others as starting points. Also, I have found that some periodicals and websites are particularly useful for discerning what the future might bring. There are even a few movies that I will recommend.

FINANCIAL MARKETS

- Lewis, Michael: *Liars Poker*, Penguin, 1900. An incredibly well–written and entertaining book about the trading culture in a bull market. You will laugh a lot and learn a little.
- Fraser-Sampson, Guy: *Private Equity as an Asset Class*, Wiley, 2007. The best technical description of private equity that is actually readable that I have seen.
- Tvede, Lars: *Business Cycles: History, Theory and Investment Reality*, Wiley, 2006. OK, written by myself, but it does give a comprehensive overview over how business cycles work, which I haven't seen else-where. Too long, perhaps, but at times entertaining. At least it got good reviews.
- Tvede, Lars: *Psychology of Finance*, Wiley, 2002. Here we go again. Written by me too, but sells really well, and explains the psychology behind financial irrationality.

- Ross-Sorkin, Andrew: *Too Big to Fail: The Inside Story of How Wall Street and Washington Fought to Save the Financial System—and Themselves.* Too big to read in some people's opinion, but by far the best account of the events during the subprime meltdown. Hilarious and instructive.
- Burrough, Bryan and John Helyar: *Barbarians at the Gate: The Fall of RJR Nabisco,* 2009. One of the best business books ever written. The dramatic story of the Nabisco buyout—the largest ever, when it occurred. Also available as a video.
- Phillips, Kenneth S. and Ronald J. Surz: *Hedge Funds: Definitive Strategies and Techniques,* Wiley, 2003. Explains the mechanics of why hedge funds work very well.
- Lowenstein, Roger: *When Genius Failed: The Rise and Fall of Long-Term Capital Management,* Fourth Estate, 2002. About the spectacular meltdown of a giant hedge fund. Among the managers were two Nobel Prize winners and top Wall Street experts; and yet they created the biggest financial meltdown on record. Explains why men with models can be a very dangerous thing. Math can describe what we know, but when dealing with fluid complex systems, computer models can get it very, very wrong. What comes out of computers is not data.

SCARES AND HYPE

- Mackay, Charles: *Extraordinary Popular Delusions and the Madness of Crowds,* Martino Fine Books, 2009. This book describes how humans time and again get captivated by weird ideas and pursue them into utter absurdity. It is about groupthink, bubbles, scares, and just collective madness, and it is as well-written as it is thought-provoking. Even though it was first published in 1864, almost 150 years ago, nothing seems to have changed since. I think every person on Earth should read it. It is at least considered mandatory reading in the better part of the financial community.
- Booker, Christopher and Richard North: *Scared to Death: From BSE to Global Warming—Why Scares Are Costing Us the Earth.* A very detailed and extremely well-researched and written book about the main scares since 1980, with a slightly U.K.-centric perspective. One author has been science writer for the *Sunday Telegraph* for several decades, where he covered all the scares in the book, and the other a research director in the European parliament. They know what they are talking about and the analysis is sharp and to the point.

- Herman, Arthur: *The Idea of Decline in Western History*, Free Press, 2007. A thorough treatise on the history of declinism. Not an easy read, but comprehensive and thoughtful.
- Goldacre, Ben: *Bad Science*, Fourth Estate, 2009. A great and funny book about pseudo-science, of which there is a lot. Mainly focused on healing/nutrition nonsense and the way the press deals with it.

DEMOGRAPHICS

- Magnus, George: *The Age of Aging: How Demographics Are Changing the Global Economy and Our World*. Short in summaries of what it all means, but does include tons of facts. It's honestly not very interesting to read books about demographics (in my view), but if I should pick one, it would be this.

INNOVATION IN GENERAL

- Kurzweil, Ray: *The Singularity Is Near: When Humans Transcend Biology*, Viking Adult, 2005. Kurzweil is a living legend, and this book has some very important points—in particular about prediction in markets that evolve exponentially. Looking at his previous forecasts, I think he has often been ahead of the curve, and not everything he expects makes sense to me. But definitely worth reading, and anyway: What do I know?
- Kaku, Michio: *Visions: How Science Will Revolutionize the 21st Century*, Anchor, 1998. A superb, broad-spectrum view into the future of technology. Unfortunately it is getting dated—I wish he would update it.
- Lewis, Michael: *The New New Thing: A Silicon Valley Story*, Penguin, 2001. When I was young I thought that what took some people a month, others could do in two weeks. Now I know that what takes some a month, others do (better) in a day. Michael Lewis follows the frantic career and lifestyle of a high-tech entrepreneur. A classic.
- Parkinson, C. Northcote: *Parkinson's Law: And Other Studies in Administration*, Ballantine Books, 1971. Story of my life, really, but explains why things take time, why the private sector is generally more efficient than the public, and why we do need decentralization.

INTELLIGENCE

- Wills, Christopher: *The Runaway Brain: The Evolution of Human Uniqueness*, Basic Books, 1994. A great book about how we became so smart, and how scientists use genomics to analyze history
- Hawkins, Jeff: *On Intelligence*, Holt Paperbacks, 2005. The best description that I have seen of how the neocortex probably works. Brilliant.

ENVIRONMENT AND RESOURCES

- Gore, Al: *Our Choice: A Plan to Solve the Climate Crisis*, Rodale Books, 2009. If you want to read Al Gore, this is the one to choose. *An Inconvenient Truth* is unbearably manipulative. *Our Choice*, on the other hand, is more down to Earth and has lots of information about what we may do to reduce the emissions of greenhouse gases and which parts to prioritize. He will hopefully update it from time to time, because the field is fortunately in a flux.
- Olah, George A., Alain Goeppert, and G. K. Surya Prakash: *Beyond Oil and Gas: The Methanol Economy*. A very good book about all types of energy explained by a Nobel Prize winner and two distinguished colleagues who actually stick to the facts.
- Rischard, Jean-François: *High Noon*, Basic Books, 2003. A good, brief overview of some of the largest problems facing mankind, and it's not as alarmist as the title may suggest.
- Lomborg, Bjørn: *The Skeptical Environmentalist: Measuring the Real State of the World*, Cambridge University Press, 2001. This is an absolute must-read. Thorough, detailed analyses of myths and facts in the debate about environments and resources.
- Svensmark, Henrik and Nigel Calder: *The Chilling Stars: The New Theory of Climate Change*, Totem Books, 2007. In discussing climate change, we do need to understand why such enormous changes happened before humans could have had anything to do with it. This book may have an answer.

POWER, EMPIRES, WAR, AND TERROR

- Murray, Charles: *Human Accomplishment: The Pursuit of Excellence in the Arts and Sciences, 800 B.C. to 1950*, Harper Perennial, 2004. Extremely important and the only one of its kind. However, potential readers should know that a large part of it is technical descriptions of how he did his studies. Apart from that, the coverage goes from 888 BC to 1950, since he correctly assumes that recent data may be biased. However, he speculates that human achievement may have declined after his cutoff date. Here I disagree. In visual arts perhaps yes, but in music no, and in technology the last decades have put everything before in the shadow, in my opinion.

- Collier, Paul: *The Bottom Billion: Why the Poorest Countries Are Failing and What Can Be Done about It*, Oxford University Press, 2007. An excellent explanation of why some countries don't work, and what it would take to get them out of their swamps.

- Johnson, Paul M.: *Modern Times Revised Edition: The World from the Twenties to the Nineties*, Harper Perennial Modern Classics, 2001. A splendid explanation of the drivers behind modern history.

- Gombrich, Ernst H.: *Art and Illusion*, Princeton University Press, 2000. The best book I ever read about art, and I suspect the best that was ever written.

- Fukuyama, Francis: *The End of History and the Last Man*. About the global trend toward liberal democracies, which he describes as our final destination. He was mocked because "history" began again with 9/11, but I think he is very right anyway. Things just take time.

SECTORS

- Thompson, Don: *The $12 Million Stuffed Shark: The Curious Economics of Contemporary Art*. Palgrave Macmillan, 2008. About the branding, illusion, and delusion in contemporary art markets. I laughed until tears were running. However, there is a serious reality behind it all, because the madness of contemporary art markets is just one recent example of Charles MacKay's "madness of crowds", and there are many others.

- Venter, Craig: *A Life Decoded: My Genome: My Life*, Viking Adult, 2007. The world's most important man today (in my view) writes about his work in genomics. What goes on in this sector is a series of great discoveries and engineering feats that will change everything. Not understanding this is like not understanding the internet when it took off or not listening to Columbus when he returned from his travels and explained that he had found new land.

- Shreeve, James: *The Genome War: How Craig Venter Tried to Capture the Code of Life and Save the World*, Ballantine Books, 2000. A well-written and well-researched book about the race to sequence the human genome

- Charles, Dan: *Lords of the Harvest: Biotech, Big Money, and the Future of Food.* Basic Books, 2002. Explanation of genomics and biotech in the farming industry. Probably the best introduction for anyone who wishes to understand this aspect of genomics.

- Henderson, Mark: *50 Genetics Ideas You Really Need to Know*, Quercus Publishing, 2009. Ultra-easy read with introductions to genetics themes. Great place to start.

- Abate, Tom: *The Biotech Investor: How to Profit from the Coming Boom in Biotechnology*, Holt Paperbacks, 2004. A solid description of what biotech companies actually are working with, how they do it, the time it takes, the money it costs, and the risks it involves (many!).

- Robbins-Roth, Cynthia: *From Alchemy to IPO: The Business of Biotechnology*, Basic Books, 2001. Another book about the realities of commercial biotech, which includes some of the relevant history.

- Moravek, Hans: *Robot: Mere Machine to Transcendent Mind*, Oxford University Press, 2000. Moravek is an institution in robotics, and a great writer too. Well-written introduction to the subject.

- Levi, David: *Robots Unlimited: Life in a Virtual Age*, A. K. Peters, 2005. He lost me when discussing the love life, marriage, and religious beliefs of future robots, but let's see. In any case, a good, detailed description of all the hardware and software robots will be made of.

- Carr, Nicholas: *The Big Switch: Rewiring the World, from Edison to Google*, W. W. Norton & Co., 2009. Compares the internet with when electricity was introduced and explains where we are going with cloud computing, as-a-service business models. etc. Very well written.

LIFESTYLES

- Florida, Richard: *The Rise of the Creative Class: And How It's Transforming Work, Leisure, Community and Everyday Life*, Basic Books, 2003. Perhaps too long for its substance, but the concept is really important, and his research is good and relevant.

- Watson, Richard: *Future Files: The 5 Trends that Will Shape the Next 50 Years*, Nicholas Brealey, 2008. A good and well-written description of coming lifestyle changes. Less relevant for investors.

Index